THE GREAT WAR

The Great War is a landmark history that firmly places the First World War in the context of imperialism. Set to overturn conventional accounts of what happened during this, the first truly international conflict, it extends the study of the First World War beyond the confines of Europe and the Western Front.

By recounting the experiences of people from the colonies, especially those brought into the war effort either as volunteers or through conscription, John H. Morrow's magisterial work also unveils the impact of the war in Asia, India, and Africa.

From the origins of the First World War to its bloody (and largely unknown) aftermath, *The Great War* is distinguished by its long chronological coverage, first person battle and home front accounts, its pan-European and global emphasis, and the integration of cultural considerations with political.

John H. Morrow, Jr. is Franklin Professor of History at the University of Georgia. He specializes in the history of modern Europe and of warfare and society. He is the author of *The Great War in the Air: Military Aviation from 1909 to 1921* (1993), *German Air Power in World War I* (1982), *and Building German Air Power, 1909–1914* (1976) and has edited *A Yankee Ace in the RAF: The World War I Letters of Captain Bogart Rogers* (1996).

Praise for *The Great War: An Imperial History*

'Morrow is an excellent military historian who follows quite strictly the war's events on the various fronts, revealing the colonial effort in troops and economics.' *Times Higher Education Supplement*

'With a staggering wealth of reference, John H. Morrow has produced a universal historical tapestry which weaves together the international threads that provide the woof and warp of the conflict that introduced and essentially shaped the most barbaric century in human history. Given his canvas, he writes with amazing clarity, never allowing the reader to feel that he is being sold short on this panoramic journey through four years when the world went mad.' *Morning Star*

'Lively, informative and based on a lifetime of reading … Morrow's history will give readers reason to think about a wide range of issues: not least the possibility that, during and after the First World War, Europeans began to apply to one another the brutality they had formerly reserved for their African subjects.' *The Independent*

'A wide-ranging narrative account of the First World War, written in a combative manner and easy style.' Hew Strachan, *University of Oxford*

'Morrow writes well, in places even evocatively, and his lucid and engaging text merits a wide readership' *American Historical Review*

THE GREAT WAR

An Imperial History

John H. Morrow, Jr.

Routledge
Taylor & Francis Group

LONDON AND NEW YORK

Centenary edition published 2014
by Routledge
2 Park Square, Milton Park,
Abingdon, Oxon, OX14 4RN

and by Routledge
711 Third Avenue, New York, NY 10017

Routledge is an imprint of the Taylor & Francis Group, an informa business

© 2005, 2014 John H. Morrow, Jr.

Typeset in Ehrhardt by M Rules

Library of Congress Cataloging in Publication Data

A catalog record for this book has been requested

British Library Cataloguing in Publication Data
A catalogue record for this book is available from the British Library

ISBN 978-0-415-71559-1

MIX
Paper from
responsible sources
FSC
www.fsc.org   FSC® C013056

Printed and bound in Great Britain by
TJ International Ltd, Padstow, Cornwall

To our beloved children, daughter Kieran and son Evan.

May you and your generation have the wisdom, strength and courage to right the wrongs of your elders.

CONTENTS

ILLUSTRATIONS

PREFACE TO THE CENTENARY EDITION

The Great War: An Imperial History is a global history that places the First World War in the context of imperialism. As a consequence, while it pays due attention to Europe, which many considered the center of the world at the time, it moves away from a Eurocentric view of the Great War to demonstrate non-European peoples' role in the conflict and to include colonial campaigns. Furthermore, the book seeks a holistic understanding of that global "total war" in all its complexity, not solely on global fighting fronts but also on the all-important domestic – or home – fronts of the warring powers. "Total" war required an unprecedented "total" mobilization of societies, as governments conscripted millions of men for military service and then pressed millions of women and youth into the production of war materiel. Combatants focused all the forces of science, technology, industry, and economy on enhancing their national capacity for war, and enlisted intellectuals in the cause of cultural mobilization of their respective populations. The four-and-a-half-year duration of the conflict placed increasing stress on the fault lines in societies – those of class, gender, and race – each of which would affect the conduct of the war.

A combat or battle history would not enable the comprehensive understanding of origins, course, outcome, and aftermath of a devastating conflict that shook the world to its very foundations. It remains the "Great War" to Europeans, the cataclysm that killed or maimed millions of its precious youth and irreparably undermined the old order. Also, despite being proclaimed "the war to end war," the conflict of 1914–18 set the stage for – although it did not inexorably lead to – the even more "total" and horrendous Second World War. For these reasons, the First World War merits as complete an understanding as possible. *The Great War: An Imperial History* strives to achieve that goal.

I am pleased and honored that Routledge is reissuing a centenary edition of this book, which first appeared a decade ago, in 2004. I owe particular thanks to Routledge's Senior History Editor, Eve Setch, for her unstinting support and encouragement of my efforts over the years, and to her editorial assistant, Paul Brotherston, for his assistance with recent tasks.

The book merits a centennial edition, I believe, because it has retained its validity since publication, with a number of recent studies reinforcing the soundness of the imperial approach. Some of these have offered new perspectives on the origins of the war. The first chapter of *Imperial History* roundly condemned the "sterile canon" of saddling Germany with the major responsibility for starting the First World War, an interpretation that Fritz Fischer's magisterial *Germany's Aims in the First World War* firmly planted in historians' minds. The English title of Fischer's work is a bland translation of the original German – *Griff nach der Weltmacht: Die Kriegszielpolitik des kaiserlichen Deutschland 1914–1918* (*Grasping at World Power: The War Aims Policies of Imperial Germany, 1914–18*) – and fails to capture the authentic tone and thrust of the book, which was first published in Germany in 1961. A few years later, Immanuel Geiss published *July 1914: The Outbreak of the First World War: Selected Documents* (German edition, 1964; English edition, 1967), in which the introduction and documents allegedly demonstrated Germany's "war guilt." German historians' willingness to condemn their own state and provide the evidence for their country's responsibility for starting the war seemed the ultimate proof of the case. Yet neither historian could compare Germany with the other European powers, whose documents remained unavailable while Germany's were exposed to all after its defeat in the Second World War.

Imperial History contended that all the powers in an era of "high imperialism" bore responsibility for the origins of the war. Now, a half-century after Fischer and Geiss, historian Sean McMeekin has shifted the focus of attention and responsibility primarily to Russia and secondly to France. His invaluable study, *The Russian Origins of the First World War* (Cambridge, MA: Belknap Press of Harvard University Press, 2011), exemplifies how an imperial perspective prevents simplistic attempts to blame a single power for the First World War. McMeekin pointedly suggests that after the Italian and Balkan wars, from 1911 through 1913, the First World War was plausibly "The War of Ottoman Succession," and consequently, "it was Russia's war even more than it was Germany's." Russia also directly challenged Ottoman Turkey with its Armenian reform campaign of 1913–14, which McMeekin labels "a scarcely disguised Trojan horse for the expansion of Russian influence in Turkish Anatolia," as a preliminary to its plans to seize Constantinople and the Straits. Russian imperialists, he asserts, were "dead serious" about dismembering Turkey and Austria-Hungary, whose army Russian generals considered a "paper tiger." In fact, McMeekin suggests that it is "naïve" to believe that Russia went to war on behalf of Serbia. All the powers anticipated Ottoman Turkey's demise, and Russia was willing to provoke a war to promote its national interests and gain control of Constantinople and the Straits.[1] McMeekin's more recent book, *July 1914: Countdown to War* (New York: Basic Books, 2013), pursues his thesis that Russia and France, rather than Germany and Austria-Hungary, bore primary responsibility for the outbreak of war in 1914.

McMeekin's work is part of a healthy tendency in recent studies of the First World War to focus on the east as well as the west, to encompass Russia and the Ottoman Empire, with the latter especially a highly significant but often forgotten power. While it may have merited the label "The Sick Man of Europe" in 1914, it was far from dead and was destined to be a significant battleground in the global war. The policies of the Ottoman Empire were a significant factor in the war's origins, and they have finally received the attention they deserve in Mustafa Aksakal's monograph, *The Ottoman Road to War: The Ottoman Empire and the First World War* (Cambridge: Cambridge University Press, 2008). Aksakal points out that the Ottoman government viewed the events from the Balkan Wars in 1912 through the crisis of July 1914 "in the context of Russian intentions to seize control over Istanbul and the Ottoman Straits." The Young Turks, reeling in the aftermath of the disastrous Balkan Wars, "feared Russia" and thus sided with Germany.[2] On the all-important topic of the struggle between the Ottoman and Russian empires, Michael A. Reynolds's *Shattering Empires: The Clash and Collapse of the Ottoman and Russian Empires, 1908–1918* (Cambridge: Cambridge University Press, 2011) yields significant insight. Finally, the unique horror of the Armenian genocide receives due attention in two recent books: *The Armenian Genocide: A Complete History* (London: I.B. Tauris, 2011) by Raymond Kévorkian; and *The Young Turks' Crime against Humanity: The Armenian Genocide and Ethnic Cleansing in the Ottoman Empire* (Princeton: Princeton University Press, 2012) by Tamer Akçam.

To return to the western powers, some of the best works on imperialism concern France, which alone among the powers shipped its colonial subjects to Europe to fight and work. France's urgent need for manpower on the Western Front coincided with the desire of the sole African representative in the French Parliament, Senegalese deputy Blaise Diagne, to use the service of African soldiers as an avenue to gain more rights in the colonies. Richard S. Fogarty's excellent book, *Race and War in France: Colonial Subjects in the French Army, 1914–1918* (Baltimore: Johns Hopkins University Press, 2008) explores and analyzes in nuanced fashion the complex relationship between France and its colonial warriors. Even more fascinating, Xu Guoqi's *Strangers on the Western Front: Chinese Workers in the Great War* (Cambridge, MA: Harvard University Press, 2011) sheds light on a hitherto ignored band of workers in France. Some 140,000 Chinese laborers formed the largest and longest-serving immigrant group on the Western Front from 1917 to 1920. The Chinese government had sent them as part of a complex, if ultimately futile, plan to establish a link between China and the west in the hope of regaining Shantung from the Japanese and forestalling future Japanese incursions.[3]

For readers attracted to accounts of famous battles, the military history of British campaigns against the Ottoman Empire continues to offer sobering and enlightening reading. In particular I would recommend Charles Townshend's *Desert Hell: The British Invasion of Mesopotamia* (Cambridge, MA: Belknap Press of Harvard University Press, 2011), and Peter Hart's *Gallipoli* (Oxford: Oxford University Press, 2011).

Finally, in reference to the wars in Iraq and Afghanistan, I wrote the preface for the original edition of this book in 2003, when the United States government had just embarked on what I termed "imperial initiatives in the Middle East." Back then, I firmly believed that the Great War offered a cautionary tale to anyone embarking on campaigns that, however euphemistically their motives and goals might be labeled, essentially mirrored those that drove the imperial powers to war in 1914. Now, a decade later, as the United States continues to withdraw from Afghanistan, that original preface still merits the attention of readers who wish to understand the continuing importance of the First World War.

1 McMeekin, *Russian Origins*, 4–5, 12, 21, 28, 31–32, 34–35.
2 Aksakal, *The Ottoman Road to War*, 3, 190.
3 Guoqi, *Strangers*, 1–6.

PREFACE TO THE FIRST EDITION

The Great War. An Imperial History presents a global perspective of a war that many people often construe narrowly as a European, even a western European conflict. It seeks to mesh the military with the political, social, economic, and cultural aspects of the history of global conflict, from the origins through the aftermath of the Great War of 1914–18. This approach to the war consequently opens and closes with overarching chapters on the origins of the war and then its aftermath within a global context. The wartime chapters follow the conflict chronologically, on an annual basis, discussing all fronts and theaters of the war and the domestic developments within the major combatant powers, with particular attention to class, gender, and race where appropriate. Chapter conclusions seek to tie together coherently annual developments.

Other works have often taken a topical approach to the war, but such an approach does violence to the interrelated nature of disparate events as they occurred chronologically during the war. Some historians focus selectively on particular powers, and omit, even in general histories, discussion of Italy, Austria-Hungary, and the Ottoman Empire in favor of concentration on the major powers. Historians sometimes so compartmentalize their study of major events that they become like the blind men who cannot imagine the entire elephant whose individual parts they confront. In regard to war, military historians accept only operational history as relevant, while other historians view war only through the lens of their particular field. Such partitioning is not only ironic in the study of "total" war; it actually impedes a more complete understanding of developments that inextricably intertwine all facets of history.

Such compartmentalization becomes even more absurd in the context of the twenty-first century, when present observers and participants can comprehend the United States' government's response to the events of 9/11, its invasion of Afghanistan, and invasion of Iraq only through a multi-faceted approach to these topics. I first conceived of this work a number of years ago and ultimately finished the manuscript in spring 2002. I had no idea that as I would be writing the prefatory comments, the United States government would have embarked upon imperial initiatives in the Middle East.

I have never taken very seriously the old adage that those who do not know history are doomed to repeat it. Historical lessons depend upon who is drawing them and their knowledge and motives, and people seldom seem to learn from their own mistakes, much less those of others. Frequently, advocates for courses of action draw their historical analogies from inappropriate precedents due to the limits of their historical knowledge, a circumstance that does illustrate the validity of the adage.

Current events fill a historian of the imperial era of the turn of the previous century with foreboding and a grim sense of *déjà vu*, because the use of war as a "handmaiden of politics" became fraught with peril and disaster in the twentieth century, starting with the Great War of 1914–18. The reluctance of most Europeans to become involved in a revived American imperialism in the twenty-first century may stem from the results of their imperial experience in the nineteenth and twentieth centuries. Whether the professed goals be the "civilizing mission," "liberation," "regime change," or "democratization," the "Great Powers'" fundamental premises have lain invariably in a determination to exploit the resources of the targeted region, whether gold, diamonds, or oil, and an arrogance toward the region's culture, society, and civilization. The end result became predictable – reinforcement of the imperial powers' "might makes right" attitude and the brutal, corrupt domination of other peoples.

Europeans glorified war and violence and feared other "lesser races" as a result of imperial conquest. These impulses undid Europe, as its powers embarked upon war for control of the continent and the world in 1914. The European masses, stoked with xenophobic nationalism, went willingly, even gaily, to a conflict which their leaders, imbued with a perverse combination of arrogance and fatalism, believed they could control. The result became an uncontrollable orgy of violence during the next third of a century. The demise of the peace settlements after 1918 demonstrated that negotiating and preserving peace demand as much determination and sacrifice as waging war, or all the blood and tears shed will be for naught. By 1945, Europeans had realized the worst of all possibilities – they had destroyed their own world and opened the door to freedom for their colonized and exploited peoples.

History, unlike a scientific experiment, does not repeat itself exactly, but it does offer lessons for those alert to them and sufficiently unbiased to avoid twisting them for political or personal gain. Furthermore, historical awareness does enable the recognition of circumstances that give rise to such sayings as "Old wine in new bottles" and "There's nothing new under the sun." Americans, including some historians, construe the present threat of terrorism and our "war against terrorism" as unique. Yet history furnishes numerous examples of previous terrorist threats and the responses of threatened governments, none more memorable than the Austro-Hungarian government's response to Bosnian nationalists' assassination of Archduke

Franz Ferdinand in 1914. In every case, one man's "terrorist" is another's "freedom fighter," and the weapons they wield are proportional in magnitude to the arsenals of the powers they confront, whether in 1914 or today.

At various times during the twentieth century America has run the very real danger of becoming a "garrison state." Government and citizens became imbued with a "siege mentality," viewing the domestic and international universe through the black-and-white lens of a "we/they" dichotomy. They declared domestic dissenters as internal enemies and curtailed civil liberties, and raged against a world deemed hostile to America's morally superior goals for it, goals which happened to coincide with American interests. Intellectuals such as Harold Lasswell long ago warned of the danger, which the post-First World War "Red Menace" and the raids and infringements on civil liberties of Attorney General A. Mitchell Palmer had exemplified earlier. These circumstances ultimately catapulted J. Edgar Hoover to a position of power at the Federal Bureau of Investigation from which he could abuse the rights of others in the name of justice for another half century. The transgressions of the McCarthy era, and, most grievously, the internment of Japanese Americans during the Second World War while their young men fought bravely in Europe, stain the history of twentieth-century America.

The Great War offers a cautionary tale for any who would resort to war or threat of war heedlessly, without thought to all potential consequences, who would stifle dissent, abridge civil liberties, and ignore cautionary advice in pursuit of an elusive and expansionist definition of national security, and who would then cloak the enterprise of war in the arrogant, triumphal, and simplistic language of good and evil. Perhaps two world wars have taught that much of the evil Europeans detected in others lay within themselves.

Many Americans know little about the First World War, much less about the era of imperialism. The youth of America, in fact, often know very little about history, even United States history, and what they do know usually comes from film and television rather than in-depth study of the subject. Their European counterparts know more about the First World War because of its great toll of their ancestors, but they know little about the global aspects of the war, because historians have chosen to concentrate on the European arena.

The Great War: An Imperial History seeks to broaden the knowledge of all readers everywhere on that seminal conflict of the twentieth century. May it provide them with new perspectives on the war of 1914–18, perhaps the single most important formative experience of the twentieth century, as the United States government embarks upon an imperial venture early in the twenty-first century.

ACKNOWLEDGMENTS

The Great War: An Imperial History is the product of more than thirty years of teaching and researching the subject of modern warfare and society. An abiding interest in aviation stimulated my research on the First World War for much of my career in academe, but the more I taught the history of modern Europe, western civilization, and warfare and society, in particular the history of the First and Second World Wars, the greater my dissatisfaction became with the available histories of these global conflicts. My students at the University of Georgia consequently suggested that I write a history myself. This book is the result.

In the aftermath of the Second World War, I grew up reading avidly about the 1939–45 conflict, in which my Uncle William fought. My interest shifted when my father, John Sr., took me at the age of 18 to visit the battlefields and monuments at Belleau Wood and Château Thierry in France. My mother Ann Rowena informed me that my Great-Uncle Thomas Davis had won the Distinguished Service Cross and the *Croix de Guerre* for his bravery in combat at Binarville, France, on 30 September 1918. Later his younger brother Harry told me about Thomas's life and showed me his medals and Colt .45 automatic pistol when I stayed with him and my cousin Nancy Davis in Washington, D.C., in the summer of 1965. In 2000 I finally visited Binarville as I walked the battlefields of western Europe.

I thank editor Heather McCallum, then of Routledge, whose interest and encouragement spurred my work. When Ms. McCallum left Routledge, Victoria Peters succeeded her and inherited me and my work. I thank Ms. Peters for her continued encouragement and advice, and feel very fortunate to have worked with two such fine editors. I have greatly appreciated the contributions of senior editorial assistant Sünje Redies and publicity manager Aine Duffy.

I owe to the large numbers of historians who have written about the First World War a debt of thanks, but in particular I would like to single out the following colleagues. I greatly appreciate John Peters's detailed and constructive assessment of the manuscript. Naval historian Paul Halpern has urged me not to forget the navy, while David F. Trask has always offered praise and encouragement. Holger Herwig's work on German and naval history and Gerald Feldman's work on First World War Germany, inflation, and Versailles have proved excellent guides. Hew Strachan's suggestions, collection of essays, and his presently in-process magisterial work on the war have also proved enormously insightful. The work of University of Georgia Masters students Christian Davis, Michael Pack, and Gregory Parsons proved quite helpful. I thank my colleague Alexei Kojevnikov for allowing me to read his excellent article on Russian science in manuscript. Jenny Wood of the Imperial War Museum graciously helped me select posters for inclusion in the book.

All pictures are reproduced with permission of The Trustees of the Imperial War Museum, London. The maps were adapted from Martin Gilbert's *Atlas of the First World War*, published by Routledge, 2002.

I owe a special debt of thanks to Annette Becker, friend and colleague in the study of the First World War, for her willingness to take a kindred spirit on a tour of monuments, battlefields and cemeteries of northern France and Belgium.

Finally, I thank my wife Diane Batts Morrow, also a historian, for serving as a rigorous critic and sole reader of my manuscript before submission. Although our fields of research differ widely, we have been a team of two in mutual support and advice for more than thirty-five years. I also appreciate the support of our two grown-up children, Kieran and Evan, who, although neither chose to enter academe, encourage our historical endeavors, and the assistance of the various furry denizens of the Batts Morrow household.

John H. Morrow, Jr.
Athens, Georgia
6 January 2003

1

The Origins of War, 1871–1914

Europe, imperialism, and power rivalries, 1871–1905

"Exterminate all the brutes."

Kurtz in Joseph Conrad, *Heart of Darkness*[1]

"There are many humorous things in the world; among them the white man's notion that he is less savage than the other savages."

Mark Twain, *Following the Equator and Anti-imperialist Essays*[2]

As the twentieth century opened, Europe, particularly the great powers at its heart – Britain, France, Germany, Austria-Hungary, and Russia – stood at the crest of its power, figuratively at the center of the world. During the nineteenth century its population had risen from 190 million inhabitants in 1815 to 460 million in 1914; its share of the world's population, from 20 to 27 percent. European industrial and technological supremacy, combined with its rising population, enabled its states to dominate much of the globe by 1914.

Historians have occasionally attempted to generalize about Europe before 1914. Eric Hobsbawm refers to it as "bourgeois," or dominated by the middle class riding the wave of industrialization and urbanization. In contrast, Arno Mayer has asserted that Europe remained under the political, social, and cultural control of the aristocracy of the *ancien régime*, which a sea of modernity had not swept away. In fact, the diversity evident across Europe renders either generalization suspect. George Lichtheim's description of Europe as a geographical entity inhabited by peoples whose only commonality was their "mutual detestation and their readiness to go to war against one another" seems more apt than the first two class-bound interpretations.[3]

Traversing Europe from west to east, one passed from densely populated and industrialized states such as Britain and Germany, and a France heavily industrialized in its northeast and predominantly rural elsewhere, to states such as Austria-Hungary and Russia, overwhelmingly rural and agrarian with pockets of industrialization around major cities or in mining areas. Britain reigned as the world's commercial, financial, industrial, maritime, and imperial pace-setter, the center of the globe in all of these realms. The island kingdom dominated an empire of 444 million people and 12.7 million square miles of territory. A plutocracy of an intertwined, intermarried wealthy aristocracy and middle class ruled this kingdom. More than 50 percent of its population of some 45 million people inhabited cities and towns, and peasants or yeomen farmers, had long disappeared from the rural landscape.

Across the English Channel lay France, whose population was stagnating at some 39 million inhabitants. France's northeastern corridor to the east of Paris was a grim industrial and mining region, but middle-class peasant farmers dominated the rest of the country and the Parliament, a result of the French Revolution. However, France's industrial expertise proved formidable. By 1914 it led the world in the new aviation industry and its automobile industry ranked second – a distant second of course – only to that of the United States. Furthermore, it ranked second only to Britain in the extent of its overseas empire.

France's stagnating population contrasted sharply with its eastern neighbor, the German Empire, 70 million people strong and growing fast. Germany was overtaking Britain in certain realms of industrial production, such as iron and steel. Germany had further established a clear ascendancy in the new science and technology-driven chemical and electrical industries due to the superiority of its educational system and its connections with industry. Germany's aristocracy observed the distinctions separating it from the middle class more stringently than did Britain's, although wealthy industrialists such as the Krupp family bought patents of aristocracy. The Krupps ruled their domain – the armaments and armor manufacturing city of Essen in the Ruhr – in much the same fashion as a Prussian junker ruled his estates.

In Europe east of the Elbe River, the unofficial boundary between western and eastern Germany and western and eastern Europe as well, society remained aristocratic, rural, and agrarian. Aristocratic landlords ruled their estates and the peasants who inhabited and worked them much as they had for centuries. Prominent but isolated pockets of industrialization existed – in Silesia and Berlin in Prussia, in Bohemia and around Vienna and Wiener Neustadt in Austria-Hungary, and around St. Petersburg and Moscow and in the mining regions in Russia. The further east one went, the punier the middle class became. Russian industrialization was so recent and the middle class so tiny that workers toiled in gigantic factories with relatively few foremen to supervise them. Such conditions rendered this first-generation working class perfect fodder for strikes and revolution, as the events of the Russian Revolution of 1905 demonstrated.

Of the major European states, only France was a republic, where Parliament governed and the president wielded essentially ceremonial and personal power. The other states were monarchies, with constitutional regimes which enabled popular participation in government to varying extents. England, and tiny Belgium, were constitutional monarchies where the monarchy retained few real powers and Parliament essentially governed. The Kingdom of Italy, unified only in 1870, was also a constitutional monarchy, though with a less developed party system than the others.

The further east one traveled, the more authoritarian the regimes became. In the German Empire, the Prussian Hohenzollern monarch, prime minister, and army command were also the German emperor, chancellor, and army command. A German Parliament (*Reichstag*) elected by universal male suffrage and an upper house (*Bundesrat*) comprising representatives of the empire's seventeen monarchical regimes completed the governmental apparatus. Yet the *Reichstag*, or glee club as some cynics referred to it, voted the budget only every seven years and primarily debated issues. The Social Democratic Party was the largest party in the Parliament, but the institution was in truth merely a constitutional fig-leaf. The emperor chose his chancellor and his power rested, as it had for the nearly three centuries of Prussia's existence, on the army and its officer corps, which the aristocracy still controlled.

In the dual monarchy Austria–Hungary, Habsburg Emperor Franz Josef, who had reigned since the revolution of 1848, relied upon the imperial army and bureaucracy to hold together a sprawling realm of more than a hundred different nationalities and ethnic groups. The two parliaments were more – in German-dominated Austria – or less – in Magyar-dominated Hungary – based on popular suffrage. As one might imagine, dealing with one parliament was difficult enough; with two, a nightmare. Nevertheless, the unwieldy system creaked, or muddled, into the new century.

The Romanov dynasty in the person of Tsar Nicholas II, an autocrat, ruled the gigantic Russian Empire, sprawling across the continental heartland of Europe and Asia, swarming with nationalities. Tsar Nicholas had granted his people a representative assembly, or Duma, after an abortive revolution in 1905, but then rescinded most of what little power it had in the years to 1914. The tsar's authority, like that of his German and Austro-Hungarian fellow rulers, rested primarily on his army and its aristocratic officer corps. The imperial army's potentially gigantic reserves of manpower, embodied in the stolid Russian peasant, only some fifty years out of serfdom by 1914, established Russia as a great power.

The last power, often forgotten because of its decline during the nineteenth century, was another empire that spanned Europe and Asia, this time southern Europe and Asia Minor: the Ottoman Empire, the so-called "Sick Man of Europe." However, it would be premature to declare the sick man dead, especially because a coup by the so-called "Young Turks" in 1908 had reinvigorated the ruling Ottoman elite.

The Ottomans' decline did have a destabilizing effect on southeastern Europe. As the independent states Bulgaria, Rumania, and Serbia expelled and replaced their former overlords, the Ottoman Turks, the Balkans became a tinder-box. The Balkan states' aspirations for further land and people, which invariably belonged to one another or to Austria-Hungary, conflicted with the strivings toward dominance in the Balkans of the Russian and Austro-Hungarian empires, the former to become the patron of the Orthodox Slavs there, the latter to protect its integrity and maintain control over the Slavic peoples within its borders.

———

Discussion of the origins of the First World War should begin with the formation of the state which historians hold responsible for the war. In 1871 the Prussian Hohenzollern monarchy's formidable Prime Minister Otto von Bismarck and army under the leadership of its Chief of the General Staff Gen. Helmuth von Moltke created the German Empire. In the 1860s Bismarck's expert diplomacy isolated Prussia's enemies, enabling the Prussian Army to win three wars quickly – against Denmark in 1864, against Austria in 1866, and against France in 1870–71. The unexpected and rapid appearance of this new industrial and military power in central Europe gave rise to a historical "German problem" because of its potential for destabilizing the balance of power in Europe.

In fact, the formation of the empire did not really create a "German problem." For centuries wars had accomplished or accompanied the rise and fall of powers in the European system, many more catastrophic than the German wars of unification. Bismarck had actually ended the Franco–Prussian War before the Prussian Army could destroy France as Moltke desired. The "Iron Chancellor," who would remain in charge of German policy from 1871 until 1890, was quite content with his creation, and Germany became the new fulcrum of the balance of power, the "balancer" in European international relationships. Bismarck kept defeated France in diplomatic isolation and allied with both Russia and Austria-Hungary, thereby checking their clashing interests in the Balkans, for which he cared not a whit, thus preserving both his new state and the peace in Europe. His focus on Europe and disinterest in naval and colonial affairs, increasingly rare by the 1880s, unfortunately accustomed the British, in their isolation from continental concerns and preoccupation with empire, to circumstances that could not endure. The world of the late nineteenth century was swiftly changing, not just in its rapid industrialization and urbanization, but also in its culture and international structure.

The second half of the nineteenth century was the time of "realist" or "scientific" doctrines, or at least doctrines that purported to be scientific. The nationalism, or devotion to the nation and to the sovereign state of that nation, of the third quarter of the nineteenth century had acquired "scientific" characteristics, exemplified by social Darwinism and "scientific" racism. These qualities transformed the liberal nationalism of the first half of the century, which had espoused the equality of different nationalities and their right to national self-determination, into a conservative doctrine proclaiming a hierarchy of nationalities and the superiority of one nation state to another. In the process nationalism became exclusive and chauvinist.

Social Darwinism left a legacy for theories of war and human aggression that interpreted war as a biological necessity and response to evolutionary pressures. Humans were pugnacious and competitive. Proponents literal-mindedly and often inappropriately applied the metaphors of relentless "struggle for existence," "survival of the fittest," and "law of the jungle" to human conflict. Historian Paul Crook demonstrates that Darwinism equally supported such opposing ideas as "peace biology."[4] Yet the tenor of the times meant that on balance Darwinism buttressed bellicosity.

Ironically, while Darwin had propounded the mutability of species, scientific racism asserted not only the fixed characteristics and hierarchy of so-called races but also the importance of preventing miscegenation. The fear of inferior races either inbreeding with their betters or somehow conquering them proved rampant. Concerns for improvement of the race led to the rise of eugenics and proposals for weeding out its "weaker" members. The rise of "scientific" racism has proven an incredibly tenacious belief despite the absence of scientific evidence supporting it. At the turn of the twentieth century it rendered national differences more exaggerated and supremacist than had the liberal nationalism of the early nineteenth century, which had propounded the ideal of national self-determination. The nationalism of the late nineteenth century had become conservative, racist, and xenophobic.

Conservatism required a ruling class or elite. In the clearly defined hierarchy of traditional society, the aristocracy reigned over middle classes and then peasants at the bottom, and all "knew their place." Women also knew their place in a patriarchal society, the few suffragettes of western Europe notwithstanding. Well-to-do women did not work, while working-class women did, either in domestic service or textile manufacture. The new working class, hated and feared by all the others, in part because the purportedly "scientific" socialism of Marx and Engels predicted that it would revolutionize society and make the other classes disappear, was unintegrated into the European society of the late nineteenth century. Another group of "outsiders," defined not by class but by race and religion, posed an even greater threat in a racist era – Jews.

Anti-Semitism manifested itself across the face of Europe. The Dreyfus affair in the France of the 1890s, in which the only Jewish officer on the French General Staff found himself condemned for spying and sentenced to Devil's Island on the flimsiest of evidence, was perhaps the most notorious single example of anti-Semitism. The army high command, backed by a rabidly racist rightist Parisian newspaper and Parisian mob, refused to exonerate Dreyfus long after evidence had proven him innocent. The civilian government ultimately pardoned Dreyfus and reinstated him in the army. In Russia anti-Jewish legislation had increased under Tsars Alexander III and Nicholas II, and the government instigated and participated in widespread and bloody pogroms against Jews from 1903 to 1906. By the turn of the century, universities in Germany and Austria-Hungary were hotbeds of anti-Semitism. In Vienna, where the anti-Semitic Christian Social Party reigned and the citizens elected political anti-Semite Karl Lueger mayor of Vienna five times, anti-Semitic Pan-Germanism was immensely popular with university students. Such rampant anti-Semitism epitomized the xenophobic and illiberal epoch.

Anti-Semitism prevailed not only in Europe, but also in the *Herrenvolk* or white supremacist democracies, such as the United States, Australia, Canada, and South Africa, that had sprung from it. In the United States, for example, famed automobile manufacturer Henry Ford was a rabid anti-Semite who freely disseminated copies of *The Protocols of the Elders of Zion*, a forged document allegedly proving Jewish plans for world domination. The so-called "white" races defined Jews and blacks as inferior and dangerous, to bar, subjugate, subordinate, banish, or exterminate. Such racism led to Kaiser Wilhelm's warning against the "yellow peril" after Japan's victory over Russia in 1905, a sentiment readily echoed and acted upon across the western world. The United States and Canada, for example, sought to ban Asian immigration. The Japanese perception of a "white" peril in Asia reflected their concern with European and American penetration of China. The end of the nineteenth century was thus a rabidly racist era that set the tone for and planted the roots of twentieth-century war and genocide.

In the 1880s a new epoch began, the era of "new imperialism," in which primarily European powers expanded their power and dominion exponentially over the globe. The reasons and justifications varied: economic, such as the pursuit of wealth and markets; geopolitical, or the strategic value of certain territories; and political and ideological, in the push to increase national prestige. European states, endowed with "surplus" population, superior technology, and naval power, conquered and then colonized the rest of the globe, particularly in Africa and Asia. Although many of the colonies brought no economic advantage, such as additional markets or raw materials for the capitalist economies of the colonizing powers to exploit, the exploiters and contemporary observers often persisted in perceiving the drive for colonies in terms of economic advantage. Great Britain and France led in this conquest of new empires, while even lesser European states such as Belgium, the Netherlands, and Portugal participated in the grab for power. By the end of the nineteenth century the United States in the Americas and in the Pacific, and Japan on the Asian continent had joined the race for empire.

This new imperialism grew from, and in turn enhanced, racist nationalism prevalent in Europe in the last quarter of the nineteenth century. The conquered and subject peoples became evidence of the racial and moral superiority of the European conquerors. Missionaries, and evangelical imperialists such as Rudyard Kipling, cloaked the goal of exploitation with a further "*mission civilatrice*," as the French referred to the hubristic goal of civilizing the "savage" native populations. Their "primitive" wards now became "the white man's burden" to Christianize and civilize. In truth, the white man now became the burden of the conquered peoples. He condemned the so-called "lower races" to serve their brutal European conquerors, who were usually too low-born or poor to have employed servants in Europe, as slave labor in the household and on the land, in mines, on railroads, or on expeditions to explore, conquer, and exploit further land. Only a very few French subjects converted to Catholicism, the first step of their admission to the ranks of the civilized few. British subjects faced clear-cut barriers, such as the "no dogs or Chinese allowed" signs outside British clubs in the Far East.

Weapons gave the European intruders a crushing superiority: gunboats armed with cannon; rapid firing artillery; automatic weapons such as the Gatling and Maxim guns; and the repeating rifle, accurate to 1000 yards. Guns used smokeless powder, which rendered hidden forces difficult to locate, and dumdum bullets, patented in 1897 and manufactured initially in Dum Dum outside Calcutta. The lead-cored dumdums exploded on contact, causing large, painful wounds that dropped charging warriors in their tracks. Europeans used them only in big game hunting and in colonial wars; conventions prohibited their use in conflicts between "civilized states."[5]

In fact, Europeans and Americans differentiated between colonial or "little" wars against "uncivilized," "barbarian," or "savage" peoples, and "major" wars between "civilized" nations. The former were necessary, as Theodore Roosevelt explained in 1899, because "In the long run civilized man finds he can keep the peace only by subduing his barbarian neighbor; for the barbarian will yield only to force."[6] Roosevelt, racist, imperialist, and militarist, believed it the duty of superior civilized races to expand in "just wars" against primitive races.[7] As imperial armies used dumdum bullets, the U.S. Army replaced the .38 caliber revolver with the .45 Colt automatic to stop charging Philippine warriors.

British and Egyptian soldiers massacred the Mahdi's dervishes at the Battle of Omdurman in the Sudan in 1898. The cannon of nearby gunboats and machine-guns scythed down the ranks of the Muslim troops long before they ever made contact with the British Indian Army, which merely completed the slaughter. The British lost forty-eight men; they killed 11,000 Sudanese, and practically none of the 16,000 wounded Sudanese survived. Observers such as Winston Churchill cast such massacres in a heroic and romantic light; poems and stories romanticized such murderous deeds to a generation of British youth raised in the Victorian era. The victories resulted not from superior courage, virtue, or discipline, but from superior technology, which the British and other Europeans took as proof of their God-given greatness. No wonder European youth set off to war in 1914 with romantic images of glory and honor in their heads. Their intellectuals and authors had spent a generation romanticizing their slaughter of other peoples; they presumed to continue this tradition in August 1914.

Europeans believed that extinction awaited the "inferior races," that imperialism aided the course of civilization by weeding out these "inferiors." Consequently, if whippings and other brutal practices did not suffice to "civilize" or break the "savages," annihilation remained, not as an unfortunate by-product of imperialism, but as an intended goal. Firearms gave even the lone European explorer the ability to subjugate, degrade, and murder Africans. Joseph Conrad's novel *The Heart of Darkness* presented a terse rendering of this vicious and murderous exploitation. The brutal deeds of famed explorers such as the British Henry Stanley and the German Carl Peters exceeded those of Conrad's fictional Kurtz, whose final utterance "Exterminate all the brutes," which meant all the "niggers," or non-white races, encapsulated Europeans' ultimate intentions.

Every European country had its brutal colonizers and its massacres, including latecomer Germany's near-total extermination of the Herrero tribe in German Southwest Africa between 1904 and 1911. Belgian King Leopold II's exploitation of the Congo, "the single most murderous episode in the European seizure of Africa,"[8] illustrated the extremes to which imperialism led. Between 1880 and 1920 Belgian atrocities – slave labor, plunder, the murderous suppression of rebellion, attendant famine – depopulated the Congo by half, from some 20 million to 10 million people. In the German invasion of Belgium and France in August 1914, the German Army's cruel treatment of enemy civilians would provoke paroxysms of outrage and sympathy for "poor little Belgium." The Belgians would suffer far, far less under their German conquerors than Leopold's African subjects had suffered under his rule, but to Europeans the life of one European equaled those of numerous "savage" colored people.

Europeans transmogrified technological superiority into biological superiority; it was God's will that Europeans conquer and civilize, or exploit, the "lesser" peoples of Africa, and, if necessary, "sacrifice," or exterminate, them in the name of progress. Charles Darwin contemplated "what an endless number of the lower races will have been eliminated by the higher civilised races" in the not too distant future.[9] From the start European expansion had entailed the disappearance of entire peoples and the appropriation of their land, or what German geopoliticians and Adolf Hitler would later refer to as gaining *Lebensraum*, or living space. Scientific racism and social Darwinism justified such developments. Struggle between the races was essential to progress and to avoid decay and degeneracy, as the superior race would win. Even within races, it would be best if inferior types disappeared along the way.

The conquered territories became part of the power bloc of European empire, an extension for the imperial power to guard, exploit, expand, or, in a very few cases, trade to another European power as compensation. Given the integral nature of empire, a seamless web linked mother country to imperial possessions. The connection of India to Britain, for example, gave rise to the belief that there were two centers of British wealth and strength. Lord Curzon explained in 1901, "As long as we rule India we are the greatest power in the world. If we lose it we shall drop straight away to a third rate power."[10] Indian markets bolstered the British economy, and the Indian Army, 220,000 men strong led by British officers at the end of the nineteenth century, served around the empire and enabled the British to avoid conscription at home.

J.A. Hobson's work *Imperialism*, first published in 1902, warned of the deleterious effects of empire on the imperialists. Attack upon "weaker or lower races" fostered an "excess of national self-consciousness" among the imperial powers. The "divine right" of might and of racial superiority justified European conquests in the constant struggle of the "survival of the fittest." Imperialism and its wars of conquest were a "perpetual necessity," as the choice was "to expand or die." The white man had to "impose his superior civilization on the coloured races," but this very process would "[I]ntensify the struggle of white races." The "parasitism" of the white rulers' relationship to the "lower races" engendered a "psychology" of imperialism. Naked aggression, conquest, exploitation, and extermination became euphemistically civilizing, "educating and elevating" the "lower races," and developing their barren lands for the good of the world. A most "perilous device" of this "parasitism" was the formation of "vast native forces" commanded by white officers, which Hobson likened to the final stages of the Roman Empire, and the "dangerous precedent" of using these forces against another white race. Ironically, Hobson contemplated the likelihood that the development of capitalism would render future wars between "civilized powers" too costly and ultimately impossible.[11]

Hobson would not be the sole prewar observer to believe that capitalism and its connections among the civilized or European powers would make a future war, or at least a long future war, impossible. To presume that economics, the touchstone of supposedly "rational" or "civilized" man, could forestall or override political, cultural, and military calculations, would prove to be wishful thinking. The boundaries between Europe and empire were permeable, and attitudes and beliefs, like financial transactions, flowed in both directions. Culture would prove stronger than capitalism.

In imperialism Europeans did not act only against other peoples. Imperial conquest and interaction reinforced certain attitudes that affected Europeans' perceptions of themselves and of other Europeans. Europeans not only divided the world into races, but also conflated nationality with race as they eyed one another warily. Constant references to the Anglo-Saxon, or the Gallic, or Teutonic, or Slavic "races," indicated the heightened hostility of one European nation toward another. Winston Churchill constantly referred to an exalted Anglo-Saxon "race"; German Chancellor Theobald von Bethmann Hollweg feared the rising power of the Slavs in 1914. Gauls feared the savage Teutons to the east, while Teutons feared the barbaric Slavic hordes to their east. The Anglo-Saxons, from their island, had reached out to conquer the globe but now perceived the ultimate threat to their existence in their Teutonic cousins across the North Sea. So-called continental imperialists, Pan-Germans and Pan-Slavs, in their determination to unite all ethnic Germans in one German state and all Slavs under Russian leadership, would upset the status quo, particularly in central and eastern Europe. Once the Europeans divided themselves into "races," into superior and inferior peoples, what was to prevent the extension of the brutal attitudes toward "colored peoples" to other Europeans for the sake of progress and survival? Hobson's concern for the brutalization of Europeans in imperialism echoed Thomas Jefferson's worries about the pernicious effects of slavery on American whites. Neither was concerned about the colonized or the enslaved, but they recognized the permeable nature of the boundaries between conqueror and conquered.

The future of one's inherently superior race and culture, and of civilization, was at stake. Men had reverted to the most ancient of imperial sentiments, the protection of civilization against the barbarians. Ironically these barbarians included the other so-called "white races" of Europe. The intertwined sentiments of racism, nationalism, and imperialism thus rendered Europe and the world a more volatile realm by the end of the nineteenth century. As historian John Whiteclay Chambers II commented, "The ruthlessness of colonial warfare, with its lack of restraints, would return to haunt Europe in the slaughter of World War I."[12]

———

Within this highly charged context, international confrontations destabilized Europe. As of 1898 two alliances existed: the Triple Alliance of Germany, Austria-Hungary, and Italy, formed in 1882, and the Dual Alliance of France and Russia, formed in 1894. In fact, there were two dual alliances, since Italy was always a tenuous partner, coveting the land and people of the south Tyrol which belonged to Austria-Hungary. Britain stood alone, in "splendid isolation" from continental alignments. In 1898, the same year that the British defeated the Mahdi, Britain confronted France over the Sudan at Fashoda. The French, who had traveled overland from West Africa, acknowledged their disadvantage against the British, who had come down the Nile, and backed down.

The British had escaped confrontation in Africa, but across the North Sea, the Germans posed a challenge closer to home. Kaiser Wilhelm had longed for "a place in the sun" for Germany, an empire to accord with its industrial and military power. The British and French, even the Belgians, had already seized the wealthiest and most fertile domains, and were naturally loath to share the imperial pie. In the naval law of 1898, the head of the Imperial German Naval Office, Adm. Alfred von Tirpitz, proposed to build a fleet to challenge British naval supremacy in the North Sea. Tirpitz, a skilled propagandist, engineered the creation of a navy league that enrolled 240,000 members by the fall of 1899 to stage a campaign for a German battleship fleet.

Just as the British began to contemplate this new naval challenge, they became embroiled in a war to preserve their dominion over South Africa in 1899. They anticipated that the war would end quickly, but it would take three years, substantial numbers of troops, and unanticipated amounts of funds to subdue the barbaric Boers. The Afrikaaners most unchivalrously resorted to guerrilla warfare, to which the British were slow to reply. Ultimately the British resorted to "concentration camps" to corral Boer families in their suppression of the insurrection. In the process much of continental Europe, gloating over this unexpected challenge to the smug British imperialists, sided with the Boers, Kaiser Wilhelm most openly in an impolitic letter to the Boer leader Kruger. Britain had pursued a policy of "splendid isolation" from the affairs of the continent since the Napoleonic Wars and concentrated on the acquisition of empire. Isolation no longer seemed splendid, but threatening.

Britain responded initially in 1902 with an alliance with Japan, the rising power in the Far East after its victory in the Sino–Japanese War of 1895. The treaty contained a secret clause providing for peacetime naval cooperation, as British industry and advisers helped the Japanese develop a first-class navy. The imperial Japanese Army, on the other hand, took as its model the Prussian and looked to conquest in East Asia. Japan gave the British a potential counterweight in Asia to the Russians, whom British India regarded as its foremost threat. Furthermore, the alliance tacitly granted a free hand in Korea and Manchuria to Japan, and tacitly acknowledged that Britain could no longer maintain global naval supremacy in general and in the Far East in particular.

Here British interests diverged from those of the United States, Australia, and Canada, upon whom the British relied for trade. The United States faced Japan in the Pacific, and all three states sought to exclude the Japanese. This sort of racism typified the *Herrenvolk* democracies that Europeans established in Africa and the Americas. Such racist attitudes as a "White Australia" did grant a sense of national identity to and militarized Dominion societies, strengthened their sense of dependence on Britain, and readied them to make themselves available to Britain in case of war.[13]

With the rise of Japan and the United States as naval powers, Britain's global naval supremacy diminished by the turn of the twentieth century. By 1903 the growth of the United States Navy, evident with the Spanish American War of 1898, had prompted the Admiralty to discard plans for the defense of Canada against the United States, a decision which it neglected to discuss with the army. The increased defense expenditures occasioned by the Boer War had exacerbated already existing fears of Britain's inability to support the cost of empire. In 1902, Colonial Secretary Joseph Chamberlain bemoaned, "The Weary Titan staggers under the too vast orb of its fate." Although Britain continued to prosper, it had fallen into a state of "relative decline."[14] Germany and the United States were displacing it in iron, steel, and coal production, and the United States had already surpassed it in manufacturing output in the 1890s.

Shadows were starting to fall across Britain's "place in the sun," and the naval challenge became the darkest. In an era dominated by the seapower theory of Alfred Thayer Mahan, which emphasized concentration and fleet engagements, navies focussed on battleships. Public interest, first and foremost in naval power, and later in air power, as symbols of national pride and achievement, heightened at the turn of the twentieth century. Britain, intent on worldwide naval supremacy for centuries, had postulated since 1817 a two–power standard, according to which the British Navy prepared to best the next two strongest powers combined. Throughout the nineteenth century those next two powers had been France and Russia. In acknowledging the naval might of both the United States and Japan in 1895 and 1904, Britain in fact relinquished both global naval supremacy and the two–power standard.

The traditional British naval rivalry with France and Russia, who were also expanding their navies, endured into the twentieth century, when the German naval buildup began to pose a more immediate threat to Britain. In 1904, the year of the creation of the Anglo–French Entente, the two armies began discussions of possible joint responses to German aggression. Lord Selbourne, First Lord of the Admiralty, planned to strengthen British naval power in European waters at the expense of the Far East and the Western Hemisphere" – "a significant shift in the strategic posture of the British Empire."[15] Britain had now come to terms, implicit or explicit, with three challengers: the United States, Japan, and France. By the time Sir John "Jacky" Fisher became First Sea Lord at the Admiralty in 1904, Germany had become Britain's major potential naval enemy.

Before 1905 the British Army focussed on the Russian threat to India through Afghanistan; and after 1905 on the German threat to France. But the British were in denial about the extensive military preparations required to fight in either place. The Boer War had demonstrated that British military power did not suffice to meet imperial needs. By 1905 military experts predicted that a two-year war in India would require Britain to send 500,000 men. While acknowledging the Russian threat, the British Army did not increase its forces to counter the threat.[16] The Japanese defeat of Russia in 1905 solved the British dilemma, at which point the British General Staff began to concentrate on Belgium.

In October 1905 the General Staff concluded that a 120,000-man army might just prevent German incursions into France and recommended that size of army to the Liberal government in 1906.[17] Eight years later a British Expeditionary Force of approximately that size would land on the continent to cover the left flank of the French Army, while the other major European powers mobilized millions of men.

In 1905 General Alfred von Schlieffen, Chief of the German General Staff, finalized the German Army's plan for fighting a future European war. The Schlieffen Plan, in the opinion of historian John Keegan, was the "most important government document" of the first decade of the twentieth century.[18] The Plan plotted the invasion of Belgium and the encirclement of the French armies within forty-two days, provided that the Belgians capitulated quickly and the French Army contested and met defeat during the German invasion.

The Prussian Army had won its victories of 1864–71 with a numerical superiority provided by universal conscription and a technological ascendancy based on railroads, breechloading rifles, and more modern field artillery. In the Franco–Prussian War of 1870–71, the campaign to annihilate the French Army nearly became a war to annihilate France, to crush it completely, when General Staff Chief Helmuth von Moltke confronted a French people's war against the German invader. Only Bismarck's intervention had prevented a longer and more disastrous war.

Between 1871 and 1905 Germany lost its military advantages as other powers modernized their armies. Moltke concluded that future wars would engage entire nations, thus making short war and rapid or decisive victory unlikely if not impossible. He predicted that the next war would last for seven or even thirty years, and advised that the Germans should defend in the west and push the Russian borders east as far as possible. General Colmar von der Goltz's influential work of 1883, *Das Volk in Waffen*, consequently advocated the militarization of society to prepare for a war of annihilation.

Schlieffen rejected both Moltke's limitations and Goltz's Armageddon. His plan would avoid France's strong eastern defenses by launching two-thirds of the German Army in an invasion from the north through Belgium and the southern Netherlands. In order to annihilate the French Army with these forces, he was prepared to allow the French to invade Alsace and even to accept the temporary loss of East Prussia to Russian troops. Schlieffen was determined to avoid a war of attrition, which he believed would cause Germany's economic collapse, and so he gambled with this risky strategy to prevent a catastrophic long war. Historian Stig Förster concludes that the plan was, in fact, "much less a recipe to win a war than an operational plan to win a campaign" at a time when politicians and soldiers were convinced that war was inevitable.[19]

In fact, the German Army no longer possessed the numerical superiority even against France necessary to achieve Schlieffen's aims. The War Ministry's preoccupation with burgeoning budgets and the dilution of aristocratic control over an army with a much larger officer corps and more urban conscripts ensured a large gap between the size of the extant army and of one necessary to execute the Schlieffen Plan. The apolitical Schlieffen did not trouble himself to solve this problem. The additional troops would pose a monstrous logistical bottle-neck in Belgium. In any case, execution of the Plan would fall to his successors. The German Army intended to win the future war as it had won its previous ones, with a rapid mobilization using the railroads, precisely timed to allow troop trains carrying millions of soldiers to move through the potential bottle-neck of Aachen on their way to the German border. German planners considered two years a long war and planned for a six- to ten-month war at the maximum.

Did this emphasis on the offensive make sense, in light of developments in warfare evident as early as the American Civil War in 1861–5 and more recently in the Russo–Japanese War of 1904–05? The modern battlefield had emerged, with barbed wire, mines, rapid firing weapons, and increasingly accurate rifles. Powerful artillery fired plunging high explosive and shrapnel shells faster and further, forced troops in both wars to go to ground, burrow in siege warfare, and to suffer sizable casualties when they launched attacks. After the Japanese advance through Manchuria, their siege of the Russian base at Port Arthur foreshadowed battles of the First World War. The clash at Mukden between armies of 300,000 soldiers was the largest battle prior to the First World War. Losses were high on both sides; the expenditure of ammunition enormous.

Military observers of the Russo–Japanese War of 1904–05 concluded that however bloody the engagements, the Japanese Army's aggressiveness and willingness to take the offensive against the Russians regardless of casualties had won the war. Observers did overestimate the value of the bayonet and underestimate the machine-gun, which they presumed would serve primarily as a defensive weapon in fixed fortifications. The military and financial cost, as well as the Russian Revolution of 1905, prompted both sides to seek a negotiated settlement from American President Theodore Roosevelt. The Russo–Japanese War thus essentially confirmed the value of the offensive and of the will of well-trained and disciplined soldiers to employ and endure the new weaponry, high losses notwithstanding. If the war confirmed the potential for exhaustion inherent in prolonged warfare, it also offered the possibility of victory in a short, brutal conflict.

Recurring crises and responsibility for war, 1905–14

"A bloody purging would be good for the country."

Sir Arthur Conan Doyle, August 1914[20]

From crisis to crisis. Plans, preparations, and readiness for war

The year 1905–6 was a watershed in the prewar era for a number of reasons. A series of crises in North Africa and the Balkans erupted that would end in war. In Germany a new Chief ascended to command the General Staff. France experienced a surge of nationalism that future crises would exacerbate, goading it to fight the foe that had crushed it some forty years before. Russia would have to recover from its defeat at the hands of the Japanese, while the British realigned their policies to face the continent, and Germany. Two armaments races would proceed simultaneously, with the Germans at the center of both, a continental one pitting Germany and a weak Austria-Hungary against France and Russia, and a naval one between Germany and Britain. The German Empire was powerful, but was it sufficiently powerful and wealthy to conduct two competitions against two powers that potentially outnumbered it on land and one that patently surpassed it at sea? The crises that occurred among the European powers from 1905 through 1914 developed in the context of political and social tensions, general cultural attitudes toward war, and, most concretely, tandem armaments races and plans for war on land and sea.

—

Social and economic historians have suggested that rapid industrialization, urbanization, and the rise of the urban masses between 1875 and 1914 strained European political systems, particularly in Germany. Governments facing internal strains might attempt to resolve them through escape into war, by posing an external enemy to paper over the internal stresses of their society. German historians of the school of *Innenpolitik*[21] have emphasized internal social and economic pressures and dynamics and their political manifestations as the primary determinants of international policy, including war. For them *Aussenpolitik* – the state's international standing and its interactions with other states – is secondary.

Historians have claimed that internal social strains and economic demands drove Germany, for example, to build a navy that it did not need and to resort to war in 1914. Interpretations of the German fleet as a "luxury" fleet[22] emphasize its alleged superfluity to a country with the most powerful army in Europe and its domestic importance to industry and the middle class. War offered an escape from a governmental impasse occasioned by the rise of Social Democracy, which confronted an essentially authoritarian regime of emperor, army, and aristocracy.

Yet such a focus on Germany appears peculiarly one-sided. As early as 1935 historian George Dangerfield pointed out that "liberal" England was in a state of disintegration by 1914.[23] An arch-conservative House of Lords had become increasingly irrelevant. Workers struck frequently and sometimes violently. The likelihood of Home Rule for Ireland after 1912 prompted Northern Irish Protestants in Ulster to arm in opposition, with support from British Conservatives and soldiers. In March 1914, in the so-called "Mutiny at the Curragh," army officers, encouraged by Conservative politician Bonar Law and Gen. Sir Henry Wilson, resigned rather than follow government orders to respond to the anticipated uprising of the Protestant Ulster Volunteers. Finally, militant suffragettes had been challenging traditional ideas of gender since 1910 and often encountered brutal fury from police and male bystanders. A war of nations in August 1914 relieved the British of contending with civil, class, and sex war.[24] The possibility of war in Ireland preoccupied London before continental events intervened. The war not only halted the suffragists' activities, but also liberated men from civilian society to escape into the masculine world of the military. War offered the opportunity to re-establish traditional separate spheres for men and women, as manly men would sally forth to engage in that manliest of pursuits.

In Russia, Romanov Tsar Nicholas II ruled through his bureaucracy and army, and granted minuscule power to the Russian Duma, a fig-leaf of a parliament. He ruled a land increasingly plagued by strikes in industry and mining. His government had failed to secure either a stable working class in its rapid but spotty industrialization or to create a stable peasantry sufficient to buttress the autocracy. Only the army's support had preserved Nicholas's throne in the revolution of 1905, but he remained determined to preserve his autocratic rule. The realities of imperial Russia make it highly unlikely that it would have evolved peacefully into a constitutional monarchy in the absence of war.

The circumstances in both Britain and Russia provide sufficient evidence that war would have offered to their governments as much of an escape from destabilizing domestic conflicts as it did Germany. In fact any government, but particularly the Russian, when confronted with the threat of war, would have to fight regardless of its readiness, or acknowledge its decline in status to second-rate power and face the consequences of severe internal unrest. Urbanization and industrialization, depressions and upswings, and their social stresses and strains consequently provide no means of assessing the responsibility of particular states for causing the war.

While historians have concentrated on the destabilizing effects of economic development, some contemporaries believed that capitalism and the rise of an international economy would prevent war among "civilized" states, as Hobson had hoped in 1902. In 1910 Norman Angell's book, *The Great Illusion*, argued that Europe could not afford and should not prepare for a long war for economic reasons. Britain and Germany were each other's primary trading partners. The pound sterling, the foundation of the gold standard, was the basis of global economic stability. A major war would destroy all of this. Europe simply could not afford a major war; consequently it would not engage in one. Historical works with Angell's title have discussed the origins of the war; other historical works have discussed at length the "short war illusion."[25]

In fact, key prewar figures would not fall prey to the "illusion." Furthermore, concern for short war was not an illusion, but an imperative in the view of those contemporary arguments. Europe was not prepared for nor could it afford a long war. Historians have made much of the very few isolated prognosticators, such as Friedrich Engels and the Pole Ivan Bloch, whose multi-volume work predicted long and debilitating war. In a certain sense these and Angell's work reinforced the necessity for a short offensive war. After all, if a long war was unaffordable and perhaps even impossible, then only a short war remained if fight they must.

The same year as Angell's work, 1910, another, lesser known study appeared in France that indicated the permeability of the boundaries between Europe and empire in plans for future war – General Charles Mangin's book *La Force Noire*. According to Mangin, France's declining birth rate made it absolutely necessary to find other sources of men. He proposed sub-Saharan Africa, whose valorous warriors had achieved significant feats of arms in the past and stood ready to repeat them for France, as a viable source. Mangin dodged right-wing racist objections to having blacks in France by averring that these troops would serve in North and West Africa. Still others doubted the value of African troops. On the other hand, individual black or mulatto Frenchmen had served as officers, even rising to the rank of general, in the French Army starting in the French Revolution. North African troops such as Moroccan infantry (*tirailleurs*) would be shipped to France in case of war. These very examples indicate the French Army's more open attitude toward non-white colonials than other white nations.

Mangin, a swashbuckling colonial officer who had been at Fashoda and served in both Africa and Indo-China during his career, had no hesitation about sending his African soldiers to fight in France. While the original idea had come from other officers in the French colonial army who recognized the fighting qualities of their West African soldiers, Mangin was the officer who advocated it at a crucial time, in the years immediately prior to the war. The *Force Noire*, the black force, would counter the Teutonic threat on the Rhine. The loss of the Franco–Prussian War had forced Mangin's family from its ancestral home in Lorraine to migrate to Algeria. Mangin, like other colonial officers, never lost sight of Europe. In their minds, imperial and European battlefields were intertwined – a French African army would help defend France's eastern frontier and gain revenge against Germany.

The first black African soldiers to visit the metropole, other than a very few officers, had come in 1899, when 150 soldiers who had been at Fashoda in 1898 participated in the parade on Bastille Day and then enjoyed hospitable tours of Paris. French colonial officers had adjusted to African soldierly customs, and the colonial army contained native (*indigène*) officers, though none above the rank of captain and few commissioned officers overall. In 1913 five regiments of Senegalese *tirailleurs* participated in the Bastille Day parade, where one soldier was decorated with the cross of the Legion of Honor, but, notwithstanding an increase in the number of Africans in the force from 13,600 to 22,600 between 1908 and 1912, it would take a war to make the black force a reality.[26]

The culture of the imperialist age not only led to French plans to import colonial soldiers for European war, it also further established an atmosphere in which European youth yearned for war. Niall Ferguson disagrees with the frequent assertion that "the culture of militarism" caused the First World War by preparing men to the extent that they desired it.[27] The evidence, however, supports the frequent assertion, not Ferguson. Sport and adventure prepared youth for war. In the words of Sir Robert Baden-Powell, founder of the Boy Scouts and hero of the siege of Mafeking in the Boer War, "Football is a good game, but better than it, better than any other game, is that of man-hunting."[28] The Scouts were intended to transform industrial society's puny offspring, who had failed in large numbers to qualify for service in the Boer War, into sturdy potential warriors.

As historian Michael C.C. Adams observed in his study of the cultural milieu in Britain and the United States prior to 1914, "war could be seen as an intrinsicially valuable human endeavor."[29] British society, divided rigidly along gender lines, raised and educated male youth, particularly of the middle and upper classes, to value violent athletics from boxing and rugby to hunting. Killing others and dying well and honorably in war inhered in this ethos. War was a "cleansing experience." Garnet Wolseley, Britain's most admired soldier, considered war "the greatest purifier" of an "overrefined" "race or nation."[30] The British Empire required an "Imperial Race," purged of "effeminate" and "degenerate" traits.[31] Sir Arthur Conan Doyle, creator of Sherlock Holmes, mused in August 1914, "a bloody purging would be good for the country."[32]

The obsessive interest in the Middle Ages, in knighthood and chivalry, to the point of staging tourneys, indicated the unease with which many greeted the modern industrial and urban society. Yet these pastimes also "obfuscated the inhuman quality of modern war" and thus actually "helped to encourage" its slaughter.[33] The arrival of war in August 1914 would release young men from the constraints of a dull, materialistic society to find their escape and fulfillment in the grandest enterprise of all. The notion of an "escape into war" that historians have occasionally applied to imperial German foreign policy[34] in fact aptly describes war's reception by a generation of educated young men of the Victorian and Edwardian era.

The German youth movement, the *Wandervogel*, also sponsored escape from the sordid urban materialism and intellectualism of bourgeois life into the purity of nature. Germans, like the British, worried that urban life made sissies of young men. The founders of the German boy scouts (*Pfadfinder*) were veterans of the Herrero War in Southwest Africa, and knightly, patriotic exhortations laced the scouting manual. Industrial continuation schools for young laborers indoctrinated them in the patriotic and monarchical spirit. Ultimately the *Jungdeutschlandbund* militarized youth work. Historian Derek Linton concludes that these organizations were "very much products of the age of imperialism," which made war seem "a heroic and glorious game, a test of a generation, and an escape from . . . urban life."[35]

In France similar currents flowed. In France and Germany bourgeois men revived dueling to restore masculine mettle, while sport in France prepared youth for the ultimate forge of masculinity: war. After the Franco–Prussian War, which had undermined France's international position, modern life, including feminism, was undermining French masculinity. War with Germany would restore France's international position and the traditional gender order. The war itself, Frenchmen believed, as did their other western counterparts, would be "chivalric, heroic, and regenerative of men and nation."[36]

French war myth, as that of other countries, excluded women, since gender concepts associated them with anti-militarism and pacifism, and they often played leading roles in those organizations. Women's duty to society and nation was maternity, and men conceived of women's role in war as the object of their protection. By 1914 nursing as well as motherhood had become acceptable roles for women in wartime, and women expected to participate in the coming war.[37] European youth was ready for war, as the primary intellectual currents of the time exalted conflict. European intellectuals actually yearned for war as a purgative for a dull, bourgeois, materialistic, and overly rational society. A little instinct, intuition, and emotion, a return to nature, a resort to violence, and *voilà*, all would be well. Social Darwinism, which nuanced analyses indicate supported a variety of positions ranging from war and militarism to peaceful evolution, tended to support the former rather than the latter.[38]

Wars begin in the minds of men. Intellectuals proved instrumental in setting the mood of the era, but neither Darwin nor Nietzsche, nor any other intellectuals, would decide for war in 1914. In fact, like Charles Péguy, a French thinker who glorified war, the intellectual's lot, if male and able, would be to join and die in the glorious crusade he advocated – an appropriate end for intellectuals who exalted violence.

———

The European arms races comprised two essential components: a German, French, and Russian race on land and an Anglo–German naval race.

On 1 January 1906 Helmuth von Moltke, the nephew and namesake of the victor of the wars of German unification, succeeded the retired Schlieffen as Chief of the German General Staff. The younger Moltke was a fatalist, a pessimist, whose views of future war resembled his famous uncle's. In January 1905, when the Kaiser offered him the chief's position, he warned of a war with France:

> It will be a people's war that cannot be won in one decisive battle but will turn into a long and tedious struggle with a country that will not give up before the strength of its entire people has been broken. Our own people too will be utterly exhausted, even if we should be victorious.[39]

Nevertheless, Moltke saw no alternative to the Schlieffen Plan, which he did modify after 1908 by weakening the right wing, limiting the offensive path to Belgium so that the Netherlands would serve as an outlet for German trade in case of a British blockade, and strengthening the forces facing the French in Alsace-Lorraine. His modifications indicated his concern that the war might not be short. In 1912, the growing armaments race with France and Russia convinced Moltke that a war would last for at least two years.

Despite his concerns, Germany continued to conscript a far smaller proportion of its youth than did France, which, with a population of slightly more than half that of Germany, would have a standing army by 1914 whose size (750,000 to 900,000) compared favorably to that of Germany. Financial concerns and social reservations about military expansion still impeded the expansion of army and armaments to the level Moltke desired, even as the armaments race intensified. France and Germany responded to one another's increases in conscription, while the Russian Army improved the armaments of its millions of men. If Germany was militarily ascendant on the continent in 1905, French and Russian efforts eroded that ascendancy over time. By April 1914, when the French Army adhered to Plan XVII's all-out offensive, the military balance was swinging toward the Triple Entente.[40]

While the French and Russian Armies certainly improved, the key to German military ascendancy lay essentially in superior training, officers, and firepower, particularly heavy artillery. The German Army had trained its reserve units so well that it incorporated them into its front-line forces, unlike other armies. German junior officers learned to take the initiative, in contrast to their peers in other armies who awaited orders from above, and could assume positions of command two ranks above their own. Finally, German officers appreciated the benefits of firepower and artillery support more fully than did their adversaries. The key to the effectiveness of artillery fire lay in the accuracy of indirect fire, as gunners had to fire precisely at targets they could not see based on coordinates provided by artillery observers. The French 75, whose hydraulic recoil mechanism rendered it accurate up to its maximum range of seven kilometers, possessed a limited elevation capability of 16 degrees and thus fired twelve to sixteen shells a minute in a relatively flat trajectory typical of cannon of its size like its inferior counterpart, the German 77 mm. gun. The relative paucity, heaviness, short range, and absence of a recoil mechanism of larger French 120 and 155 mm. field guns rendered their indirect fire inadequate and inaccurate.

The Germans, on the other hand, had emphasized the development of howitzers with hydraulic recoil mechanisms that fired a shell at a greater angle (45 degrees) over a shorter range than a field gun of comparable caliber, thus generating plunging fire on targets to penetrate them from above. The German 105 and 150 mm. howitzers were practically the same size and weight as their 77 mm. field gun and thus equally mobile, but the Germans also possessed a 210 mm. howitzer for deployment in the field using either horses or tractors. They consequently outgunned the French and British with heavier shells at ranges of up to 10 or 12 kilometers. For close-range fire of less than 900 meters, the Germans had developed the *minenwerfer*, mine-thrower or mortar, equipped with hydraulic recoil and deployed by *pioniere*, or combat engineers. Their squat high-angle barrels could lob shells up to 170 mm. caliber that packed an enormous high explosive punch. The French 75's shell had .688 kgs. of high explosive; the German 105 mm. howitzer, 1 kg.; the German 150 mm. howitzer, 6 kgs.; the 210 mm. howitzer, 18 kgs.; the 170 mm. mortar, 37 kgs.

Niall Ferguson interpreted Germany's conscription of proportionally fewer men than France as evidence of less rabid support of the military in Germany, proof that militarism was "in political decline" with the rise of "overtly anti-militarist socialist parties." "Europeans," he concluded, "were not marching to war, but turning their backs on militarism."[41] Yet both assertions prove misleading.

Ferguson himself states that overstretched finances and the political inability to raise higher taxes constrained Germany relative to Britain and France. He notes Moltke's contemplation of war in 1913 as "deliverance from the great armaments, the financial burdens, the political tensions." Ferguson explains further that contemporaries deemed the cost of the arms race so intolerable – although it ranged as a percentage of GNP from only 2 percent in Austria-Hungary to a high of 4.6 percent in Russia in 1913 – because the regressive tax systems of the continental powers, compounded by the complex federal governmental systems in Germany and Austria-Hungary, set political and fiscal limits to the level of armaments.[42] But Ferguson fails to connect fiscal restraints and social considerations – the War Ministry's concern to preserve the budget and the aristocratic nature of the officer corps – with the German concept of militarism, which was alive and well. The German officer corps generally did not believe in the *levée en masse* or "people's war."

Second, the rise of socialist parties, as the outbreak of war would make abundantly clear, did not necessarily counter nationalism or militarism. The warlike sentiments suffusing European culture and the escalation of the arms race after 1912 do not show a Europe turning its back on war. In fact, the armaments race expanded between 1910 and 1914 into a new realm – the air – as the airship and airplane demonstrated their potential for military use as reconnaissance and perhaps fighting vehicles. By 1914 every European military establishment had an air service of a few hundred aircraft and a few airships.[43]

The German government undertook no economic preparations for war, but then, neither did any other power. No country was prepared economically for a war of any duration. Britain actually depended on Germany for ball-bearings, magnetos, optical glass, and chemicals essential to manufacture explosives. In general Britain lacked precision machinery and a modern machine-tool industry, and relied on the United States, Sweden, and Switzerland for such supplies.[44] Russian industry's economic, scientific, and industrial dependence upon Germany, in the words of historian Alexei Kojevnikov, "bordered on the colonial." Russian Gen. A.A. Manikovskii, in charge of wartime supplies for the Russian Army, complained that "Germany had supplied the entire world, including Russia, with tools of war, and we had paid our money for the development of expensive German military industry."[45] Germany, in turn, had benefitted from patenting scientific inventions of foreigners, including Russians, in such realms as synthetic dyestuffs, because the Russian university scientists were preoccupied with "pure" science to the neglect of "applied" research in the absence of connections to Russian industry. The domination of Russian civilian industry by foreign investors, particularly French, led it to rely on imported technologies, and Russian state munitions factories tended to buy and copy foreign innovations.

The economies, industries, science, and technology in all the European powers would suffer from the fragmentation of international relations that the war would cause, and none was prepared for the magnitude of the disruption. Germany, at least, was fortunate in the extent of its dominance in leading scientific, technological, and industrial realms, in its superior system of technological education, and in the highly developed links among German science, industry, and military embodied in state and private research institutes.

If economic preparations lay beyond the range of vision of governments, naval armaments, in particular in Britain and Germany, loomed large. The Anglo–German naval race has received more attention than the land arms contest from historians as a causal factor of the Great War. The commercial rivalry between the two, as well as the fact that they were each other's primary trading partners, paled after 1905 before the naval competition.

Britain's First Sea Lord of the Admiralty from 1904 to 1910, the ruthless firebrand Sir John Fisher, introduced the dreadnought, the all-big-gun battleship, in 1905 and then the large, fast, heavily armed, and lightly armored battlecruisers in 1908. These powerful ships presupposed a fire control system that would enable British guns to strike accurately at long range, which was not the case, but the naval race entered a new phase with their introduction.

The introduction of the dreadnought seemed to offer the Germans a chance to compete on equal terms in the construction of battleships. But Tirpitz would learn that the British had no intention of brooking a challenge to their naval supremacy. Whatever number the Germans attempted to build, the British invariably exceeded to preserve their margin of superiority. Tirpitz's risk theory proved problematic from the start, and fleet construction deflected funds from the foundation of German might, the army. Historians have judged the program's assumption – that the British would not meet the challenge of Germany's building program – fundamentally flawed.[46]

British and Dominion historians have often condemned the German Navy as a "luxury fleet," unnecessary and unnecessarily provocative, in a sense an extension of the perspective of a "German problem." John Keegan, for example, after noting that rivalries abounded and that Britain and France ruled "much of the rest of the world," asserted that "the worst of the rivalries had been provoked by Germany" in its decision to rival the British

Navy. Britain, Keegan asserted, "rightly" judged the German naval law "an unjustified threat to its century-old command of the seas."[47]

The naval race and the consequent Anglo–German antagonism certainly inflamed passions and created an atmosphere conducive to war. Fisher's threat to "Copenhagen" the German fleet, or sink it in port, and the imagined invasions in the prolific and often bombastic "future war" literature in Germany and England, heightened the sense of reciprocal threat to their readers before 1914.[48]

Historian Avner Offer labels German naval armament "a fundamental cause of the Anglo–German war" and condemns Germany for not using the navy as a diplomatic tool. Yet, Offer at least acknowledges Germany's need for a fleet to protect its growing maritime trade interests so that it would not be at the mercy of others, such as Britain.[49] Niall Ferguson corroborates this in his assessment that the British simply refused to acknowledge the legitimacy of any challenge to their "absolute supremacy at sea."[50] Such refusal smacks of the absurd. Britain was not exempt from challenge on the seas. No rule of international relations stipulated that powers should not have armies and navies, both of which constituted necessary parts of a military arsenal in the new era of world power and overseas empire.

Winston Churchill, First Lord of the Admiralty from 1911 to 1915, switched the fleet from coal to oil fuel, a decision driven by consideration of technological advantage which would later impel British drives to control the oil reserves of the Middle East and Central Asia. In 1912 the British fleet deployed to home waters. Churchill revealed in Parliament that Britain had abandoned the old "two-power standard" and was focussing solely on Germany. The Haldane mission to Germany in 1912 failed to stop the race, but Britain and particularly Germany could not afford to maintain the pace of battleship construction. After 1912 the German government turned its concentration back to the army. The Anglo–German naval race ran out of steam and died of its own accord, too expensive to continue at full speed. Tensions lessened. Niall Ferguson observes that Britain had decisively won the Anglo–German naval race, to the extent that even Churchill recalled that by 1914 "naval rivalry had ceased . . . to be a cause of friction."[51] The naval race was over; the British victorious.

In 1914 Britain had superior numbers of new and older ships of all types in its navy, a volunteer service, plus its large merchant marine. The newest British battleships carried 15-inch compared to German 12-inch guns. However, Germany constructed better ships for its conscript navy and equipped them with superior armor, excellent gunnery and optical systems, and better shells, mines, and torpedoes. Ironically the British and the Germans in their concentration on battleships and the clash of great fleets ignored a weapon of great potential in a war on commerce: the submarine. The Anglo–German naval race has loomed large as a pressure for war, even as a cause in some interpretations, and Germany always appears as the villain of the piece.[52] Both interpretations prove debatable.

The overweening concentration on the naval race has also obscured other key developments in British war plans, which shifted and bifurcated in the prewar era after 1905. In addition to landing the expeditionary force in France and Belgium, the Naval Intelligence Department contemplated economic warfare as an offensive weapon against Germany. Vice-Adm. C.L. Otley, Director of Naval Intelligence, informed First Lord Reginald McKenna in 1908 that a blockade offered a "certain and simple means of strangling Germany at sea," that in a protracted war "grass would sooner or later grow in the streets of Hamburg and widespread dearth and ruin would be inflicted."[53] The British blockade was thus not a wartime reprisal for German actions but an aspect of Britain's preparations for war. While the Admiralty fixated on its battle fleet and a single great naval encounter, Intelligence Department members such as the intellectual Royal Marine Maurice Hankey concentrated on victory by economic blockade, a close blockade of the coast to strangle German commerce, as Britain had done in the past. Ferguson asserts that a "hubristic" Admiralty knew a trade blockade would destroy Germany and that Tirpitz was aware of that danger if the war lasted for eighteen months.[54]

The navy's lack of interest in wartime convoys of merchant ships stemmed from the sheer size of the British merchant fleet, which comprised nearly half the world's tonnage, thus leaving plenty of margin for losses. British cruisers, meanwhile, would track down and destroy enemy commerce raiders, and thus protect Britain from class warfare and economic disaster. Hankey and "Jacky" Fisher also desired a bond with the United States and the Dominions' agricultural economies as the basis for British policy against Germany. They planned further to avoid military intervention on the continent and the consequent enormous need for manpower.[55]

Nevertheless, to take effect the blockade would require a protracted war and would not save France from Germany in the short term, so the Committee of Imperial Defense conditionally approved the need for an expeditionary force in France in 1909. The British Foreign Office and General Staff, presuming that blockade was at best an auxiliary and not a decisive weapon, dismissed "commercial strategies" and advocated a stronger "continental commitment." Ultimately, both strategies coexisted uneasily through the declaration of war, when Britain prepared for blockade, the possibility of a naval battle, and the transport of a small professional force to the continent. Fisher, and Hankey, who became Secretary of the Committee of Imperial Defence (CID), planned to face the Atlantic, not Europe, and to rely on Britain's overseas assets, the Dominions and the United States. Avner Offer concludes that Sir Edward Grey chose to enter the war, but in order to fight a naval and economic conflict with only a token military commitment to the continent.[56]

Some historians have praised British policy as "a triumph of prudence, realism, and sound diplomacy," one which, according to Robert Gilpin, "brought its resources and commitments into balance."[57] To Aaron Friedberg, such appraisals overstate the coherence and intentionality, and ignore the disjunction between commitment and threat. Ultimately, British policy fell between two stools: its army was too small to deter a German attack on France or to play a decisive role early in the war, but it sufficed to draw Britain into a land struggle for which it proved "woefully unprepared." Friedberg contends that Britain needed to increase its military capabilities substantially to contain German expansion, deter German aggression, or participate meaningfully and early in a European war. He concludes: "Instead the British got the worst of both worlds. Their commitment to France was not sufficient to prevent a war or to win quickly once one had begun, but it was more than enough to draw them into a struggle for which they were woefully unprepared."[58]

Niall Ferguson also condemns British policy, but for other reasons. For centuries British policy had resisted Russian expansion toward the Black Sea Straits and Constantinople, into Persia and Afghanistan, and in the Balkans. Liberal imperialist Foreign Secretary Sir Edward Grey and Foreign Office Germanophobes such as Eyre Crowe broke with established policy to create a counterpoise to Germany. They transformed the entente with France into a "de facto defensive alliance." By the meeting of the Committee of Imperial Defence of August 1911, Britain had become France's "active ally." This meeting, Ferguson contends, was a "real war council" in contrast to a similar German meeting of December 1912 which historians have often claimed was a council of war. A further CID meeting in December 1912 led Ferguson to conclude that, "If Germany had not violated Belgian neutrality in 1914, Britain would have."[59] Britain's greatest illusion, in Ferguson's opinion, was Grey's belief that it could conduct a European policy with a minuscule army, which meant that Britain was unprepared for war. Ferguson concludes that ultimately war between Britain and Germany resulted from British perceptions and machinations.[60]

These interpretations raise several crucial points. First, historians have overemphasized the importance of the Anglo–German naval race as a cause of war in 1914. Second, the British government bore more responsibility for the Anglo–German confrontation than historians have previously acknowledged. Third, German desires for a fleet constituted a reasonable policy, even though Tirpitz's pursuit of this goal proved dysfunctional. Finally, British military and naval policy between 1905 and 1914 included disjunctive and aggressive elements similar in motive to those that British historians have attributed to other powers.

—

In the period from 1905 to 1914, two flashpoints gave rise to intermittent crises that heightened tensions among the European powers: Morocco and the Balkans. Both regions were the site of imperial contests: Morocco, primarily between the French and Germans; the Balkans, between the Austro-Hungarian and Russian empires. Other major powers played key roles in the confrontations that arose, and although Morocco served merely as a pawn in the imperial game of chess, the Balkan states, which were freeing themselves from declining Ottoman rule, played increasingly significant roles in the Balkan crises. At first glance, the two locales seem to have no connection, but Morocco and the Balkans shared a history – both had belonged to the Ottoman Empire.

France and Spain planned to reform the governments in their respective spheres of influence in Morocco with the ultimate intention of incorporating these territories into their empires. These initiatives precipitated the Moroccan crisis of 1905–06. In the negotiations, the French had ignored the German government, so the Kaiser responded with a dramatic visit to Tangier, Morocco. The Germans protested the violation of Moroccan sovereignty and demanded equal access or an "open door" in Morocco. Disrupting and splitting the recently formed Entente Cordiale between France and Britain formed the underlying German aim. The Germans gained an initial diplomatic victory in forcing the resignation of French Foreign Minister Delcassé, but then attempted to force an international conference over the issue.

German diplomats asked U.S. President Roosevelt to intervene in the Moroccan crisis of 1905–06, presuming that his support of "open-door" policies in China would extend to Morocco. Roosevelt intervened, since he feared that Europe was close to war. Ironically, the militarist and imperialist Roosevelt, who praised wars between civilized and primitive peoples as improving man and race, abhorred war between civilized races as calamitous, "tragic and deplorable" because it would weaken "civilization as a whole."[61]

The Germans' bullying tactics led the British to stand firmly with the French. Roosevelt perceived a real danger of war stemming from German paranoia of "encirclement" and British paranoia of a continental coalition. In light of Russia's recent defeat, Germany held a decisive military advantage in Europe, but they retreated diplomatically, unwilling to resort to war. The ultimate results were a French nationalist revival and *rapprochement* among England, France, and Russia. German pressure had resulted in the very encirclement they feared. By 1907 an Anglo–Russian convention eased their rivalry over Persia, although it did not end friction in Central Asia, where the two powers had long played "The Great Game" with diplomats, explorers, and adventurers to control the region.

In 1908–09, the Austro-Hungarian empire determined to annex Bosnia-Herzegovina, which it had administered since the retreat of the Turks in the

1870s. Yet the dual monarchy would have to compensate Russia, the other great power interested in the Balkans. In discussions between Foreign Ministers Aehrenthal and Isvolski, Russia requested assistance in approaching the British to achieve a centuries-long aim, access to the Straits at Constantinople, connecting the Black Sea to the Aegean and ultimately the Mediterranean Sea. Aehrenthal acknowledged the request, then quickly annexed Bosnia and even more rapidly "forgot" his negotiations with Isvolski. The neighboring Balkan state Serbia mightily resented Austria-Hungary's annexation of a territory which the Serbs believed belonged to them.

More crucially, the Russians, enraged, began to fulminate. Pan-Slav idealogues believed that protection of the Slavic peoples in the Balkans was Russia's duty, and that Austria-Hungary's incursions threatened Russia's great power status. Germany promptly intervened on behalf of its ally and informed the Russians that Germany would support Austria-Hungary in any ensuing confrontation. The Russians backed down, but the German–Austrian diplomatic victory proved a pyrrhic one. Russia, now wed even more firmly to France, undertook military reform and expansion that would make the Russian Army the most powerful in Europe by 1917. The Russian Empire would not tolerate another such humiliation.

In 1911 the French and Spanish intervened further in Morocco, prompting the Germans to send the gunboat *Panther* to Agadir to reinforce their demand for compensation. In response to complaints that Germany was negotiating "with a pistol on the table," the German government sought to reassure the other powers. But British politician David Lloyd George pre-empted their attempt in a dramatic speech warning Germany that Britain's "national honor was at stake." In the ensuing negotiations, Germany received small compensation in the French Congo for France's annexation of Morocco, and departed resenting the British intervention.

French nationalism surged higher. The British and French Navies concluded an agreement stipulating that in case of war, the French Navy would cover the Mediterranean, thereby allowing the British to concentrate their fleet in the North Sea against Germany. The French Navy had to control the Mediterranean to move troops from North Africa to France, but found itself faced with a potential combination of a developing Austro-Hungarian Navy and a new German Mediterranean division of two cruisers in 1912. This agreement further cemented the Entente, as the armies had been discussing joint operations on the continent since 1905. After the second Moroccan crisis, Europeans began to believe that a war was inevitable and launched further extensive preparations for it. Wars begin in the mind. Once people, particularly those in power, believe that something is inevitable, it invariably happens.

The Italian government, stimulated by French success in Morocco, determined to conquer its own slice of North Africa from the Ottoman Turks, in Libya. The Italian campaign to conquer Libya, or Tripoli and Cyrenaica, constituted a direct attack on the Ottoman Empire. In April 1911 Italian Prime Minister Giovanni Giolitti, who recognized that the integrity of the Ottoman Empire was integral to the peace of Europe, presciently observed:

> And what if after we have attacked Turkey the Balkans begin to stir? and what if a Balkan clash provokes a clash between the two power blocs and a European war? Can it be that we could shoulder the responsibility of putting a match to the powder?[62]

Such musings, of course, did not prevent Italian aggression in September, and the war lasted for more than a year. Yet Giolitti would prove to be correct. The trail of the origins of the war would lead, just as he predicted, from North Africa via the Ottoman Empire into the Balkans.

In October 1912 the powers of the Balkan League – Serbia, Bulgaria, Greece, and Montenegro – declared war against the Turks. The Russians, goaded by the French, prodded the Balkan powers. To the surprise of all, and to the utter dismay of Austria-Hungary, within a month the Balkan powers defeated the Turks, driving them practically from Europe, to Constantinople. The peace treaty signed after lengthy negotiations in May 1913 satisfied no one and lasted only a month, until the Bulgarians attacked the Serbs over the disputed territorial spoils. The other Balkan states, and the Turks, then turned on Bulgaria, which quickly lost the war, from which everyone emerged once again dissatisfied.

Despite reawakened apprehensions of a general European war, it did not occur. Russian Foreign Minister Sazonov reined in the Serbs, at the price of tendering future support for Serb aspirations against Austria-Hungary. Austria-Hungary, although confronted with a second disastrous *fait accompli* and threatened increasingly by Serb strength, took no action. Heir to the throne Archduke Franz Ferdinand, who hoped to turn the dual monarchy into a triad by granting more power to the Slavs in its territory, opposed action against the Serbs.

A year later, while on inspection of the army garrison on 28 June 1914, Franz Ferdinand and his morganatic wife Sophie Chotek fell to the bullets of a young Bosnian nationalist, Gavrilo Princip, in Sarajevo, the capital of Bosnia. The highly secret organization Union or Death, also called the Black Hand, led by the megalomaniacal Col. Dragutin Dimitrievitch, or "Col. Apis," had trained, armed, and dispatched the assassins. Individual members of the Serb Cabinet knew of the plot, but were not behind it and dared not divulge any knowledge of it in the terrorist atmosphere that reigned in Serbia at the time. After all, in 1903 Serb officers had murdered the King and

Queen, the Queen's brothers, and two Cabinet ministers, then chopped the bodies of the King and Queen into bits with sabers and thrown the pieces out of the window into the royal garden. In a footnote to history, the Serb government in exile would execute Apis in 1917.

The Serbian press callously applauded the murders and denounced the Dual Monarchy, which mourned but did not respond. When it did at last with an ultimatum on 23 July, the die had been cast. After inaction in the earlier crises, and with Franz Ferdinand now dead, Emperor Franz Josef, Foreign Minister Berchtold, and General Staff Chief Franz Conrad von Hötzendorf, long an advocate of attacking Serbia, had now decided on war, and Germany had extended a blank check of support to them. At the time of the ultimatum French President Raymond Poincaré and Prime Minister René Viviani were *en route* from a state visit to Russia, but Poincaré had assured the Russian government of French support. Russia, after its own inaction in earlier crises, was ready to support Serbia unconditionally. The Serb reply to the ultimatum was conciliatory, but the Serbs refused to allow Austria–Hungary a free hand to investigate the assassination in Serbia, which would have constituted a violation of the sovereignty of any self-respecting state.

Austria–Hungary consequently responded with a declaration of war on 28 July. The Russian government declared general mobilization on 30 July, which occasioned German mobilization and declaration of war against Russia on 1 August, France on 3 August, and Belgium on 4 August. Britain, which had kept its fleet on station since a review in home waters on 26 July, declared war against Germany on 4 August. In all, thirteen declarations of war occurred throughout the month of August by European states large and small, and by Japan against Germany and Austria–Hungary. Italy chose neutrality, since the territory it coveted belonged to Austria–Hungary. The war that most had anticipated since 1905, that many had considered inevitable since the second Moroccan crisis of 1911, had finally begun.

Historians have studied the July crisis and the declaration of war repeatedly, examining in great detail the discussions within and between European governments, the roles and attitudes, often shifting under the pressures of the moment, of the individual monarchs, statesmen, and generals involved. Regardless of the nuanced and varying assessments of responsibility, the histories all end the same way, with the opening of the war.

In an oft-cited scene, Sir Edward Grey, British Foreign Secretary, looks out of his office window the night that Britain declared war on Germany and utters the famous and poignant statement: "The lights are going out all over Europe and we shall not see them lit again in our lifetimes." Far less well known, but equally revealing, were Moltke's sentiments expressed in a letter of 28 July urging Bethmann Hollweg to move quickly toward war. He referred to the coming conflict as a "world war," in which Europe's civilized nations would tear each other to pieces and "destroy civilization in almost all of Europe for decades to come."[63] Despite strong reservations about the Schlieffen Plan and constant concerns about a lengthy war, Moltke had long demanded a pre-emptive strike as soon as possible. He believed a conflict to be inevitable, and that it would "purify" the German nation in a struggle of the fittest. Grey's and Moltke's sentiments belie the mythical contention that everyone expected a short war.

The war plans of all the powers entailed an offensive against the enemy: in the cases of Russia and Austria-Hungary, against two enemies simultaneously; in the case of Germany, against one and then the next sequentially; and in the case of France, against Germany alone. Germany planned to invade France and Belgium; France, Germany; Britain, to support France in Belgium; Russia, both Germany and Austria-Hungary; and Austria-Hungary, both Russia and Serbia. Austria-Hungary's intentions were certainly the most absurd of all in light of its military capabilities. However, the weakest of the forces had for its Chief of Staff the most rabid warmonger of the generals, Franz Conrad von Hötzendorf, who had constantly urged war in the half decade before 1914. Had Italy had the audacity to enter the war on the Entente side in August 1914, Conrad might have attacked all three at once, with an army unable to fight even one.

Historical observers have condemned this cult or "ideology of the offensive."[64] Certainly in France the elevation of the attack in all circumstances, the emphasis on *élan vital*, on will over material circumstances on the battlefield, and on training with the bayonet, smacked of a cult. The defensive, however, was also costly, but without the redemption of offering victory. In 1914, with the survival of one's very culture and civilization against lesser European "races" who would plunge the world into ruin seemingly at stake, all the powers launched offensives aimed to win the war quickly.

Keegan explains that war plans of the European armies assumed "mathematical rigidities" and "inflexibility."[65] However, the movement of armies of millions of men bound in alliance necessitated some stability and planning impervious to any one ruler's whim. Historian Gerhard Ritter believed that the Schlieffen Plan overestimated the capabilities of German troops marching and fighting their way into France, and underestimated Russian capabilities to mobilize quickly and invade East Prussia.[66]

Other critiques of the Schlieffen Plan condemn its mechanistic and fanciful nature. Yet, recently Antulio J. Echevarria demonstrates that the Schlieffen Plan was not the rigid, inflexible, and mechanistic structure that many previous historians have postulated, but a new way of viewing individual battles as part of a greater whole, or *Gesamtschlacht*.[67] The war plans of the other powers were no paragons of realism and flexibility, as Friedberg's description of "fanciful war games" in the War Office and India mechanically treating "units like men on a chessboard"[68] indicates. Moltke

was not prepared to consider alternatives to the Schlieffen Plan when
Wilhelm inquired about such possibilities in 1913. In 1914 the Russian
generals informed Tsar Nicholas that partial mobilization solely against
Austria-Hungary was not feasible. The French Army ignored evidence of the
extent of the German right wing's swing through Belgium, and its Plan 17
stipulated attack through Alsace Lorraine, the most heavily fortified region
in western Europe. In Austria-Hungary, Franz Conrad von Hötzendorf was
determined to attack in two directions at once, against Russia and Serbia. The
offensive reigned, and the key to success was the rapid execution of
mobilization and attack, most of all for Germany, which lay between its
enemies.

Historians have condemned the Schlieffen Plan because it alone made no
distinction between mobilization and attack and because it disregarded
political considerations in its violation of Belgian neutrality. Both assessments
ring hollow. What technically was a German advantage becomes somehow
damning, as if the plan's seamlessness pushed men to make decisions that
they would otherwise not have taken, or all the powers, given a short
intermission between mobilizing and attacking, might miraculously have
called a halt to the entire drama. The violation of Belgian neutrality was not
what brought Great Britain into the war, although the British government
used the invasion as a political excuse justifying British entry to the masses.
France and Britain also contemplated invasion of Belgium.

A myth that holds a unique fascination for western culture concerns the
role of technology and the demands of armaments races and mobilization in
driving statesmen and generals to war. The state of technology and resulting
conditions of mobilization did not cause the outbreak of the war. Technology
may create imperatives, but humans, who possess agency, choose whether and
how to exploit technology. Men created military technology and formulated
the plans for its use. Perhaps all generals and politicians did not realize that
military technology might imply a long war, but some of them did in 1914.

Some historians argue that arms races actually caused the war, or, in Sir
Edward Grey's words, "The enormous growth of armaments in Europe . . .
made war inevitable."[69] Military historians have reviewed the significance of
the prewar armaments races with increasing nuance and complexity, defining
armaments to include manpower and materiel. Such evidence indicates
German motives in 1914 that stemmed less from aggressive expansionism
and more from a fearful and desperate pre-emption of rising Russian power.
Furthermore, arms races do not lead automatically to war, as nearly fifty years
of the Cold War demonstrated. Consequently, historians should seek the
cause of and responsibility for the First World War in the arms race only with
the utmost caution.

In a further variation on this theme, some historians, looking back with the
knowledge of future technological developments, often contemplate what

might have happened had later technologies been available in 1914. For example, John Keegan observes that radio communication, or wireless telegraphy, was not available to help the statesmen of August 1914, whose capacities "events successively and progressively overwhelmed."[70] He laments the lack of communication within governments, of which he considered Germany to be the most extreme example. Avner Offer also condemns Germany for its lack of coordination at the top under an "unbalanced" Kaiser.[71]

Yet, to the statesmen and soldiers of the time, the conditions, technological and otherwise, under which they labored were givens. Furthermore, to construe the German government as the most egregious example of poor communication overlooks equally formidable examples of lack of communication among British politicians, generals, and admirals before the war. The Kaiser, with all his foibles and prejudices, offers an easy target for simplistic accusations. The course of recent history, when the technology of communication has become incredibly sophisticated, continues to provide numerous examples of lack of communication within and between governments, of statesmen whose capacities are patently not up to the task at hand, and even of a further phenomenon, "information overload."

RESPONSIBILITY. PERSPECTIVE AND A STERILE CANON

The Second World War concluded an energetic and politicized interwar debate over the origins of the First World War by reinforcing the case for German responsibility in the origins of the war of 1914–18. Starting in 1961, Fritz Fischer's two magisterial works, *Germany's Aims in the First World War* and *War of Illusions*,[72] asserted dramatically and unequivocally that Germany was responsible for starting the First World War. The first work, *Germany's Aims*, concerned the war, and the second examined the prewar era – a clear indication that Fischer assumed *a priori* German responsibility for the war in its imperialist aims. Neither work compared Germany to the other European powers, whose documents were unavailable, while German loss of the 1939–45 war had thrown their documents open to all. None of this mattered; such German *mea culpas* essentially closed the case. Ever since, western historians, including Germans, have concentrated on the "peculiarities" of German history that led it to cause both wars and generate the Holocaust. Numerous books have appeared concerning, some even titled, "The German Problem." Such perspectives strike a thoughtful reader as ironic, since any major power invariably poses a "problem" to other powers, and all powers have their "peculiarities."

In recent decades historians have essentially accepted this canon of interpretation of the origins of the war. Simply stated, Germany bears the main responsibility for starting the war of 1914 to 1918. Some historians conjectured that the war stemmed from a tragedy of miscalculation, or that timetables of military mobilization propelled the actors in the drama of July 1914. Yet even in those views, Germany had committed most of the miscalculations, while the necessities of rapid German mobilization forced the pace toward war. Some authors, while accepting the main premise, suggest that Austria-Hungary or Russia acted more independently of their allies than historians have heretofore acknowledged, and consequently bear more responsibility for the outbreak of war. The end result is that the losers remain responsible for the war.

Niall Ferguson acknowledged that a "jingoist and expansionist" Serbia risked European war in hopes of profiting from it, and placed responsibility further on Britain for transforming a continental into a world conflagration. He believes that British perceptions exaggerated the German threat and that Britain could have lived with German war aims.[73] Ferguson's assertions about Britain are scarcely believable, as Britain could not allow one state to dominate the continent and could not retreat from commitments to its allies. More peculiarly, Ferguson still attributes principal responsibility for the war to the Germans for encouraging an Austrian military response and contemplating a pre-emptive strike in their pessimism about the future military situation,[74] although the very evidence he presents implies a further re-evaluation of that fundamental premise. His Eurocentric and particularly Anglo-German focus prevents that reassessment.

James Joll's work of 1984 remains the most satisfying attempt in the past twenty years to discuss the origins, but he accepts German responsibility for the war. Avner Offer condemned the German leaders for "flying in the face of economics," and of "fundamental incompetence," and "reckless, fatalistic abandon."[75] In John Keegan's view the Kaiser, who failed to bring order to the disarray at the top of Germany and to rein in the military, bore ultimate responsibility for the war.[76] Keegan, while blaming the Kaiser, contradictorily deems the origins of the war "mysterious" and the entire First World War "a tragic and unnecessary conflict."[77] The general public, like Keegan, seems to consider the war an unnecessary and tragic waste of millions of men. On the ninetieth anniversary of the armistice, the News Services report from Paris in *The Atlanta Journal-Constitution* of 12 November 1998[78] was headlined "In solemn pomp, Europe recalls 'a useless war.'" A teenage girl reiterates, "It was a stupid war," while 101-year-old French veteran of the conflict Robert Gelineau muses, "It was a useless war."

In contrast to Keegan, Australian historians Robin Prior and Trevor Wilson, with enviable clarity, assert the canon unequivocally. The leaders of one great power acted in a manner most likely to cause a European conflict. "All roads," they conclude, "lead to Berlin." The German Kaiser and General Staff were responsible for the war.[79]

Paradoxically, the fixation on the very existence and policies of Germany as the root cause of the war contradicts the other prevailing notions of tragedy, mystery, and uselessness. The first belief has as its premise that an aggressive, authoritarian, militaristic, and expansionist Germany threatened to dominate Europe, whatever the means or cost necessary. Given this premise, the war could certainly not be mysterious or useless. Yet the very coexistence of these two attitudes, sometimes in the same work, indicates historians' inability to come to grips clearly with the origins of the war.

Western Europeans in particular, who still pride themselves on their superiority to the rest of the world, over much of which they ruled in 1914, have difficulty coming to grips with the fact that they undermined that very authority in an unparalleled orgy of self-destruction which began in 1914 and concluded in 1945. This very arrogance, this hubris, renders the origins of the war and the war itself so incomprehensible to so many still, as a new millennium begins. Something this horrible should never have happened on a continent as marvelously progressive as Europe. The impossibility of reconciling this attitude with the historical evidence of nationalist, racist, and imperialist European powers that valued and glorified war, and had reasons, aims, and obligations to go to war in 1914, has prevented further progress in understanding the origins of the war.

The First World War may seem senseless; it was and is so only for those who refuse to face the reality of the era prior to 1914, which in retrospect is termed *La Belle Époque* (the beautiful epoch). It was beautiful only for the wealthy, and only in retrospect. It was, in fact, riven with instability and tension, both domestic and international.

European historians also persist in believing in the alleged separation and hierarchy between European and imperial issues and the primacy of continental matters, with the consequent belief that the war could not have and did not start over imperial concerns. Joll, for example, asserted that "immediate motives" were "not directly imperialist" but that the "frame of mind" stemmed in part from earlier imperialist policies.[80] This contention simply does not fit the facts. In the era of imperialism and colonialism, Europeans' concept of empire viewed mother country and possessions as an indissoluble whole. Statesmen viewed colonial and continental issues as inextricably intertwined, the two merging indistinctly, and in the British official mind, with the imperial often of greater import.

Only a Eurocentric perspective refuses to understand the signal importance of imperialism in the origins of the war. In the era of the new imperialism from 1880 to 1914, Europe forged relationships with the wider world that were, on balance, destructive of other societies. Consequently, as a few contemporary observers such as Hobson recognized, Europe was potentially self-destructive. The clichés of "chickens coming home to roost" or "sowing the wind and reaping the whirlwind" apply to the relationship of European imperialism and the origins of the First World War.

All the imperial powers eyed one another predatorily and warily, intent on expanding or defending their empires. Britain was concerned that its ally Japan looked to extend its possessions in East Asia, at the expense of other Asian countries and, if possible, at the expense of its European competitors in Asia. Russia and Great Britain had long played "the Great Game" in central Asia, a rivalry that the Anglo–Russian convention did not suddenly and miraculously halt. England, France, Germany, Russia, and Austria-Hungary, as well as lesser powers such as Italy, and even Serbia, covetously eyed the Ottoman Empire, the "sick man" of Europe. While the Ottoman Empire may have been "sick," its illness did not mean that the Young Turks who seized power in 1908 did not have plans to restore the imperial glory of the empire. They harbored, in fact, grandiose designs, at Russia's expense. Both friend and foe deemed Austria-Hungary, with its mix of nationalities and ethnic groups, the next empire likely to disintegrate, with the spoils going to its ever greedy neighbors, both large and small. The existence of Pan-Germanism and Pan-Slavism demonstrated most clearly the penetration of the continent by imperialist ideas. No major power remained satisfied with its circumstances. Even England and France were intent upon, and in the process of, expanding their empires further around the globe, and circumscribing German territorial acquisitions. As the events of 1914 demonstrated, all proved willing to fight to achieve their goals.

Aggression and fear saturated the entire imperial world view. A vaunted sense of superiority coexisted with the haunting fear that one's lesser competitor might somehow gain the upper hand, unleashing disastrous consequences for civilization. The introductory plaque on the origins of the war at the *Historial de la Première Guerre Mondiale* in Péronne, France, decries the disproportion between the relative insignificance of the war's causes and its monstrous magnitude, a tribute to the war's absurdity. Yet the causes of the war were not insignificant. The European powers went to war to determine who would control Europe and the world. The stakes proved enormous, and statesmen and generals such as Grey, Moltke, and Bethman Hollweg knew it. There were no innocents in power in Europe, only civilian and military leaders culpable and complicitous in causing the war. Prior to August 1914 Europeans had presumed to control the world; they were now to learn that they could not control themselves.

2

1914. The "Big Show" opens

"Even if we perish, it will have been exquisite."

German War Minister Gen. Erich von Falkenhayn to Chancellor
Theobald von Bethmann Hollweg, Berlin, 4 August 1914[1]

"This is pure murder, not war."

Cpl. George Matheson, BCo., 1st Bn, Cameron Highlanders, BEF, Ypres,
11 November 1914[2]

Upon the declaration of war and mobilization in August 1914, ecstatic crowds gathered to cheer off the troops in major cities around Europe. As the German Army expanded to some three million men, troops assembled to depart for the front in trains with *nach Paris* hastily scrawled on the coaches. Civilians greeted the outbreak of hostilities with such enthusiasm that press and photographs immortalized the "August days" of 1914. Kaiser Wilhelm proclaimed that he recognized "only Germans," capturing the pervasive sense of unity that seemed to permeate the time. Sharp-eyed observers of photographs of the crowd on the Odeonsplatz in Munich have even located a young Adolf Hitler among the exuberant throng.

In Vienna people paraded through the streets as young recruits marched away. As three million soldiers, representing eleven different nationalities, reported to the Austro-Hungarian Army, spontaneous enthusiasm erupted in the major cities of the empire. In a Russia plagued by strikes and demonstrations through July, relative labor peace reigned as 96 percent of conscripts reported in the capital St. Petersburg. There, Tsar Nicholas and Tsarina Alexandra appeared on the palace balcony, and the crowd sang the national anthem on bended knee, as a sense of patriotic unity surged through the multitude.

The British, French, and German governments expected riots and resistance from the working class because of socialist influence, especially in France where a right-wing gunman assassinated leading socialist Jean Jaurès. In Düsseldorf, Germany, July had ended with workers' anti-war demonstrations, while the women of the peace movement continued to advocate their beliefs. The governments and the right wing need not have feared, as conscripts and volunteers, socialists included, flocked to the colors in unexpectedly large numbers. Some deserters even reported for duty. In France, as church bells pealed and drumbeats resounded through communities calling men to the colors, more than three million men, out of a French population of some thirty-nine million, gathered to leave for war. Some rear echelon officers, swept away in the enthusiasm of the moment and overcome by the prospects of glorious combat, left their posts for the front in order to participate in the anticipated short, sharp clash. They would be fortunate to survive to return to the rear. Chalked on the side of French boxcars was the slogan *à Berlin*.

In Britain, which did not have conscription, the numbers of volunteers caught the army without sufficient uniforms. A few unfit unfortunates whom recruiters rejected summarily for physical shortcomings committed suicide in despair. Had they but waited, the declining standards for military service as the war continued might have offered them the opportunity to die for their country. The small 120,000-man British Expeditionary Force set sail for Belgium, soon to appropriate the Kaiser's reference to them as a "contemptible little army" for their own label, the "Old Contemptibles." In all countries soldiers, professional and conscript, set off to perform their duty. In the bellicose atmosphere of the war's opening days, troops prepared to confront enemies that threatened the very existence of their country and culture.

The crowds, rather than the soldiers, have excited the interest of historians. The more historians probe the nature of the crowds, the more they have qualified their composition. The legendary crowds, under the historical microscope, have now become primarily an urban middle-class phenomenon. Rural folk did not celebrate the prospect of war. The harvest preoccupied them, just as all their able-bodied men reported for duty in armies that comprised primarily peasant farmers. In Bavaria, in southern Germany, they reacted with worry and fear, anxiety and uncertainty, as farmers called up for service wondered how long they could hold out in a long war. Urban workers, facing widespread unemployment as peacetime industries abruptly closed early in war, were not much in evidence in the crowds. They reported as conscripts, ready to do their duty. Finally, in cities in border areas, which faced the prospect of invasion, crowds were noticeably absent.[3]

Historians, using police reports and press accounts, now distinguish three primary groups in the crowds: adults, seized with or anticipating panic and rushing to banks and stores; riotous youth, exploiting the occasion for juvenile rowdiness; and ardently patriotic middle-class professionals and students, caught up in the moment and mobbing the squares and troops, and then rushing off to volunteer themselves.[4]

In Austria-Hungary, an image of unity overlay the Austro-Hungarian government's discrimination against certain "unreliable" nationalities, specifically Serbs, Ruthenes, and Poles, who had potential links with the empire's enemies. Austrian Prime Minister Count Karl Stürgkh had ruled by decree since March 1914. Now government by military authorities and civilian bureaucrats foreclosed any political forum for non-Germans in Austria, while a new army "Surveillance Office" watched for subversion. In Hungary Parliament continued to function, but did not represent non-Magyar nationalities anyway. Early in the war "unhealthy political conditions" in Bohemia undoubtedly influenced Czech soldiers, who soon gained a reputation for unreliability.[5]

What happened at home mattered little to most Europeans in August 1914; all eyes focussed on the fighting fronts. In 1912 a newly minted military aviator had encouraged a friend to learn to fly with the invitation to come see men "like ants crawling." In August 1914 armies of millions of human ants crawled across the landscape of Europe to clash on three fronts: the western, between Britain, France, and Germany; the eastern, between Germany and Russia in the northeastern sector, and between Austria-Hungary and Russia in the southeast; and the Balkan front, between Austria-Hungary and Serbia.

In the midst of the rush to war, some governments in Europe, and across the Atlantic the United States, remained neutral. The Italian government, calculating that its alliance with Germany and Austria-Hungary deprived it of any prospect of gaining the territory it most coveted in the Austrian Tyrol, shrewdly chose to remain neutral in August 1914. In the Balkans the monarchs of Bulgaria and Rumania also decided to wait and see how the war progressed before throwing in their lot with the side they thought more likely to win and award them the territory they coveted.

In the United States President Woodrow Wilson urged American neutrality on 19 August, an easy proclamation to make in August, but harder to espouse when the war did not end quickly. North America led the world in grain and livestock production, while the United States led in steel, coal, wheat, and petroleum products. Europe would inevitably approach it for financial and material aid. If the United States denied loans and credits and fulfillment of orders for food and materiel in a long war, it would cripple its own economy and forgo enormous economic benefits that the European war offered. In October the government allowed short-term loans and credits in connection with trade to the warring countries, although in fact the British blockade would mean that the United States was trading with the Entente alone, hardly a neutral outcome. Nevertheless, for the United States, which had intervened in a Mexico riven with domestic turmoil and whose tiny army was now hard-pressed to contain Mexican bandit Pancho Villa on its southern frontier, and whose population comprised so many immigrants from various European countries at war, neutrality, however defined, made sense.

These neutrals notwithstanding, the potential for conflict beyond Europe loomed. Further east lay possible additional fronts if the Ottoman Empire entered the war. Across the wide expanse of the oceans of the globe ranged potential naval and colonial theaters of conflict. From the very start of the conflict, it became evident that the major fronts would lie in Europe. However, the war's naval and imperial components would render it global in scope almost immediately. Furthermore, the inability of the combatants to terminate the conflict quickly would require the mobilization of their home fronts, a prospect that the near universal conviction of a quick war had indeed precluded.

THE WESTERN FRONT. FROM MOBILE SLAUGHTER TO STALEMATE

On the Western Front, the German juggernaut exhibited superb efficiency. The High Command assembled its troops, incorporated its reserves into the ranks of first-line troops in a step other armies could not match, loaded them into trains, and moved them with precision by rail to the Belgian frontier. "War by timetable" was under way. According to Moltke's modification of the Schlieffen Plan, the right wing, some 60 percent of the German Army, would have to seize the Belgian fortress cities and then march and fight its way through Belgium and into France, defeating the French and British forces on the way. They would encircle Paris from the northwest, then come around south of Paris, heading east to strike the French armies in Alsace Lorraine from the rear. Meanwhile, the bulk of the French Army, adhering to Plan 17, formed up on the frontier of Alsace Lorraine to thrust directly into the heart of Germany through the most heavily fortified region in Europe. The rest of the French forces moved north to counter the German thrust through Belgium, where the British Expeditionary Force joined them on their left flank.

The German Army encountered unexpected opposition in Belgium, first from the fortresses. They brought up giant Skoda mortars to crush the offenders. In Liège a general staff officer, Erich Ludendorff, distinguished himself by taking command of soldiers in disarray after their general had been killed and successfully seizing the fort. Throughout Belgium and northeastern France, German troops who came under fire and could not locate enemy soldiers presumed that *franc-tireurs*, or civilian snipers, were the culprits, as such incidents had occurred in the Franco–Prussian War. In their highly charged frame of mind and under orders to display German *Schrecklichkeit*, or frightfulness, to minimize resistance, German soldiers brooked no such underhand tactics as popular participation in warfare. According to Lt. Fritz Nagel, they responded to the extremely "nerve-racking" conditions with "savage and merciless slaughter at the slightest provocation."[6] German soldiers consequently shot civilians, burned down towns, and, most egregiously to defenders of western civilization, major libraries and cathedrals. Their behavior became grist for the propaganda mill of their enemies.

In the war of movement through Belgium and northern France, the initial encounters evoked memories of glories past. British and French cavalry, the latter clad gaudily in red and blue with the sun glinting off their armor, skirmished with Prussian *Uhlans*, with occasional jubilation from having blooded a saber or lance. The first British casualties to die in France fell to friendly rifle fire from other British soldiers, while the first German killed fell to the saber of a British cavalryman.[7] The Germans, marching forward in close formation and in waves, presented incredible targets to British artillery and to professional soldiers capable of fifteen rounds of accurate rapid fire a minute, at encounters such as the Battle of Mons, Belgium on 23 August. British officers recounted how their soldiers and machine-gunners mowed down German cavalry patrols and advancing masses of German infantry, killing as many as 500 in two minutes, while German artillery and machine-gunners decimated British units.[8] British soldiers at Mons reported the appearance of an angel, above battlefields that some compared to hell.

The volume and accuracy of British soldiers' rifle fire misled attacking German forces into thinking that they confronted machine-guns. Conscripts, of course, were incapable of such feats. Nevertheless, a skilled machine-gunner could more than compensate for soldiers' rifle fire, and the British and French could stem the German tide only momentarily before beating hasty retreats. Cavalry galloped away, horsedrawn artillery wheeled and retreated, while the poor bloody infantry, exhausted, walking wounded, and hungry, followed on foot, leaving behind their seriously wounded comrades. Lt. K.F.B. Tower of the Royal Fusiliers called the retreat "a veritable rout," which "Had the Germans only taken advantage of this, the Expeditionary Force must have surrendered."[9] The Germans did not, and the BEF retreated in disorder.

The encounter at Mons was small. In fact, despite valiant British action in 1914, the BEF itself was too small to pose serious opposition, and on 25 August the Germans once again defeated the BEF at Le Cateau. Often ignored in English-language accounts of the encounter at Mons is the contemporaneous battle of 23 August between French and Germans at Charleroi, Belgium, where the French lost 130,000 men killed or wounded,

more than the total British force in Belgium. Concentration on relatively
small Anglo–German encounters obscures the fact that the French bore the
brunt of the German onslaught on the Western Front in 1914. In the
standard image of these major battles, masses of men usually blundered into
one another and then, eschewing the finesse of maneuver, attempted to
bludgeon the other side into submission by sheer weight of numbers. The
resulting charges of French soldiers into German machine-gun fire and
German troops at French rapid-firing 75 mm. cannon – the "father, son, and
holy ghost" of warfare – yielded horrendous losses.

In fact, the slaughter tended to be quite one-sided in favor of the Germans
due to their superior heavy artillery and the accuracy of its indirect fire at
targets. German shellfire supported German infantry and annihilated French
infantry. Attacking French soldiers found themselves under devastating fire
from German artillery which outranged their own and destroyed them before
they could ever reach German infantry with their weapon of choice, the
bayonet. Undeterred, French soldiers, led by officers occasionally wearing
white gloves and brandishing swords, launched repeated assaults without
artillery support directly into German artillery fire. Succeeding waves of
attackers trampled on their comrades' maimed and mangled bodies that
littered the battlefield, in the din of whining and bursting shells heightened
by shouts of the attackers and the demoralizing shrieks and screams of the
wounded, who lay where they had fallen. Survivors of the shellfire still faced
a hail of machine-gun and rifle fire to bring their bayonets to bear. The
courage and spirit of French infantry, officers and men, all trained to obey
orders without question, resulted in their slaughter in encounter after
encounter, and on many more occasions than their German counterparts,
whose officers by training exercised responsibility of command and their own
discretion in combat. French 75s and machine-guns wreaked the same bloody
losses on German troops who charged them headlong, but the French relied
ultimately on their infantry, while the Germans relied on their infantry
supported by superior firepower. The French would pay an enormous price
for this inequity.

Confronted with the German onslaught from Belgium and beaten at
Charleroi, French General Lanrezac withdrew his Fifth Army so quickly
toward the south that he left the BEF's right flank hanging, nearly causing
BEF commander Gen. John French a nervous collapse. French Commander-
in-Chief Gen. Joffre later sacked Lanrezac for the latter's lack of sang-froid.
Yet Lanrezac's precipitous retreat had actually saved the French Fifth Army,
pulling the BEF with it, to fight another day, instead of giving combat and
being destroyed by the Germans, the fate of those who did fight. The
Schlieffen Plan's success presumed the willingness of the French Army to
fight and not flee, as retreat shortened French and lengthened German lines
of supply. An imperturbable Joffre, who never missed his daily three meals

or nightly eight hours' sleep, roared round to rally his generals in his powerful Hispano Suiza staff car, chauffered by a former Le Mans Grand Prix victor, as his armies retreated. Ultimately the retreat would redound to his advantage.

Schlieffen's rendering of his plan had provided for an exceedingly strong right wing, perhaps 90 percent of German troops, swarming through Belgium and northern France, and a much weaker left wing that would allow the French armies to penetrate into Alsace Lorraine and then hold them there. The right wing would then envelop Paris and strike the rear of the French troops caught in Alsace Lorraine. Moltke's adjustment to a 60–40 percent ratio between the right and left wing of the German armies on the Western Front did not allow the right wing sufficient numerical margin to envelop Paris or the left wing a sufficient inferiority to enable much French success in Alsace Lorraine.

The French armies' initial attacks into Alsace Lorraine on 20 August encountered heavy opposition and failed disastrously. Gen. Noel de Castelnau, army commander in Gen. Ferdinand Foch's XX Corps, lost a son in these abortive attacks. Only the necessity of opposing the German advance through northeastern France prevented Joffre from launching another disastrous attack in Lorraine. French corpses littered the battlefields, their red pants and blue coats having offered better targets than British khaki or German field gray. Among the dead lay North and West Africans. On 4 August 1914, French War Minister Messimy ordered the transport of ten West African battalions, or some 10,000 men, to France. The French isolated the African *tirailleurs* in training camps away from French civilians, until they marched to the front. On 21 August the first Senegalese battalions joined combat on the Western Front, with the nearly immediate loss of 250 soldiers killed and more than 600 total casualties. Instead of drawing French armies further into the provinces to fight, German forces ejected them from Alsace Lorraine. The French regrouped and turned their left flank to face the German onslaught from Belgium. During their retreat, Gen. Maurice Sarrail, a staunch supporter of the republican government and thus a rarity among the French army command, defied Joffre and refused to surrender the fortresses around the city of Verdun even when the Germans had nearly enveloped it. Verdun would become the anchor for the French attacks on the Marne and assume even greater significance later, in 1916.

Large gaps appeared between the German armies as they drove south, prompting their commanders to wheel southeast to close the gaps and to pass Paris to the northeast. They thereby exposed their right flank to French and British troops who had retreated toward Paris. French airplanes, one actually piloted by aircraft designer Louis Breguet, spotted the German Army's turn to the east of Paris, and a new instrument of war truly came into its own. Joffre, most ably assisted and encouraged by the elderly, energetic, and incisive commander of the Paris garrison, Gen. Joseph Galliéni, gathered his forces for a counter-attack against the flank of and into the gaps of the German armies in the first week in September. A number of over-age generals on all sides retired or were sacked early in the conflict, as the stress of command in a war of this magnitude proved too much for their constitutions. Galliéni, a striking exception to this rule, commandeered the taxis of Paris to transport troops to the Marne, a first case of motorized infantry, with truly French flair.

As the exhausted German troops of Gen. von Kluck's First Army on the right wing advanced toward the Marne River, they found themselves under assault on their right flank by regrouped French and British forces, whose counter-attacks brought the Germans to a stuttering halt. The German soldiers were certainly close to the end of their tether. The French and British had retreated toward their sources of supply and had regrouped. The Germans had had no respite from the war of movement's blistering heat and all-enveloping dust. Their infantry – clothed in tattered wool uniforms, lugging their rifles and sixty-pound packs, grimy, thirsty, hungry, their feet blistered, bloody, and swollen inside disintegrating boots – had reached a critical juncture.

If Kluck chose to wheel west and face the British and French, he would widen the gap between his and Gen. von Bülow's Second Army to his east. When German General Staff Officer Col. Richard Hentsch, whom Moltke had sent by car to serve as liaison, decided with Bülow to withdraw the latter's Second Army in the face of the attacks, Kluck had no choice but to retreat or be left hanging. Another staff officer might have counseled a more aggressive response to test the resolve of their battered enemy. The results would not have been a foregone conclusion. But Hentsch, like his chief Moltke, who concurred with the decision, chose otherwise, so the Germans retreated to shorten their lines and close their gaps, and then entrenched. The Battle of the Marne (5–10 September), which in fact encompassed a series of five crucial and separate battles fought over some 125 miles of front along the Aisne and Marne Rivers, signaled the failure of Moltke's modified Schlieffen Plan. During the "miracle" of the Marne, as the French referred to the struggle, the battles followed the course of earlier encounters and French infantry paid dearly for their attacks. As Col. Emil Driant, parliamentary deputy and a hero of Verdun in 1916, observed, "The miracle of the Marne" is due to "the courage of the common soldiers and the lower ranks, an astonishing contempt of danger and death that repaired the horrors, the crimes in high places. At the top, nothing was anticipated."[10]

War Minister Gen. Erich von Falkenhayn became Chief of the General Staff on 14 September, as Moltke became the highest placed victim of the Schlieffen Plan's demise. Yet the German Army had overrun Belgium and northeastern France, and the French and the small BEF now confronted the task of ejecting them. French politician Georges Clemenceau observed in retrospect that the most dangerous time had been at the beginning of the war. French losses of 329,000 men in August and September 1914 far exceeded those for any other two-month period of the entire conflict, including the Battle of Verdun in 1916. By late September the army was even running short of shells for the vaunted 75 mm. cannon, their essential field piece.[11] Still, they fought on.

After a short respite, both sides attempted repeatedly to outflank each other to the north, which led to a leap-frogging movement sometimes labeled "the race to the sea." The end result extended the trench lines across northeastern France to the Channel coast between Dunkirk and Ostend, Belgium. Unfortunately, the BEF's move north was not rapid enough to prevent the Germans from seizing the city of Lille, a major center of French industry and an important railway junction.

In early October, First Lord of the Admiralty Winston Churchill ordered the Royal Naval Division, many of whom lacked training, to Antwerp, Belgium to help defend it against the encroaching Germans. When the Germans forced the Belgian surrender, the Division had suffered fewer than 200 casualties. But when it retreated to sail for Britain, some 2,500 men never received the order to retreat and ended either captives of the Germans or interned in Holland, where they had fled. Parliament and press blamed Winston Churchill for the disaster.[12]

The "race" officially concluded at the last gap in the front, with the Battle of Ypres in October and November. In an effort to reach the channel ports supplying the BEF, the Germans attempted to punch through French, French African, British, and Indian troops, the latter having arrived recently to buttress the BEF. In early November soldiers of the Thirty-ninth Garwahal Rifles of the Indian Corps assaulted the German trenches in a night raid, a traditional method of attack on the Indian frontier that would later become primarily a British and then a general practice on the western front. The British and French hoped to break through to the industrial city of Lille and march on to Brussels. The fighting was ferocious; the casualties, high; the prisoners taken on both sides, few. Some five weeks of unrelenting combat reduced four battalions of West African troops to one. Both sides failed to reach their objectives, although the Germans ended in possession of the high ground around a British salient at the focal point of the battle. Entente engineers' flooding of the area around Ypres, which if done earlier might have avoided the costly struggle, prevented any further German advance.

If the British had met disaster at Antwerp, Ypres gave rise to a German legend. Some proclaimed it a "day of honor" of German youth that would set "a glowing example for the young generation"; others, the *Kindermord bei Ypern*, or the "Massacre of the Innocents at Ypres." Although reservists recalled to service comprised most of the German dead at Ypres, a German high command communiqué of 11 November announced to the public that young regiments singing *Deutschland, Deutschland über alles* had broken through the lines west of Langemarck and taken prisoner some 2,000 French infantry and six machine-guns. The German Volunteer Corps, composed of bourgeois university and high school student volunteers with only one or two months' training, had in fact essentially committed suicide. The Corps, advancing arm in arm and singing, its members wearing their student caps, marched straight into British and French artillery, machine-gun, and rifle fire. The German High Command had sacrificed potential young company officers uselessly, at a time when any illusions of a short war should have shattered against the reality of the Western Front. Yet the German command's generation of a heroic Langemarck legend turned a military defeat into a moral victory.[13]

The armies dug in, the Germans most often with an eye to the high ground and strong positions, since they stood on enemy territory. They burrowed deep and well, creating two and three lines of defense with fortified bunkers for first-line troops and reinforcements and concealed positions for artillery observers, fronted by barbed wire, with concrete machine-gun nests, for they had come to stay. The French and British dug less well, for any sign of permanence might have signaled resignation, and the French had every intention of ejecting the invader from their sacred soil as soon as possible. Everyone dug, probably, with a sense of relief, for the trenches offered refuge and respite, however temporary, from the frenzied war of movement. These lines would move but little and only with Olympian effort for nearly three and a half years.

Cavalry now became useless, since only aircraft could see into the enemy's rear. Aircraft had observed over enemy lines from the beginning of the war. French airplanes had provided information key to the success at the Marne. The Germans employed their vaunted Zeppelins to reconnoiter, but the giant airships proved vulnerable to ground fire. During the war of movement, troops located by artillery spotters had come under crushing bombardment soon thereafter. The air arms of all countries had suffered from problems of supply early in the war. Now, like the front, supply stabilized, and the airplanes became the primary means of operational reconnaissance over the front lines. Once the war settled into the trenches, these fragile, flimsy, wood and fabric biplanes and monoplanes soared over the lines to keep watch on enemy movements and concentrations.

As German Zeppelins bombed towns and cities in Belgium, France, and even along the British coast, French and British planes bombed military and industrial targets, often Zeppelin or other army installations, in western Germany in reprisal for enemy attacks. After haphazard strikes against military targets, the French determined to wage a systematic strategic air campaign in the fall against military and industrial targets with the creation of a First Bombardment Group. But primitive aircraft offered no prospect of breaking the stalemate.

On 4 August the prospect of war had so thrilled Gen. von Falkenhayn that he exclaimed to Chancellor Bethmann Hollweg: "Even if we perish, it will have been exquisite." By November, with the failure of his assault on Ypres and a dangerous shortage of ammunition looming, Falkenhayn's sanguinity had vanished. He gloomily opined that attacks on trenches were a senseless and "useless waste of human lives" and that Germany needed to seek a separate peace with one of the allies. Without such a political solution, Germany would simply slowly exhaust itself, as it could not defeat all three enemies. Neither Bethmann Hollweg nor the commanders of the Eastern Front, Hindenburg and Ludendorff, all of whom desired a victorious peace of annexations, agreed with Falkenhayn's dismal but prescient prediction of the outcome of a war of attrition.[14]

The German Army now occupied Belgium and northern France, regions swarming with refugees from their recent advance through the region. Military governors ruled through a military administration, although they left some officials such as mayors in place as conduits to the population through which they obtained labor for local work. The governors proceeded to seize most of the 1914 harvest, farm produce, and livestock, to feed German troops and the people of Germany. In Lille, a city of half a million inhabitants in northern France, the Germans shipped textiles and food reserves to Germany by the train-load, and then dismantled and shipped the looms, along with machine tools, heavy equipment, and any other raw materials or machines they deemed useful. They destroyed the giant steelworks at Denain, which would take ten years to rebuild after the war, and blew up other factories. Soldiers also requisitioned even household items for their own use or transport to Germany. A German mine management directed French and Belgian coal-mines.

The Germans strictly regulated the lives of the occupied population and controlled any commerce. They treated the citizens of Alsace Lorraine even more brutally than those in other regions, since some had greeted the French as liberators in August 1914 after more than forty years of German rule. The Germans consequently stepped up their policies of Germanization in the two provinces, and further deported many key citizens to camps in Germany, where they spent the war, like convicts, breaking stones and working on roads.

In the fall of 1914, Belgian food supply failed because of wartime disruption, and some seven million Belgians faced a severe crisis. The British government was reluctant to intervene or ease its blockade, as it considered Belgium to be Germany's problem and believed that the Germans might well take any imported food for themselves. Into the gap stepped wealthy American mining engineer Herbert Hoover, who was living in London at the time. Hoover became chairman of the Commission for Relief in Belgium (CRB), an international public agency founded on 22 October to secure food for Belgium. Hoover, working without pay, brought to the daunting task

Quaker principles, financial and political acumen, and stubborn determination. In December he traveled to Belgium to observe his organization and conditions there, and compared his entry through the barbed wire border, during which he was strip searched, to entering a prison. Yet the CRB's efforts were feeding Belgians, and Hoover returned to London determined to make it even more effective, as the Germans were proving to be merciless in occupation.[15]

THE EASTERN FRONT. GERMANY EXCELS RUSSIA EXCELS AUSTRIA-HUNGARY

In the east the speed of Russian mobilization stunned Germany and Austria-Hungary, particularly the military and civilians in East Prussia who faced imminent invasion. *Stavka*, the Russian Army supreme command, determined to save its French ally at all costs by forcing Germany to defend its eastern border. Despite such a commendable motive, *Stavka*, under Grand Duke Nicholas, a towering and impressive figurehead, existed mainly to communicate with the allies. Conflict between Nicholas and War Minister Sukhomlinov bitterly divided Russian generals. Real power lay with the separate army groups, or fronts: the northwestern under Gen. Zhilinski against Germany; the southwestern under Gen. Ivanov. These two separate commands would fight two separate wars.[16] Finally, from day one of the war, the Russian Army suffered shortages of weapons and supplies, a lack of motorized transport, outmoded communications, and inadequate training of many of its troops.

On the German eastern front – the Russian northwestern front – in August the Russian armies, slowed only by a minor German victory at Stallupönen on 17 August, advanced into East Prussia, sweeping the Prussian armies and masses of refugees before them. Russian reports of the capture of fleeing Prussian officers dressed in women's clothing impugned the masculinity of their opponent and aroused mirth in the Russian ranks. The Russian Army then defeated the Germans at the Battle of Gumbinnen on 20 August, where German Gen. von Mackensen learned the hard way that head-on attacks against prepared Russian positions without prior artillery bombardment simply slaughtered his own men. The German front commander, Gen. Max von Prittwitz, under orders to delay the Russians, feared that they would smash his smaller army. He panicked, and asked Moltke for permission to withdraw, which would have left Prussia to the Russians. Moltke, who had never trusted the fat Prittwitz, a favorite of the Kaiser, promptly sacked him.

The Russian success would be short-lived. The sheer weight of their numbers had told initially. Now, as they moved into broken country, dense forests, and marshes, confusion within the front command, inadequate supplies, and misleading intelligence on German positions robbed the advance of momentum and order. German general staff planners ably directed by Col. Max Hoffmann exploited the railway system in East Prussia, their reconnaissance airplanes, and the Russian penchant for sending uncoded radio messages to thwart the Russian offensive. Only aerial observation could locate Russian armies in East Prussia's vast, dense forests that swallowed up entire divisions. Russian cavalry greatly outnumbered German, and both failed to locate enemy forces in forays into the forests. German airplanes tracked the Russian armies in the forests with the help of Russian soldiers, who could not resist firing at the droning pests above, thereby giving away their otherwise undetectable positions.

The Germans left a single cavalry division to screen Russian Gen. Pavel Rennenkampf's more slowly moving army advancing from due east. The bulk of German troops moved by rail to strike Gen. Alexander Samsonov's faster moving army advancing from the southeast in its northern flank. Rennenkampf and Samsonov, who disliked one another intensely and whose armies the marshy terrain of the Masurian Lakes separated, were about to suffer a severe shock as late August approached. Samsonov, misinformed by Zhilinski at headquarters that he faced an insignificant German force, ploughed ahead despite burgeoning supply problems.

Moltke, upon receipt of Prittwitz's distressing reports from the east, later detached two army corps from his right wing on the Western Front for service in the east. These troops would arrive too late to affect events in East Prussia, although they further deprived the Western Front of sorely needed manpower. More crucially, Moltke immediately assigned new commanders to the Eastern Front. A train with Gen. Erich Ludendorff of Liège fame on board rolled east. On the way Ludendorff's new superior, Gen. Paul von Hindenburg, a retired general reinstated in the wartime emergency, joined him. The older Prussian would balance his impetuous, emotional, and brilliant subordinate. They approved Hoffmann's plans, which concurred with their own assessment of the situation, and steamed toward the Eastern Front, and destiny.

Hindenburg and Ludendorff arrived in time to preside over the German armies' decisive victory at the Battle of Tannenberg (26–31 August), a name chosen for its historical resonance. A crushed and despondent Gen. Samsonov, unable to keep pace with his retreating staff because of heart problems and asthma, wandered alone into the forest and shot himself. Tannenberg was Germany's first decisive victory, and when Moltke released the news in September, it catapulted its commanders to instant fame and popularity. As a retired general after the war, an overshadowed and annoyed Hoffmann would guide tours of the Tannenberg battlefield, pointedly showing his audiences where Hindenburg and Ludendorff had slept during the battle he had planned.

The remains of Samsonov's army reeled back across the Russian border. The Germans then concentrated on Rennenkampf's force, and at the Battle of the Masurian Lakes (9–14 September) forced him to retreat from Prussia. The Russians suffered some 250,000 casualties and prisoners to German casualties of 25,000 in both battles, which established German military superiority over the numerically superior Russian forces. The threat to East Prussia receded as rapidly as it had appeared. Gen. von Rennenkampf became *Rennen von Kampf*, or "Gen. Run from Battle," to his German opponents, as his staff led his army in precipitous flight. Yet the German Army, suffering from serious losses, problems of supply, and troop exhaustion, could not give pursuit. It also needed to look after its Austro-Hungarian ally on the southeastern front.

Of the "Great Powers," only Austria-Hungary lurched away from the starting line in the great race for conquest. General Staff Chief Franz Conrad von Hötzendorf determined to punish the Serb "bandits," although he was fully aware that the Russians would be coming in the east. After bombarding the Serbian capital Belgrade to signal the beginning of hostilities, the Austro-Hungarian Army delayed assembling its forces so that the peasants could bring in the harvest. On 12 August General Potiorek attacked Serbia with some two-and-a-half armies, nearly 500,000 men, many of them substandard militia units. They met a Serbian army of equal strength, but battle-hardened in the recent Balkan wars and led by the elderly, sickly, but skillful Serb Gen. Radomir Putnik. In three offensives, in August, September, and November, Potiorek failed to sustain an invasion of Serbia. Finally, after suffering casualties of 150,000 men, the Austro-Hungarian Army fled back across the border in mid-December, leaving 75,000 prisoners in the hands of the Serbs, who sustained 170,000 casualties.

In August 100,000 of the soldiers engaged in the Serbian campaign were supposed to participate in the attack on Russia. But Potiorek, who was Conrad's rival, was slow to release these men for Conrad's planned launching of four armies into Russian Poland through the flat, dusty, and trackless plains of Galicia. Conrad underestimated the strength of the Russian armies opposite him, and his offensive dispersed his troops too widely.

Gen. Alekseev, Russian commander Ivanov's chief of staff, was in fact competent, and their subordinate generals included Aleksei Brusilov, perhaps the ablest Russian commander of the war. The August struggles included the war's largest cavalry battle, a bloody and costly, but indecisive clash of a Russian and Austro-Hungarian division. In late August, at the same time the Russians were losing at Tannenberg, they also suffered two defeats at Krasnik and Komarow. Then the Russian armies pressed against Conrad's flanks and proceeded to crush his armies, leaving battlefields piled with corpses and wounded. Conrad's initially victorious army had to break off its attack and retreat.

By September the Russian armies had the Austro-Hungarian forces in full flight, as the latter reeled back some 150 miles, losing most of Galicia, though leaving 150,000 men to hold the fortress city of Przemysl. Once the front stabilized, Conrad had lost some 250,000 casualties and 100,000 prisoners – one third of the army's combat strength, including substantial numbers of irreplaceable frontline officers, among them his son Herbert, a cavalry officer. The victorious Russians had lost 250,000 men, casualties or prisoners. Austria-Hungary had begun its war poorly, its invasion of Serbia bloodily repulsed, its offensive on the Russian front routed. The incompetence of the Austro-Hungarian Army, which the humorous tales of the good soldier Schweik would immortalize, was anything but laughable as it lurched from defeat to defeat, debacle to debacle, its soldiers dying in droves.

Conrad further neglected to coordinate with the Germans, who needed a focussed and strong Austro-Hungarian attack into Galicia to distract the Russians from East Prussia. Now the Austrian retreat exposed the German flank in Silesia to Russian attack in late September. Confronted with some sixty Russian divisions to eighteen German, Ludendorff launched two spoiling attacks in September and again in November, toward the Vistula River and ultimately Warsaw. In both cases Russian numerical superiority enabled them ultimately to counterattack successfully, but Ludendorff had successfully preempted a Russian invasion of Silesia. As earlier at Tannenberg, the German rail network combined with the Russian penchant for sending uncoded messages worked to German advantage. Hindenburg and Ludendorff had avoided disaster with two well conceived and executed countermoves, but their inability to secure reinforcements from Falkenhayn, himself preoccupied with Ypres, thoroughly annoyed them. Kaiser Wilhelm, anxious to placate his popular duo, created a High Command Eastern Front (*Oberkommando Ost*, or *Ober Ost*) which rendered them more independent from the OHL.

Conrad's Austro-Hungarian forces struggled on, demonstrating surprising resiliency in the face of staggering losses, and managed to force the Russians back from Cracow, the farthest west they would reach during the war. The Russians answered by counter-attacking in the Carpathian Mountains in the dead of winter, and Conrad, who preferred the offensive and was not about to retreat,[17] contested what would become a devastating battle of attrition. The war on the Eastern Front ended the year in stalemate.

OTTOMAN ENTRY INTO THE WAR

The Turkish government observed the early course of the conflict. The poor state of the army – deficient in essentials from artillery and machine-guns to non-commissioned officers and medical support, totally lacking in motorized transport and aviation – justified such caution. The country itself, with practically no industry, much less war industry, few roads or railways, and thus no home front as it existed in the industrial powers, lacked the infrastructure to wage a major war. Finally, the state was still exhausted from the Balkan wars, which had shifted the center of gravity of the empire from Europe to Asia.

Historians have long credited the German government with manipulating the Ottoman government into the war to foster German aims of an empire from Berlin to Baghdad, with the famous railway line as a link. More recently, historians have realized that the ruling Committee of Union and Progress, the Young Turks, had their own aims, and, if anything, manipulated the Germans.[18] A European war would provide the opportunity for the Ottomans to throw off the European yoke of privileges for foreigners in the empire, recoup their imperial losses, and expand against Russia in association with Germany and Austria-Hungary. Although the Grand Vizier Sait Halim was uneasy about ties to Germany and preferred to keep his options open, most of the Young Turks, in particular the three who dominated the government in 1914 – Enver, Talaat, and Kemal Pasha – were pro-German. After the humiliation of the Balkan wars, they had turned to Germany as the model for their military and received a German military mission under Lt. Gen. Liman von Sanders late in 1913. While events from August onward indicated that the right hand in the Ottoman government often did not know what the left was doing, these key individuals, encouraged by German Ambassador Wangenheim, pressed first for an alliance with Germany and then for entry into the war.

Germany and the Ottoman Empire signed a secret treaty of alliance on 2 August 1914, but the following day the Ottomans openly proclaimed themselves neutral. Almost simultaneously, First Lord of the Admiralty Winston Churchill reneged on delivery to the Turks of two modern, powerful battleships built in British shipyards and claimed them for Britain. Circumstances then enabled the Turks to respond to Churchill's act and gain further concessions from the Germans supporting Ottoman independence. Entente ships were pursuing two powerful German cruisers, the *Goeben* and the *Breslau*, from the Mediterranean toward the Straits. The Turks allowed the two cruisers to enter the Straits and shelter at Constantinople in early August. They then claimed to buy the ships, which henceforth flew the Turkish flag, although their crews remained German. Further bargaining elicited future secret deliveries of gold from Germany.

Churchill, enraged that the German cruisers had escaped, urged an attack on Turkey and ordered a blockade of Turkish vessels leaving the Dardanelles in early September. The Turks replied by sealing off and mining the Straits. By that time, the Turkish government had abrogated foreign privileges in the empire. In early October the Pashas secretly informed the Germans that they would open hostilities and attack Russia as soon as two million Turkish pounds in gold arrived. On 29 October 1914 the two "Turkish" cruisers bombarded Russian Black Sea forts. The Ottomans had entered the war.

The British responded immediately with an ultimatum, which the Turks did not answer, and Britain opened hostilities against Turkey on 31 October. On 3 November British warships bombarded the forts at the Dardanelles. Britain, Russia, and France were all at war with the Ottomans by 5 November, and the Russians were already asking the British for aid against the Turks.

The British declaration of war reversed Britain's traditional policy of preserving the existence of the Ottoman Empire as a barrier against Russia. Britain now determined to destroy the Ottoman Empire and use portions of it to lure Italy and Balkan states into the war on the Entente side. Britain's newly appointed Secretary of State for War Lord Kitchener viewed Ottoman Turkey and the Middle East as sideshows of no importance in the war, and the British government did not take the Ottoman Empire seriously as an enemy. British imperial offices believed that they understood foreign peoples everywhere, but they were, in fact, ignorant of the Middle East. Contrary to their wishful thinking, the Muslim Middle East of the Ottoman Empire was not ready for revolt. In fact it supported the empire and certainly did not desire non-Muslim rule.

Kitchener presumed that after the war the British, in order to keep the Russians out of the region, would need to control much of the former Ottoman Empire, specifically the Arab part. They would install a puppet Caliph through whom they could reign. Kitchener's men in Cairo, ignoring Arab disunity, were proposing a unified Arab world which they presumed to control. The British looked toward Mecca, the center of the Muslim world, for their potential puppet. Its sherif and emir Hussein ibn Ali might be interested in securing the position for his family, in particular his two politically active sons, Abdullah and Feisal, if Ottoman power waned.

In a war of empires, the potential demise of one inevitably prompted a struggle for its holdings, as others sought to protect and increase their own territories. Some European power would replace the Ottomans in the event of an Entente victory. The Russians had long coveted Constantinople and access to the Straits. Yet if the British government in England might contemplate allowing the Russians such a reward, the British government in India, long accustomed to regarding the Russians as *the* threat to Indian security, would not tolerate it. Furthermore, the government in India desired a weak and fragmented Arabia. Britain, and no one else, would have to replace the Turks, most particularly in the Middle East.

The British government of India attacked the Turks in Mesopotamia to protect its interests, particularly the pipeline, refinery, and terminal of the Anglo-Persian Oil Company, in the Persian Gulf. By late November the

British imperial forces had captured the port of Basra, 70 miles up the Shatt-al-Arab channel. Then, lured by further possibilities in Baghdad, they advanced another 45 miles up the channel to the junction of the Tigris and Euphrates Rivers, and seized the city of Kurnah, the Turkish commandant, and 1,000 prisoners in early December.

Meanwhile, it took the Turkish Army nearly two months to prepare for war on disparate fronts. Elsewhere, the Turks took the offensive. On 11 November the Sultan proclaimed a *jihad*, or Holy War, against the Entente, but to no effect, although the British feared the possibility. More concretely, the Turks launched an offensive toward the Russian Caucasus in December. The Russians retreated into and through the Caucasus Mountains, where the Turks impetuously followed. Winter was fast approaching, and the Turkish troops, who were not equipped for it, began to freeze to death. A smaller offensive launched against the Suez Canal offered little prospect of success. Yet these ambitious efforts demonstrated that the so-called "Sick Man of Europe" was not dead. The Young Turks had begun the war badly, however, and if their military adventurism continued, they seemed likely to finish themselves in suicidal fashion.

A GLOBAL WAR AT SEA.

At the outbreak of war a major Anglo-German naval engagement seemed likely, as the British fleet sailed to battle stations in the North Sea. The British, however, well aware of the danger from mines, submarines, torpedoes, and coastal artillery, eschewed their traditional close blockade of the enemy coast in favor of a distant one blocking the exits from the North Sea. In August the British government began restricting the legal transport of goods through the Netherlands to Germany. The German fleet command expected a close blockade and had had no answer in May 1914 to Tirpitz's query "What will you do if they do not come?"[19]

Both fleets would join battle only if both anticipated favorable outcomes – a highly unlikely and almost mutually exclusive circumstance. The naval war in the North Sea was thus reduced to one of sweeps, ambushes, small clashes, and minelaying. The British Grand Fleet began a pattern of fruitless sweeps off the northern coast of Europe on 4 August and transported the BEF to France from 12 to 18 August. British cruisers attacked German destroyer patrols in the Heligoland Bight and sank three German light cruisers off Heligoland on 28 August.

The Germans pursued a *Kleinkrieg*, or "little war," of mine laying and submarine patrols. On 22 September Lt. Otto Weddigen, patroling in the obsolescent U.9 off the Dutch coast, sank three British cruisers with the loss of over 1,400 officers and men. A month later on 27 October a mine sank the

British dreadnought *Audacious*. The submarine and the mine, not the German High Sea Fleet, now became the greatest threats to the Royal Navy's control of the North Sea. The British mined parts of the North Sea in November to facilitate control of shipping, but they lacked both an adequate minesweeper force and efficient, reliable mines. They would develop them only in 1917 from copies of German mines.

When Prince Louis of Battenberg resigned as First Sea Lord of the Admiralty on 28 October, Sir John "Jacky" Fisher, recalled from retirement at the age of 74, replaced him. Fisher, endowed, according to a compatriot, with "courage . . . fine zeal, energy, and determination, coupled with low cunning,"[20] anticipated a long war and began a huge building program. In the fall the Admiralty intelligence division under Adm. Reginald "Blinker" Hall acquired German code-books and consequently the ability to read German wireless communications. On 5 November 1914 the Admiralty declared the entire North Sea a war zone, subject to patrol by cruisers and armed merchantmen ready to intercept and board shipping at will.

In Germany Tirpitz advocated offensive action, but the fleet commanders opted to continue mine laying off the British coast and battlecruiser raids against British coastal towns. Human error and stormy weather foiled a German raid of 16 December intended to lure British capital ships into a trap of mines and submarines. In the absence of naval action, the Royal Naval Air Service launched seaplane raids against Zeppelin hangars in the fall, culminating in an attack on Christmas Day on Cuxhaven. Stalemate reigned in the North Sea.

In contrast to the powerful fleets and defenses concentrated in the North Sea, the Royal Navy deployed insufficient numbers of cruisers and destroyers to protect the sea lanes around the globe. The British and their dominions owned 43 percent of the world's shipping; the Germans, in second place, only 12 percent. The British had to protect their shipping from German cruiser attack, while supporting overseas expeditions against German colonies and transporting Dominion and colonial troops to wartime theaters. The British dispersed their merchantmen to make them more difficult to locate, but escorted troop-ships in great "imperial convoys" from Canada, India, Australia, and New Zealand. Australian and New Zealand and Indian troop convoys sailed for Suez, while convoys brought home most British troops from abroad and Canadian troops to England. The German Navy was powerless to affect any of these troop movements. The threat of German auxiliary cruisers against merchant shipping never fully materialized, as the Germans lacked overseas bases to supply their warships.

One reason for Britain's success and Germany's failure was Japan's entry into the war in late August. The Japanese government viewed the "European War" as an opportunity for expansion in China and in the Pacific. Japanese statesmen had various motives, from honoring the alliance with Britain despite their admiration for Germany, to securing China as a junior partner in the future likelihood of a race war against whites in the East. The army coveted further territory and influence in China, while the navy eyed Germany's Pacific possessions – the Marshall, Mariana, and Caroline Islands.

On 5 August Britain requested Japanese naval assistance to protect their merchant vessels from German cruisers. The Japanese government's enthusiastic reaction to the British request – they were prepared to declare war against Germany – elicited Foreign Secretary Lord Grey's reluctance and suspicion. First Lord of the Admiralty Winston Churchill, however, welcomed Japanese support and later even desired a Japanese battleship squadron for back-up in the Mediterranean. The Japanese ultimatum to Germany instructed it to clear eastern waters and give Japan its leased territory of Kiaochow. Meanwhile the Japanese assured the western powers that they intended merely to drive Germany out, not to seek territorial aggrandizement. Germany did not reply by the expiration of the ultimatum on 23 August, while the German ambassador to the United States condemned the British for "seeking help from yellow men."[21] One day later Japanese forces, acting quickly in case the war was short, landed on the Shantung peninsula, and blockaded and besieged the port of Tsingtao, which fell on 7 November. The Japanese now turned toward China, where the President of the Chinese Republic, Yuan Shikai, had legitimized the Japanese seizure of Tsingtao by declaring the German leasehold around Kiachow in Shantung a war zone. This encouraged the Japanese to occupy all of Shantung, and Yuan demanded their total withdrawal.

The Japanese Navy helped convoy British troop-ships, pushed German ships out of the Pacific, and freed the British to pursue them. The British concentrated on the East Asiatic Cruiser Squadron (EACS) of Adm. Graf von Spee, with its two new armored cruisers *Scharnhorst* and *Gneisenau* based at Tsingtao. The Germans also had a total of three light cruisers in the Caribbean and on the east coast of Africa.

Spee, who was cruising the Pacific when the war began, disappeared into its vastness, while one cruiser, the *Emden*, made for the Indian Ocean. The *Emden*, under the able leadership of *Fregattenkapitän* Karl von Müller, sank sixteen British steamers, a Russian light cruiser, and a French destroyer before the Australian light cruiser *Sydney* sank it on 9 November. The German cruiser *Königsberg*, lacking coal, stayed trapped in the Rufigi River on the east coast of Africa. A fatal internal explosion on 4 November abruptly terminated the successful cruise of the German raider *Karlsruhe* about 300 miles from Barbados in the Caribbean.

Spee's two armored cruisers and three light cruisers steamed for South America, to the waters off the west coast of Chile. There, at the Battle of Coronel on 1 November, he defeated an inferior British cruiser force under Rear Adm. Christopher Cradock. This first defeat of the Royal Navy in action for more than a century caused British loss of life of 1,600 men. But at his next stop for coal, Spee acknowledged a female admirer's bouquet with the comment, "Thank you, they will do very nicely for my grave."[22] A superior British force cornered his small squadron, now down to four cruisers, and brought him to bay off the Falkland Islands. In the ensuing encounter, only 215 men survived of the German cruisers' complement of 2,200 men. Spee and two of his sons were among the lost.

Surrender in naval surface encounters was unthinkable, so the superior force pounded the inferior to a pulp. Plunging shells tore both men and metal apart, detonating in white-hot flames if they hit explosives and powder in turrets or in magazines below decks. Dismembered, bleeding bodies rendered decks slippery with blood, guts, and brain. Men roasted in fires hot enough to melt metal. Scalding water from ships' ruptured boilers doused hands below deck. It was almost merciful when the pummeled burning hulk keeled over and sank, taking its crew to a watery grave. Few sailors escaped death on vanquished ships and captains invariably chose to go down with their vessels.

The few German surface raiders that prowled the sea lanes vanished one by one. An exciting and romantic era of naval warfare was passing, when the lone ship had hunted its prey, boarded and captured merchant vessels, then either plundered and sunk the ship after taking its crew, or manned it with a prize crew to sail it home. Later in the war the Germans would persist in launching occasional raiders, but while they might elude British patrols in the North Sea to reach the trackless realm of the world's oceans, their forays would be furtive and unsuccessful.

As the German surface fleet disappeared from the high seas, the submarine announced its presence, launching a new era of naval warfare. Ironically, the Anglo–German naval race over battleships culminated in a war where British and German dreadnought fleets primarily avoided combat and spent their time jockeying for advantage in case of an encounter. Both fleets feared these primitive tiny submersibles, which paradoxically began to dwarf the behemoths that reigned in the Mahanian era of seapower. Dirty, stinking, and unshaven crews labored under oppressive conditions, in foul and fetid air, in the dank, cramped confines of their metal tanks, which could quickly become their coffins. These scruffy but intrepid submariners became the navies' new elite.

The few torpedoes which early submarines carried often ran neither straight nor true. They might not explode on contact with the target. They might even curve round and target the submarine. No one, including the British, had an answer to the new weapon. Germany's most potent naval weapon of the 1914–45 era – the *U-Boot*, or *Unterseeboot* – had debuted, a predator far more deadly than its surface predecessors, and potentially subversive of the rules and etiquette of commerce raiding. As German troops on the Western Front burrowed under the earth's surface to build concrete bunkers impervious to shells, German submariners submerged to strike at the enemy's navy and commerce.

CONFLICT IN THE COLONIES

The submarine, however, could do nothing to defend Germany's small empire around the globe. In Africa the Entente colonies promptly invaded their German neighbors, although German colonial governors had pleaded in vain for neutrality. The Germans had argued against the use of African troops in colonial warfare to forestall armed black troops killing white adversaries. Although white Rhodesians shared such fears, all the imperial powers, including the Germans, mobilized their African subjects, either as soldiers or as porters, to such an extent that the war led to depopulation and famine in some regions. The indigenous African peoples were about to become involved in a war that would significantly affect their land and lives.

The British intended to seize German colonies as spoils of war. Their limited objective of defending maritime communications quickly escalated into territorial conquest and the seizure of prizes to balance any German gains in Europe. The British Cabinet, in a fit of war fever, appeared to Prime Minister Asquith "more like a gang of Elizabethan buccaneers than a meek collection of black-coated Liberal Ministers."[23]

The South African government coveted German Southwest Africa, which the British would use to ensure South Africa's loyal participation in the war. In West Africa the French planned to seize Cameroon, a small portion of which they had ceded as compensation in the Moroccan crisis in 1911. Even Belgium took the offensive to secure a bargaining chip in any future peace conference. The allies either occupied or bombarded German ports in Africa to deny them to the German fleet.

In August 1914 German colonies in West and East Africa found themselves under assault from French, British, and Belgian colonial armies as well as white South African and Rhodesian forces. Togoland, the smallest German colony in Africa, lay sandwiched between British and French colonies, had a powerful German wireless station like other German colonies that the Entente determined to seize, and no army to protect it. It surrendered unconditionally on 26 August after a three-week campaign.

To the east of Togoland lay Cameroon, sandwiched between British Nigeria, French Equatorial Africa, and the Belgian Congo. Some 2,000 Europeans ruled 500,000 Africans with a *Schutztruppe* of 200 German officers and NCOs and 1,550 African *askaris*, or soldiers. The British colony alone could muster three times the German force, and in mid-August an Anglo-French conference in London authorized a joint attack on Cameroon. With cruisers and gunboats in support, the British seized the key port and wireless station at Douala in September, forcing the Germans to retreat inland. British and French colonial forces consisting mostly of black Africans pursued the Germans into the interior along river and railway corridors. By the end of 1915, despite Anglo-French discord and competition over the colony, occasional German ambushes, and assaults by mosquitoes and stinging bees and ants, the Entente forces had penetrated deep into the Cameroonian interior.

German Southwest Africa formed Germany's second largest colony with an area of more than 300,000 square miles bordered by Portuguese Angola in the north and South Africa elsewhere. The *Schutztruppe* there, unlike elsewhere in German Africa, included no black Africans, according to precedent set by the first German imperial commissioner, Ernst Göring, father of Hermann. In this it resembled the forces of South Africa and Rhodesia that resolutely refused to arm black soldiers. The opposing South African forces totaled 50,000 whites, supported by 33,000 black Africans, under the leadership of Louis Botha, Prime Minister of the Union of South Africa, and his colleague Jan Smuts. The first South African invaders, however, encountered a much larger German force and consequently surrendered. Some 11,500 Afrikaners in Orange River Colony and the Transvaal, who had not forgotten the Boer War and preferred the Germans to the British, revolted. Botha and 30,000 men crushed the rebellion by November, with under a thousand total casualties on both sides. South Africa was now ready to resume the offensive in German Southwest Africa.

German East Africa was Germany's largest possession with more than 380,000 square miles in area, thus larger than France and Germany combined, and inhabited by some 5,000 Europeans, 15,000 Indians and Arabs, and 7.5 million Africans. Early in 1914 Lieut. Col. Paul von Lettow-Vorbeck arrived to take command of the *Schutztruppe* of 260 European officers and NCOs and 2,472 African *askaris*, or soldiers, including 2 officers and 184 NCOs. Hostile colonies surrounded German East Africa: British East Africa in the north; the Belgian Congo in the west; Rhodesia in the southwest; and Portuguese Mozambique in the southeast. The governors of British and German East Africa preferred to remain neutral, as they feared using black troops against white men would destroy the tradition of the "inviolability of the white man." Still, the British Colonial Office had established the King's African Rifles (KAR) of 62 British officers and 2,300 black troops, and when the war began, volunteers formed the East Africa Regiment and the East African Mounted Rifles (EAMR).

Neutrality evaporated rapidly. In September both sides launched small offensives against one another. In September the German cruiser *Königsberg*, lately of Adm. von Spee's squadron, took refuge in the Rufigi delta south of Dar-es-Salaam, where British naval forces blockaded it. In November the British attacked inland in the foothills of Kilimanjaro and focussed on landing a seaborne force at the port of Tanga. British Expeditionary Force "B," with 8,000 British and Indian troops under the command of Maj. Gen. A.E. Aitken, spearheaded the invasion. Although his Indian soldiers lacked adequate training and equipment, Aitken was confident that they would make "short work of a lot of niggers" and that he would "thrash the Germans before Christmas."[24] They landed unopposed on 3 November, and the following day advanced toward Tanga, Aitken observing from the bridge of a converted liner.

Lettow-Vorbeck, who had arrived during the night and bicycled around the German perimeter, counted on "the clumsiness" of the British troops in battle that he had observed during his tour of duty in East Asia. His forces, outnumbered eight to one, waited until the British forces advanced, then opened fire on them. Stunned, some of the Indian troops broke and ran, but others and British troops fought their way into Tanga, where at one point angry bees attacked and drove off both forces. Lettow-Vorbeck ended the struggle with a determined counter-attack that won the day and the battle. Aitken withdrew, leaving his arms, ammunition, and supplies. The British suffered 10 percent casualties of their 8,000-man force; the Germans, about 150 soldiers. Aitken lost his command, while Lettow-Vorbeck's victory attracted white and black volunteers, whom he equipped with British arms. The war in East Africa was just beginning.

In the Pacific the British Navy convoyed Australian expeditions to New Britain and Rabaul and a New Zealand force to Samoa in August and September. The German government had stridently protested its encirclement by the Entente powers since 1905. That potential encirclement was now real, as the Entente ringed Germany on the continent and the British blockade severed German commercial ties to the overseas world. By the end of 1914 Germany no longer had any secure overseas possessions, its thirty-year struggle to gain a "place in the sun" hopelessly defeated. Now it could realize its aim of world power only by bringing the British, French, and Russians, and their empires, to their knees. Isolated German forces in the colonies continued fighting, buoyed only by the hope that they might draw enemy forces and resources from the main front in Europe for as long as they survived.

THE EUROPEAN HOME FRONTS. STUMBLING TOWARD MOBILIZATION

On the home fronts in Europe, the excitement and exuberance manifest in August 1914 yielded slowly as the war continued to the realization of the high price of glory. As casualties mounted, local papers began to carry the lists. The number of black–clad war widows, grieving parents, and orphans grew, for each death deprived a family somewhere of loved ones. The concept of a "blood tax" (*impôt du sang*), as the French grimly expressed it, paid directly by the soldier and indirectly by his family, contrasted to the more uplifting ideal of a brave and gallant sacrifice for the motherland, fatherland, or the empire. At first the public held war widows in respect. In time they would become commonplace. Then public concerns about income, food shortages, and rationing combined, particularly in Germany and Austria, to render them suspect for deriving an unfair advantage from their status.

The outbreak of war had occasioned widespread unemployment and a financial crisis on the stock exchanges of all the major European countries.[25] The war's continuation ended the widespread unemployment that its outbreak had caused, and factories manufacturing war materiel were soon running full bore and preparing to expand their production. Such growth would necessitate tapping women and youth as sources of industrial and agricultural labor. Working-class women had already labored in domestic service or menial jobs before they entered temporary wartime work in munitions industries; consequently contemporary observers focussed on the entry of previously unemployed middle-class women into the wartime labor force. On the land, women, children, and the elderly worked to compensate for the loss of males of military age.

The opening of the war and mobilization severely disrupted the labor and housing markets in Germany. Some important firms lost one-third to one-half of their workforce, causing a slump in production. As non-essential industries closed, unemployment shot up from 2.9 percent among trade union members to 22.4 percent in August. It would not regain the low prewar levels until spring 1915. The chronic shortage of housing in German cities eased as many wives, absent their husbands, could no longer pay their rents and had to move in with in-laws.[26]

The German government paid no heed to economic preparations at the outbreak of war, as a short war necessitated none. Through the fall, food supplies seemed even over-abundant. By late in the year, however, the first shortages loomed, and not simply of ammunition at the front. Government authorities concentrated on public campaigns to encourage Germans to consume less, and by December they had progressed from introducing "war bread" with additives and maximum prices to rationing bread in Berlin.[27]

Jewish industrialist Walther Rathenau, head of the giant German firm AEG (*Allgemeine Elektrizitäts Gesellschaft*), advised the army that Germany was not economically prepared to fight a long war. "Long" to the military meant two years, after which they feared that the British blockade would throttle Germany. Rathenau counseled close military–industrial cooperation to organize Germany's slender raw material reserves and a focussed scientific-technological-industrial effort to create and manufacture substitute, or *ersatz*, materials. In August 1914 the German War Ministry established a War Raw

Materials Department (KRA, or *Kriegsrohstoffabteilung*) and appointed Rathenau its director. The KRA would become "a pivot of the German war economy."[28] Without this early initiative, Germany would never have survived nearly four more years of war and blockade. German Chancellor Bethmann Hollweg drafted the government's war aims program in September, while German heavy industry and right-wing economic interests presented their war aims to the Chancellor in November. They planned to annex not only much of Belgium and reduce it to a vassal state, but also the Longwy-Briey mining and industrial area from France, and extensive territory in the east.[29]

The early stages of the war produced the first floods of refugees, from Belgium and eastern France, now under German occupation, from East Prussia during the Russian invasion, and in southeastern Europe, as Austro-Hungarian and Russian armies clashed. Their numbers would increase, particularly at the end of the war, when it seemed that entire empires were on the move, trudging with any belongings they could carry in bags or carts to escape the sound of the guns. As the German armies approached Paris in August 1914, even the French civilian government assumed refugee status, fleeing to Bordeaux, and leaving Paris and northeastern France under the army's control. When the government returned after the German tide receded, northeastern France remained the zone of the armies for the rest of the war, beyond the orbit of the civilian government.

Despite the precipitous retreat, French leaders such as President Raymond Poincaré made no plans to surrender. In the invasion of northeastern France, German armies had swept through Poincaré's village and destroyed his family home. He vowed to achieve total victory and refused to entertain the notion of a compromise peace because of the bonds of alliance, Germany's aggression, and his determination to retrieve Alsace Lorraine.[30]

As it became evident that the war would not end quickly, the French government, like the German, improvised piecemeal the mobilization of industrial production to support the armies at the front. In Bordeaux on 20 September, French War Minister André Millerand called a conference of bankers, railway and mine owners, and industrialists in order to increase armaments manufacture. He shifted arms production from state arsenals to private industry, which organized a network of employer associations to promote industrial concentration and specialization. The War Ministry became the middleman between the army and these industrial associations.

The British case remains most striking, because they eschewed conscription and filled the ranks of their military services with volunteers. The promulgation of the Defence of the Realm Act (DORA) in August granted the government the power to requisition the production of essential war materiels – a far-reaching prerogative from which the government recoiled. Instead, the British Cabinet began the war with the attitude of "business as usual," which meant no planning. Minister Herbert Asquith appointed the legendary Lord Horatio Kitchener, victor of Omdurman, Sirdar of Egypt, as Secretary of State for War. The tall, striking soldier, whose face would grace many a recruiting poster and who loomed over his political counterparts, promptly stunned them by predicting a long war with the need for millions of British soldiers. On 6 August, before the BEF had arrived on the continent, Kitchener articulated his intuition that Britain needed to begin by raising an army of 500,000 men. Kitchener's decision to raise the New Armies became a shocking discontinuity, or break with past tradition for Britain, although he relied initially on voluntary enlistments and the free market to secure soldiers and munitions.[31]

The raising of these New Armies required some mobilization to support their existence, but the British government approached it in piecemeal fashion. Many of the volunteers came from the labor force in industries essential to war production, equivalent to 16 percent of small arms factory employees and 25 percent of chemical and explosive factory employees. Their enlistments actually undercut the army's production of materiel, and they would one day gain exemption for war production, provided they survived that long.[32]

The British government hoped to concentrate on economic and naval warfare for two to three years. Kitchener planned to raise the British Army while the continental powers engaged each other and exhausted themselves by 1917. Britain would then enter the military struggle on the continent, win the war, and make the peace. Upon American entry into the war in 1917, Woodrow Wilson would hope to follow the same path. The war would thwart first Kitchener's and later Wilson's plans.

The volunteer army scheme met with early success, as men flocked to the colors, driven by unemployment, the thrill of adventure, the patriotic desire to protect their country in danger. Some joined perhaps to avoid vigilant women waving white feathers – the symbol of cowardice – in the faces of male civilians. Many enlisted in groups, from trades, professions, cities, towns, and regions, which laid the foundation for particularly close bonds of friendship in such units of "Pals." The "Old Contemptibles" were fighting and dying on the continent; "Kitchener's Mob" would take their place in 1915.

In Ireland both Unionists and Nationalists volunteered: the former because they identified with British interests; the latter because they identified with little Belgium and looked forward to Home Rule, enacted on 18 September but then suspended for the war's duration.[33] Throughout the empire emigrants came home to defend the mother country. All willingly committed themselves to an army that, "drawing on the ethos of British society, regarded people as expendable."[34]

In eastern Europe, the Russian government also pursued a policy of "business as usual." Russia's puppet parliament, the *Duma*, met for one day on 26 July for a demonstration of patriotism, then adjourned until the beginning of 1915, leaving the conduct of the war to the Cabinet. The Russian Unions of *Zemstvos* and Towns formed to provide for the relief of wounded soldiers. Yet the war's beginnings proved particularly disruptive to an economy that was less highly developed than its western European counterparts. Its economic isolation led to a precipitous decline in exports and imports. The closing of the border with Germany in August 1914 brought chaos to Russian industry because of its economic and scientific dependence upon Germany. The wartime rupture of scientific communications among the belligerent nations led to Russia's virtual isolation in science until 1921. In general the domination of Russian civilian industry by foreign investors had led to reliance on imported technologies, and state munitions factories tended to buy and copy foreign innovations. Russia had imported nearly 50 percent of the prewar products in the machine and chemical industries. Now the army turned to its allies and neutral powers for technology and supplies, placing orders even in Japan and the United States. Russian industry and commercial agriculture suffered greatly from the labor shortage caused by the mobilization of some five million men in 1914, while its railway system proved inadequate to supply both urban areas and the front.

What few policies the government enacted made conditions worse. At the end of July 1914 it temporarily prohibited the sale of intoxicating liquor. On 22 August it decreed prohibition for the duration of the war. Fully one-quarter of annual prewar revenues had derived from the state monopoly of the sale of spirits, so the decree caused a considerable loss to government coffers and contributed to the financial deficit. Like the later introduction of prohibition in the United States in 1918, the law did nothing to contribute to the temperance its advocates had preached. Finally, a law on wartime military administration promulgated in July 1914 granted wide powers to the army commander-in-chief and to the military authorities in general, but did not delineate the relationship between military and civilian authorities, which led to confusion and conflict as the army arrogated undue power. Its monopoly of Russian industrial production, for example, severely impaired the manufacture of agricultural machinery, which in turn exacerbated shortages in food supplies.

The dual monarchy of Austria-Hungary fractured politically from the very start of the war. In Hungary, parliament continued to function under Minister President Tisza. In Austria, Tisza's counterpart, Count Stürgkh, did not summon Parliament and ruled with his Cabinet of bureaucrats by imperial decree, responsible only to Emperor Franz Joseph. Very few parliamentary deputies challenged Stürgkh, and politicians and people accepted the situation and Stürgkh's stated intention to forget politics in order to concentrate all the powers of the state on the war effort. The first war loans in the fall of 1914 proved extremely popular and well subscribed, indicating substantial support for the war effort. Yet the government itself did not consider the people's rights sacrosanct. The Cabinet ministers and the military command, which would soon engage in a struggle for power as the army sought to enlarge its wide-ranging powers even further, agreed on the removal of basic rights and even some personal freedoms in wartime.

Reflecting the political fissure, the Austrian and Hungarian governments pursued separate economic measures in the absence of a central agency for the war economy. Austria had difficulties securing essential food supplies from Hungary, which had instituted border controls to prevent the outflow of food, so the two halves of the monarchy entered negotiation over this thorny matter in September. The military mobilization, which took large numbers of skilled workers even from war industry, first led to the collapse of many firms and unemployment, and later to a permanent labor shortage. Extensive transportation shortages, so severe that some historians have highlighted transport as the Achilles heel of the monarchy's war effort, impaired supplies to the large cities. The army's demands came first, and in Austria-Hungary the military's extensive controls rendered civilian authorities such as the commerce ministry impotent. An imperial order of 1 August 1914 assured the citizens of the supply of necessary goods, but ordering did not ensure enactment in the context of shortages of transport and raw materials, and internal trade barriers between Austria and Hungary. Attempts to set price controls on scarce goods simply caused the items to disappear from stores, to reappear on the black market. Finally, the Dual Monarchy entered economic isolation, able to trade only with its ally Germany.

All the powers had seriously underestimated the munitions necessary for war in 1914 and had no manufacturing plan once the war began. Governments initially left the conduct of the war to their army commands. As the war continued interminably, the universally inadequate preparations for the huge amounts of shells and supplies that armies would consume became quickly evident already in 1914. The combatants needed to increase production dramatically, and consequently continuing, much less winning, the war would necessitate mobilization at home. Government intervention in the economy and society of the warring countries had begun.[35]

Not only did war prompt economic mobilization, it also led to socio-cultural and intellectual mobilization. "Real" war provided an escape for men from the "civil . . . sex . . . and class war"[36] of prewar Britain into a manly realm that reinforced gender distinctions under assault from suffragettes before 1914. Men went off to war to kill and destroy, while women retreated into passive and traditional roles, knitting socks and mufflers for the fighting men.

Some women also accosted men in civilian clothes to present them with white feathers for cowardice. F.P. Crozier, on leave and in civilian dress in London in December, accompanied one such harpy to the recruiting office in Trafalgar Square after she challenged him, "Afraid to fight?"

The condescending recruiting officer judged him "A bit on the short side! However, times are hard!" When Crozier admitted under further questioning that he was already serving in the army, the recruiter brusquely queried, "What the hell are you doing here then?"

Crozier replied, "I don't know, I'm sure. Better ask the lady." After a stunned silence, she finally asked Crozier who and what he was. He answered, "A major in the Royal Irish Rifles."[37]

Separate spheres now ossified – the front for men, the home for women. The women's suffrage movement promptly accepted its domestic responsibilities to the nation of mothering, nursing, and saving lives. It fragmented between patriotism and pacifism, the latter the ultimate "feminine" stance in a world at war. Initially, then, the war appeared as a "remasculinization" of an English culture grown "degenerate, effeminate," as women remembered that their place was at home.[38] This reinforcement of traditional gender roles and separate spheres occurred in all countries.

The atrocity propaganda justifying the war reflected these traditional roles.[39] During the First World War, the dissemination of harrowing accounts of enemy atrocities occurred on a hitherto unprecedented scale, accounts that employed "the conscious use of gendered violence to justify military, foreign, and domestic policy."[40] Germany's violation of international and civil law, and German Chancellor Bethmann Hollweg's comments that "necessity knows no law" and treaties were "a scrap of paper" lacked the drama that a "yellow press" required for its readership. The necessity of popularizing the war to the masses led to a shift in concentration from legalistic to human issues of the safety of women and the family, to the defense of "mothers, wives, and sisters from the horrors of war."[41]

By the end of August 1914, the "rape" of neutral Belgium had become the *cause célèbre* of the war, and British propagandists resorted to more powerful and graphic images of alleged crimes against women and children. Representations in lurid detail of German atrocities, of women raped, mutilated, and murdered, children with their hands sliced off, babies bayonetted, were rife in the press, posters, even in woodcuts. Titillating images and tales of the "rape" of Belgium and of its women, and the consequent necessity to protect a "feminine" Belgium from the atrocities committed by a "masculine" Germany, pushed men to enlist. Paradoxically, at home the British government believed that it had to protect its servicemen from aggressively promiscuous working-class women out to seduce any man in uniform.

A crucial aspect of this cultural and intellectual mobilization was that governments had only to harness, not to generate it. Artists and writers quickly produced a lurid popular art and literature of atrocity. Intellectuals undertook "self-mobilization" in 1914–15.[42] Even many of the Russian intelligentsia, writers and artists frequently at odds with their government, rallied to support it and the war effort.[43]

German intellectuals blatantly and enthusiastically fell into step in the struggle for national unity. A Declaration of German University Teachers renounced their British academic degrees on 7 September 1914 because Britain had incited war against Germany. A further proclamation "An Appeal to the Civilized World," or the Manifesto of 93, on 4 October denied that Germany had started the war or, for that matter, violated Belgian neutrality and disturbed any Belgian citizens. Academic journals published attacks, even in rhyme, against Germany's enemies.[44]

The German proclamation provoked a mobilization of French intellectuals in response. On 3 November the Manifesto of French Universities appeared, and various responses continued through spring 1915, when a French Manifesto of 100 appeared. Intellectuals condemned Pan-Germanism and published pamphlets documenting German atrocities from German soldiers' diaries. Opposing conceptions of human civilization warred.

Austrian intellectuals followed the lead of their German counterparts, celebrating the *Grosse Zeit*, or "Great Time." They extolled the regenerative value of war. Yet they differed from their counterparts in Germany in viewing Russia, not England, as the primary antagonist, the instigator of a war it had duped the western powers into joining. If German intellectuals believed that their *Kultur* was fighting soulless and materialistic western powers assisted by barbarous Russia for the salvation of humanity, Austrian intellectuals perceived the crucial moral struggle to be against a dark and despotic Russia.[45] Russian intellectuals could claim that Russia would free itself from the yoke of dependence upon Germany.

As the intellectuals of the combatant nations assaulted their opponents verbally, Romain Rolland's essay "Above the Fray" of September 1914 condemned French and German intellectuals for abandoning their intellectual objectivity to serve the state as apologists for war. Needless to say, Rolland's stance proved unpopular in this monstrous struggle of good and evil.[46]

CONCLUSION. HUMANITY PLUNGES HEADLONG INTO HELL

The year 1914 drew to a close with no end of the war in sight either on land or at sea. On the Western Front, a steadily increasing complex of front-line, reserve, and communication trenches on both sides, with no-man's land in between, carved a deep and suppurating wound across northeastern France into Belgium. Shells and mines cratered the earth until it resembled a human face ravaged by the pox, or, as many envisaged it, a moonscape. Bare of foliage, the jagged stumps of blasted trees jutting skyward, the earth's torn surface became infested with millions of burrowing men, staked with mile upon mile of barbed wire, and littered with rotting bodies and rusting equipment. In places the scars remain visible to this day, like the scars on the populations who inflicted this scourge upon themselves and the land.

In the vast spaces of the Eastern Front, another pattern of warfare took shape. The Germans could send the Russians' northern armies reeling backward until German exhaustion and overextended supply lines prevented further advance against stiffening Russian resistance. In the south the Russians had pounded their Austro–Hungarian adversary. Great battles, lengthy retreats and advances, punctuated by sieges, set the pattern on the southern sector of the Eastern Front.

Severe losses occurred on all sides, with the exception of the British, whose entire expeditionary force was smaller than the number of casualties suffered by each of the other combatant countries. Yet the BEF's losses in proportion to the size of the force remained staggering. Historians once asserted, dramatically if erroneously, that the old Prussian Army died at the Marne. The BEF's "Old Contemptibles," however, had suffered such severe losses – some 30,000 dead and total casualties of some 90,000 officers and men – that they no longer constituted an effective force by the end of the year. Some units had ceased to exist. The Royal Welch Fusiliers, in three weeks of combat at Ypres, had eighty-six survivors of a 1,100-man battalion; the 1st Battalion of the Queen's Own Cameronian Highlanders, eighty men of those who had begun the campaign.[47] An engineer sergeant upon finding his younger brother, a 19-year-old "old soldier," inquired of his unit, "Well, where's the rest of your mob?" The brother's reply – "There isn't no [sic] more. They've all copped it"[48] – strikes a wider resonance applicable to the BEF itself, and many another unit in European armies. Those who had survived and the cadres that Kitchener retained at home would train the multitude of British volunteers.

The French Army, having suffered its highest losses of the war in the first six months, stood bloody if unbowed. Its vaunted élan, its worship of the offensive, and its colorful red and blue uniforms had almost proved its undoing. In the first four months of the war the French Army had lost over 450,000 men dead and missing, the Belgian Army some 70,000 men, and the BEF some 44,000 men, to the German Army's losses of 200,000 men.[49] France now confronted the task of defeating a powerful German foe whose losses, if substantial, had less effect on a country with a population nearly double that of France. The German male population of 32 million was substantially greater than the French of 20 million. But the Germans faced a two-front war.

In the east the Austro-Hungarian Army's severe losses, particularly irreplaceable among its officer corps, rendered it capable of battlefield success only with the help of German armies led by German generals. That circumstance generated resentment on the part of the Austro-Hungarian high command and contempt on the part of the Germans. The Russian Army had also suffered grievously, losing a million and a half casualties and prisoners, in particular infantry officers, commissioned and non-commissioned. Yet, despite shortages of officers, ammunition, rifles, and even uniforms, the Russian Army had acquitted itself well. Its early offensive into East Prussia helped spare its French ally, and its offensives had established its clear military superiority over the Austro-Hungarian foe. In the Caucasus it faced a Turkish army which would be fortunate to survive the winter.

The sheer violence and scale of the war in comparison to earlier conflicts was evident from the starting engagements. In the midst of the violence, quite unnoticed, both the German and French armies had experimented with small quantities of non-fatal gas by October, and both planned to employ gas, but of a lethal variety, in 1915. The volume of artillery, rifle, and machine-gun-fire wrought terrible carnage upon all armies, literally driving them first to ground, and then underground, especially in the confines of the Western Front. Troops emerged to attack and counter-attack, reconnoiter and raid. On the Anglo–German front the soldiers also emerged at Christmas to celebrate spontaneously, sharing rations, liquor, and addresses, playing rugby and soccer. During a football match between Scots and Saxons, Lt. Johannes Niemann and his soldiers "really roared when a gust of wind revealed that the Scots wore no drawers under their kilts – and hooted and whistled every time" they glimpsed a Scotsman's "posterior."[50] In some sections of the front this soldiers' truce lasted for a week, until their commanding officers drove them apart. The Brigade Commander ordered 2nd Lt. Cyril Drummond's artillery battery to fire on a farm behind the German lines to end the truce. They did, but only after warning the Germans.[51] Commanders reminded their men that the other side was a perfidious enemy with whom fraternization should not recur. It would not, as in December 1915 the commanders on both sides forbade any repetition of the "regrettable" events of the previous Christmas and investigated any reports of attempted communication or fraternization.[52]

The lines froze in place, as soldiers endured their first winter of the war. The war of movement's blistering heat and all-enveloping dust of the late summer and early fall had yielded to the trench warfare of the fall and winter, as the infantry settled into trenches that passed from sodden mud to frozen ground, where they suffered from trench foot and frostbite and huddled together for warmth. On no front did the fighting cease in the winter, as

French, Russians, and Turks launched offensives in December. At least by December some French generals such as Maunoury and Franchet D'Esperey complained to Joffre about wasting their men in poorly prepared and inadequately supported attacks which resulted in high losses disproportionate to their gains. Joffre, however, seemed unaffected by these repeated failures and obsessed with the notion that continued offensives, however wasteful, would keep the troops ready for future offensives. The troops, who were, in fact, exhausted, discouraged, resigned, and fatalistic, believed that the staff held them in contempt, a scorn they returned readily.[53]

The Langemarck legend demonstrated the valiant patriotism and bravery of German youth and symbolized the sense of national unity evident in all the warring countries in August 1914. In another sense, however, their exploit, like the repeated assaults against strongly held positions, exemplified the wanton callousness of army commanders seeking rapid and complete victory, whatever the cost. Armies expended their troops with no regard for class or education. French law required students of the prestigious *Ecole Normale* to serve in the infantry, and as junior officers they went straight to the front line. In six months of combat, of the 255 *normaliens* called up since August 1914, only ninety-five remained unscathed: fifty-five were dead; sixteen missing; sixty-four wounded; and twenty-five prisoners.[54] Men became mere cannon-fodder.

French intellectual Charles Péguy had exalted the blessed good fortune of men who fell in combat, and during the Battle of the Marne in early September, on the Ourcq River, Péguy fell, his body joining the multitudes strewn about the battlefields of 1914. The fortunate Péguy realized his dream early of dying in "glorious" combat and avoided the lingering death or maiming that proved the fate of so many soldiers. He perished before the patina of war's glory eroded to show the true face of a monstrous slaughter gnawing away at the vitals of European society.

Péguy, a 40-year-old lieutenant, also exemplified a fact often forgotten – the men mobilized to fight ranged in age from 18 to 45 to 48 depending upon the country. The standard conception of the front-line soldier of the First World War remains one of youth. In fact, men in their late twenties, thirties, forties, and occasionally even fifties – far into middle age – served in the front-line trenches. Their bloated, putrefying bodies in the hundreds of thousands, left to rot in mounds in the sun because they were too many to bury, unleashed a horrid stench assailing those who had to carry on the great conflict, but now without any exalted illusion about the nature of war.

Many British youth greeted war with a zesty enthusiasm. Oxonian Julian Grenfell, who perished in October 1914, wrote home that he *"adored"* war, found it "the best fun," like a "big picnic," and enjoyed nothing better than sniping at the enemy, commenting "One loves one's fellow man so much more when one is bent on killing him."[55] Such youthful civilian "idealists" flocked to the colors in 1914 and 1915. Péguy and Grenfell were dead by October, when the mood began to change at the front. Notes of despair began to creep into soldiers' letters home that once brimmed with patriotic enthusiasm. One German university student wrote on 28 October from Dixmude in Belgium: "With what joy and pleasure I was drawn into the struggle, which seemed to me the greatest opportunity, to release my longing and zest for life. With what disillusionment I sit here, with dread in my heart."[56] A British professional soldier, suffering from no romantic illusions, echoed the German student more tersely: "This is pure murder, not war."[57]

Troops in all armies suffered under difficult conditions that worsened the further east one ventured. The Austro-Hungarian Army under siege from the Russians in the fortress of Przemsyl was running short of supplies, while the stolid Russian peasant besiegers once again demonstrated their legendary endurance of deprivation. Meanwhile, Turkish soldiers were freezing to death by the thousands in the Caucasus Mountains, sacrificed to the stupid zeal of their commander to pursue retreating Russians through impassable mountain passes. For soldiers on all sides, an incredible test of their endurance and will to survive against terrible odds had begun. Failed commanders retired, were sacked, or even "kicked upstairs," promoted above battlefield command. The soldiers paid a higher penalty: their lives and limbs.

No army medical service could treat the number and diverse nature of casualties. The soldiers themselves carried minimal bandages, and their corpsmen, even in the most advanced armies, might at best be able to stanch the flow of blood of some wounds, pour iodine or other compounds into the wound to prevent infection, and carry the soldier to a field hospital. From there, evacuation proved perilous and painful. The high velocity of rifle and machine-gun bullets ensured that the resulting wounds were deep. Shrapnel from shells and grenades created jagged wounds that blew clothes into the body as it tore away bone and muscle, thus compounding the injury with the likelihood of secondary infections. A shell might tear off a man's leg, or part of his face, or slice his stomach open, leaving him struggling vainly to keep his intestines from spilling out of his body as he died. The very blast could kill a man without leaving a mark on him, or the concussion might cause bleeding from every bodily orifice.

Many of the badly wounded miraculously did not die, only to endure the rest of their lives as horrific reminders of the struggle. Overwhelmed field hospitals struggled to save as many as possible, and loaded the thousands that might live to receive better treatment at home on munitions trains returning from the front. At home, they would offer medical science new opportunities for rehabilitation and prosthetics. The phenomenon known in France as *les gueules cassées*, the "broken mouths," men who survived without jaws, cheeks, noses, or mouths, whose faces shells and bullets had mutilated horribly and permanently, began in 1914. Those whose wounds healed faced return to the front for more of the same. By December 1914 medical officers were encountering more traumatized cases – mute, deaf, trembling men, unable to stand or walk – produced by the anxiety and terror of living constantly with violence and death from bullets, shells, and mines.[58]

If casualties overwhelmed medical facilities on the Western Front, wounded troops in the Austro–Hungarian, Russian, and Turkish armies faced hellish conditions. Russian soldiers traveled from the front to the capital with little medical attention, and what attention they received at any time was primitive. As winter approached, wounded men lay in the cold rain and mud in Warsaw as they awaited trains for Russia. Men needlessly crippled in crude operations recuperated, or likely died, in inadequate hospitals. Soldiers, as well as potential conscripts, began to mutilate themselves, slicing or shooting off the index or trigger finger of their right hand. Civic efforts by the Russian local councils, or *zemstva*, to raise funds for medical aid could not stem the bloody tide.[59]

The war engendered mass, indiscriminate slaughter. The various fronts or theatres constituted the slaughterhouses; the military commanders, the butchers; and the civilian governments, whether authoritarian or democratic, the mobilizers of the fodder and implements for the slaughter. The industrialists and masters of science and technology supplied and created implements of destruction in astounding quantity; intellectuals, the press, the cinema, and the arts prepared their subjects psychologically for the butchery. The eligible male population became the fodder; the rest of the adult males, women, and youth, the labor to manufacture the implements to kill them; and the children, potential participants in future wars to socialize through patriotic instruction. The war enmeshed entire societies.

3

1915. An Insignificant Year?

"This is not war. It is the ending of the world."

Hindu soldier on the Western Front.[1]

"The war? It'll last until I get killed. The rest makes little difference."

French officer Blanchard, 22 January 1915.[2]

"I've only got to survive a few more hours to reach twenty. I hope I make it. I know I'll never reach twenty-one."

French soldier Personne, June 1915.[3]

"I do not expect you to attack, I order you to die."

Lieut. Col. Mustapha Kemal, Gallipoli, 25 April 1915.[4]

The year 1915 appears comparatively insignificant in the Great War, sandwiched between the dramatic beginning of the war in 1914 and its cataclysmic and costly battles on both Western and Eastern Fronts that led to stalemate, and the gigantic battles in 1916 of Verdun and the Somme on the Western Front and the Brusilov offensive in the east. The latter arguably constitute the most monstrous examples of a war of materiel and attrition that portended an unending conflict until one or both sides collapsed. However, 1915 deserves far more attention for a variety of reasons. To English-speaking observers, the Entente's invasion of Gallipoli and the German sinking of the liner *Lusitania* loom as the most significant events. Certainly, the Gallipoli campaign, unrestricted submarine warfare, Germany's introduction of poison gas on the Western Front and of a strategic bombing campaign against England figure prominently in military events. British and French landings at Gallipoli and Salonika, a British incursion into Mesopotamia, and ongoing conflict in Africa indicate the strongly imperialist nature of the war. Furthermore, the entry of Italy into the war creates another European front, a southwestern theater against Austria-Hungary. Finally, and perhaps most critically, 1915 witnesses the mobilization on the home fronts, the initiation of a collective effort to prepare the combatants to wage a war of escalating proportions with the intent not merely to endure but to emerge victorious.

THE WESTERN FRONT. "NIBBLING" AWAY AT EACH OTHER'S VITALS

With deadlock came fortification of the front lines, which on the Western Front stretched for nearly 500 miles; on the Eastern, another 800. The ratio of troops to space varied from high in the west to low in the east. The no-man's land separating front-line trenches in the west usually ran 200 to 300 yards wide, though in places, such as the brickyards at Cuinchy, it narrowed to 25 yards; on the Eastern Front it frequently spanned two miles.

In November 1914 German General Staff Chief Falkenhayn had ordered the troops to fortify the Western Front's main trench line so that small numbers could resist attacks by superior forces. Hindenburg, Ludendorff, and Chancellor Bethmann Hollweg pressured Falkenhayn to focus more on the Eastern Front. Consequently, he planned to defend in the west and send more first-line troops to the Eastern Front. In January 1915 the German Army had grown to 4,357,934 men, of whom 2,618,158 fought in the field, despite the losses of the 1914 campaign.[5] The burrowing German troops dug shell-proof shelters equipped with electric light and other comforts of home, connected underground command posts by telephone lines to artillery batteries, and constructed iron and concrete machine-gun positions behind them in support. The Germans intended to hold these fortified trench lines and to retake them by immediate counter-attack in the event of their capture. While the Germans planned to defend, the French intended to attack, to retake the ten *départements* containing most of France's industry and mines, and ultimately, to rout the Germans from France.

Joffre ordered two barbed wire belts, 10 yards in width and 20 yards apart, with gaps for patrols, built along the entire front. On active fronts, French soldiers manned strong-points behind the wire, then sheltered positions for counter-attack companies further back, and finally, two miles to the rear, a second line. The French invariably looked to their artillery, especially the 75 mm. cannon, for defensive protection. To economize on manpower the army held the front with as few men as possible, and positioned outposts a circumspect distance from German lines. Yet the very manpower Joffre took such pains to husband, he intended to expend on repeated offensives. The

French Army could expect little respite from its commanding general's determination to attack in 1915.

In contrast to the Germans, the British attempted to dominate no-man's land – an oxymoronic undertaking – by entrenching closer to the Germans and staging trench raids to seize prisoners and enhance troop morale through offensive action. Their small but increasing numbers ensured that they would play a supporting role to their superior French ally. In January 1915 BEF commander Sir John French wisely declared the supply of materiel the decisive factor in trench warfare, but his awareness did not effect any improvement in his troops' equipment.

All front-line soldiers lived, like the rats and other vermin that shared their positions with them, in a muddy maze of trenches. All trenches zigzagged to make it impossible for shell blast or enfilading fire to sweep them clean of men for any distance. Behind the front-line trenches lay parallel support lines 200 yards back and finally reserve lines another 400 yards to the rear, all of which communication trenches connected for the movement of troops and supplies to and from the front. Soldiers continually improved these trenches or dug new ones, and every cycle of attack and counter-attack necessitated digging and shoring up new trenches. Beyond these man-made demands, rain, rain, and more rain sometimes flooded whole sections of trench lines, necessitating shoring up existing trenches against encroaching mud and water and building new ones to escape. This maze of trenches required signs and guides to negotiate, especially as aerial reconnaissance increasingly forced night troop movements. Around Ypres in January British troops had to drain their low-lying trenches, build, fortify, and fix barbed wire belts the length of it, all the while dodging German snipers.

In certain sectors of the Western Front – along the 160 miles of the Vosges Mountains at the southern end, for example – the inhospitable terrain rendered large-scale operations untenable. There the front became relatively quiet or "inactive." Yet even in the "quiet" Vosges, French and German elite mountain troops contested the summit of Hartmannsweilerkopf in murderous but inconclusive fighting throughout 1915. In fact, the French were expending some of their best troops by attacking repeatedly up mountain crests that the Germans had heavily fortified and increasingly held with reserve troops. Furthermore, the Germans used the inhospitable mountain terrain, which impeded the use of artillery, to experiment with new infantry tactics. *Sturmbattailon Rohr*, named after its captain, combined elite infantry and engineers to develop more powerful infantry units, primarily grenadiers supported by machine-gun, mortar, and flame-thrower platoons.[6]

The Entente deemed the Argonne Forest too dense, the coastal zone in Flanders too wet for major undertakings. Yet, while the major battles of 1915 raged around these regions, German troops in the Argonne Forest under the command of Gen. von Mudra spent the year to September 1915 perfecting new tactics in a series of small offensives that essentially ejected the French from the Argonne. Mudra's attacks focussed on small sections of the front, which his infantry and engineers would infiltrate after a short massive artillery bombardment had surprised and stunned the French. Once these leading units had cleared the area using grenades, flame-throwers, mortars, and explosives, more infantry and machine-gun teams would establish the new positions. A gifted young Swabian lieutenant who spent most of 1915 in the Argonne under von Mudra, and then joined an Alpine unit that fought in the Vosges, would later distinguish himself. Erwin Rommel, like other men who rotated through these test battalions and then joined other units on other fronts, disseminated and implemented these "stormtroop" tactics throughout the German Army.[7] A "quiet" sector of the front proved "inactive" only in comparison to sectors where major battles raged. Under cover of relative inactivity, the Germans were developing new tactics and staging small and murderously effective attacks, as the French battered themselves to death in suicidal infantry attacks often unsupported by artillery. Even "inactive" sectors generated deadly combat.

Furthermore, the German General Staff reorganized its divisional structure in 1915. Standard European divisions had two brigades, and each brigade comprised two infantry regiments of some 3,000 men each. Regiments in turn consisted of battalions, then companies, and platoons. In 1915 the German Army reduced the number of regiments in each division to three, then added a second machine-gun company to each regiment and additional howitzers to each division. This restructuring produced a smaller division with more firepower, in particular 50 percent more machine-guns than its predecessor. The Entente misinterpreted the reorganization as a sign that their attacks were killing far more Germans than was the case, and that Germany was running out of manpower.

In fact, the German Army was husbanding its manpower, as the new division proved far more potent than the old. German superiority in firepower, with their increased reliance on mortars, grenades, and flame-throwers, enabled them to stage operations without overwhelming numerical superiority. The brigade disappeared, thereby eliminating a layer of command, while command decentralized as the basic tactical unit devolved from the regiment to the battalion. Battlefield commanders at battalion and company levels gained more autonomy and could pull back under bombardment, then return in time to face an attack, a tactic which gave attackers the impression of an empty battlefield until German soldiers suddenly reappeared to engage them.

While German reorganization and tactical development proceeded apace, the French and British focussed on major offensives. The dry, chalky terrain of the Somme and in Champagne offered ideal staging areas for major operations, and both sides held key railway lines behind the front for logistical support. The railway lines, in fact, determined the strategic plans that the French and British formulated in January for the year. The Germans held a great bulge, or salient, into Entente lines between Flanders and Verdun. In the spring the French planned to attack in the south in Champagne, and the French and British in the north in Flanders and Artois in an attempt to cut the rail lines supplying the salient and ultimately to pinch it off. French Prime Minister René Viviani and Senator Aristide Briand, President and Vice-President of the War Council respectively, believed that the high command lacked a strategic plan and remained skeptical about the success of the coming offensives. They preferred Generals Galliéni's and Franchet D'Esperey's proposals about offensives at Gallipoli and Salonika and even diverted troops to those theaters. Nevertheless, they simultaneously pushed Joffre to finish the war.

The Germans knew of French intentions and resorted to a ploy that they would use repeatedly during the war. In response to the French attacks in Artois and Champagne of December 1914 and to forestall future Entente attacks, the Germans counter-attacked at Soissons, west of the French attacks in Champagne, and at la Bassée in the north against the British in January and February. In March the French and British implemented their plans of attack. The French continued their offensive in Champagne and then initiated a further attack in April against the St. Mihiel salient south of Verdun, while the British launched an offensive at Neuve-Chapelle on 10 March.

The French attacks proved abortive and costly. The French had manufactured more field guns and munitions. French 75s could destroy German machine-gun nests, and French sappers and artillery could destroy barbed wire to prepare the way for the infantry. The Germans, however, had manufactured even more and heavier artillery, and these guns and their mortars preserved their mastery of the battlefield. Furthermore, inadequate French aerial direction of artillery fire caused French guns to fire on their own troops. The numbers of French wounded overwhelmed their medical services. The French advanced nearly two miles.

In the struggle at Les Éparges, a small hill southeast of Verdun, two authors whose writing on the war would make them famous numbered among the wounded. The young German Ernst Jünger, hit in the shoulder and knocked to the ground, thought initially that a flying clod of earth had struck him, until he felt warm blood flowing down his torso. He lay surrounded by other German victims, dead and wounded, of French 75s, and noted that he had seen no living Frenchmen, only dead or wounded. On the other side Maurice Genevoix, on the attack, stumbled to one knee, then felt a hard shock in his left arm. He looked down to see it bleeding in spasmodic streams. He tried to rise but failed. He was still looking at his left arm when another bullet struck it, leaving him bleeding from another hole. His body felt like lead, his head inclined forward, as Genevoix, stupefied, watched another scrap of uniform jump, as a third bullet carved a deep furrow of red flesh on the left side of his chest close to his armpit. Medics retrieved the fortunate Jünger and Genevoix, placed compresses on their wounds, and ultimately transported them to hospitals where they could recuperate.[8]

At Neuve-Chapelle the BEF achieved a twofold feat: they assembled some 60,000 British and Indian troops in complete secrecy and their thirty-five-minute artillery bombardment caught the German defenders unaware. They seized Neuve-Chapelle and broke into open country, but then the British junior field commanders had to request further orders to advance from headquarters, which took six hours. Their German counterparts, acting on their own initiative, moved machine-guns and reserves to attack the flanks. In two hours two German machine-guns slaughtered a thousand British soldiers before they were put out of action. When the British finally received their orders, it was too late in the day to do more than secure their positions. The next morning mist impeded their resumption of the attack. The third day brought the inevitable German counter-attack, which twenty machine-guns the British had emplaced to consolidate the position cut down. The battle now petered out, with 11,652 British casualties to 8,600 German. The debilitating losses of Indian infantry in particular undermined their effectiveness as offensive troops. British artillery had also expended some one-third of their artillery shells.

Falkenhayn staged a limited offensive in April against the British in the Ypres salient to seize the initiative, straighten his line, and cover the movement of troops to the Eastern Front. He would hammer away for over a month (22 April to 25 May), but the opening salvo of the attack on 22 April took warfare to a new level, as for the first time the Germans used a killing gas – chlorine – in sufficiently high concentrations to affect the enemy. The German Army intended the attack only as a diversion, but when pressurized cylinders released the yellow-greenish cloud of gas into French lines held by Algerian troops both white and African, it opened a five-mile gap in the French lines.

Chlorine gas drowned its victims through the excessive production of fluid in the lungs. Victims experienced a stinging irritation of the nose, throat, and eyes, then chest pains, sensations of suffocation, and violent coughing. Some keeled over on the spot, others struggled back, vomiting phlegm tinged with blood. If they reached the rear, they often died of asphyxiation from pulmonary lesions. The gas blinded others, sometimes permanently, and the lines of sightless men, their eyes covered with bandages, their hands on the shoulder of the man in front, etched a searing image of the effect of gas in the war.

Gas attacks against the Canadians and British on 24 April and 1 May had less effect, since diagnosis of the gas as chlorine led to improvisation of water-soaked cloths over the mouth and nose, and the soldiers fought back fiercely. Before the gas attack the inexperienced Canadian division had occupied a part of the front consisting of mere holes and mounds instead of trenches. Water-rats inhabited the many rotting, stinking bodies left unburied from the battles the previous fall. In their first major encounter since entering the lines in March, the Canadians suffered severe casualties in a determined defensive struggle that contained the German penetration to two miles. The soldiers of the embryonic Canadian Expeditionary Force served as part of the British Army, with British soldiers and sergeant-majors to train and enter combat with them. The fighting left the region covered with "a mass of dead bodies." Lance-Sgt. J.L. Bouche of the Coldstream Guards noted that at night, "You sat on something, and it moved up and down. You knew perfectly well that underneath you was a dead body that had swelled up."[9] The British retreated to shorten their lines, and held, although Falkenhayn staged a larger gas attack on 24 May.

The Entente suffered twice as many casualties as the German forces' 35,000 losses in this Second Battle of Ypres, although British propaganda now justifiably could excoriate German brutality and inhumanity. Ironically, Falkenhayn had doubted the effectiveness of gas and had amassed insufficient reserves to exploit its surprise. In general, German soldiers distrusted gas warfare and viewed gas with disdain and doubt, because its dependence upon winds made it unpredictable. The prevailing winds of the Western Front, furthermore, blew from west to east, advantaging the French and British, who quickly adopted gas. German scientist Fritz Haber, the father of the gas cloud, had assured the soldiers that an Entente riposte would require six months. In fact, both sides quickly developed gas and gas masks, as the vile cloud became just another weapon in the arsenal of the combatants.[10]

In May and June the French and British attacked in the Second Battle of Artois against German high ground at Vimy and Aubers Ridges. Both met with little success in return for high losses from German artillery and machine-gunfire. Pétain's troops advanced well, led by mountain troops, foreign legionnaires, and African assault units, but brutal German artillery fire decimated their ranks. French infantry did reach the summit of Vimy Ridge before a counter-attack by German reserves threw them off decisively. Joffre believed that his soldiers had inflicted critical casualties on the Germans, but in fact he had broken the back of French assault forces with losses of more than 84,000 casualties between 6 May and 18 June in return for an advance of two and a half miles. Joffre's generals – Foch, Dubail, and Castelnau – reproached him for depriving them of all initiative, while French politicians reproached War Minister Millerand for protecting Joffre. On 1 July Millerand did provide French soldiers with their first leave – eight days – since the beginning of the war. Joffre, meanwhile, persisted in preparing his next attack, replenishing his stock of Moroccan and French shock troops. He refused to contemplate a defensive strategy, since he feared that it would erode French soldiers' physical and moral qualities.[11]

The failure of the May offensive prompted BEF commander Sir John

French to censure the War Office for inadequate supplies and materiel. French's condemnation initiated a public "shell scandal" in Britain that would lead to the fall of the Asquith government. In fact, nearly every combatant experienced a shortage of munitions in 1915, as their artillery might fire as many shells in one day's barrage as both sides in the American Civil War expended in the entire conflict. Shell production temporarily lagged behind front-line expenditure.

In the spring and summer, as the battle of materiel intensified, both sides struck at the enemy homeland from the air. German Zeppelins bombed towns in southwest England and planes struck the French towns of Nancy and Verdun. British and French biplanes, dropping primitive bombs made from 90 mm. artillery shells, bombed war industries in west German industrial cities. The French then struck Karlsruhe in June in reprisal for German attacks, and a vicious circle of reprisal and retaliation from the air began in 1915 that would last the entire war. The tiny bomb loads of these primitive aircraft rendered early attacks rather harmless. German anti-aircraft guns and embryonic fighter defenses proved effective, while the prevailing westerly wind would often blow underpowered French Voisin bombers backward into Germany as they struggled to regain the French lines. Zeppelins actually carried a larger bomb load and could outclimb and thus escape extant airplanes, so they proved effective raiders. These strategic air attacks struck directly at civilian populations. Along with the submarine, aircraft transformed the civilian population into a direct and indirect target of military operations in 1915.

In June Joffre requested that the British take over more front, and the BEF proceeded to man the front from Ypres in the north to the River Somme. Although the British government, plagued by a shortage of munitions, wanted to postpone any major attack until spring 1916, Joffre insisted on keeping the pressure on the Germans with a fall offensive. The British prepared to meet this test of their steadfastness. Meanwhile the Germans prepared a second line of emplacements behind their first line and on the reverse slope of the high ground they occupied to protect them from Entente shell fire. With concrete machine-gun pillboxes in between these lines, these defensive belts now extended for three miles. German artillery would shell Entente troops as they assembled and attacked through no-man's land, leaving the remnants to the machine-gunners and counter-attacking infantry.

On 25 September the French and British attacked again in Champagne and in Artois, in both cases behind a gas cloud. French shock troops, colonial soldiers in khaki, French in "horizon blue" uniforms, had received the first metal helmets, the *casque Adrian*, which one soldier labeled derisively a "salad bowl to scare crows and owls."[12] In Champagne twenty French divisions attacked on a twenty-mile front, some regiments actually flying their colors and marching to the music of their bands in the front-line trenches. They never reached the German second line. Gen. Mangin was organizing an attack when he was shot in the chest. Mangin returned to duty ten days later; thousands of his men could not. The Germans counter-attacked to regain any lost territory, and the battle ended on 31 October. In Artois the French attackers once again reached the crest of Vimy Ridge only to fall victim to German artillery. They had gained another mile or so of ground in Artois, but nothing in Champagne, except casualties.

At Loos six British divisions attacked, but quickly needed the help of two reserve divisions, which BEF commander French had positioned so far in the rear that the attack was halted until the following morning. They then marched forward, bayonets fixed, in ten columns of a thousand men each, as if on parade. German machine-gunners had a field day, opening fire at nearly a mile range, their bullets scything down the ranks of marching men. The wind blew British gas back into the trenches before Capt. W.G. Bagot Chester and his Gurkhas attacked. He and his men had all fallen dead or wounded before they covered the 200 yards to the German trenches. The wounded were hit repeatedly as they lay exposed or in shallow holes on the battlefield. German fire annihilated entire units as they advanced. When the British finally retreated, the Germans actually held their fire, nauseated at what they labeled "the corpsefield at Loos." That night the survivors lay in their trenches listening to the cries and screams of the wounded left to die in agony.[13] Loos had provided a grim initiation to battle for "Kitchener's Mob," since two of the New Army divisions suffered 8,000 casualties of 15,000 infantry. The British, undaunted, continued their attacks for three more weeks. When the battle in Artois petered out, the French and British had suffered 190,000 and 60,000 casualties respectively to some 140,000 German. Among the casualties was the career of Sir John French, whom Douglas Haig replaced as commander of the BEF.

Entente casualties included thousands of Indian soldiers serving with the British and Africans in the French colonial forces. In 1915 both the French and the British used colonial troops on the Western Front: the French, north and west African infantry; the British, Indian infantry and cavalry. African combat troops would serve the French in Europe in increasing numbers through to the end of the war, but 1915 marked the height of Indian combat service on the Western Front. The British had dispatched Indian Army expeditionary forces in the fall of 1914 to Basra, Egypt, and East Africa, but primarily to France, where they had entered combat in October. The Indians' first encounters with the Germans on the Western Front in 1914 had caused heavy losses, and the brutally cold winter undermined morale. Nevertheless, during the winter of 1914–15, the Indian Corps grew to include two infantry and two cavalry divisions composed of some 16,000 British and 28,500 Indian troops, who participated in the attacks at Neuve Chapelle in March 1915, at Festubert in early May, and at Loos in late September.

The Indian Army, a colonial force of 150,000 men, comprised mainly illiterate peasants from the north and northwest of the subcontinent, whom the British deemed the most "martial" of the Indian "races." The deliberate recruitment of the least educated men also served to minimize the penetration of "dangerous" western ideas into the minds of Indian troops. The Indian Corps's command structure typified that in colonial armies, in which, in essence, no Indian officer could command a European. The corps figured prominently in the Battle of Neuve Chapelle in March, where their attack resulted in losses of 12,500 of 30,000 men engaged. At the Battle of Loos they incurred additional debilitating losses, which further undermined their effectiveness as assault infantry or shock troops, the favorite use of colonial troops on the Western Front.

The Indian soldiers' letters home prove poignant and revealing. Scribes often wrote the letters, while the censors' concentration on the suppression of accounts of sex with white women and slighting references to whites in order to preserve white prestige in India[14] allowed the occasional transmission of dramatic sentiments about the front. Already in January, individual soldiers were writing that "it would be difficult for anyone to survive and come back safe and sound from the war . . ." where "The bullets and cannon-balls come down like snow."[15] Hindu soldiers commented that "This is not war. It is the ending of the world,"[16] as the front far surpassed in scale and intensity any combat they had experienced on the Indian frontier. On the other hand, soldiers were winning medals for acts of heroism that made them, their units, and their ethnic groups proud and cast glory upon their families at home.

A rifleman wounded in the head in the attack at Neuve Chapelle described events when they reached the German trenches:

> we used the bayonet and the *kukri* [a large, curved knife], and blood was shed so freely that we could not recognize each other's faces; the whole ground was covered with blood. There were heaps of men's heads, and some soldiers were without legs, others had been cut into, some without hands and others without eyes.[17]

Many had given up all hope of returning to India, because the British sent home only those who had lost limbs or were so wretchedly wounded that they could no longer serve. One soldier whose war was over wrote from Kitchener's Indian Hospital in Brighton in September, "There is nothing but my corpse left. They have cut off the whole of one leg, and one hand too is useless. What is the use of my going to India thus? They have given me a leg, but it is made of wood, and vile. I cannot walk. . . . What am I to do?"[18] By May some companies and regiments had suffered 100 percent casualties. As the year and battles wore on, some soldiers despaired, others remained concerned to comport themselves honorably, while some remained determined to come to grips with the enemy using the sword.[19] As a Sikh observed disappointedly in October, it is "the religion of Sikhs to die facing the foe," but in the war of machine-guns, cannon, mines, and bombs, "There is no fighting face to face."[20] One particularly poetic individual wrote his wife, "Our life is a living death. For what great sin are we being punished? Kill us, Oh God, but free us from our pain! We move in agony but never rest. We are slaves of masters who can show no mercy. . . . Many sons of mothers lie dead. No one takes any heed. . . . God the Omnipotent plays a game, and men die. Death here is dreadful, but of life there is not the briefest hope."[21] The censor suppressed it.

Finally, the prospect of another winter delivered the *coup de grâce* to Indian infantry presence on the Western Front, as the Imperial General Staff sent what survived of the two infantry divisions to the Mesopotamian theater. The cavalry divisions remained, usually in reserve but occasionally in combat, and endured until the spring of 1918. In an ironic twist of fate, in December 1914 the British government assigned territorial, or home defense battalions, to garrison duty in India and Burma to replace Indian Army units destined for service in France. Assigned to garrison duty in south Asia, these battalions spent most of the war there, isolated from the main theaters of war, policing rebellious hill tribes. Snakes, scorpions, tarantulas, giant bugs, and the heat posed more danger than did the tribes, as most untended bites proved fatal.[22]

While Indian infantry departed, more West African *tirailleurs* would be arriving on the Western Front to fight for the French in 1916. French casualties since August 1914 had been horrendous: as of 5 November 1915: officers – 15,201 dead, 28,513 wounded, 6,046 missing; troops – 507,897 dead, 876,726 wounded, 375,537 missing.[23] Such losses occasioned serious worry about adequate numbers of effective troops, and consequently the demand for West African recruits for use on the Western Front increased steadily in 1915. The Governor of French West Africa, Jost van Vollenhoven, worried about the debilitating loss of manpower from the colonies, urged diplomatic efforts to persuade the British to recruit in their African colonies.

The British absolutely refused to use African combat troops in Europe or outside Africa, although they did import numbers of Asian and African labor battalions. For the English, having Indian soldiers in England constituted sufficient threat; the presence of black colonial soldiers would prove insufferable. In France, however, contrary to Vollenhoven's concerns, Mangin wanted more shock troops, and Senegalese deputy Blaise Diagne regarded service of African troops in France as the avenue toward more rights for the colonies. A law of 19 October 1915 consequently introduced conscription in Senegal, so that its vaunted warriors could serve in Europe and elsewhere, while the French used Madagascan and Annamite (Indo-Chinese) troops as laborers behind the Western Front and as combat soldiers in the Near East.

Troop color certainly mattered less to the French and more to the British, but it made no difference to the furnace of the Western Front, which consumed all colors with equal relish in its roaring inferno.

By the end of the year 391,000 Entente and 114,000 German soldiers had succumbed on the Western Front.[24] Joffre described his policy as one of *grignotage*, or nibbling, in which he, through his relentless offensives, ate away at the Germans. The rather rotund general, who never missed a meal, clearly believed that his French soldiers were devouring the Germans and exacting more casualties than they incurred. The actual casualties indicate otherwise – French offensives, confronted with superior German firepower and tactics, consumed French soldiers, while smaller scale German attacks effectively gnawed at the French and British. Joffre, it seemed, was rather a gourmand, who serenely and indiscriminately launched offensives that ingested more French than German soldiers.

In occupied Belgium and northern France, starvation threatened. Hoover managed to convince Lloyd George in Britain and Poincaré in France of the necessity to feed the populations of the occupied territory, regardless of whether the British and French governments considered them the responsibility of the occupying Germans. In four months Hoover had managed to create an international network to feed Belgium, and now that the British and French governments added significant funds, the CRB was importing tens of thousands of tons of food monthly.

Hoover likened the occupied territories to a "vast concentration camp."[25] The German occupation forces required the registration of all males between 17 and 50 years of age for labor in the region or in Germany in January 1915. They shot resisters, including women, caught helping Entente soldiers to escape from the occupied territories or keeping pigeons, which were forbidden on grounds that they might carry messages across the lines. In Lille a monument to its executed citizens stands to this day. Edith Cavell, the British nurse executed by the Germans for espionage, was only one of many the Germans shot, but British propaganda ensured her fame. The international outcry at her death did result in the commutation of death sentences for women such as Louise de Bettignies, who had formed a network of spies, to life sentences of hard labor in Siegburg prison in Germany. Life grew increasingly harsh under the German occupation.

EASTERN AND BALKAN FRONTS. GERMANY TAKES CHARGE

Hindenburg, Ludendorff, and Conrad began the year by planning a gigantic pincer movement in winter battles to envelop the Russians, in the north with a German attack east from the Masurian Lakes, in the south with an Austro-

Hungarian attack through the Carpathian Mountains to free the besieged fortress at Przemysl. In a preliminary feint on 31 January the Germans first employed gas, but the cold weather negated its effect. The Second Battle of the Masurian Lakes began on 7 February, and the Germans fought through blizzards and cold temperatures to beat back the Russians seventy miles and inflicted nearly 200,000 casualties, half of them killed, upon them. At that point the Germans could push no further and went over to the defensive.

In the south Conrad's offensive failed to relieve Przemysl, whose 120,000-man garrison surrendered on 22 March after a siege of 194 days. Instead the Russians seized the initiative and began to threaten western Galicia and Hungary. At this juncture Falkenhayn realized that Germany would have to save Austria-Hungary from disaster, but without getting too involved because of the demands of other fronts. He consequently rejected Hindenburg's and Ludendorff's grandiose plans of pincers and adopted Conrad's proposal to strike in the foothills of the Carpathians in northwestern Galicia. Kaiser Wilhelm supported Falkenhayn's decision.

Falkenhayn moved his headquarters east to direct the campaign, which entailed an offensive by a new 11th Army under Gen. August von Mackensen comprising eight German and four Austro-Hungarian divisions on a thirty-mile front in the south between the towns of Gorlice and Tarnow. Falkenhayn, like Hindenburg, held Conrad's forces in contempt, but Mackensen, who commanded the joint army, respected the Austrians. This 66-year-old cavalry general, wearing the skull-and-crossbones shako of the regiment in which he fought the Franco-Prussian War, his white hair and mustache flowing, cut a dashing figure. Yet Mackensen possessed substance as well. He had learned from his earlier losses at Tannenberg, and he had assembled a brilliant staff, among them Col. Hans von Seeckt. Mackensen planned a rapid, deep penetration by the infantry followed by the artillery.

The attack on 2 May caught the Russians, deficient in artillery shells and even rifles, completely by surprise. The German bombardment, the most devastating to that time on the Eastern Front, pulverized the Russian defenses and panicked the Russian troops. Mackensen's troops tore a gaping hole in the Russian line and advanced rapidly, forcing the Russian troops around the breakthrough to flee. Late in May, and twice again during the summer, the German Army used gas, this time a chlorine-phosgene mixture, against the Russians. Despite its killing power, capricious winds and continued Russian resistance neutralized the effect of the gas. Still, the Germans recaptured Przemysl on 3 June, and Lemberg on 22 June. At this point the Central Powers' commanders once again disagreed on the next steps. Conrad wanted to attack the Italians, who had entered the war in May, but the Italians would be attacking Austria soon enough. Hindenburg and Ludendorff proposed a major attack on their front in East Prussia. Falkenhayn, however, preferred to launch Mackensen northeast toward

Brest–Litovsk, passing Warsaw to the south, while the German armies struck from the north. Once again Falkenhayn prevailed with the Kaiser and even offered the Russians a separate peace, which Tsar Nicholas rejected. Conrad also had other ideas, since he resented the German successes, which were establishing Germany as senior partner and Austria-Hungary as subaltern in the Central Powers.

The German offensive began in mid–July. The Germans seized Warsaw on 5 August and took Brest-Litovsk and three other Russian frontier fortresses by 4 September. In late September the fall *rasputitsa*, heavy rains which transformed the primitive roads to impassable mud, halted the German advance. In late August Conrad, to compete with the Germans, launched his great "black-yellow" offensive toward Kiev. Conrad's forces charged forward for a week, but the Russians withdrew and then allowed the Austro-Hungarian armies to expend themselves in fruitless but costly frontal assaults, after which they retook the lost territory in late September. Understrength and exhausted Austro-Hungarian units surrendered to the Russians in great numbers. Conrad's staff nicknamed the offensive *Herbstsau*, literally translated "autumn swinery"[26] but more loosely "fall fuck-up." Once again German divisions had to stabilize their ally's front, confirming their superiority within the alliance, the German generals' contempt for their Habsburg ally, and their conviction that they would have to dominate Austria to stave off the Slavs.

The Russians destroyed the territories they lost; looting, shipping entire factories, and often driving the people east as they retreated. The Russian Army treated Jews and Lutherans particularly harshly. *Stavka* and front commander Mikhail Alekseev, acknowledging the army's untenable positions and inadequate munitions, retreated 300 miles and thereby shortened their front from 1,000 to 600 miles. They sacked numerous Russian generals and even imprisoned some for dereliction of duty, but the ultimate scapegoat for the Russian disaster in Poland became commander-in-chief Grand Duke Nicholas. Tsar Nicholas himself left the capital Petrograd to assume supreme command in late August, with Alekseev as his chief of staff. The Russians had suffered nearly a million casualties and another 750,000 prisoners lost, but Russia itself remained intact and could still draw on substantial population reserves. The Central Powers had lost some 650,000 casualties in their victories.

In August the German government assigned a civilian governor general to Poland, prompting Ludendorff's resolve to keep the conquered lands to the northeast under the army's control. When the German Army entered the ravaged and refugee-filled cities of northeastern Europe, Death's Head Hussars, wrapped in their grey cloaks, gazing haughtily down from their mounts at the rabble about them, recalled the advance of the Teutonic Knights a half millennium before, their skull-and-crossbones insignia replacing the Knights' Cross. The German Army planned to bring order to *Ober Ost*, an area of some 42,000 square miles including Kurland, Lithuania, and Bialystok-Grodno which was twice as large as Prussia and contained an ethnically diverse population of three million. *Ober Ost* became the army command's feudal fiefdom. On 1 November Hindenburg became field marshal in command of all German and Austro-Hungarian forces on the Eastern Front.

Before the war Germans had perceived Russia as a unified, absolutist state that became more barbarous the further east one went. Such attitudes encouraged a sense of German mission in a *Drang nach Osten*, a "Drive to the East," to bring culture and civilization to primitive peoples as the Teutonic Knights had once attempted. However, German troops now encountered a confusing variety of lands and peoples in this "war land," where eastern Jews spoke a German dialect and aristocratic Baltic Germans greeted their conquerors as liberators, and vast empty spaces of primeval forest and marshes awaited the advancing troops. The soldiers conjured up images of themselves as *Landesknechte*, the rootless and brutal freebooters of the Thirty Years' War, who confronted a weak and prostrate population that seemed to offer the opportunity to build a new world.

The German Army planned to rule the east like a colony, with an iron hand, and in 1915 it used press-gangs of POWs and native inhabitants to exploit the region's gigantic reserves of lumber. It sealed off the region from the east, disinfecting and delousing everything, including German soldiers, that came from the Eastern Front. The army railroad directorate, which became a virtual state within a state in *Ober Ost*, mapped the region, re-established transport routes, registered everyone for a system of passes, and established a press section to produce propaganda in December. *Ober Ost* also assumed control of all education, in order to produce obedient, ordered, and disciplined youth respectful of German authority and might.[27]

Meanwhile Falkenhayn, having driven the Russians from Poland and eliminated the threat against Austria-Hungary, began to move troops west to France and south toward Serbia. Hindenburg and Ludendorff, however, insisted on continuing the attacks in the north, and ultimately reached the Baltic at the gulf of Riga, close to the port of Riga, in Latvia. Having acquired 62,500 square miles of territory, they now consolidated a rather straight front south from there, 100 miles east of Brest-Litovsk and to Czernowitz in the Carpathian Mountains.

Falkenhayn focussed on Serbia, now that Bulgaria had decided to join Germany and Austria-Hungary, the Central Powers, and to attack Serbia from the southeast. Germany desired to open communications and an overland supply route to its Ottoman ally through Belgrade, Serbia, and Sofia, Bulgaria, and the main railway to Turkey ran through Serbia. King Ferdinand of Bulgaria, noting the Central Powers' successes against Russia and the stalemate at Gallipoli, allied with Germany and Austria-Hungary on 6 September, committing Bulgaria to attack Serbia in concert with them in return for financial subsidies and Serb territory. Gen. von Mackensen assumed overall command of the Serbian front, while German General Staff Col. Richard Hentsch, advocate of withdrawal at the Marne a year earlier, planned the campaign to envelop Serbia from the north, east, and southeast.

Serbia desperately needed Entente help, and in November 1914 the French had proposed the use of the Greek port of Salonika to move Entente troops into the Balkans. Greek Prime Minister Venizelos invited the allies to send troops, but Greek King Constantine, the German emperor's brother-in-law, preferring Greek neutrality, refused to honor a prewar commitment to defend Serbia against Bulgaria, and dismissed Venizelos. The French and British still landed an expeditionary force and began to build a base at Salonika. Joffre seized the opportunity to export to Greece French commander Gen. Sarrail, a favorite of the politicians and the focus of political opposition to Joffre.

None of this affected Serbia, which German, Austro-Hungarian, and Bulgarian troops invaded in overwhelming numbers in early October, blocking any allied expedition from Salonika and severing any Serb line of retreat to the south. The Serbs consequently retreated southwest through the mountains of Montenegro and Albania in the dead of winter, and only 125,000 of their original army of 200,000 men survived for the Entente to ship to Salonika. With the fall of Serbia, the British wanted to withdraw from Salonika, but the French preferred to remain to protect their interests in the Balkans. Sarrail and two divisions that arrived in October would receive steady reinforcement in what the German High Command and German journalists described as the "largest internment camp in the world."[28] If the French remained, so did the British, as neither ally planned to allow the other to gain an advantage on these far-flung fronts. Although the Central Powers posed no threat to the Entente troops in Salonika, the anopheles mosquito would take a toll of as many as 80 percent of the men there at any given time with malaria.

OTTOMAN FRONTS. DISASTERS AND DEBACLES

In 1915 the Ottoman Empire drew the increased attention of the Entente, which seized the strategic initiative by attacking the Empire in the Caucasus, at Gallipoli, and in Mesopotamia. The year began with Turkish forces attacking Russia through the Caucasus Mountains and the British at the Suez Canal in Egypt from Syria via the Sinai Desert. Russian troops under Gen. Nikolai Yudenich trapped Enver Pasha's 95,000-man invasion force in mountain passes, then counter-attacked and encircled them. Enver and

18,000 Turks escaped in mid-January; some 30,000 of his troops had frozen to death in the mountains. In the Middle East Kemal Pasha's 20,000-man force fared no better, arriving at the Suez Canal exhausted in February. Indian and ANZAC (Australian and New Zealand) forces soon drove the Turks back into the Sinai.

After the Turkish disaster in the Caucasus, the Turks expected a Russian offensive, but before it occurred, in May, the Russo–Turkish conflict unleashed genocide. Armenia, the region of the struggle, straddled Russia and Turkey. The Ottomans had already massacred some 200,000 Armenians in 1894–6 and another 25,000 in 1909, as the nationalism and Pan-Turkism of the Young Turks confronted a rising Armenian nationalism. A division of Christian Armenians fought with the Russian Army against the Turks and then declared a provisional Armenian government on Russian territory in April. The Turks believed that the Armenian population in eastern Anatolia, the scene of civil unrest, was preparing to revolt with the active conspiracy of the Russians.

The Ottoman Army had formed a Special Organization to monitor and control separatist movements in the empire. This agency disseminated propaganda emphasizing the danger the Armenians posed to the Empire and then deployed officers to lead units of brigands and convicts, essentially "an army of murderers," to "destroy the Armenians and thereby do away with the Armenian question."[29] In fall 1914 the Russian Army and Armenian volunteers had taken a toll of units of brigands, or guerrillas, in the Transcaucasus; now some 30,000 brigands, led by officers encouraged by bounties and spoils, enjoyed ample opportunity for revenge upon defenseless Armenian civilians.

When Russian offensives and armed Armenian revolts occurred in spring 1915, the Ottoman Army crushed the rebels brutally and then concluded that an armed, rebellious population located where it could disrupt Turkish military operations required further subjugation. In June the Turks deported Armenians en masse permanently to Mesopotamia and Syria. The Armenian rebellion in concert with Russian forces continued, in the midst of the Entente attacks on all fronts. In the process of the deportations, the Turks massacred Armenians and marched them into the desert to die.[30] On 24 May 1915 the Entente powers warned the Ottoman government that they would hold them "personally responsible" if implicated in these "crimes . . . against humanity and civilization."[31] By June 1915 both the Russian and Turkish Armies had exhausted themselves, and both sides ceased operations to recuperate and plan for 1916. The Special Organization continued its slaughter of the Armenians, however, and in the coming two years the Ottomans would kill some 800,000 Armenians.

In Mesopotamia the British government of India forged ahead in their defense of British interests in the Persian Gulf, specifically the pipeline, refinery, and terminal of the Anglo–Persian Oil Company. Having seized the city of Kurnah at the junction of the Tigris and Euphrates Rivers in December 1914, Indian Army forces in early 1915 determined to eliminate Turkish threats further inland on the river system to oilfields across the border in Persia. Riverine warfare with armed small sloops and paddle steamers, barges, tugs, and motorboats had begun in 1914, as the water's depth in these regions ranged from two to three feet, making the use of shallow–draft vessels imperative. The conflict expanded in March 1915 into the marshy waterways of the interior, as British boats hunted Arab sailing vessels, or dhows, supplying the growing Turkish forces.

A Turkish attack from the west toward Basra in April incurred a rapid British counter-attack that routed the Turks and opened up the possibility to Gen. Sir John Nixon, the recently appointed theater commander, of further advance up the Tigris and Euphrates Rivers to secure lower Mesopotamia as well as the Persian oilfields to the east. At the end of May the 6th Indian Division under Maj. Gen. Charles Townshend attacked up the Tigris River toward Amara supported by a large and motley flotilla of small armed craft for fighting and supplies, as well as paddle canoes carrying ten men each for any amphibious assaults. Within a week they had captured Amara.

They now turned to secure their western flank by attacking up the Euphrates and within a month, by the end of July, had seized their objective of Nasiriya. The Turks offered stronger resistance, while more British imperial forces succumbed to disease and the heat, but the British advance seemed irresistible. After a diversion to secure a cable communications station in the Persian Gulf linking Basra and India, Baghdad beckoned. Townshend's troops had advanced some 140 miles inland along the torturous waterways. Now they planned to proceed another 180 miles by river to seize the town of Kut as the first stage of the grandiose plan. Kut fell within three weeks by the end of September, as the Turks retreated toward positions they had fortified at Ctesiphon, thirty miles below Baghdad.

Late in October the War Committee in London determined to strike for Baghdad, although it left the task to the imperial government in India and provided Nixon with no further reinforcements beyond more gunboats. Not only would the seizure of Baghdad sever German communications with Persia and Afghanistan, but it offered the potential salvation of British prestige in the Muslim world during a disappointing year. The desire of the *Raj*, the British government in India, to impress Muslim opinion in Afghanistan and India, to counter German intrigues in Persia and Afghanistan against India, and to stop a potential Pan-Islamic movement in all three countries drove British forces toward Baghdad.

In late November Townshend assaulted the Turkish positions at Ctesiphon. This time, however, the Turks held, as their artillery kept the gunboats at bay, forcing Townshend to retreat back down the river. The

Turks had turned the tables on the British, and Townshend and his British and Indian troops now found themselves under siege in Kut in December. In Mesopotamia the British imperial forces, overreaching, had gone from victory to defeat in what one general referred to as the "Bastard War." They had pressed so hard to seize Baghdad to compensate for a debacle of the first order – Gallipoli.

Late in 1914 the British and French had begun to search for new fronts to break the deadlock in Europe and to aid the Russians. Although the French preferred Salonika, Kitchener and Churchill believed that the Dardanelles offered a more plausible place for an attack, from which they could eliminate the weakest of the Central Powers and open up a supply route to Russia. Even before the war the British Committee of Imperial Defence (CID) had contemplated amphibious landings on the Gallipoli peninsula to control the straits and protect the Suez Canal in the event of war against either Turkey or Russia. The Royal Navy, following Churchill's orders, had bombarded the Dardanelles forts upon the declaration of war against the Turks in November 1914. Such shelling proved counter-productive, since the Turks, with German assistance, had repaired and reinforced the forts and mined the straits.

By January 1915, Chancellor of the Exchequer David Lloyd George, Secretary of the CID Maurice Hankey, and Adm. Fisher determined to attack Turkey. Although Fisher proposed an assault on land and at sea, Churchill, in response to Kitchener's declaration that he could spare no soldiers, decided to bombard and then force the straits using large numbers of older battleships and battle cruisers. The naval commander, Sir Sackville Carden, began the bombardment on 19 February, using twelve of the twenty-two battleships at his disposal. The shelling silenced some forts but failed to silence mobile Turkish artillery batteries that prevented British minesweepers from clearing a channel through the straits for the battleships. Royal Marines suffered heavy casualties attacking one fort on 4 March. By March the nervous strain had overcome Carden, who resigned on 16 March in favor of his second-in-command, John de Robeck.

Robeck continued what Carden had begun. On 18 March he ordered sixteen British and French battleships, including the new super-dreadnought *Queen Elizabeth*, preceded by minesweepers, destroyers, and cruisers, to "force the Narrows." This ponderous force advanced for three hours. Then, disaster struck as mines sank three battleships, badly damaged and put out of action a British battlecruiser and two French battleships, and damaged four other capital ships. Robeck withdrew with the dark, but the die was now cast.

With British prestige at stake, on 10 March Kitchener, who had already sent ANZAC troops to the Greek island of Lemnos, fifty miles from the Dardanelles, ordered the British 29th Division there as well. He appointed

Gen. Sir Ian Hamilton to command the force. Including a French division, the Mediterranean Expeditionary Force on Lemnos totaled five divisions and 70,000 men. The British estimated that 170,000 Turkish troops awaited them. In fact, they would face the Turkish 5th Army of six divisions totaling 84,000 men under German commander Liman von Sanders. The ensuing events prompt one to recoil in horror at the potential magnitude of the disaster had the Turks actually possessed the numbers the British anticipated.

By D–Day on 25 April, the British improvised a plan using a motley fleet of some 200 merchant ships to land the 29th Division on five narrow beaches at Cape Helles around the southern tip of the Gallipoli peninsula and the ANZACs six miles up the west coast. The 29th would move to seize a ridge six miles inland, while the ANZACs would seize the heights off their landing beach and attack east across the peninsula, trapping the Turkish forces and forts to the south between them. French and other British imperial troops staged two feint attacks in the north of the peninsula to lure the Turks away from the landing beaches.

The preliminary naval bombardment began at 5 a.m. "Tows," or lines of rowboats that sailors crewed and small steamships towed, would transport the infantry from ships until they were close enough to row to shore. A coal ship, or collier, would beach, to disgorge its passengers through holes cut in the bow on to gangplanks that would descend across the decks of barges to the beach.

On the three beaches on the flanks of the attack, 29th Division troops encountered little or no opposition, but, instead of moving inland, they enjoyed a spot of tea, sunbathed, and trekked about, while moving supplies on to the beach. At the two beaches in the center at the tip of the peninsula, a hail of machine-gun and rifle bullets slaughtered the troops. The Turks had opened fire on them as soon as the rowboats reached 100 yards from shore or as packs of men attempted to descend the gangways from the collier. The sea turned red with blood to 50 yards from the shore, while bodies floated in bunches like schools of dead fish. Amidst the slaughter, the remnants of the first waves managed to wade through the crimson waters, past the bodies, and secure precarious footholds on the beaches. The First Battalion of the Lancashire Fusiliers Regiment won six Victoria Crosses, Britain's highest award for valor, that morning, establishing the legend of "Six VCs before Breakfast," an outstanding feat.[32] However, they had fallen victim to fire from fewer than 100 Turkish defenders, who stalwartly faced some 4,000 soldiers in the first wave of the assault force before they retreated.

Up the peninsula the ANZACs landed erroneously, if unopposed, a mile north of their designated location, on to a small beach whose slopes rose precipitously on three sides. They moved inland into a maze of ridges and gullies, penetrating a mile and a half before a Turkish company of 200 men began to counter-attack in the afternoon. By the following day the Allies had landed 30,000 troops on Gallipoli, but the Turks, led by one man in particular, determined to yield not one yard more of the peninsula.

Lieut. Col. Mustapha Kemal, 34-year-old commander of the Turkish 19th Division, encamped four miles north of the ANZAC beach-head. He led a regiment of his men at forced march toward the sound of gunfire and reached the crest of the ridge above the landing area just as the Turkish company began to flee. Australian troops fired at Kemal but missed, and then they failed to seize the crest before Kemal's men, bayonets fixed, counter-attacked the ANZACs repeatedly and beat them off the high ground. Catholic Chaplain Father Eric Green busily ministered to "poor fellows, with wounds of every description, all disfigured and defiled with blood, and clay and dirt, in many cases unrecognizable, often features blown away."[33] By early May the exhausted Turks and ANZACs dug in, the Turks on the high ground around a tiny ANZAC beach-head a mile and a half wide and 1,000 yards deep. To the south, the 29th Division, reinforced with Indian troops and the Royal Naval Division, managed to penetrate only some three miles before both sides went to ground.

There they would remain for the next eight months, through bloody attacks and counter-attacks, as both sides launched ferocious and suicidal assaults against each other. The troops not mown down by shell or machine-gun and rifle fire fell in frenzied hand-to-hand combat, as men bit, punched, bludgeoned, and stabbed each other to death, all to no avail. Those who survived the combat often fell victim to diseases such as malaria, dysentery, and enteric fever, which proved deadly in the summer heat when fresh water was often at a premium. Others bore septic sores, while half of the soldiers longest at Gallipoli "showed symptoms of cardiac debility."[34] Another Allied landing in August fell prey to the same circumstances: Kemal responded to the bridgehead as he had in May, and Turkish counter-attacks contained the threat while holding the other Allied forces on their beaches. Fourteen Turkish divisions faced fourteen Allied divisions in a stalemate as vicious and debilitating as any on the Western Front.

Finally, as summer yielded to fall and a bitter winter, and vicious storms drowned soldiers in their trenches, a new commander, Gen. Sir Charles Monro, recommended withdrawal. In eleven days ending 9 January 1916, the Allied forces withdrew under cover of night. Ironically, evacuation proved the Entente's greatest success in the entire Gallipoli campaign, in which the Allies had suffered some 265,000 casualties; the outnumbered Turks, 218,000.[35]

Gallipoli, the subject of numerous histories, remains to this day one of the most remembered and memorialized battles of the First World War. The image of brave and gallant ANZACs and Englishmen sacrificed by bungling commanders to a resolute Turkish foe and disease in a disastrous campaign resonates still. English-speaking histories highlight its particular significance for the evolution of an Australian and New Zealand nationalism separate and distinct from that of the mother country. Certainly, the Australian media interpreted Gallipoli as a seminal event in the birth of the nation, although some, including Australian Prime Minister William M. Hughes and British war correspondents, deemed it proof of the Australian right to be British, true exemplars of the British race rather than mere colonials.[36] In 1915 the Australian government also began a campaign against "enemy aliens" at home, particularly German Australians. The Australian government and people proceeded to register them, appropriate their businesses, intern, and even deport them.[37]

Such mutual contradictions mattered little; in contrast to British incompetence, ANZACs had demonstrated leadership and superb soldierly qualities.[38] Furthermore, the ANZACs, ultimately formed into the five divisions of the Australian Imperial Force (AIF) under Gen. Sir John Monash, would go on to display such qualities on the Western Front from 1916 through 1918. Starting in 1916, Australians celebrated 25 April as ANZAC Day, "the natal day of Australia's entrance into the world's politics and history,"[39] and Gallipoli would become the symbol of Australian national identity as it became a sovereign dominion after the war.

Gallipoli, however, proved equally important in the evolution of modern Turkish nationalism. It heralded the rise to fame and leadership of Mustapha Kemal, whose endurance and repeated bravery contributed greatly to their success. Kemal became the symbol of the Turkish nation – a leader whose courage had rendered Turkish troops more than a match for European armies.

The failures of the Gallipoli campaign are legion: the tentative first bombardments from battleships in January 1915 which merely alerted the Turks; the abortive naval attempt to force the straits; the landings at incorrect sites and the failure to move inland quickly where possible; the ensuing slaughters in countless fruitless head-on attacks and counter-attacks uphill in forbidding terrain; and the persistence in the wasteful venture long after it clearly promised no positive results.

In comparison to the campaign, the withdrawal seemed a victory, in the same fashion that in 1940 Churchillian propaganda would transmogrify the withdrawal of a defeated army from the continent at Dunkirk into a victory, but after a campaign on the continent of only five weeks. Of course, Winston Churchill figured prominently in the origins and execution of the Gallipoli campaign, but he took more blame for the disaster than he deserved. British and French forces landed in part to respond to their Russian ally's plea to distract the Ottoman Turks from the Caucasus. However, both powers had other reasons for the strike at the Dardanelles. The British had accompanied the French to Salonika and remained to preserve their interests in the region. At Gallipoli the British led, and the French presence ensured their interests should the Ottoman Empire fall. Salonika entrapped the

Entente powers, but Gallipoli degenerated into outright disaster. Instead of conquering and dismembering Turkey, the British, in their obsession to enhance their prestige in the Muslim world, blundered badly.

Repeated British improvisations, hesitations, and outright mistakes stemmed ultimately from their underestimation of the Ottoman Turks. They believed that the "sick man" of Europe had fallen prey to "Asiatic decay." British imperial troops had anticipated with jaunty enthusiasm the opportunity to administer a thrashing to a non-white, barbaric foe, reminiscent of their past chastising of colonial opponents. British officers, steeped in the classical tradition, identified romantically with the theater of the assault. To fight where their ancient Greek forebears had launched the western tradition, to defeat an alien foe in the war to defend western civilization – the mere prospect would suffice to drive such noble warriors to victory, regardless of how well or how poorly their leaders planned and executed the enterprise. Unfortunately, no one had informed Mustapha Kemal and his soldiers that they were supposed to fall victim to thousands of years of the western tradition. If the Ottoman Empire was sick, the western powers for the moment proved insufficiently healthy themselves to put it out of its misery.

SOUTHWEST EUROPE. ITALY ENTERS THE FRAY

It was no coincidence that on 26 April 1915, the day after the Gallipoli landing, the Italian government signed the Treaty of London committing it to join the Entente cause. Britain and France had promised land in Austria-Hungary, the Ottoman Empire, and in German Africa. The Italian government had remained neutral in August 1914 on the grounds that German and Austro-Hungarian offensives violated the defensive nature of the Triple Alliance and voided any Italian obligation to its allies. Territory was the price of Italian participation in the war; whichever side offered the land it most coveted – the Austro-Hungarian territory in the Trentino to the north and around the Adriatic coast to the east – would likely gain Italian support. While the Germans urged their Austro-Hungarian ally to cede territory to Italy, Britain and France could obviously play far faster and looser with such promises. Italian Prime Minister Antonio Salandra and Foreign Minister Sidney Sonnino believed that only by joining the Entente powers could they satisfy the "sacred egoism" of Italy. Italy declared war on Austria-Hungary on 23 May.

Austria-Hungary had only some 100,000 soldiers to spare from its other fronts to confront the Italians, but the Italian Army faced some of the most forbidding terrain in Europe. From west to east, along a border, now a front, of some 400 miles, rose the highest mountains in Europe, the Tyrol and then the Julian Alps. Only on the eastern frontier, where the Isonzo River flows to the Adriatic, does the land rise only some 2,000 feet to two desolate plateaux, the Bainsizza, rippled with steep ridges, and the Carso, surfaced with sharp stones above limestone caves. The Austrians held the high ground everywhere.

The Italian Army fielded 875,000 men, most of them poorly trained and equipped, lacking in machine-guns and artillery, in sum the weakest of the major powers in the war. Their mountain troops proved excellent but few – only two brigades. The Italian officer corps came primarily from the kingdom of Savoy, or Sardinia, which had unified Italy as Prussia had unified Germany and provided a solid professional military nucleus. The troops, however, came largely from rural and poor backgrounds, and those from southern Italy, from a region not well integrated into an Italian state that had existed for only half a century. Chief of Staff Gen. Luigi Cadorna, a 65-year-old martinet of an artilleryman, proposed to launch these legions of dubious quality against the Isonzo Front, through the mountain pass of the Ljubljana Gap and into the heartland of Austria in the Danube River plain.

The Italian Army attacked on 23 June and broke off the attack two weeks later. It attacked again on 18 July and halted again after two weeks. After a respite to bring up more artillery, it attacked again in October and in November. By the end of the year the first four battles of the Isonzo had netted the Italians some 250,000 casualties, the Austro-Hungarian Army 160,000. Multitudes on both sides incurred head and eye injuries caused by jagged limestone rock splinters propelled by exploding shells. The Austrians, under the able command of Gen. Svetozar Boroevic von Bojna, held their positions skillfully against the brave assaults of the untrained Italians. The onset of winter ended the battles, but the future year held the grim prospect of more bloodshed on the Isonzo battlefield.

AFRICA. REBELLION AND WAR

The ravages of diseases that felled troops at Salonika paled in comparison to the deadly impact of disease on troops in Africa, where European colonial administrators and military officers waged war against each other and African insurgents primarily with African soldiers. By 1915 some African chiefs and recruiters impressed men into service in ways reminiscent of, although in numbers far exceeding, the slave trade. In some regions, Africans, aware of the diminished numbers of Europeans, revolted in resistance to conscription, the war, and the colonial regime. In Nyasaland in East Africa in January 1915 John Chilembwe, a Malawian educated in mission schools and in the United States, led a small uprising with strong Christian and millenarian expectations against the British. Enlisted Nyasas had already suffered severe casualties in the war against the Germans in 1914. Chilembwe feared the war, and interpreted forced recruitment of soldiers and particularly laborers as European enslavement of Africans "to die for a cause that is not theirs." The British crushed his movement easily.[40] In North Africa the Ottoman summons to *jihad* aroused the Senussi brotherhood in Libya, who invaded Egypt in 1915. The British beat them back. Another revolt in southern Tunisia required 15,000 French soldiers to suppress it.

Such rebellions remained isolated. Furthermore, the colonial powers suppressed information on the true scope of such "rebellions" or "insurrections," which the indigenous peoples called "wars." If revealed, the brutal suppression of the "rebels," which entailed a "total war" against the resisting tribes, would have demonstrated the hypocrisy of the French and British, who condemned German prewar atrocities in Africa as proof of German unworthiness for the "civilizing mission" in which the western imperial powers supposedly engaged.[41]

One struggle in particular, the Volta–Bani War in French West Africa from late 1915 through 1916, demonstrated the extent and savagery of these struggles. By 1915 a tenuous French occupation of the region had endured for only seventeen years. The indigenous peoples had expected that the French would behave as had previous African intruders and form alliances while avoiding interference in local affairs. Instead, the French, exploiting their military superiority, demanded domination, which the African communities expediently acknowledged without accepting French sovereignty. The onset of the European war drained French and native forces from the region. The entry of the Ottoman Empire into the war on the side of Germany prompted the violent and impetuous French colonial administrator Henri Maubert, who had waged repressive campaigns in the region since his arrival in fall 1914, to humiliate, torture, and whip Muslim leaders publicly to prevent any conspiracies. In light of the weakened state of colonial forces in the region, a campaign in fall 1915 to conscript local men into the colonial army proved to be the last straw for the inhabitants of the region. On 17 November, after much planning and preparation, the representatives of a league of eleven villages in the region gathered outside the village of Bona and declared war on the French colonial administration with the words "We will rise against the white man and we will fight him." They would wage war "without respite, without taking account of their loses or of the success of the white man, until the final victory."[42]

In the last week of November a meeting of even more villages divided the responsibilities for defense of the region among the autonomous village leagues. Bona had already defied the canton chief selected by the French, who replied by dispatching first forty and then more than 200 African *tirailleurs* and auxiliaries, including horsemen, armed with rifles, muskets, bows and arrows, and spears. In a gruesome two-day struggle, the French, although they killed some 400 tribesmen for the loss of only a few soldiers, failed to seize Bona and retreated in the face of reinforcements. The tribesmen then besieged a force led by Maubert in the village of Bondokuy. After eight days, Maubert's force, despite killing about 1,000 tribesmen, beat a fighting retreat on 5 December, killing another 1,000 in the process.[43]

Late in December, the largest colonial army the French had ever assembled in West Africa, a force of 800 soldiers led by twenty-three French commissioned and non-commissioned officers and supported by an artillery unit of four 80 mm. mountain guns, set forth to pacify the rebels. They met some 10,000 highly disciplined warriors at the village of Yankaso early in the morning of 23 December. By noon the French colonial force, having expended most of their artillery shells, retreated, their superior firepower nullified by the numbers, organization, and courage of their opponents. This time the French force suffered more than 100 casualties, and, more critically, the shattering of the myth of their invincibility.[44] Both sides prepared to continue the struggle in the new year.

Elsewhere in Africa, although the German colony of Togoland had surrendered quickly, in others the German *Schutztruppe* determined to resist the invasions of their Entente colonial neighbors. In the German West African colony of the Cameroon, major French and British forces invaded from all directions, but in uncoordinated fashion, because the two allies did not trust one another and the French wanted to recoup the territory they had ceded to Germany in 1911 in the Moroccan negotiations. Black Africans constituted the rank and file in the three colonial forces, to whom the British added Indian and West Indian regiments. The German force resorted to guerrilla warfare as the French and British first advanced in the spring, then retreated in the early summer as rain forest, rain, and disease sapped their expeditions. Reinforced Anglo-French forces unleashed offensives designed to finish the Germans and seize the Cameroon in early October, at the end of the rainy season. This time their relentless offensive ultimately drove the remnants of the German colonial force and administration into neighboring Spanish Equatorial Guinea, where the authorities interned and then sent the Germans to Spain. The campaign ended in January 1916, and the British and French divided the Cameroon, the French receiving most of it, in March. Most of the few thousand military casualties had fallen to disease, but no one bothered to count the thousands of carriers, or porters, who succumbed during the campaign.

Having suppressed the Afrikaner revolt in Orange River Colony and the Transvaal, the South African Army returned to conquer German Southwest Africa in 1915. Botha commanded regular army and volunteers, the latter in a Mounted Burgher Corps, undisciplined and unsanitary but tough, a regiment from Rhodesia, and an assortment of imperial troops and freebooters. They advanced into the vastness of Southwest Africa, tiny forces in a colony over 300,000 square miles in area. On the way they encountered poisoned wells and mines, as Botha inexorably advanced his infantry in the center and his mounted troops around the flanks. The German colonial forces surrendered unconditionally on 9 July 1915, although Botha, always alert to preserve white supremacy, allowed German reservists to return to their farms with rifles and ammunition to protect themselves from the blacks. Casualties in the fighting forces of both sides totaled under 2,000 men, with the German colonial forces suffering the bulk of the losses.

Only on the east coast, in German East Africa, did the Germans continue the struggle. A German blockade runner, the *Rubens*, under the Danish name *Kronborg*, managed to reach the East African coast in April and beach itself, where African and Arab laborers succeeded in salvaging arms, ammunition, and supplies intended originally for the cruiser *Königsberg*, which remained blockaded in the Rufigi delta. Lettow-Vorbeck's little army reaped the benefit. Many of the crew and shipboard marines had joined the *Schutztruppe*, while sailors on board succumbed to malaria and typhoid. In July two British monitors towed all the way from England blasted the German cruiser, which had survived from 30 October 1914 to 11 July 1915. Yet the *Königsberg* lived on, as the Germans salvaged all ten of the cruiser's 10.5 cm. guns, placed them on wheeled mounts, and Lettow-Vorbeck divided them among his three main forces in the north, southwest, and west.

Lettow-Vorbeck acknowledged the inevitability of defeat in East Africa, but he planned to prolong the fight there as long as possible to deflect Entente forces from the Western Front. He demanded the best from his officers and men, and they gave it unstintingly to this unusual commander. His African soldiers (*askaris*) in particular proved extremely loyal, perhaps because he alone among European officers in Africa believed that "the better man will always outwit the inferior, and the colour of his skin does not matter."[45] Lettow-Vorbeck, always alert to find the best men, placed Africans in white companies and whites in black, and, as they fought side by side, mutual respect and camaraderie grew.

A small victory won at disproportionate expense in January reinforced Lettow-Vorbeck's decision to restrict himself to guerrilla warfare, and the Germans concentrated on small raids north to disrupt the Uganda railway. Occasionally, in this war of patrols, both sides encountered enemies bigger than both of them. In one firefight, an enraged rhinoceros charged first the British, then the German unit, putting them both to flight, and finished by attacking spectating Masai tribesmen. In the west, the British transported small armed boats overland to seize control of Lake Tanganyika, while in the southwest the German and Rhodesian forces fought to stalemate. By the end of 1915 Lettow-Vorbeck had 3,000 white and 11,000 black soldiers in his little army. In contrast, in British East Africa the government refused to arm black troops on a large scale and formed no new King's African Rifle battalions in 1915.

THE NAVAL WAR. STALEMATE AND SUBMARINES

First Lord Churchill and First Sea Lord Fisher, the dynamic duo at the British Admiralty, began the year by proposing an amphibious attack on the tiny North Sea island of Borkum, from which they would seize control of the Kiel Canal and the Baltic Sea, and ultimately land Russian troops on the Baltic coast of Germany 100 miles from Berlin. The Gallipoli landings took precedence over this fantastic plan, though not before one naval officer denounced it as "idiotic" and "*quite mad*."[46] The navy also contemplated a blockade of the Belgian port of Zeebrugge and did shell Zeebrugge and Ostend, but powerful German artillery positions protected the locations of the German Flanders Submarine Flotilla. These ideas yielded to the reality of the naval war, primarily in the North Sea and around the British Isles, and secondarily in the Dardanelles.

In the North Sea and the Channel, where the Anglo-German naval confrontation loomed largest, the German submarine U.24 began the year by sinking the pre-dreadnought battleship *Formidable* in the Channel on New Year's Day. The British ability to read the German code enabled them to recoup within the month. Adm. Hipper sortied with his battlecruisers to reconnoiter the Dogger Bank, a shallow area off the east coast of England where he hoped to find vulnerable British forces. Instead he encountered a superior force of Adm. Beatty's battlecruisers on 24 January. Alert to the possibility of a trap, Hipper fled, leaving the older and slower armored cruiser *Blücher* to its fate. Beatty's battlecruisers, plagued repeatedly by botched signals, concentrated on the doomed *Blücher* and allowed the other German cruisers to escape. The widely disseminated photograph of German crew scrambling over the capsizing hull of the *Blücher* confirmed a British victory, however limited.

In Germany, Dogger Bank reinforced the Kaiser's determination not to risk his High Sea Fleet and encouraged the naval command to wage submarine war against British trade. In November 1914 the Chief of the German Naval Staff Adm. von Pohl had advocated unrestricted submarine warfare, but objections even within the navy, particularly from Tirpitz, who correctly deemed the submarine fleet inadequate to strike a decisive blow against Britain, held sway. By February 1915 the pendulum swing reversed: the naval command decided to back Pohl; the army command backed the navy; and the German public, persuaded by a barrage of propaganda, supported a submarine offensive. Chancellor Bethmann Hollweg assented, and on 4 February the Germans declared the waters around Great Britain and Ireland a war zone.

In March the Entente introduced the policy of unrestricted blockade against ships and goods moving to and from the Central Powers, even through neutral ports and countries. The Entente reached agreements not only with the Dutch but also with the Swiss and Swedish governments to restrict trade with Germany in certain raw materials. After the German declaration of unrestricted submarine warfare, Entente demands for blockade elicited only mild objections.

The Kaiser refused to risk his surface fleet, and the British also stopped exposing their capital ships, battleships, and battlecruisers to the mines and submarines in the North Sea, except for specific exercises or offensive operations. Naval historian Paul Halpern appropriately likened the North Sea to a watery no-man's land.[47] Older, lighter cruisers could not withstand the rough seas. Consequently armed merchant cruisers, under the command of Royal Navy officers and with Royal Marines and sailors supplementing the regular crew as boarding parties and prize crews, enforced the blockade. These merchant cruisers, if vulnerable to a potential strike by German battlecruisers, went about their work protected by the British Grand Fleet, which still sortied more frequently than its German counterpart or any other fleet in operation around the globe, regardless of submarines or mines.

The threat of a chance encounter with superior British forces kept the German High Sea Fleet in harbor, much to the dismay of many of its officers, who considered such inactivity dishonorable in the midst of a great and bloody war. Yet, after Dogger Bank even Tirpitz preferred a submarine blockade, the aerial bombing of London, or cruiser attacks on British merchant shipping in the Atlantic. In the fall of 1914 German submarine officers had already begun striking at British coastal commerce. In contrast to the seizure of ships by Entente cruisers, German submarine operations produced sinkings with loss of life and potential accusations of atrocities, with resultant propagandistic and diplomatic repercussions. Nevertheless, the declaration of 4 February launched unrestricted submarine warfare around the British Isles.

Lest the term "unrestricted" evoke visions of a monstrous effort, the German Navy had only twenty-five submarines available, with only one-third of them on patrol at any given time. Furthermore, it could not commission the manufacture of additional boats rapidly enough to alter this circumstance. The immediate objections of neutral powers, particularly the United States, did prompt the Germans to spare neutral and hospital ships. From March to May an average of nearly six U-boats at sea daily sank twenty steamers for every one of the five subs lost during that time, while the British failed to counter the subs effectively.

From the beginning the German submarine attacks provoked criticism from neutral countries, but the sinking of the Cunard liner *Lusitania* by the U.20 off the coast of Ireland on 7 May produced outrage. The speedy, four-funneled liner, one of the most famous afloat, sank in eighteen minutes after Lt. Walter Schwieger put one torpedo into her bow. In 1912 the *Titanic* had taken more than three hours to sink after striking an iceberg. Consequently, the *Lusitania*'s rapid disappearance beneath the waves after a second internal explosion, caused either by munitions or coal dust in empty bunkers, surprised everyone, including Schwieger. Some 1,201 people died, including 128 United States citizens, and bodies floated ashore on the Irish coast for the next week.

Despite German advertisements in the United States warning American passengers not to travel in the war zone on British ships, the American government became indignant. Over the objections of the German Navy, German Chancellor Bethmann Hollweg persuaded the Kaiser on 5 June to halt submarine attacks on large passenger liners, and thereby avoided the possible breakdown of German–American relations. Restrictions notwithstanding, the average number of U-boats at sea increased to nearly nine, taking a higher toll of ships by the fall. Sub-commanders had always preferred to use their deck guns and explosives and to conserve their few torpedoes. They consequently sank fewer ships with torpedoes and more with gunfire and explosive charges set by boarding parties.

During the summer the British countered with Q-ships, harmless-looking tramp steamers that would lure the U-boats in close, then drop facades on deck to reveal guns that promptly sank the unsuspecting *U-Boot*. Initially working with British submarines, and then primarily alone, the Q-ships sank five German subs from late June to late September. The submarine war became more brutal. The U.24 sank the White Star liner *Arabic* on 19 August. Later that day the Q-ship *Baralong*, flying an American flag, came to the rescue of a small steamer under attack from the U.27. Under the guise of rescuing the ship's crew, it approached, keeping the steamer between it and the submarine, then hoisted the battle ensign and opened fire. After sinking the U.27, the *Baralong*'s commander dispatched a Marine boarding party that killed six German submariners who had managed to climb aboard the steamer.

The sinking of the *Arabic* led to another German diplomatic confrontation with the United States. Neither Bethmann Hollweg nor Falkenhayn desired problems with neutral countries, so the Kaiser forbade the sinking of even small liners and kept the subs away from their shipping lanes. The Admiralty staff, on the other hand, advocated forcing Britain out of the war through a submarine blockade, so Pohl resigned as Chief of the Admiralty Staff. Tirpitz attempted to resign as well, but his popularity ensured his retention, although with diminished power. The new Chief of the Admiralty Staff, Adm. Henning von Holtzendorff, terminated the submarine offensive in mid-September, shifting some boats to the Mediterranean to minimize encounters with United States' vessels. The acrimony within the German naval leadership, which Tirpitz exacerbated by labeling his colleagues with uncomplimentary nicknames, did not subside until he resigned in March 1916.

The submarine campaign of 1915, especially the sinking of 107 ships totaling 182,772 tons in August, had demonstrated its potential. Fortunately for Britain, new construction and the seizure of enemy ships offset total losses at the height of the campaign. However, construction of merchant ships ceded precedence to warship manufacture, jeopardizing Britain's future mercantile capacity should the Germans resume their submarine campaign. Ironically, "restricted" submarine warfare between September 1915 and January 1916 took a monthly toll of an average of 120,000 gross tons of shipping, actually higher than the monthly average of 116,000 gross tons during the "unrestricted" campaign from March to September. The August sinkings indicated that German capability was improving dramatically.[48]

The combination of Gallipoli, submarine sinkings, and the shell scandal ultimately had political repercussions in England. In the Dardanelles in May the loss of another old British battleship to a nighttime torpedo from a Turkish destroyer prompted Fisher, who preferred to focus on the North Sea anyway, to insist on the withdrawal of the superdreadnought *Queen Elizabeth*. Churchill, committed to reinforce Gallipoli, demurred and was forced from office, and Fisher resigned as First Sea Lord on 15 May, just after the sinking of the *Lusitania* and news of the shell scandal.

As Churchill departed the government, the German submarine U.21, one of three sent to the Dardanelles, announced its arrival by sinking two British battleships. British and French submarines also experienced some success, but the submariners' exploits, however daring, did not affect the course of the Gallipoli campaign. By September German submarines were striking effectively at Entente shipping in the Mediterranean and more were arriving from the North Sea, as the undersea war took precedence in the region.

In focussing monolithically on the Anglo-German naval war, historians frequently neglect other naval campaigns on the seas around Europe, from the Arctic to the Adriatic. Paul Halpern's fine naval history of the Great War, on the other hand, includes these other naval fronts. The German Navy paid little attention to Arctic waters, where Entente and neutral shipping carried 1.2 million tons of cargo to the Russian ports of Archangel and Murmansk. British trawlers swept the few German mines laid in the Arctic and White Seas, but the severe weather posed more threat than the Germans. In 1915 the Baltic Sea remained a secondary theater to the North Sea for the Germans, who needed to protect the crucial trade in raw materials with Sweden. The Russian fleet's primary objective remained the defense of Petrograd and the Gulf of Riga. The Russians integrated their naval forces with minefields and coastal artillery in a form of naval trench warfare,[49] while the German Navy supported its land forces as they advanced up the Baltic coast. The German Army and Navy found Riga and the Gulf of Riga impregnable in 1915 with their available forces. Both British and Russian submarines operated in the Baltic, the British with some success, disrupting German trade, and sinking and damaging ships, including three German cruisers, with mines and torpedoes. Small naval encounters during mine-laying expeditions punctuated an active year of naval operations in the Baltic Sea.

If the Russians held off the Germans in the Gulf of Riga in the north, they dominated the Turks in the south, in the Black Sea, where they disrupted Turkish communications, staged amphibious landings on the Caucasus front, and launched seaplane raids on the Turkish coast from seaplane carriers. The presence of German cruisers the *Goeben*, with its ten 28 cm. guns, and the *Breslau*, certainly posed a threat, but the Russian Black Sea Fleet outclassed its Turkish counterpart, and the *Goeben* spent part of 1915 under repairs from mine damage suffered during a sortie in late December 1914. The opposing fleets spent their time shelling enemy ports and enemy shipping, and clashing occasionally during these raids. In coordination with the Entente landings at Gallipoli, the Russian fleet sporadically bombarded the Turkish forts at the Bosporus and employed large, fast destroyers to attack Turkish coal convoys in the Black Sea. By the end of the year the arrival of two new Russian dreadnoughts that outgunned the *Goeben* threatened to upset the balance of naval forces, but the Germans responded by sending more submarines.

The Adriatic Sea became a potentially critical naval arena with Italian entry into the war. Its narrowness – 60–100 miles wide – militated against large sweeps and classic naval encounters between the four Austro-Hungarian and six Italian dreadnoughts. Consequently, the war became a "naval guerrilla war" between submarines and high-speed motor torpedo boats.[50] Italy insisted upon command of any Entente naval forces in the Adriatic; therefore the naval convention of 10 May established a "First Allied Fleet" under Italian command, and a "Second" fleet under French command. Divisions – internal ones within the Italian naval command, and external ones among the Entente fleets – plagued Entente naval efforts in the Adriatic.

On 24 May the Austrians struck first, bombarding northern and central Italian coastal cities with ships and aircraft in a number of raids. The Italians countered with raids on Austrian coastal bases in the mid- and lower Adriatic. Then, within two weeks in July, the Italian navy lost two armored cruisers to Austrian and German submarines, the latter bearing an Austrian insignia because Germany and Italy would not be at war for another year. These losses and constant Austrian air and naval raids upset Italian plans to seize two islands in the Adriatic and prompted their retreat from the venture. The retreat sent British naval liaison Capt. Richmond into paroxysms of rage, as he considered the act an unwarranted surrender of command of the Adriatic to an inferior Austrian force. He ranted of the Italians, "They had better sell their Fleet & take up their organs & monkeys again, for, by Heaven, that seems more their profession than sea-fighting."[51]

The Austrian fleet had no intention of risking combat with the Entente forces, preferring to use its very existence to hold them in the Adriatic. Submarines made sorties of capital ships on both sides highly dangerous, and so the war in the Adriatic settled into stalemate by the end of the summer. In September the British began to establish the so-called Otranto barrage at the straits at the base of the Adriatic, a line of armed trawlers connected by anti-submarine nets to blockade German and Austrian submarines. By the end of the year only some forty boats functioned, but another forty were on the way.

By then the course of the Serbian campaign had stirred Adriatic waters. First, the Bulgarians had severed Serb supply lines to Salonika, forcing the Entente to supply Serbia through Balkan ports on the Adriatic. In response the Austrians moved their newest and fastest cruisers, destroyers, and torpedo boats to the southern Adriatic base of Cattaro, where they remained for the rest of the war. These ships, and submarines and aircraft, took a toll on Entente shipping. In the winter, the evacuation of the defeated Serbian Army became the priority of the Entente's Adriatic force. The Austrians riposted by attempting to ambush supply ships, but on 29 December lost two modern destroyers and barely escaped destruction by a superior Entente force after a high-speed chase. Afterwards, a combination of Entente deterrence and bad weather neutralized the Austrian Navy, and by April 1916 the Entente navies had evacuated 100,000 Serb civilians and Austrian prisoners-of-war and 160,000 Serb soldiers to the Greek island of Corfu, where they would prepare to join the Entente forces in Salonika to fight another day.

HOME FRONTS. MOBILIZATION

The prosecution of the war in 1915 placed increasing demands on the belligerent governments. They met these only with great difficulty. On the home front, the year witnessed concerted attempts at mobilization, as not only had the war not ended, it also seemed likely to continue for a very long time, and survival would depend upon the state's ability to mobilize its human and material resources for the conflict.

Britain and France. Politics, production, and gender

By the beginning of 1915 the British government's policy of "business as usual" was proving an inadequate principle of response to wartime necessities. In the Cabinet, Chancellor of the Exchequer David Lloyd George resorted increasingly to improvisation, forming a Cabinet Committee on Munitions in October 1914 to increase production. By early 1915 he attempted to regiment the armaments industry and place it under centralized government control.

In March 1915 the government extended its powers under DORA in order to concentrate on essential production and intervene in labor matters. A "Shell and Fuses Agreement" secured the unions' acceptance of "dilution" – the employment of semi-skilled women and youth – for the war's duration in return for the employers' commitment not to use dilution to dismiss skilled workers or lower wages during wartime and to return to the status quo *ante bellum* after the war. A government Committee on Production undertook an investigation of the arms industry in February that culminated in March in the government's Treasury Agreement with the unions. The unions essentially agreed to an industrial truce – their cooperation, acceptance of dilution, the renunciation of strikes in war industry, and acceptance in principle of compulsory arbitration. Lloyd George had provided the impetus behind negotiations to introduce government control through guaranteed profits to employers.

Mobilization in England increased the power of trade unions and shop stewards. Wartime law endowed the British government with far greater power over industry than the French government would ever enjoy, but Lloyd George chose to negotiate with industry and organized labor over arms production. The signal importance of skilled workers, in particular through the Amalgamated Society of Engineers, meant that employers had to have their full cooperation to reorganize and rationalize industry.[52] Thus the strength of craft and trade unions in Britain ensured a continuity unlike France.

Kitchener's New Armies represented a tremendous break with the past, yet the old soldier relied on voluntarism to raise the manpower and market mechanisms to supply the munitions. In 1915, however, the peak and decline of voluntary enlistments and the burgeoning "shell scandal" forced Kitchener to accede to the politicians' demands for more government control through a Ministry of Munitions. In April Lloyd George chaired the newly created Munitions of War Committee, which did not include Kitchener because Lloyd George had concluded that the War Office was not running wartime procurement effectively.

The "shell scandal" and Gallipoli disaster prompted British Conservatives to demand a coalition government, which Liberal Prime Minister Asquith enacted on 25 May. Conservatives demanded and got the head of First Lord of the Admiralty Winston Churchill for his role in the Gallipoli fiasco. Sir John Fisher had already resigned as First Sea Lord on 15 May. On the other hand, Lloyd George's star ascended, as he became the new Minister of Munitions in June 1915. He recruited industrialists to the Ministry to organize a controlled economy based on semi-public "national factories" and "controlled establishments," private arms producers under government contract.[53] The Welsh dynamo's flurry of activity to increase munitions and relieve the shell shortage ultimately placed him before the British public as an alternative to Asquith.

Improvisation was yielding to organization, as the government gathered its powers to coordinate war production. The new Ministry operated on the premise of the "seamless interdependence of the home and the fighting fronts,"[54] with civilians at the helm of the entire enterprise. The state now directed capital and labor and collaborated closely with industrialists in formulating armaments policy. Industrialists played key roles in the Ministry of Munitions, a "businessman's organization" as Lloyd George called it, with labor leaders in at best advisory capacities. The Ministry's contracts fueled the expansion not only of the private arms industry, but also a public sector of government munitions factories. It thus secured lower prices for the production of shells in quantity. The Munitions of War Act in July 1915 gave the government wide-ranging powers over labor, confirming in law the earlier voluntary agreements with labor and employers. Lloyd George failed to secure compulsory service for civilians, which would have enabled the absolute control of labor, but the government had taken major strides in Britain's industrial mobilization.

In 1915 the boundaries between and the distinct identities of the home and fighting front, civilians and soldiers, women and men blurred, not only because of the increased importance of industrial mobilization but directly from air raids on cities and submarine attacks on merchant ships. Lloyd George realized already in late 1914 that the economy needed more civilian workers, and women wanted to serve and work. This congruence between the state's needs and women's desires meant that the war's demands as of mid-1915 overturned the prewar gender system, as women began to do men's work in factories and in the economy in general. Nevertheless, this development did precipitate anxiety among men, and the notion of women in uniform aroused outright scorn and distaste for such "mannish Amazons." Furthermore, fears of female promiscuity as women became as assertive as men, images of women drinking, smoking, and gambling publicly – manly pursuits all – threatened traditionally separate gender roles.[55]

The arrival of Indian soldiers in England prompted efforts to constrain and control their mobility and sexuality and those of white working-class women.[56] The government and army focussed on controlling the Indian soldiers' access to white society, in particular white women. Authorities feared that these two groups, whom stereotype portrayed as highly sexual, might experience a mutual attraction that would affront family and national values, result in miscegenation and ultimately racial degeneration, and undermine the stability of imperial racist rule in the colonies. Long before the war the arrival of white women in the colonies had led to anxiety and efforts on the part of the authorities to prevent their relationships with black men, while eugenics and fears of miscegenation and racial degeneration antedated the war at home and in the empire. In England, the myths of "uncontrolled black lust" and "white proletarian women's curiosity about . . . interracial sex" "made for an explosive anxiety" about the presence of colonial soldiers in Britain, as the "wrong" ideas about English women "would be most detrimental to the prestige and spirit of European rule in India."[57] Consequently, authorities confined wounded Indian soldiers to the hospital precincts on Britain's south coast, where controversy arose over the use of white women nurses. Authorities resolved the problem by limiting the nurses to supervisory positions, and confining Indian forays to London to highly organized Cook's Tours.

Yet all the regulations in the world could not ensure absolute separation. The censor kept another letter informing a soldier's family that "if any one wishes to marry, I can get a nice wife for him. Marriage in England is very cheap. If it be necessary I can get thousands of women for your brothers."[58] A soldier in France commented that "The ladies are very nice and bestow their favors freely upon us."[59] From Brighton another wrote that "The girls of this place are notorious and very fond of accosting Indians and fooling with them. They are ever ready for any purpose."[60] Still another offered from France, "If you want any French women there are plenty here, and they are very good looking. If you really want any I can send one to you in a parcel."[61] None of these letters escaped vigilant and humorless censors. Other soldiers, however, had no intention of violating their faith by consorting with Christian women,[62] while an Indian assistant surgeon, finding the English of Bournemouth "charming," wondered "why they become so bad on reaching India."[63]

In contrast, white Dominion soldiers never faced such restrictions in any theater. Canadian and ANZAC soldiers ran amok in London, the former achieving the highest levels of venereal disease of any allied troops on the Western Front. ANZAC troops in Cairo contracted high rates of venereal disease in the brothels of the Wazza district, on their way to Gallipoli. In contrast, the battlefield exploits of Canadian and ANZAC soldiers at Ypres and Gallipoli respectively provided the very real foundation for the future national myths establishing the Dominions' independence from Britain. The memorable lines "In Flanders fields the poppies blow/Between the crosses, row on row" of Canadian military doctor John McCrae's immortal poem "In Flanders Fields," penned at Ypres in May and published in *Punch* in December, epitomized for those at home in Canada the awakening pride in their role in the great crusade and the importance of keeping faith with those who lay forever in Flanders.[64]

France was not immune from crises resulting from the bloody stalemate on its soil. The army's urgent demands for men, munitions, and heavy artillery meant that the War Ministry would need parliamentary cooperation to secure them. In May the government took critical steps in industrial mobilization. The Cabinet formed an Undersecretariat of Artillery within the War Ministry under moderate socialist Albert Thomas. Thomas, who regulated the supply and distribution of mobilized men to industry, reduced the number of mobilized men by replacing them with women and youth in order to send the men to the front. Thomas became the "architect of state policy in the war factories,"[65] as he balanced attention to labor wages and conditions with industrial concentration and technological innovation. French unions had collapsed at mobilization in August 1914, and Thomas's policies reinforced the power of management.[66] The government concentrated production in larger, efficient firms and promoted specialization and the division of labor among firms producing rifles, for example. The labor shortage evident in all countries led the French government already in September 1914 to accord the munitions industry priority over the armed forces, and by the end of 1915 some 500,000 skilled workers had returned from the army to their jobs.[67]

Women entered the metalworking industry when the government acknowledged that the war would not end in six weeks or months. The loss of the industrialized northeast to the enemy forced the need for rapid mobilization in France. French industrialists attempted initially to secure as many skilled men as possible, but by mid-1915 they recognized the need for new workers, and women in particular. The Parisian metal industry increased its female workforce from 8–9,000 women in 1914 to 30,000 in the summer of 1915, and by December women composed almost one-fifth of the national metal industry's workforce.[68]

In regard to manpower, West Africa offered a potential reservoir to France. On 10 May 1914 Senegalese voters elected Blaise Diagne, a brilliant 42-year-old Senegalese, educated in France and married to a French woman, deputy to the French National Assembly from Senegal. The war offered Diagne the opportunity to improve the political status of West Africans, in return for their service to France. Initially, the War Ministry under Millerand and his fellow deputies resisted the notion that *originaires* (inhabitants of the four urban communities in Senegal) should serve in metropolitan units, which would entail the integration of the relatively small number of blacks who were *originaires* with white Frenchmen. The *originaires* possessed legal rights and privileges that separated them from other Senegalese, and Diagne persisted, arguing his case brilliantly in Parliament. On 19 October 1915, Parliament voted into law not only the conscription of the *originaires* but also their incorporation into French units. By the law of 29 September 1916, they would become French citizens.[69]

By the fall, with nothing to show from major offensives except constant casualties, the French High Command, residing in their palatial residence at Chantilly, had given Parliament and the press the impression of remoteness, arrogance, and indifference to casualties. French impotence in the face of the invasion and defeat of Serbia was the straw that broke the government's back, because War Minister André Millerand had protected Joffre in Parliament. In the change of cabinet, French President Poincaré intended that the civilian executive branch would control the war effort. Consequently, in October he engineered a new parliamentary ministry of Aristide Briand with Gen. Galliéni as War Minister that encompassed a broader span, from a right-wing Catholic monarchist to a Marxist, than any previous government.[70]

Italy. A late arrival with grandiose plans

The most recent Entente power, the Italian constitutional monarchy, was a predominantly rural country in which industry located primarily in the north, the "iron triangle" of Turin, Milan, and Genoa, while the south remained rural, poor, and backward, even in agricultural techniques. The government had very close ties with powerful industrialists and with the army, while within the government the very conditions of Italy's entry into the war demonstrated the limited control that Parliament had over the executive, the prime minister, and his cabinet. The living conditions of the rural peasants and the urban working class, who bore a heavy tax burden, were abysmal, and unrelieved by governmental measures, as the Italian government lagged behind other industrialized countries in social reform. Violent rural and urban popular revolts, which the government and bosses brutally crushed, recurred in the prewar years. The hostile peasant and working masses consequently distrusted the state, while Italy, because of its class and regional divisions, lacked the sense of national and collective identity that was evident in states such as Britain, France, and Germany at the onset of the war.[71]

The democratizing policy of Prime Minister Giovanni Giolitti, who preferred neutrality, allowed the freedom to strike and ignited demonstrations that had caused his fall from power in March 1914. His successor, the conservative agrarian Antonio Salandra, an authoritarian who opposed democratization, used the occasion to bring Italy into the war in 1915 in defiance of the wishes of the majority of political forces, from socialists and liberals to many members of the Catholic Party, and the majority of the people, from the middle class through the urban and rural poor. Salandra and Sonnino, with the connivance of King Victor Emmanuel III, signed the treaty with the Entente, but without submitting the decision to Parliament. When Parliament objected, Salandra appealed to nationalists such as Gabriele D'Annunzio and Benito Mussolini. The resulting mob violence and demonstrations cowed any opposition.

Italy was unprepared for war politically, industrially, economically, and militarily, but Salandra, the king, and the army generals had strong reasons for intervention. They hoped to profit from a brief war and Entente victory to gain the status of a leading power, reap the spoils promised in the treaty, and gain the authoritarian social control of rural and urban workers desired by their social allies and supporters, the large agrarian landlords and the iron and steel industrialists.

The outbreak of war brought with it extensive state contracts for the iron and steel industry, which attracted many new workers from the countryside. This wartime development exacerbated the shortage of workers on the land caused by the mobilization of Italy's largely peasant army. Two decrees, in June and August 1915, established an Under-secretariat for Arms and Munitions in the War Ministry under Gen. Alfredo Dallolio to centralize industrial mobilization, guaranteeing high profits and much independence to industrialists while planning to militarize, discipline, and control labor and limit its mobility and wages. Italian mobilization differed from its French and British allies in a military control more similar to German practice and a focus on labor prompted by concerns about socialist support given the circumstances of the declaration of war.[72]

The government chose to finance the war through inflation, so prices rose from the start. Yet the government planned to repress any opposition and to rule above Parliament with the collusion of the king and the army.[73] The peasant and working-class population responded to the war with resignation, and strikes declined in 1915, as the government forbade them and inducted militant workers.[74] If successful, Salandra essentially would have executed a "coup from above," but he and other interventionists counted upon a short war with imminent Austrian collapse. They composed a minority in Parliament, yet could not agree among themselves on whether to wage war against Germany or merely against Austria-Hungary, and whether to form a wider coalition government or, as Salandra preferred, to rule in a wartime dictatorship. The first battles of the Isonzo brought no victories for Italy, just as the wider war yielded no victory for the Entente in 1915. The coming year would confront Salandra's government with a continuing conflict they had not anticipated.

Germany and Austria-Hungary. Scarcity and bureaucratic discord

Germany suffered no shell scandal as did the other combatant nations, since the army, with Rathenau's assistance in the KRA, essentially controlled the German war effort. The army possessed the only bureaucracy in Germany that reached from the central government down to the regions and cities, in the general commands located throughout Germany and outside every major city monitored. These general commands were the fundamental agencies in troop mobilization, and when they departed for the front with the troops, they left behind deputy general commands, whose generals answered to the Kaiser alone. This left them autonomous, insulated even from the War Ministry's control, much less that of the Chancellor and civilian agencies. The civilian government, in contrast, consisted of a central imperial bureaucracy perched upon the bureaucracies of the seventeen federal states. The fragmentation of authority in Germany, even of military authority, rendered the German home front a "bureaucratic nightmare," in contrast to the "bureaucratic cohesion" the Ministry of Munitions achieved in Britain.[75]

In Germany labor quickly became a particularly scarce commodity, so that by mid-1915 the government was exempting skilled workers from military service to work in the war industries, which were also employing and training large numbers of women. German working-class women suffered a loss of income at the beginning of the war because they formed a disproportionately high percentage of workers in industries the war effort made idle. Unskilled, immobile, and concentrated in the textile industry, working-class women encountered factory closures in the conversion to the war economy due to the shortage of raw materials, particularly cotton, and consequent government restrictions.[76] Food prices began to rise early in the war, but fortunately by 1915 many of these women would find work in war industry. The war proved particularly difficult for war widows, and the wife of a conscripted worker had to have nine children before war welfare actually granted them an increase in funds.

The German bureaucracy, when confronted with its most intractable problem – food supply – proliferated, as the Imperial Office of the Interior created its own agencies which naturally came into conflict with the military. The German population expected the state to intervene in the economy to meet their needs. A poor potato harvest in 1914, followed by increasingly inadequate grain harvests starting in 1915, posed tremendous problems, especially for the working class, since potatoes and bread formed the staples of the German diet. By February and March mobs of women and children waged battles for potatoes in Berlin, and consumers in general, confronted with increasing shortages, began to identify with the plight of poorer women. The rapidly rising price of pork, the "German meat of choice," rendered it increasingly inaccessible to more consumers, for whom it provided an essential source of fat and protein. Then, by the fall, butter became scarce. Urban consumers, embittered toward the rich, the farmers, and merchant middlemen, began to take to the streets, demonstrating and rioting in Berlin in October, and demanding the appointment of a "military food dictator." The police and the press, rather than repressing or ignoring these outbreaks, reported and publicized as valid the concerns of the crowds of irate women, concerns which eclipsed interest in military matters and implicitly threatened the German war effort from within if the state did not act to allay them.[77]

Early in 1915 the government rationed all bread, or "*K-brot*," which contained potato flour, and the adulteration of milk became commonplace. The government attempted to control food prices by setting national price ceilings and to replace the market with bureaucratic controls, which the farmers evaded quite creatively. Furthermore, its fixed grain prices and unrestricted meat prices worked against its intended goals. For example, in the worst fiasco, the "pig massacre" of early 1915, the government had two million pigs slaughtered as it attempted to gear stock farming to the country's fodder capacity to reduce consumption of grain. The farmers, of course, shifted to cattle and sheep to benefit from meat prices. Government measures were just as likely to exacerbate the food shortage as to alleviate it. From the spring of 1915 onward, it restricted distilling and rationed malt to breweries to decrease production. Given the importance of pork and beer in the German diet, particularly in Bavaria, it remains a wonder that these measures did not provoke a cessation of the German war effort. Furthermore, a thriving black market in food eluded government control, so that the food supply difficulties called into question both the efficacy and legitimacy of the German government in the public mind.

With the need for increased mobilization of the home front came ever larger demands for annexations in war aims. Industrialists and academics supported a war aims movement in society and in the Reichstag. Industrialist Hugo Stinnes, for example, desired ardently to colonize Belgium, seize its industry from Belgian management, and rule Belgium dictatorially.[78] In May 1915 industrial and agricultural interest groups sent Chancellor Bethman Hollweg a "memorandum of the six Economic Organizations," a petition demanding control of industrial and mining regions in Belgium and northern France and expansion into the agrarian lands of the east. A "petition of the Intellectuals" in July emphasized Germany's cultural mission in the east and its struggle against Russian barbarism, while annexationist literature proposed the seizure of the Baltic provinces and Lithuania and their settlement by *Reichsdeutsche* from Russia. Propagandists emphasized the importance of geography in "War geography" or "Geopolitics," and in October 1915 Friedrich Naumann published his book *Mitteleuropa*, which advocated German control of a central European economic zone.[79]

By early 1915 the Austro-Hungarian High Command (AOK) judged the civilian government actions too late, too weak, and inadequate to support the war effort. The AOK wanted to take direct control of Bohemia and the Sudeten areas, supposedly to improve the reliability of Czech troops, but faced the resistance of the civilian government under Count Stürgkh. Military and civilian agencies and the Austrian and Hungarian governments challenged each other, and, with the opening of Austria-Hungary's third front against Italy in May, another military center of power arose. As Austria was the rear of the Italian front, that command was closest to the imperial capital Vienna, while Hungary was the hinterland of the Russian and Balkan fronts.

In May Conrad at AOK took the initiative in both internal and foreign policy. He arrested two prominent Czechs and charged one, Karel Kramář, a parliamentary deputy close to Stürgkh, with high treason for meeting with the Italian consul in Prague. Conrad, eager to demonstrate that the civilian government treated the Czechs too leniently, acted hastily and foolishly, because he had no proof of treason. In May he also advocated a negotiated peace with Serbia, the incorporation of the South Slavs with representation in Parliament into the monarchy, as well as peace with Russia. On 18 June, Franz Joseph suggested that Conrad relent. Conrad did, but his ambition for military power in the civilian realm mushroomed. He yearned to govern Bohemia and dictate equality between Germans and Czechs by military fiat, to control Galicia and Bukovina and establish a military borderland around the empire, to distribute food to industrial centers, to monitor civilian administrators for patriotism, and to militarize education, youth, and ultimately society. Incredibly, in the fall the AOK even participated in a court intrigue against Stürgkh that failed.

With all these civilian ventures percolating in his brain, Conrad may have had difficulty concentrating on military planning, especially since in October the 63–year-old general married his 36-year-old mistress, whom he had ardently pursued and written on nearly a daily basis for years. Clearly Conrad spent too much time attempting to insert the army into internal affairs and foreign policy. Yet he also believed, and openly proclaimed, that an inept dualistic and parliamentary civilian government, inadequate munitions and supplies, and unreliable Czech, Ruthene, and Italian citizens – not the army – were responsible for Austria-Hungary's defeats.

Relations between Austria and Hungary worsened as the war continued. Tisza and the Hungarian Parliament zealously guarded Hungary's independence in all realms, a policy which impeded intergovernmental negotiations. The issue of equal sharing of the wartime burden reared its ugly head. Hungary was hoarding food for its own use instead of shipping supplies to Austria. In the fall Tisza accused Austria of exempting more men to work in industry so that Hungary bore proportionally higher losses at the front, an allegation which Stürgkh refuted by producing statistics to show that Austria was in fact sustaining a higher proportion of losses.

If Austria and Hungary grew further apart, the Dual Monarchy's government drew closer to Germany, especially through their military plenipotentiaries and central procurement agencies. Germany had been sending Austria-Hungary weapons and munitions in return for raw materials since the beginning of the war. In 1915 the two allies began to unify armaments production, and Austro-Hungarian industry fell increasingly into dependence on its stronger German counterpart. The two powers negotiated trade treaties in 1915 despite difficulties with Hungary. German loans to the Dual Monarchy enabled the latter to tender loans to Turkey and Bulgaria, often in return for raw materials.

Already in 1915 shortages of coal, labor, and transport plagued Austria-Hungary. While the iron and steel industry shifted rapidly to war production, other firms shut down. Still, demand exhausted the reserve of male workers, and the munitions industry turned to refugees, prisoners, and finally to women. Despite long hours in the factories, workers exhibited no unrest in

1915 and unions adhered to the civil peace. Although the government imposed limits on meat consumption in early 1915, proclaiming two meatless days a week, and rationing led to higher prices and black marketeering in the midst of currency inflation, civilians seemed determined to persevere until victory and heavily subscribed to a second war loan in May 1915.

Russia. The autocracy mobilizes without its autocrat

By 1915 it became evident that the Russian government's policy of "business as usual" amounted to no policy at all. It simply bought at inflated prices whatever large industrial firms delivered and made no effort to increase production. Government economic policy was "opportunistic, inconsistent, and incoherent."[80] The retreat from Galicia in April combined with the depreciation of the ruble, disorganization of transport, and the munitions shortage to prompt middle-class opinion to reject "business as usual" in favor of mobilization. In the Western and Central Powers the impetus for mobilization came from the government; in Russia it arose in unofficial circles outside the government.

In the face of mounting criticism of the war from the middle-class businessmen in the spring of 1915, the government established commissions for various supplies, but the commissions did not intervene in industrial or labor affairs. In May the entrepreneurs, still concerned about incompetence and corruption, established "War Industry Committees" to mobilize industry more efficiently. These committees included representatives of government, industry, commerce, and labor, and attempted to encourage a wider and better planned distribution of war contracts. While the owners of small and medium-sized firms did secure a percentage of contracts for their factories, the government, the large armaments producers, and labor ignored them. The first two did not want their relationship disturbed, while the workers, who were beginning to question the war effort, boycotted. From spring onwards, workers' wages fell behind rapidly rising food prices, and food shortages caused strikes in industrial areas. In mid-August the formation of four Special Councils of National Defense, Transport, Fuel, and Food Supply, which comprised representatives of the Duma, the State Council, Unions of *Zemstvos* and Towns, reinforced the committees.

Barely a week later, on 23 August, an event occurred that some historians have labeled a turning point in the war, although in fact the deed, however momentous, simply underscored the disarray at the top in Russia. Tsar Nicholas left the capital Petrograd to assume command of the army, thereby leaving the autocracy without an autocrat. His Cabinet had pleaded with him to remain in the capital, but to no avail. He ignored them, just as the army high command had been doing since the beginning of the war. Neither the tsar nor his army paid any attention to the civilian government. Nicholas hoped to rally the Russian people to the war, but he lacked military training and talent. His departure left the government in the hands of his wife Alexandra, her personal advisor the sleazy monk Rasputin, and the aged, reactionary, and corrupt Prime Minister Goremykin, all of whom, particularly Rasputin, incurred the ire of Russian progressives.

The Duma, in session from June until September, nurtured a growing mistrust of the government, and, with the formation of a progressive bloc within its ranks, called for a government responsible to Parliament. Instead, the Cabinet prorogued the Duma. A government already noted for its corruption and inefficiency sank further into the mire, and front-line troops went without arms and supplies, not just because industry had failed to produce them, but because civilian and military officials neglected to deliver them.

Nevertheless, by the end of the year, Russian industry was increasing armaments production with the assistance of supplies from its allies.[81] Furthermore, in November the army, after a year of contracting with foreign industry, including 300,000,000 rubles for foreign automobiles, with inadequate results, decided to develop Russian industry in realms as diverse as automobiles, aircraft, chemicals, radios, and optical devices. To remedy the gravest problem, namely the shell shortage, the Army Artillery Procurement Commission reversed its initial decision to purchase crucial chemicals abroad. In 1915 it developed state plants and turned to private industry for the manufacture of chemicals for explosives. Scientists who had previously scorned "applied" research in favor of "pure" science responded to Russia's isolation by establishing national scientific societies like their western counterparts and working with industry to develop the practical and military applications of scientific knowledge.[82]

The United States and Japan. Entente affiliates

The United States played a crucial role in Entente success in mobilizing resources in 1915. J.P. Morgan, New York's foremost bank, became purchasing agent for Britain and France and organized American war production for them. In the fall it floated an Anglo–French loan in the States and arranged a credit for British purchases which began the substantial increase in the flow of munitions to the Entente over the next two years. The United States officially adhered to a policy of neutrality, but the effects of these arrangements, combined with British control of the high seas, proved anything but neutral.

In January 1915 Woodrow Wilson sent his advisor Col. Edward House to Europe to discuss a negotiated peace, but to no avail. Also in January Jane Addams called a meeting in Washington that some 3,000 women attended to form the Women's Peace Party. "Don't Take My Darling Boy Away" and "I Didn't Raise My Boy to Be a Soldier" were two of the year's most popular songs. The American press condemned the sinking of the *Lusitania* in early May as a barbarous act. Wilson's severe warning to the German government that he would consider the repetition of such an illegal and inhuman deed as "deliberately unfriendly" prompted the resignation of his pacifist Secretary of State William Jennings Bryan, who considered American language and actions too strong for a neutral power. Although a few like Teddy Roosevelt demanded a stronger response, Wilson's speech of 10 May took the high road, "a man . . . too proud to fight," a nation . . . so right that it does not need to convince others by force that it is right." He was not too proud or right to advocate "reasonable preparedness." However, proposals to double the size of the regular army and replace the National Guard with a federal army of 400,000 men in late fall 1915 aroused strong opposition from southern and western rural Democrats, who committed to protecting states' rights and avoiding war more than rectifying America's obvious military weakness.

Neutrality, in fact, remained a wise policy for the United States. A gigantic land with a rapidly growing population of some 100 million inhabitants by 1917, the United States' population had increased by 9.5 million people in the years 1900 to 1914. Demographic diversity proved as significant as its size, with some 10 percent of it African-American and substantial numbers of recent immigrants from southern and southeastern Europe. Still more than 50 percent rural in population, it was rapidly industrializing and urbanizing. Pronounced inequality characterized the society, as a small group of very wealthy industrialists, reigning over powerful monopolies, dominated politics and government, while millions lived in dire poverty on the land and in the cities. These magnates had chosen to import European immigrants to labor in their factories rather than employ African Americans, 90 percent of whom still lived in the agrarian South at the beginning of the century. After the turn of the century, as African Americans migrated from South to North, they led lives segregated from white immigrants, although all were crowded together in unsanitary slums and performed demanding and dangerous work in factories. As historian Neil Wynn states succinctly, "Class conflict, poverty, squalor, disease, and suffering persisted everywhere."[83]

Employers resorted readily to murderous violence, whether in the form of the national guard, state police, or paid enforcers, to keep order in their factories and mines. Labor fragmented along racial, ethnic, and class lines, and its representatives ranged from the conservative craft unions, the labor elite of Samuel Gompers's American Federation of Labor (AFL), to the radical International Workers of the World (IWW) or Wobblies.

Historians have labeled the epoch from the turn of the century to the war the Progressive Era, for its diversity of social movements that advocated the solution of problems such as drunkenness, prostitution, and vice through government intervention. Issues from women's suffrage to nativist anti-immigration coexisted under the umbrella of progressivism. Ironically, the title "Progressive Era" for prewar United States resembles *La Belle Époque* for prewar Europe, in that both proved misnomers to a certain extent. European laboring classes experienced no more beauty than blacks and poor whites in the United States witnessed progress.

In contrast to white women's attainment of political representation, African Americans experienced a deterioration in their position. Whites reinforced "Jim Crow" laws and segregation with intimidation, mob violence, and lynchings to repress blacks. Neither Theodore Roosevelt nor his successor Woodrow Wilson, a Republican and Democrat Progressive, respectively improved conditions for black Americans during their presidencies. In fact, Wilson's so-called "New Freedom" did not apply to African Americans, as his administration did not reapppoint black officeholders, segregated blacks in civil service jobs, allowed the introduction of discriminatory bills in Congress, and did nothing to discourage lynching. Progressives in general did not concern themselves with the plight of blacks. They believed in the superiority of the white race and were intent on preserving the "Wasp," or white Anglo-Saxon Protestant, tradition.

The titles of such books as Charles Carroll's *The Negro is a Beast* (1900), Robert Schufeldt's *The Negro a Menace to American Civilization* (1907), and Thomas Dixon's eulogy of the Ku Klux Klan *The Clansman* (1915) illustrate the rampant racism of the time. The last provided the basis for D.W. Griffith's film *The Birth of a Nation* (1915), which portrayed blacks as ignorant, violent, and depraved. The United States seethed with racial, ethnic, and social tensions.

In East Asia the Japanese government exploited the continuation of the war in Europe to pursue its interests in China. With Germany out of the way in early November 1914, the Japanese government responded to Chinese President Yuan's demand that they withdraw from Shantung by presenting the Chinese in January with Twenty-One Demands. The Demands continued not only the great powers' earlier imperialist practices in China but also Japan's climb to the status of a great power. Japan demanded recognition of its right to seize German interests in Shantung and the extension of its own lease over Manchuria for ninety-nine years. The most extreme demands compromised China's sovereignty by requiring the Chinese to hire Japanese financial and political advisors and to allow the Japanese to police important cities. They sought the Chinese government's dependence on Japan and the other great powers' recognition of Japanese hegemony in China. The demands focussed on achieving Japanese economic supremacy in China. The Japanese Army sought military and political control, and conspired to undermine the regime of President Yuan Shikai in order to instigate a civil war in China, which would serve as the excuse to send the Japanese Army into China. Although the Japanese government eventually withdrew these extreme demands and relinquished some of the territorial concessions they had gained, the demands occasioned Chinese resentment and alienated the United States.[84]

The Japanese ruling elite comprised both admirers of "Anglo-Saxon civilization," who desired parliamentary government in Japan and a continuation of the alliance with Britain, and "German admirers," adherents of authoritarian government, the military, and imperial expansion that had begun when the Meiji governments emulated imperial Germany. Japanese politics replicated in microcosm the European struggle.

Sino-Japanese negotiations over the Twenty-One Demands reached a climax in May 1915, when, after some modification on the part of the Japanese, the Chinese government agreed to the ultimatum. In September Japan, at the urging of British Foreign Secretary Sir Edward Grey, further reaffirmed its commitment to the alliance with Britain by adhering to the London Declaration of September 1914, in which the Entente powers proclaimed their solidarity against Germany and pledged not to consider a separate peace. Certainly the Entente knew not only that strong pro-German sentiment existed among certain elements in Japan, particularly the military, but also that Germany had approached Japan about a separate peace in January. This awareness prompted not only the reaffirmation of the commitment to the Entente, but further Russian overtures for an alliance with Japan in the summer of 1915, which Japan rejected. The Japanese government remained wary of its Entente connections, and rightly so. It knew from its London ambassador of Grey's anti-Japanese sentiments and recognized that its British ally was intent on limiting Japanese incursions in China.

CONCLUSION. A VERY SIGNIFICANT YEAR

Such events indicate the crucial nature of 1915, as governments responded to the challenges of an increasingly total war with varying degrees of effectiveness. In an economic history of the war, Gerd Hardach observed that despite Germany's steady increase in armaments production, it began to fall behind in the summer of 1915 when British industrial production increased, although the gradual shift in relative strengths went unnoticed.[85] In a sense, this development reflects the general understanding, or lack of it, of 1915. The dramatic opening of the war in 1914, and the cataclysmic and famous battles to come in 1916, overshadow the year 1915, except for the drama of Gallipoli and submarine warfare. Nevertheless, the nature and extent of the mobilization undertaken in 1915 in the major warring powers laid the foundation necessary for the powers not only to fight great battles in 1916, but to endure the further demands of a monstrous war of attrition. In 1915 the warring nations of Europe adjusted to the burgeoning conflict. Improvisation proved the order of the day in 1915, both on the home and fighting fronts. At home "business as usual" attitudes yielded to economic mobilization, often in a flurry of measures.

Labor shortages everywhere resulted from the military mobilization of essential skilled workers, and forced government and industry to turn to women to perform wartime jobs unavailable to them in peace. Women workers played key roles in the wartime mobilization and modernization of European industry. Their roles in the metalworking industries, the key to war production, were primarily the "de-skilled, machine-driven labor of the fully rationalized factory" according to the principles of Taylorism and the scientific reorganization of labor.[86] Although skilled craftsmen, the labor elite of prewar European industry, resisted rationalization, government and industry required additional labor to increase production as rapidly as possible. Rationalization fragmented or divided skilled tasks into their component processes with appropriate machinery and then women performed these tasks under the supervision of skilled male workers. Women thus entered mass production under the aegis of government needs and would ultimately form a pool of trained workers. Everywhere across Europe, the labor shortages created by the mobilization of millions of men forced governments to turn to women and youth, as well as refugees and prisoners-of-war, and eventually forced labor in Germany, to power the war effort.

Governments everywhere quickly tied themselves to industry and the employers in the effort to mobilize war production. Unions derived varying benefits in different countries over time, but they invariably remained the weakest of the three – government, management, and labor – in the wartime mobilization relationship, because of their relative weakness in comparison to the other two before the war. As the war continued, labor would have the opportunity to register gains as production demands and labor shortages increased.

The armies fought desperately to adjust to the new style of warfare, and high casualties and the constant demand for more troops reduced training to truly on-the-job experience, which further exacerbated the vicious circle. The armies' emphasized masses of men and increasing numbers of guns and shells. The French and German Armies dismounted their cavalry, and infantry began to prefer the grenade to the bayonet. In 1915 armies, led by the Germans, began to introduce "platoon technologies" – light machine-guns, hand and rifle grenades, portable mortars, light cannon such as the French 37 mm. gun – for small unit operations.[87]

Artillery concentrated more on accuracy of fire as well as mass. The crowded conditions of the Western Front assumed the nature of an urban environment, a new development in warfare. Men from mining and industrial conditions, who inhabited urban slums, were suited better to trench conditions than the peasants who had always formed the bulk of European armies. Coal-miners commented that life in the trenches was certainly healthier, and no more deadly, than life in the mines. Yet men from farm environments continued to make excellent soldiers, accustomed as they were to life outdoors and the deprivation that troops often had to endure.

Cases of war neurosis and shell shock rapidly increased in 1915, as heavy artillery fire, which particularly led to severe emotional distress, proliferated. Psychiatrist Ernst Wittermann reported in 1915 that resisting the temptation to run at the sound of approaching shells and witnessing the hideous effects of shell explosions enormously strained the nervous system. A German soldier observed from hospital that after surviving enemy shell fire that had destroyed his shelter, his right arm and leg became painful and paralyzed.[88]

The ability of soldiers to adjust to this new and terrible warfare, like the wider ability of the fighting powers to mobilize their entire resources, both human and material, to create this warfare, testified, however frighteningly, to the adaptability of the individual and society to the incredibly stressful conditions of this "war of nations," or of society against society. It is also a testimonial to the failure of these individuals and their societies to comprehend the effects, the sum total, of their deeds and endurance.

The Indian soldier who observed that the conflict by 1915 was no longer war, but the "end of the world," and his comrades' references to Armaggedon, demonstrated a better understanding of developments than his supposedly more "civilized" European counterparts and their leaders. The British soldier in 1914 had merely termed the war "murder," but in 1915 the war's barbarism, attributed by the opposing sides to one another, proceeded apace. Shooting civilians and random atrocities on the various fronts in 1914 now developed into sinking them by submarines, bombing them from aircraft, annihilating them in the case of the Armenians in Turkey, and potentially starving them over the long term in the case of the Entente blockade. The war became steadily more atrocious, and the governments and propagandists of the warring great powers exhorted their populations, who responded willingly to even greater exertions in the quest for victory.

From the beginning the war affected western culture, as intellectuals dedicated themselves openly to and willingly produced propaganda to further the cause of their particular nation-state. If many dedicated themselves to passionate advocacy, others found the war stultifying. T.S. Eliot lamented in a letter to Conrad Aiken in 1915, "The war suffocates me." Certainly the war released and focussed tremendous demonic energy in the single-minded pursuit of victory, but in another sense it not only literally suffocated many of its combatants, it also stifled other pursuits, as all ceded precedence to the engine of war. Europeans ferociously and determinedly engaged in the potential process of ending their world as they knew it in their all-out attempt to win the "war for civilization." In a supreme and sublime irony, they might destroy the very objective for which they fought.

The Entente commanders met at French General Headquarters at Chantilly in early December and agreed to carry out Joffre's agenda of coordinated offensives on an even larger scale than in 1915, not only on the Western Front but also on the Italian and Russian fronts. They would wait to attack until June or July 1916, when France and Britain would have strengthened their artillery on the Western Front, the British raised and trained their growing army, and Russia recovered from the severe defeats of 1915 and improved its army's supplies with help from its western allies. In the summer of 1916, the French and British would launch a joint offensive at the juncture of their forces on the Western Front; the Russians, an offensive on the Eastern Front; and the Italians, on the Isonzo Front.

Joffre unabashedly demanded a focus on the French Army and Western Front and advised the Russians that their attacks would be diversionary and unsupported from the west. Gen. Galliéni, now Minister of War, was concerned about defending the fortresses at Toul and Verdun, but Joffre deemed the old general's fears unjustified. Since August 1915 he had reduced the importance of Verdun, transferring artillery, equipment, and troops to other sectors of the front. As of October 1915, Joffre planned to blow up the fortress if the Germans broke through at Verdun. Then the concerns of Galliéni and parliamentary deputies in uniform stationed at Verdun goaded Joffre to begin to reverse the flow of troops and weapons from Verdun. As of December 1915 the French Army had lost almost a million men since the start of the war, 600,000 killed and 400,000 missing. Joffre had 1.2 million men in line, and would add 400,000 more in 1916. More African and older French soldiers would head for the front, while younger troops of 19 years of age would help form the assault units for the summer attack.

Entente prospects for success in 1916 were steadily improving by the end of 1915. French industrial mobilization and military reorganization meant that the army would be 25 percent stronger than it had been in 1914. Britain would contribute the bulk of the increase in manpower on the Western Front, as "Kitchener's Mob" would take the field, some thirty divisions strong, of which twenty-four would go to join the BEF in France and Belgium. The Italian Army was expanding by some 50 percent, to 1.5 million troops. Finally, Russia would have made good its losses in 1915 and have some two million soldiers, now well equipped with rifles and artillery.

In the Central Powers, Conrad was planning an Austrian offensive to "punish" the hated Italian foe, but the key to their plans lay in Germany. By December 1915, Falkenhayn had concluded that a battle of annihilation or breakthrough was impossible on the Western Front, the decisive theater of the war, and that the Central Powers must lose a long war of attrition. Consequently, Germany had to convince the Entente to quit the war by forcing at least one of them to sue for peace. Falkenhayn decided to lay the military foundation for a compromise peace, contrary to Hindenburg, Ludendorff, and even Chancellor Bethmann Hollweg, who presumed a victorious peace.

Unrestricted submarine warfare might starve Britain into submission, but the island proved immune to Germany's military power. The vastness of Russia made total victory there unlikely. Yet the German leadership clamored for a major offensive in 1916. A France under great strain since 1914 became Falkenhayn's logical target. Germany had stood primarily on the defensive for long enough, however successful that strategy had been in allowing the French Army to attack itself to death. Falkenhayn became convinced that if he could destroy the French Army, the British would quit. Germany's leaders believed that the French were ineffective soldiers, and the French in general weak, morally inferior, and unstable in national character – and thus ripe for breakdown and collapse.[89]

Falkenhayn had only twenty-five divisions in reserve, so he devised a macabre plan that took into account the desires for a victory and the limitations he faced. He decided to attack Verdun, the strongest position in the French fortress system and the anchor of the French defense at the Marne. With numerous fortresses, infantry positions, and supply depots, Verdun remained a formidable target, although the French had transferred many of its guns and infantry elsewhere on the front. The Germans surrounded the Verdun salient on three sides and could supply their forces easily by rail, while French lines of communication from Verdun to their rear proved inadequate.

Using only ten divisions from the reserve supported by powerful artillery, Falkenhayn planned to seize the hills on the east bank of the Meuse River, which flows through Verdun, and from a range of four kilometers his artillery, the key to his plan, could dominate any movement to the town and fortresses. Abandonment of Verdun would ruin French morale, and Falkenhayn calculated that the French would attempt to hold the fortresses and retake the hills at any and all cost. Standing on the defensive and pounding the French with superior artillery, the German Army would "bleed them white." He would hold the rest of his reserves for a counter-attack against the inevitable English offensive to follow and win the war.

All of Falkenhayn's colleagues, including the Chief of Staff of the Fifth Army, Gen. von Knobelsdorf, who would have to plan and execute the attack, believed that the army should broaden the attack to seize the hills on the west bank of the Meuse as well. They could thus sever Verdun's supplies and prevent the French from emplacing artillery there to shell German soldiers on the east bank of the river. Falkenhayn refused, on the grounds that he lacked the necessary troops and artillery. Operation *Gericht*, or "place of execution," would begin in February 1916.

4

1916. Total War

"If we do not lose the war, we will have won it."

Falkenhayn prior to Verdun[1]

"Ah, I wish to hell I was in France! There one lives like a gentleman and dies like a man. Here one lives like a pig and dies like a dog."

25th Lancashire Fusilier in East Africa[2]

A year of great battles loomed, and millions of men across Europe prepared to meet their destiny in combat. The outcome of the war hung in the balance, and both sides anticipated victory in 1916. In February all hell would break loose on the Western Front. Would the German inferno consume enough French soldiers to break France's will to resist before the Entente's firestorms fell upon the soldiers of the Central Powers? How would the powers accumulate materiel and men to feed the fires? And what would happen if all their plans proved wrong, and no one emerged victorious?

THE WESTERN FRONT. VERDUN AND THE SOMME

Verdun. Hell on Earth

The Germans planned to seize the initiative; however, fog, snow, and rain postponed Falkenhayn's offensive for more than a week, until the skies over Verdun cleared. During that time, on 12 February, two French divisions arrived at Verdun. On 14 February 1916, Joffre and Haig decided to attack on the Western Front in June near the Somme River to the east of the French city of Amiens. They remained unaware of German intentions.

At dawn on 21 February 1916, Crown Prince Wilhelm personally ordered the firing of the first shot at the Battle of Verdun. Falkenhayn had accumulated some 1,200 artillery pieces, including Austrian 305 mm. mortars, "Big Bertha" howitzers, even 15-inch naval guns, and used 1,300 ammunition trains in seven weeks to bring up more than 2.5 million shells. The Germans had also constructed new railway lines and depots to import men and munitions. They had concentrated their air service, including Fokker monoplane fighters, at Verdun in order to prevent French aerial reconnaissance of their buildup and to locate targets for their artillery. They began the battle with mastery of the air over the battlefield.

Tens of thousands of shells rained on the French soldiers on 21 February, followed by the appearance of German patrols, whom the French resistance surprised after the thunderous bombardment. In fact, the artillery bombardment made retreat impossible for the French, and isolated pockets of French soldiers fought where they stood. Amidst the bodies of their dead comrades, often covered with the blood, guts, brains, and bones of the cadavers, small units fought to the death, including Col. Emile Driant and the survivors of his two battalions. Heavy bombardment reduced French regiments of 3,000 men to fifty survivors in one day's combat. Nevertheless, some units counter-attacked. The French command ordered fresh French units arriving in these first days to advance until they met the Germans, dig in, despite the frozen ground, and fight. The huge numbers of wounded who survived to reach aid stations overwhelmed the French doctors, who in the process of triage left many out in the snow to die.

French resistance notwithstanding, the Germans made difficult but steady progress, and by 25 February had seized Fort Douaumont, a key position left essentially undefended. The previous day, the Germans had overrun the trenches as French troops fled and would have seized the town of Verdun but for their exhaustion. Falkenhayn had no reserves to exploit the success. On 25 February Joffre, urged by his deputy Gen. de Castelnau, who had already lost three of his sons in the war, committed to hold Verdun. In a sense he picked up the gauntlet that Falkenhayn had flung at his feet. Gen. Philippe Pétain, a taciturn and stubborn 60-year-old who stood out among his peers as an isolated proponent of the defense, assumed command at Verdun. He and his newly created Second Army would have to fill the breach and stem the German tide.

Although Pétain maintained an icy exterior toward his peers and politicians, he appreciated two things: women, for whom the elegant bachelor held a certain charm; and his soldiers (*poilus*, or "hairy ones"), who returned his concern for their welfare with a resolute devotion. Pétain ordered his troops to "Hold Fast," took personal command to coordinate the artillery, widened and improved the sole avenue of transport to Verdun, the road from Bar-le-Duc fifty miles away, and then requisitioned thousands of trucks to supply Verdun using this *Voie sacrée*, or sacred route.

With massed artillery support from the west bank of the Meuse, the French contested the German advance on the east bank, and by 27 February had stopped the Germans in their tracks four miles from the city. A young captain who had begun the war as a lieutenant in Col. Pétain's 33rd Regiment numbered among the soldiers of the French XX "Iron" Corps leading the desperate counter-attacks. Charles De Gaulle fell in hand-to-hand combat from a bayonet wound in the thigh and spent the rest of the war in a German prisoner-of-war camp. Now the German soldiers were caught in the same punishing position as the French. Should they retreat, or commit more troops?

Falkenhayn reversed his earlier decision in December and decided to attack the west bank of the river, where behind Dead Man's Hill (*Le Mort Homme*) and Hill 304 the French artillery had taken such toll of his troops, and Fort Vaux on the east bank. In March the Germans rationalized their attacks, as young elite troops equipped with flare guns marked the infantry advance for German artillery, which would precede the infantry with a rolling barrage as well as cut off any avenue of retreat or reinforcement for the French troops under attack. French morale flinched, some units surrendered, soldiers cracked under the strain. An officer informed one regiment, "the day they [the Germans] come, they will massacre you to the last man and it is your duty to fall."[3]

Pétain responded by hastening reinforcements to the battle and rotating divisions through it more rapidly. In the air war the French had quickly contested German aerial dominance by massing their best pursuit, or fighter units, at Verdun. The two sides clashed in the first struggle for air superiority. The first immortal fighter pilots, the ultimate individual heroes in a war of the masses, began to emerge. On the German side Max Immelmann, the Fokker monoplane ace, paired with Oswald Boelcke, a cool, handsome, aerial killer who would codify German fighter tactics that would endure for both world wars. On the French side, the frail yet iron-willed Georges Guynemer would become the most idolized of French heroes, followed by Charles Nungesser, ex-boxer and soldier of fortune whose iron constitution enabled him to endure multiple wounds.

Mercy and chivalry found no place, if they had ever existed in more than the romantic imaginings of a few correspondents. Albert Deullin avenged the death of a fellow French pilot when he fired twenty-five rounds into a Fokker monoplane's cockpit at a range of less than 30 feet, with the result that "the fellow was so riddled that vaporized blood sprayed on my hood, windshield, cap, and goggles." Deullin found the results "delicious to contemplate."[4] The presence of such redoubtable hunters made the sky over Verdun a very dangerous place for two-seater observation planes on both sides. By May the French, with superior numbers and aircraft such as the Nieuport biplane, wrested superiority from the Germans. Nieuport Squadron N.124 of

American volunteers, the future Lafayette Escadrille, flew among the French units at Verdun.

The French fought on, and the Germans struggled in the hell they had created. It would take the Germans two and a half months, until late May, to seize the two hills, by which time German artillery fire had lowered Hill 304, so named because of its height, 20 meters. Fort Vaux fell in the first week in June.

In the same fashion that the French High Command had constantly overestimated German losses during the offensives in 1915, the Germans presumed that their artillery fire was even more deadly than it in fact was. In the casualty race the French led the Germans, but only barely: 89,000 to 82,000. Because of Pétain's policy of rotating divisions through Verdun, more units absorbed French casualties, while German divisions remained in the line longer and replaced their casualties while there.

By March and April the battle was taking a toll on the generals sending their troops to die. Falkenhayn, aware of his severe losses, wavered between continuing and halting the battle. Other German generals, monitoring their officers' reports of exhausted and "morally broken" soldiers, already considered the battle a defeat by the end of March. On 8 April the French high command ordered Pétain to take the offensive. The next day Pétain announced the famous lines "Courage – on les aura!" ("Courage. We'll get them.") Eleven days later, on 19 April, Joffre, tired of Pétain's incessant demands for more troops, promoted Pétain to command the army group and placed Gen. Robert Nivelle in charge of the Second Army at Verdun. At 58 years of age Nivelle, unlike his successor and commander, advocated the offensive and proved an astute politician, unconcerned about losses and prepared to abandon Pétain's policy of rotation. Nivelle proclaimed equally memorable words "Ils ne passeront pas!" ("They shall not pass!") He disbanded units that retreated and had junior officers shot who ordered even tactical retreats, however reasonable they seemed.

The French decision to limit the contingent of divisions at Verdun enabled the Germans to renew their offensive in May and seize the hills and Fort Vaux. Yet Nivelle was equally determined on an offensive and supported a proposal by Gen. Mangin, commander of the fifth division and known increasingly to his men as "The Butcher," to retake Fort Douaumont.

On 8 May a series of tremendous explosions rocked Douaumont. German soldiers had been heating coffee using fires started with oil and gunpowder, next to French 15-cm. shells. The fire got out of control, and, covered in black powder dust, the men had bolted down the corridors of the fort. Other German soldiers, seeing these "blacks" running toward them, promptly concluded they were Senegalese soldiers and hurled hand grenades at them. The blasts and inferno killed 700 or 800 men in a grisly, painful fashion. The Germans simply bricked off these passageways. The dazed survivors suffered from nervous disorders, or mental derangement.[5]

With late spring the Senegalese had returned to the front, and Mangin, hoping to take advantage of the disaster, attacked on 22 May, only to have his troops turned back and decimated by the following day. The French command sacrificed its troops, whether white, brown, or black, at Verdun. Behind the lines in caves surgeons amputated ceaselessly, limbs dumped in piles outside, while amputees often died of gangrene waiting for days before evacuation to hospitals. Male nurses beat back rats with sticks from those too badly wounded to defend themselves left on their stretchers in corridors or outside to die. No one died in peace at Verdun.

In early June the Germans attempted to seize the last two forts, Souville and Tavannes, with the aid of a new, more deadly gas – diphosgene – named "Green Cross" gas because of the shell cases. Verdun was proving to be a milestone in chemical warfare, as the French and German artillery fired poison gas shells, a more convenient and accurate mode of delivery than gas clouds. The French had showered the Germans with phosgene gas shells in the spring; now the Germans drenched the French with diphosgene.[6] After the bombardment silenced critical French artillery positions, the elite *Alpenkorps* stormed to the attack, only to falter around the forts in the summer heat less than a mile short of the last ridge overlooking Verdun, two and a half miles away. The Germans would launch a final attack on Souville in early July, only to break it off two days later. The German offensive at Verdun expired, and in August, after Rumanian entry into the war, so did Falkenhayn's term as chief of the High Command.

The French, however, had other plans for Verdun. Pétain vowed to retake key Forts Douaumont and Vaux when he amassed superior forces and artillery, among the cannon two new Schneider-Creusot 400-mm. railway guns even more powerful than their German counterparts. For the infantry advance, Nivelle introduced the "rolling" barrage, in which the artillery laid down a curtain of steel that moved steadily forward across the battlefield at a pace of 100 yards per minute. The infantry followed, not in waves, but in smaller units of specialists, armed with portable machine-guns and grenades, rushing forward and using what cover existed on the battlefield. The French had adopted German tactics, and in this fashion the infantry would confront the German defenders before they had a chance to recover from the artillery barrage. The tactics demanded a high degree of precision from the artillery and coordination with the infantry.

The preliminary bombardment began on 19 October and lasted for five days, during which time it destroyed German artillery and forced the Germans to retreat Verdun. On 24 October Moroccan and Senegalese assault troops of the French Colonial Army routed the remaining German defenders and retook Douaumont that same day. The Germans evacuated Vaux and the French retook it on 2 November. In mid-December the French pushed the

Germans back two miles to the east of Douaumont. The Germans still retained perhaps half of the area in the east that they had conquered earlier in the battle, but the French could now proclaim victory at Verdun.

Victory or not, shortly afterward, at the end of December, the French government promoted Joffre to marshal, or "kicked him upstairs," the most highly ranked victim on the French side, like his counterpart Falkenhayn. In both cases, Verdun constituted the essential reason for the dismissal: in Joffre's, his denuding of its defenses and the terrible price that France had paid for his failure to anticipate the possible consequences; in Falkenhayn's, the failure of his plans for victory and the terrible price that Germany had paid. Falkenhayn, replaced by Hindenburg and Ludendorff at OHL, relocated east to further command; Joffre would see no more wartime command and would later travel to the United States to encourage the American war effort.

The greatest and most terrible battle of attrition (*Materialschlacht*) of the First World War and the longest field battle in history, involving the largest number of combatants – 1,200,000 French to 700,000 German soldiers – the greatest density of shell fire, and the largest number of casualties per square yard of battlefield thus concluded. The flame of battle finally abated, although fighting would continue on the Verdun battlefield after the struggle ended officially. The inferno had consumed at least 337,000 German and 377,000 French soldiers, including 100,000 and 162,000 respectively dead or missing. The "blood mill" of Verdun had laid waste the battlefield, destroyed all vegetation, cratered the land, and alloyed human and earth in a glutinous mud that sucked men under to drown when it rained.[7] Neither side had won, but the Germans most clearly had failed to eliminate the French presence before the Entente's summer offensives.

The Somme. Carnage in Picardy

Starting at the end of June, the Entente powers launched their massive offensives against the Central Powers. Russian General Brusilov targeted the Austro-Hungarian Army on the Eastern Front, as would the Italian Army on the Southwestern, while the British and French assaulted the Germans on the Western Front.

In July the scene of carnage shifted northwest, to the Picardy region around the Somme River. Although still a joint Franco–British operation, the Somme, in the wake of Verdun, would prove a British offensive. The BEF had grown from a 265,000-man force holding twenty-five miles of the 450-mile front in January 1915 to one of 1.1 million soldiers holding 60 miles of a 404-mile front.[8] Ironically, Haig had agreed to the Somme, where the two forces joined, in deference to Joffre and French dominance, when he would have preferred Flanders. Now his inexperienced force, with eleven out of fourteen attacking divisions the volunteers for Kitchener's Mob in 1915, was about to attack the strongest defensive position on the Western Front.

Ironically, no strategic objective lay east for the British attack to secure, just villages and dense forest, difficult objectives for attackers. The Germans had divided the high chalk ridges into two, and in some places three and nearly four, main defensive systems of trenches and underground bunkers, with 40-yard-deep barbed wire barriers before each. Any suitable position – villages, woods, chalk quarries – between the main systems harbored a deathtrap of machine-gun nests for approaching forces. Gen. Sir Henry Rawlinson's British Fourth Army would attack this thicket full of wasps' nests head-on. To the north the Third Army would launch a diversionary attack, and to the south the French Sixth Army would attack. The attack front totaled nearly nineteen miles, twelve British and seventeen French, along which the British arrayed eighteen divisions, the French five, against six German divisions. German aerial reconnaissance units had detected the British buildup in June, but the army did not heed their warnings. By July British and French aircraft outnumbered the Germans by nearly four to one.

Joffre did not expect a breakthrough, merely further attrition, but Haig, a self-righteous spiritualist and fundamentalist, an aloof and cold paragon of efficiency, believed in his ability to achieve a major breakthrough. The BEF's camp sprawled over miles behind the front, and Haig had accumulated almost three million shells for his more than 1,400 artillery pieces. A week-long artillery barrage of a million shells would cut the barbed wire, and destroy enemy artillery and fortified positions. Then on the day of attack a "creeping" barrage would provide a curtain of protection and enable his inexperienced infantry to march in straight lines right through the flattened German defenses. Haig's beloved cavalry, which included Indian units, would then burst into open country beyond and roll up the German lines.

The very coordination between artillery and infantry necessary to execute a creeping barrage presumed experienced gunners and assault troops. Although the volunteer divisions had enlisted in 1915, they remained not only inexperienced but also inadequately trained, a circumstance reflected in their simplistic and outdated tactics. Poor training organization and facilities explain part of this inexcusable situation. The determining factor, however, proved to be the regular army officers' conviction that rank amateurs not only could not master more sophisticated tactics, but also could not execute them in the field if granted any independence in tactical decision-making. As a result, the British Army instructed the best educated, most literate, and most educable and ardent force it would ever assemble to march in waves across no-man's land, burdened with sixty-pound packs. At least the soldiers now sported metal helmets that offered some protection for the head and face. The

British failure to train intelligent soldiers adequately and the decision to curtail their battlefield mobility with empty tactics and full packs remains as inexplicable as it was damnable. The British had been learning from ally and enemy in every realm of land warfare, from the use of artillery to that of aviation. They failed to adopt new practices in infantry training for the volunteer army. In comparison, French and German soldiers, who now wore the *casque Adrian* and *Stahlhelm* metal helmets respectively, attacked without full packs in small, well-armed units, rushing from point to point, providing covering fire for their comrades as they advanced, and taking advantage of ground cover.

The bombardment began on 24 June, with the offensive due to start on 29 June. Heavy rains forced postponement until 1 July, so the Germans on the eighteen-mile front endured further shelling. Although the British damaged the trench line, they lacked the heavy cannon necessary to penetrate the thirty-foot-deep troop bunkers. The 1.5 million mostly shrapnel shells fired failed to destroy the barbed wire, because they exploded upon hitting the ground and often blew the barbed wire maze into denser thickets. One general reported the wire on his sector eliminated, while one of his junior officers, probably a little closer to it, perhaps endowed with superior eyesight, pronounced the wire to be perfectly fine. That meant attacking troops would not be.

On 1 July, south of the focus of the offensive, French heavy guns and howitzers, including the 400-mm. giants, manned by experienced crews, had blasted German wire and positions, as well as most of the dugouts, to smithereens. When the French infantry attacked on the Somme on 1 July, the 1st Corps of the Colonial Army included twenty-one Senegalese battalions. As in earlier offensives, black and white troops suffered high losses. Officers encouraged the Africans in particular to close with the Germans and use their knives, and French soldiers the bayonet, although their offensive tactics, in emulation of German practices, had become more refined. Gen. Pierre Bedoulat, commander of the Colonial Army Corps at the Somme, believed that the Africans' "limited intellectual abilities" made them useful "for sparing a certain number of European lives at the moment of assaults."[9] The Senegalese knew only that their duty required them to fight for France, that they could not turn and run even if they so desired, and that they desired to prove their valor in combat. The desire to kill their own abusive officers during combat motivated some further,[10] a goal they shared with some soldiers in all armies during the war.

French platoons seized the German first line, in some places even the second, and the British troops just north of them benefitted from the artillery to advance as well. To the north of the main attack, the British diversionary attack amounted to only a cautious probing that the Germans repulsed. Between these flanks, the main force launched its attack early in the morning.

At 7.30 a.m. on that hot summer day, 100,000 British soldiers rose from their trenches to advance at a walk in four lines at 50 to 100-yard intervals toward the German lines. They might just as well have been on parade. The battlefield appeared empty of enemy. The creeping barrage preceded them. In high spirits, some battalions kicked footballs ahead of them, with a prize to the first to boot the ball into the German trenches. The "Big Push" was under way.

Enemy artillery and German machine-guns hit some men as they emerged from their trenches, while still within the British lines. Elite German machine-gunners ranged up and down the British lines, destroying entire brigades before they reached their front line. Other British troops advanced, only to see the barrage creep away from them, as inexperienced gunners, fearing that they would shell their own men, moved on to more distant targets too soon and left the infantry in no-man's land, facing uncut barbed wire and an unscathed enemy. German artillery tore holes in their formations. German soldiers, at the shout of sentries left above ground to warn of approaching enemy, seized their helmets, belts, rifles, and machine-guns, rushed from their dug-outs as they had drilled, set up the guns, and began to fire into the advancing horde, sometimes from ranges as short as twenty yards. Their fire scythed through the British ranks. In only a few places did the British actually capture the German first line and even advance beyond it, but they had to retreat from exposed positions before murderous German counter-attacks. Corp. W.H. Shaw and Pvt. W. Hay described the attack of their units as "slaughter," with "heaps of men everywhere, all dead." Hay concluded bitterly, "We always blamed the people up above. We had a saying in the Army, 'The higher, the fewer'. They meant the higher the rank, the fewer the brains."[11] A Canadian soldier, Robert Correll, who would be dead within two months, confessed in a letter to his sister that officers who "used the men dirty over here sometimes get 'accidentally' shot during a charge."[12]

News filtered slowly back from the front, as the hail of shells and bullets rendered retreat impossible, and runners did not survive to reach the British lines. Some wounded men remained in no-man's land for three days before rescue, enduring multiple wounds as gunners ranged up and down the battlefield. In other cases German machine-gunners, so incredulous and revolted at the British sacrifice and slaughter, ceased fire to allow the wounded to crawl back to their lines. Thousands expired where they fell, fortunate if their death came quickly. Others simply crawled into shell holes, wrapped themselves in their waterproof groundsheets, and bled to death in agony from their wounds.

Behind the front, Haig acknowledged a setback, but believed that his forces had taken *only* 40,000 casualties, losses he considered acceptable. In reality his men, who now referred to the "Big Push" as the "Big Balls-up," suffered 57,470 casualties, including 19,240 dead, "the greatest loss of life in

British military history,"[13] on 1 July. Haig refused to quit, and Rawlinson, appalled by the initial casualties, mounted a surprise attack before dawn on 14 July. The British captured German second positions on a three-mile front and even threatened a breakthrough, but German reinforcements sealed the breach before British cavalry could exploit it.

Later that month ANZAC veterans of Gallipoli and South African soldiers advanced further, but to no avail. After a later abortive attack, New Zealander Pvt. H. Baverstock, his thigh shattered by shrapnel, lay for hours until two stretcher-bearers without their stretcher bandaged his wound, "a gaping hole with a terrific bulge on the opposite side." He languished in his blood-soaked clothes in no-man's land for another two days until two other medics brought him in, crossing a battlefield "strewn with the bodies of New Zealanders."[14]

The dead inhabited the dreams of CSM W.J. Coggins, whose unit had spent a week's rest at an aid station. There they carried the stretchers of doomed men, whom doctors had labeled with a red tab, under a large tent and then each morning sewed up the dead in blankets and carted them away for burial. He recalled, "I used to hear them poor sods at nighttime, moaning and crying for water. Nobody went to them, you know, nobody went anywhere near them."[15] Attrition had come to the Somme.

Haig's mounted troops thus participated little at the Somme. Indian cavalry fought in limited fashion, but by 1916 some Indian soldiers had begun to think beyond the war, to what they might gain and had learned from service in Europe. One wrote in August: "If we Indians bring back to India the flag of victory which we have helped win for our King George, we shall have proved our fitness and will be entitled to self-government."[16] This sentiment echoed the words of Senegalese representative Blaise Diagne in the French Parliament, as he claimed such rights for Senegal in return for the sacrifice of Senegalese troops for the French cause.

In November an Indian lancer expressed a sentiment increasingly popular among his comrades in reproaching his grandfather for not educating the girls in the family. He observed the European custom of educating both men and women and concluded: "you ought to educate your girls as well as your boys and our posterity will be the better for it."[17] Despite every British intention to keep progressive ideas from Indian soldiers, their very presence in Europe spawned revolutionary ideas in their heads.

By November the Somme battle neared its conclusion, and if cavalry played no role in it, the airplane, and another even newer weapon, did. Entente aerial superiority enabled British and French reconnaissance planes to photograph German positions for accurate artillery barrages while protecting their own. The British, in particular, under their commander Maj. Gen. Hugh "Boom" Trenchard, pursued a "relentless and incessant offensive," determined to dominate the air far over the German lines. They bombed and strafed German troops, who cursed the British, French, and German air services in the same breath.

The German air service, like the French at Verdun, responded by concentrating its force at the Somme. British losses remained high from the start of the battle, but in mid-September the balance of losses tipped in favor of the Germans, as Oswald Boelcke arrived with a handpicked squadron of pilots (Fighter Flight 2, or *Jagdstaffel* 2) flying a formidable new fighter aircraft, the twin-gun Albatros D.1 biplane. Boelcke crashed to his death on 28 October with forty kills to his credit after a collision with another German fighter, but his legacy included his example, his dicta, and his most adept pupil, Manfred Freiherr von Richthofen.

British pilots, flying offensive patrols far over German lines in obsolete DH2 fighters for lack of newer British Sopwiths and French Nieuports, proved no match for these new opponents. In November, for example, squadron commander Lanoe Hawker, VC, Britain's premier pursuit pilot and a two-year veteran of the Western Front, encountered one of the new Albatros fighters. They maneuvered for thirty minutes, an incredibly long time, but the Albatros's superior speed and climb enabled the German to end above and behind him. Maj. Hawker finally bolted for his lines, zigzagging at low altitude, pursued relentlessly by his foe. He dodged 900 rounds, then, struck in the head, Hawker plummeted from an altitude of 90 feet into the Somme battlefield just on the German side of the lines. Manfred von Richthofen had claimed his eleventh victim.

Attrition notwithstanding, Haig possessed a secret weapon, one that he anticipated would achieve his treasured breakthrough. English, French, and Russian inventors had been pursuing the concept of a caterpillar track or treaded armored vehicle. The British War Office rejected Col. Ernest Swinton's proposal in October 1914, but Winston Churchill, invariably a fan of new weapons, had diverted Admiralty funds for the "landship." In the summer of 1915 a desperate army joined the project, which yielded a first prototype named "Little Willie" in December 1915 and a larger, armed one named "Mother" in January. The War Office ordered 150 Mark I "tanks," the new machine's code-name, and "Mother"'s offspring came in a "male" version armed with two six-pounder cannon and three machine-guns, and a "female" one armed with five machine-guns. One hundred-horsepower engines propelled the twenty-eight-ton monsters to a maximum speed of three or four miles per hour, but at an incredible strain on the motors of these grossly underpowered vehicles.

Haig demanded tanks for a September offensive, and received them with the support of Imperial General Staff Chief Sir William Robertson, another Scotsman, but one of working-class background who had risen through the ranks. Lloyd George, the Cabinet, and the inventors would have preferred to wait until they had more. Haig had forty-nine in September. Thirty-two led the offensive, twenty-three of which broke down or sank in shell craters. The last nine scattered the panicked German defenders and spearheaded a 3,500-yard advance until they too either broke down or German artillery destroyed them.

Absent a breakthrough, the British and French continued their attacks through October. By October the Canadian Expeditionary Force had expanded to an army corps of three and then four divisions, now separated from the British Army. After the casualties at Ypres in 1915, Canadian Prime Minister Sir Robert Borden had begun to assert Canada's status, not as a "subservient colony," but as a "junior but sovereign ally."[18]

In November snow and mud led to the Entente's official termination of the Battle of the Somme on 19 November. In five months the Entente had pounded a bulge in the German lines some thirty miles long and seven miles wide at its maximum and taken a toll of some 450,000 German casualties, at the expense of some 420,000 British and 200,000 French casualties. The French had taken twice as much territory for many fewer losses than the British incurred.[19]

The year 1916 ground to a close on the Western Front as it had begun, in stalemate. Total casualties for the year on both sides soared – approximately 1.8 million men killed, wounded, and missing. The number killed on both sides during the year, although still atrocious, may be more comprehensible: 150,000 British, 268,000 French, and 143,000 German dead, for a total of 561,000 men killed. An average of 46,750 men died a month, or 1,540 a day; an average of 150,000 men a month had become casualties, or 4,932 a day.

Haig and Robertson contented themselves with the erroneous belief that they had inflicted more casualties on the Germans than they had suffered. They had turned the tables of the war of attrition, or *la guerre d'usure*, as the French called it, on the Germans. The Germans had now endured two *Materialschlachten*, or battles of materiel, in the west. Hindenburg and Ludendorff worried about their losses and the breaches in places of two out of three of their defensive systems. They decided to build a more powerful fortified line twenty-five miles to the east of the Somme battlefield, to shorten their front, and husband their dwindling manpower reserve. After all, they had other fronts to tend, with no end to the war in sight on any of them.

The Germans would use French and Belgian male labor to build their new fortifications, as they had no compunction about the use of forced labor in the occupied territories or in Germany. They had required village women as young as age 15 to work starting in 1915. In spring 1916 the military governor of Lille decided to evacuate urban residents of the region to help with agricultural work. Soldiers rounded up some 25,000 young women and girls in a street-by-street dragnet of the cities, shipped them all – innocents, prostitutes, criminals together – to rural areas, and ordered them to walk to nearby villages. The women found no accommodation, because the Germans had characterized them either as immoral or criminal to the local farmers. The Germans commandeered not only people, but literally everything. In Lille they had also requisitioned mattresses, lighting, plumbing and heating fixtures, leather – anything not nailed down and many objects that were.

Even without the requisitions, life became difficult enough for the inhabitants of the region by 1916, as available food, shelter, and all the necessities of life dwindled. By 1916 the Committee for the Relief in Belgium (CRB) obtained 42 percent of its food for Belgium and northern France from the United States, 25 percent from the British Empire, 24 percent from Great Britain, and 9 percent from other countries, particularly the Netherlands. Six million people depended upon its supplies to supplement their daily rations and to ward off the increasing malnutrition and desperate living conditions. Diseases such as scurvy and beri-beri afflicted the elderly, while undernourishment undermined the health of children. However, the CRB operated at a deficit of nearly US$5 million monthly, reflecting inflationary food prices everywhere. Conditions would only worsen in the coming year.

THE EASTERN FRONT. THE BRUSILOV OFFENSIVE AND THE DECLINE OF AUSTRIA-HUNGARY

In December 1915, when the participants at the Chantilly Conference agreed to a coordinated summer offensive, *Stavka* had planned to resume its offensive against the Germans on the northern sector of the front in June, immediately prior to a Franco-British offensive. The German occupation, exploitation, and planned Germanization of the Baltic states and Poland, and the threat they ultimately posed to Petrograd, required confronting the German rather than the weaker Austro-Hungarian Army. However, the German attack at Verdun in February caused Joffre to plead for an earlier Russian attack to distract the Germans. Alekseev had anticipated that the Germans would attack as early as possible, and, although he resented Joffre's arrogance, he responded. *Stavka* ordered the northern and western army groups under Generals Alexei Kuropatkin and Alexei Evert respectively to attack on a ninety-mile front around Lake Naroch in the direction of Vilna in eastern Poland.

At the beginning of 1916 the Russian Army stood in far better condition than the disasters of 1915 would have suggested. By 1916 Russian industry had increased its production of war materiel dramatically since 1914: from 1,100 machine-guns to 11,000, and from 80,000 shells to more than 20 million. Rifle and cartridge production had caught up with military needs. Imports ranging from artillery and grenades to armored cars from Entente and neutral powers supplemented Russian production. The Russian air arm remained small, but adequate enough to reconnoiter and photograph the front. Its few giant Sikorskii "Ilia Muromets" multi-engined biplanes stood ready for long-range reconnaissance and bombing missions. Its German opponent, which regarded the Eastern Front as a reprieve from the Western, would continue to outclass it.

Furthermore, in the huge manpower drafts War Minister Aleksei Polivanov had held sufficiently large numbers of men for four to six months' extensive training that by the end of the winter 1.75 million trained Russian soldiers, with more than 750,000 in reserve, all armed, confronted just over a million German and Austro-Hungarian soldiers. Nevertheless, significant improvements in the rank and file of the army could not offset the large numbers of incompetent Russian generals who owed their positions to connections to Nicholas, Alexandra, and Rasputin.

Kuropatkin and Evert outnumbered and outgunned the Germans, and Russian infantry stormed through swamps and mud to seize the first two German positions. But feuding commanders had failed to coordinate artillery with assaulting infantry; therefore the soldiers found themselves under fire from German and Russian artillery, which also blasted Russian reinforcements. The Russians lost 100,000 to Germany's 20,000 soldiers by the end of the offensive on 31 March. In late April German counter-attacks introduced Lieut. Col. Georg Bruchmüller's *Feuerwalze*, or "creeping barrage," that destroyed targets such as artillery and reserves identified by aerial reconnaissance with centralized fire from German batteries in a brief hurricane bombardment and then launched infantry fifty yards behind the moving curtain of shells. The Germans quickly recouped the lost territory.

Afterwards Kuropatkin and Evert planned to remain on the defensive indefinitely, or for as long as they could stall. The customarily silent Tsar Nicholas had once characterized his brain as at rest at *Stavka*. Nevertheless, he roused it from its stupor and convened his generals for a Council of War on 15 April, during which the cautious duo Kuropatkin and Evert declared any offensive doomed to failure. The new commander of the Southwestern Front, Aleksei Brusilov, energetically advocated a general Russian offensive, in which he would strike the Habsburg Army first to divert German forces to the southwest, at which point Evert could attack the German forces to the north. *Stavka* approved Brusilov's plan, but stipulated that he would receive no further men or munitions.

Undaunted, Brusilov returned and instituted a rigid training regimen for his soldiers, for he planned to attack all along his 200-mile front. After a short, intense bombardment, shock troops would emerge from trenches dug as close as 75 yards from the Austrian lines, infiltrate the enemy first position, and then cede to troops moving through to attack the second and third positions. AOK chief Conrad presented the perfect opportunity when his troops attacked on the Italian front in May.

On 4 June the Russian Eighth Army smashed through the Austro-Hungarian lines on the northern end of Brusilov's front and opened a twenty-mile gap, and in three days had smashed the opposing Austro-Hungarian Army and widened the breach to some forty-five miles. At the southern end of the front the Russian Ninth Army routed its Austro-Hungarian foes and made even greater progress, while the armies in the center of the front, drawn along, advanced. The Austro-Hungarian retreat turned into a rout, as units surrendered or fled. Brusilov's northern wing advanced forty miles, his southern sixty, as his forces chased the Habsburg Army before them.

A desperate Conrad recalled some of his divisions from the Italian front and appealed for help to Falkenhayn, who sent nine divisions, four from the hard-pressed Western Front and another five from the northeast. In return Conrad had to relinquish control of the remains of his three northern armies to his despised German ally. The Germans now controlled the Habsburg Army and its military destiny, a condition developing since the war's beginning and now formalized by the change in color of Habsburg uniforms from the original light blue-gray to the German *feldgrau*. Hindenburg realized that not only the Habsburg, but also the German Army would be stretched to breaking point if Evert or Kuropatkin initiated another major offensive.

Unfortunately for the Russians, Evert, scheduled to attack ten days after Brusilov, delayed a month, only to have the Germans rebuff his half-hearted and poorly planned attack. Brusilov, cursing both of his incompetent colleagues, forged ahead. He did receive reinforcements, including the 65,000-man elite Russian Guards Army, under the command of the aged and incompetent Gen. Bezobrazov, chosen by Nicholas. Bezobrazov launched them straight at German lines through a swamp from which 80 percent of them, machine-gunned from strafing German planes, never emerged. Still, by August Brusilov's southern forces had reconquered Galicia, seized the Austrian province of Bukovina, and had once again reached the Carpathian Mountains. He continued in September, but the Central Powers held, and the fall rains in October halted any further attempts.

Nevertheless, not only had Brusilov won Russia's greatest victory of the war, he had won one of the great overall victories of the war. His armies had inflicted 700,000 Austro-Hungarian losses, including 400,000 prisoners, and another 350,000 German casualties, and captured some 15.6 square miles of enemy territory. Historian Holger Herwig considered the Austro-Hungarian defeat "a blow from which the Habsburg Army never recovered," one which "marked the end of Austria-Hungary as a great and independent power."[20] Prior to the summer of 1916 the Habsburg Army had more battalions, three times the machine guns, and twice the artillery pieces as at the beginning of the war. Then, in July and August alone, it suffered 300,000 casualties. Worse still, almost 60 percent of its losses, those prisoners, were deserters. By the end of 1916, total losses on all fronts mounted to some 1.75 million Habsburg soldiers, with the great majority victims of the Russians.[21]

Brusilov had resolved to suffer considerable losses to defeat the enemy, and he had done both. The Russian Army had suffered a million total casualties at this point. The ranks of junior officers necessary to lead the men in battle had died. As the year drew to a close, some regiments mutinied and refused to fight, even at the risk of summary execution; others were willing to defend Russia but refused to attack. Brusilov had gained a truly Pyrrhic victory, for he had driven the Russian Army to exhaustion and desperation. Its soldiers knew now with certainty that if the war continued they would die, as so many around them had already perished. They proved no longer willing to fight for a weak and incompetent tsar who surrounded himself with bungling generals who heedlessly sent them to slaughter. Furthermore, they heard rumors that their families were starving at home. Upon the heels of their greatest victory, Russian soldiers plunged to the depths of despair.

One of the greatest ironies of Brusilov's success was that it had lured Rumania into the war on the side of the Entente. Rumania, under Prime Minister Ion Bratianu and King Ferdinand, had played a waiting game since 1914. It coveted in particular the Austro-Hungarian territory of Transylvania, where three million ethnic Rumanians lived. Bratianu sought, and France and Russia promised, Transylvania and further territory, supplies and men from Russia, and an offensive from Salonika against neighboring Bulgaria to distract the Central Powers. They signed an alliance on 17 August, and on 27 August Rumania declared war.

Bulgaria struck first, against the forces at Salonika, and Gen. Sarrail's response of a limited offensive conquered only a small piece of southern Serbia. Instead of attacking Bulgaria as the Entente desired, the Rumanian half-million-man army assaulted Hungary through the Transylvanian Alps to seize their desired territory. The attack, as the Brusilov offensive slowed, drew the Central Powers like a swarm of angry hornets. Falkenhayn, dismissed as Chief of the General Staff after the culminating blow of Rumanian entry into the war, led the charge to destroy Rumania. The redoubtable Mackensen and he combined, in command of German, Austro-Hungarian, Bulgarian, and even Turkish troops, to attack Rumania from three directions in September. The capital Bucharest fell to the invaders on 5 December, and ultimately the Rumanians, supported by Russian Armies, held only the eastern province of Moldavia, having lost most of their army and most of their country.

In Rumania the Central Powers, primarily the Germans, secured oil and grain essential to their continuation of the war. In the east in general, after enduring their worst defeat, they had recouped by the end of the year. However, both the Russian and Austro-Hungarian armies had suffered horrendous and irreplaceable losses, their morale was rapidly deteriorating, and many of their units no longer remained reliable. Total exhaustion loomed in both powers. A desperate race, in a sense, took form, to see which army would collapse first.

THE SOUTHWESTERN FRONT. "PUNISHMENT"

AOK chief Conrad had asked Falkenhayn in December 1915 to send German divisions to the Eastern Front to enable him to shift more forces to his southwest front for an offensive against the Italians. He intended to strike southeast from the Trentino to seize the railway center at Padua, twenty-five miles away, and then hoped to proceed another twenty miles to the sea, severing the Italian salient in the northeast along the Isonzo River and seizing the fertile and industrialized Po River valley region. Falkenhayn, preoccupied with planning for Verdun, refused. Without informing Falkenhayn, Conrad simply shifted nine divisions and artillery from the Russian front. Conrad, seemingly oblivious to the weather in the Alpine Trentino, initially planned to attack in March, but ice and snow postponed the attack until May. Nevertheless, with a total twenty new divisions in the Austro-Hungarian Army, more artillery and munitions, Conrad believed that his *Strafexpedition*, or "punishment expedition," of fifteen divisions would chastise the perfidious former ally appropriately.

Italian Gen. Cadorna realized that his growing army outnumbered his Austrian enemy and pressed his dogged offensive on Isonzo in the summer, in alignment with the agreement of the Entente at the Chantilly conference in December 1915. Joffre's request for diversionary attacks once Verdun began prompted Cadorna to launch the Fifth Battle of the Isonzo on 11 March, regardless of the weather. With little success to show, the battle ended on 29 March, by which time the massing of Austrian forces in the Trentino warned Cadorna of Conrad's intentions.

On 15 May Conrad's artillery barraged the Italian lines, dislodging rocks and snow in avalanches that buried part of the Italian front. However, impenetrable mountainous terrain and stalwart Italian defense thwarted Conrad's drive after ten miles. By June the offensive stalled, and Brusilov's attack in the east forced Conrad to transfer eight divisions from Italy, just as Cadorna counter-attacked and regained half the lost territory. The Italians' higher casualties – 141,000 to 81,000 – failed to deflect Cadorna from the Isonzo. In four more battles of the Isonzo – the Sixth through the Ninth – from August through November, the Italian Army managed to capture the town of Gorizia and a salient of some fifty square miles, in return for 126,000 Italian and 103,000 Austrian casualties. During the year, Austria-Hungary concentrated its armed forces increasingly on the Italian front. Its small military and naval air services confronted the small Italian air services, which, however, had more multi-engine operational bombers than any other power. Italian Caproni bombers, spurred by theorist Giulio Douhet's ideas about aerial supremacy, aggressively bombed cities and railway stations. At the end of 1916, neither side, despite their expenditures of men, appeared to gain any advantage in southwestern Europe.

OTTOMAN FRONTS. FROM THE CAUCASUS TO THE MIDDLE EAST

The Ottoman Turks fought on far-flung fronts in 1916. Western historians pay the most attention to the war in the Middle East, but in fact the Caucasus constituted the Turks' primary front that year against a revived Russian Army. The Turks also launched offensives against the British in Sinai in July and against the Russians in Persia in June, but both offensives stalled and stalemated. Nevertheless, significant events transpired in Mesopotamia, and in particular Entente negotiations concerning the Middle East occurred whose consequences resonate in that region to this very day.

The Russian Army had risen like the phoenix from the disasters of 1915 to score a great victory against Austria-Hungary and Germany in the summer. *Stavka* explicitly relegated the Russo-Ottoman front to secondary status in allocation of men and materiel. In January 1916 the Russian Army of the Caucasus under former *Stavka* chief Grand Duke Nicholas Nikolaevich, and led by Caucasus front commander Gen. Nikolai Yudenich, staged a surprise offensive along the entire Caucasus front against the Turks. Yudenich intended the offensive to pre-empt any Ottoman offensives using troops that the Turkish victory at Gallipoli freed.

The attack did surprise the Turks, reveling in the evacuation of the Entente at Gallipoli and the establishment of a continuous line of communications with the rest of the Central Powers after the fall of Serbia. The Turks also believed that the fortress at Erzerum would withstand any Russian siege. The Russian seizure of Erzerum early in February consequently boded well for the Russians, and revealed to the Turks the tenuous nature of their position in the Caucasus. The Russian Army, supported by coordinated naval operations, moved from victory to victory through the spring into the summer along the Lazistan coast, despite Turkish resistance. Meanwhile, the Turks struggled with their deficient rail and road network, unimproved since the beginning of the war, to move troops to the front. Divisions took nearly seven weeks to move by rail and on foot from Constantinople to the Caucasus front.

In July the Russian offensive destroyed the Turkish Third Army. Only in August, with the transfer of Ottoman divisions from Gallipoli to the front in eastern Anatolia, could the Turks counter-attack. Instead of concentrating their forces, the Turks squandered them in a series of offensives that by September inflicted 30 percent casualties on the Turkish Second Army of some 100,000 men, hardened veterans of the Gallipoli victory. The Ottoman command's poor strategy as much as Russian offensives had destroyed two Turkish armies sequentially, inflicting total casualties of nearly 100,000 trained and irreplaceable Turkish soldiers. The offensive of the Turkish Second Army would be the last major Turkish offensive of the war. The Caucasus front had stabilized, but it had proved a difficult year for the Turks. By the end of 1916, nearly half the Ottoman Army confronted the Russian Army.

In incredible defiance of the circumstances, the Ottomans responded to an urgent request from German General Staff Chief Falkenhayn to send troops to bolster his Eastern Front in Galicia. The Turks ultimately sent seven divisions, instead of holding them in reserve to fight the Russians and British as their German advisor Liman von Sanders recommended. The Turks fought well and repulsed repeated Russian attacks through August 1917, when the Turkish General Staff finally brought them home to contend with British offensives in Palestine and Mesopotamia. This diversion compounded that of three Turkish divisions to the five-month campaign against Rumania and a later one in the fall of 1916 of two divisions for six months to the Macedonian front against the Entente troops at Salonika. Certainly an aspect of this impetuous and optimistic diversion of forces stemmed from Turkish victories early in 1916, not just at Gallipoli, but also on the far-flung battlefields in the Middle East. The year 1916 proved to be the most victorious for the Turkish Army.

In Mesopotamia British Gen. Townshend's imperial forces lay under siege in Kut after 9 December 1915 by Ottoman forces under the command of German Field Marshal Colmar von der Goltz. The Ottoman forces had also severed Kut from British forces further down the river. For four months into 1916 the British attempted repeatedly to break through the Turkish defenses and relieve them. They failed, although they did manage to drop small quantities of supplies from airplanes. Indian cavalry transferred from France to the forces in Mesopotamia found the country "absolutely uninhabited and desolate" and the heat "unbearable."[22] In February 1916 the 15th Lancers Regiment, under orders to march to the front from Basra, refused because of their religious objections to fighting the Turks near the Holy Places of Karbala. The cavalrymen requested any assignment, even the deadliest fighting in France, rather than this violation of their religious beliefs. The Authorities summarily punished the 429 soldiers involved: three NCOs received penal servitude for life; the rest of the NCOs, fifteen years; and the men, imprisonment on the Andaman Islands for seven years. The military released the men in summer 1917 to serve in the regiment's depot.[23]

Finally, after a last desperate and abortive attempt to supply Kut in late

April, Townshend and more than 13,000 troops surrendered to the Turks on 29 April 1916. Von der Goltz had died of cholera ten days before. Townshend, deranged as a consequence of a fever suffered in the 125-degree Fahrenheit heat the previous summer, spent the rest of the war in luxury in Constantinople, the honored guest of the Ottomans. The Turks force-marched his troops brutally over the most desolate of territory, first 100 miles to Baghdad, then 500 more to Anatolia, where the survivors labored in chain-gangs in prisoner-of-war camps. The British had already suffered 33,000 casualties by the time they surrendered; 4,000 of the British and Indian troops were taken prisoner, and 70 percent of the British died during the death marches or in the camps.

The captured forces would not benefit from the lessons the British government learned from the Kut disaster. Already in February 1916 the War Office had wrested control of the Mesopotamian campaign from the British government of India, and new commanders began to prepare for future campaigns. More artillery and ammunition, boats more suited to the river war, improved medical facilities, railroad construction to ease shipment of supplies – all set the stage for the arrival of a new commander of the Mesopotamian Expeditionary Force. Lieut. Gen. Sir Stanley Maude assumed command in August, and in September began a slow, methodical, and steady advance toward Kut that would proceed into the following year.

In the Middle East, at the end of 1915, Kitchener's advisors in the Cairo office devised a so-called "Egyptian Empire" scheme, in which the British High Commissioner Kitchener would rule a single Arab state with two front men, the Sherif of Mecca as spiritual leader and the monarch of Egypt as political figurehead. The Cairo Intelligence Department further established a subordinate Arab Bureau, whose ranks included Thomas Edward Lawrence, a young man from Oxford who was the protégé of the bureau chief. By the end of 1915 Sherif Hussein of Mecca, who had learned that the Young Turks planned to remove him after the war, was proposing himself as ruler of the Arab world.

In a world of complex intrigues, the Arab Bureau convinced itself, and then the Cabinet in London, that the Arabs in the Ottoman Empire might join the British side and play a significant role in the war if they could enlist Hussein. This scenario required the British Army to invade Syria and Palestine, because Hussein had no army and the allegedly powerful Arab secret societies little or no following or unity. Such a policy, however, would bring Britain into conflict with her ally France, not only because of the diversion of force from the Western Front, but also because it would threaten French interests in the Middle East.

The British government, represented by Mark Sykes, the staunchest proponent of this imperial plan, and the French government, represented by François Picot, representative of French colonial interests in their government, met late in 1915 and hammered out the Sykes–Picot Treaty in January 1916, which the French and British governments approved in February. The treaty and its terms remained secret for two years, but in essence the British and French partitioned the Ottoman Empire. France would rule or control Lebanon and Syria far enough to the east to provide the British with a buffer against the Russians, while Britain would control Mesopotamia and part of Palestine with ports that connected to Mesopotamia. Some international arrangement would administer the rest of Palestine. Of course, the Arabs desired a unified state that they controlled, and the Arab Bureau in Cairo desired a unified Arab state that it controlled, so the Sykes–Picot Treaty satisfied neither side.

The French then turned to the Russian government in secret, and in March secured Russian support for French instead of international rule in non-British Palestine. Before Sykes went to Russia, naval intelligence reminded him that he had forgotten the Jewish, specifically the Zionists' interest in returning to Palestine. The Anti-Semitic tsarist government, which considered the Zionists an internal danger, dismissed Sykes's concerns. Nevertheless, Sykes left convinced of Jewish international power and now of the existence of not only secret Arab but also secret Jewish societies.[24]

In June Hussein, who was receiving money from the Turks and the British, announced an Arab revolt against the Ottoman Empire, although he had only a few thousand tribesmen and no army with which to fight. The British would pour some £11 million into subsidizing the revolt, while Sykes began popularizing the concept of the "Middle East." The British and French sent missions to the Arabs starting in summer 1916. Among the British mission was a small, quiet, junior intelligence officer whose size had led the army to reject him for service – T.E. Lawrence. By the fall Lawrence had won the confidence of Hussein's sons Abdullah and Feisal. Feisal, with Lawrence as British liaison, would become the commander of Hussein's tribesmen in the Hejaz revolt, waging guerrilla warfare against the Turks. In November Lawrence, with the money to buy an army of tribesmen, joined Feisal, but the new year arrived with nothing to show for the British investment.

AFRICA. SUPPRESSION OF REBELLION IN THE WEST;
PURSUIT OF AN ELUSIVE PREY IN THE EAST

In West Africa, the French, frustrated by their inability to crush the tribes in the Volta–Bani region in 1915, amassed 1,500 infantry (*tirailleurs*) and more than 2,000 auxiliary soldiers, supported by six 80-mm. cannon and a machine-gun section, to finish the task in early 1916. In a vicious campaign lasting for more than a month from mid-February to mid-March, the French colonial columns inflicted losses estimated at 3,000 soldiers on the tribes while suffering fewer than 200 casualties. They followed with a two-month campaign from mid-April until mid-June using more *tirailleurs* and machine-guns, first wiping entire villages off the map and then concentrating on destroying the tribesmen and their food sources. As the people resisted fanatically, the colonial forces transformed the region into a "desert."[25] By the end of April, the colonial forces had already killed more than 3,500 opponents against slightly more than 400 dead of their own. These slaughters continued, as the people chose "death" over "slavery."[26] The anti-colonial tribes also fought bloody battles against people who remained loyal to the French, while the French ground them down, capturing or killing the rebel leaders, imprisoning women and children, and winning a last major military encounter in August. After a final sortie early in 1917, the French continued to execute captured rebel leaders throughout 1917.

To fight the Volta–Bani War, the French had mobilized by far the largest force in their colonial history – some 2,500 West African *tirailleurs* and another 2,500 auxiliary troops equipped with cannon and machine-guns. They confronted enemy villages with a total population of approximately 800,000 to 900,000 people. The French slaughtered an estimated 30,000 inhabitants in a "total war" – seizing women and children as hostages, destroying crops, rustling livestock, and poisoning wells. Too few inhabitants often survived to bury the dead, who lay rotting on the roads and in the fields. The French colonial forces had completed the "pacification" of the region.[27]

In the last region where the Entente–German conflict continued in Africa, in German East Africa, South African Jan Smuts, who had led guerrilla forces in the Boer War against the British, took command late in 1915 and arrived at Mombasa in February 1916. A German force of 1,300 men had just defeated a 6,000-man force of Indians, Africans, English, Rhodesians, and white South Africans, the last of whom, new to war, had turned and run in the face of a bayonet charge by yelling German *askaris*. Only a stand by Indian troops, whom the white South Africans despised and denigrated, prevented a total rout.

Smuts launched four columns totaling 40,000 men to encircle and defeat Paul von Lettow-Vorbeck's 16,000-man African force. Two British columns came from Kenya and Nyasaland respectively; a Portuguese from Mozambique; and a Belgian from the Congo. Lettow-Vorbeck divided his force, retreated south, fighting when necessary, before disappearing, always destroying railways and bridges behind him. His indigenous *askaris* tolerated the diseases and climate that felled white and Indian Entente soldiers at a rate of thirty-one non-battle casualties to one battle casualty. Smut's campaign looked impressive in terms of territory captured, especially when compared with the stalemate on the Western Front, but he could not achieve the essential goal of running Lettow-Vorbeck to ground and destroying the German Colonial Army. Smuts replaced his generals with three of his own choosing, two of whom were South African, but to no avail. Lettow-Vorbeck demonstrated his superiority as commander and invariably remained one step ahead of his pursuers. Furthermore, German *askaris*, or "damned kaffirs [niggers]" as Smuts called them,[28] proved to be better soldiers in the bush than Smuts's white or Indian troops.

After Smuts had seized the northern frontier around Kilimanjaro, Kitchener in the War Office proposed to halt the campaign. After all, the British would gain the German territory at the end of a victorious war, and the Western Front needed the manpower. The rest of the Cabinet, in desperate need of "victories" somewhere, encouraged Smuts. The impatient South African consequently ordered his forces forward, into constant ambushes, not only by *askaris*, but swarms of bees or tsetse flies that killed their horses.

Supplies remained sporadic, and half-starved soldiers succumbed to malaria, dysentery, and blackwater fever, while the constant rain precluded evacuation. The abysmal conditions reduced the combatants to a miserable existence. The British imperial forces, who persisted in wearing shorts and loose, open-necked shirts which made them perfect targets for insects, suffered in particular. A Lancashire Fusilier, if somewhat misled about conditions on the Western Front, understandably lamented, "Ah, I wish to hell I was in France! There one lives like a gentleman and dies like a man. Here one lives like a pig and dies like a dog."

As if disease did not suffice, parasitic infestation from chiggers, a flea that burrows into the skin and lays eggs, and guinea worm, ingested in water containing infected fleas, plagued the troops. Chiggers, unless extracted by needle, could infect, reduce to a pulpy mass, and even consume one's feet and toes, and they occasionally lodged in other body parts. The guinea worm bores through the intestinal wall to various parts of the body and finally releases its larvae either under the skin, which causes deep abscesses and further infections, or externally after emerging through the skin. The interval from invasion to emergence might exceed a year, during which time the unfortunate host suffered from debilitating symptoms. At the time of emergence treatment entailed hooking the worm on a stick and winding it gently and gradually out of the body over a two- to three-week period. If one tore the worm while removing it, its young would penetrate bodily tissues and spread further infection. African women, who had years of experience performing such operations, enjoyed a higher rate of success than army doctors.[29]

The lice, trenchfoot, and frostbite of the Western Front paled in comparison to such grisly horrors, and medical facilities in western Europe, however problematic, appeared luxurious compared to those in the bush. On the Western Front combat, not disease, prevailed as the overwhelming killer and incapacitator of men, while on other fronts such as Africa and Gallipoli, reminiscent of earlier wars, disease held sway.

Ironically, in April and May Lettow-Vorbeck received supplies from another blockade runner, the *Maria von Stettin*, delivered by some 50,000 porters. German forces consequently remained better supplied than British forces, and German officers had five porters to carry their equipment in comparison to the one allotted their British counterparts. The very number of carriers indicates their importance to both sides in the war for East Africa. Yet these noncombatants, who served all armies in tens of thousands, often disappear from the record. Their impressment and losses, though incalculable, depopulated the regions through which the armies fought, created social instability, and often led to famine. The destruction the forces wreaked on primitive lines of transportation and communication also had a deleterious effect on the territory.

Smuts obtained both new airplanes and new troops in 1916. The new airplanes proved useless, not merely because the German colonial force easily camouflaged its positions and movement, but also because wood and fabric machines, the majority of the available craft, rapidly decomposed in the humid climate. The new, black troops, on the other hand, proved very useful. Smuts grudgingly acknowledged their effectiveness and enlarged the size of the King's African Rifles (KAR). In the fall black Africans, in particular the Nigerian Brigade, replaced some 12,000 white South Africans. By September the British imperial and a Belgian colonial force had captured key cities and the railway, and surrounded Lettow-Vorbeck.

The British forces now numbered some 80,000 men, pitted against Lettow-Vorbeck's 10,000. The German commander, infected with chiggers, relentlessly pushed on into the southern half of the colony, where Smuts presumed to corner him in December. Once again, however, the German eluded the South African's trap and escaped from what appeared to be a hopeless position. The Kaiser awarded Lettow-Vorbeck Germany's highest medal for valor, the *Pour le Mérite*, late in 1916. At the end of 1916 the German's black African force continued to elude its pursuers. Smuts, for all his brilliance as a guerrilla commander against British white forces in the Boer War, had more than met his match in Lettow-Vorbeck's black army.

NAVAL WAR. SUBMARINES AND SKAGGERAK

Starting in January the Russian Navy, coordinating with the Russian offensive against the Turks in the Caucasus, staged naval sweeps in the Black Sea, bombarding Turkish positions along the southeast coast of Lazistan. Then in March and April the Russians staged amphibious landings using small craft well suited for the operations and capable of carrying 700 men and, when necessary, protected by Russian dreadnoughts and battlecruisers. A successful series of these operations through June drove the Turks from other positions, and caused them to summon their two former German battlecruisers and submarines to transport supplies and then to support a Turkish counter-offensive in late June. The Russian Black Sea Fleet benefitted from knowledge of the German codes and interception of wireless messages between Germans and Turks, enabling superior Russian forces to intercept and thwart German naval operations.

With Rumanian entry into the war on the Entente side, the Russian Black Sea Fleet shifted its focus to the west coast in the second half of 1916. Russian mine-laying, although it severely disrupted Turkish coal supplies and posed serious danger to German and Turkish submarines and ships, could not save Rumania from the savage onslaught of the Central Powers. Still, the Russian fleet clearly predominated in the Black Sea throughout 1916.

In the eastern Mediterranean, with the collapse of the Gallipoli expedition, submarine warfare took precedence. Nevertheless, the Royal Navy did stage raids on the desolate Anatolian coasts to put Greek irregulars ashore to rustle cattle and other livestock from the Turks. It beggars description that the Royal Navy, violating international law, ignoring protests from the Greeks and the Turks, would sink to such depths. The rustling raids lasted from March through October.

Meanwhile, the German Navy increased its submarine strength in the Mediterranean, because British imports flowed through the sea while neutral shipping, particularly American, was sparser than in the Atlantic. The British and French lacked sufficient destroyers to protect troop transports, much less merchant shipping. The German submarines began the year slowly, as they refitted for patrols during winter weather. By April, however, under the command of Lt. Lothar von Arnauld de la Perière, and operating from the bases at Cattaro and Pola in the Adriatic, newer and larger German submarines began wreaking havoc in the Mediterranean. They easily ran the Otranto barrage at night, and then roamed freely about the shipping lanes in the western reaches of the sea. On one cruise from 26 July to 20 August, Arnauld de la Perière in U.35 sank fifty-four ships totaling more than 90,000 tons, the most successful submarine cruise of the war. His exploits in the Mediterranean would make him Germany's most successful U-boat commander of the war.

In the second quarter of 1916 (April to June), the Mediterranean force sank nearly 50 percent of the total of nearly 400,000 tons sunk by subs everywhere, and in the third quarter (July to September) they sank 65 percent of the total of nearly 500,000 tons worldwide. They suffered only light losses – two boats – in return, as the force grew by October to fourteen submarines, including seven large ones, with others in the Black Sea and more on the way. The Entente had no effective countermeasures, other than to divert traffic to longer but safer routes around the Cape or overland. As the weather grew worse, the U-boats returned to refit at Cattaro and Pola for the coming year.

At the northern end of Europe, the Entente powers and the United States shipped some 2.5 million tons of supplies by way of the Arctic Sea to the Russian ports of Archangel and Murmansk. The Central Powers had closed other avenues of shipping to Russia: the Ottomans, the Black Sea; the Germans, the Baltic Sea. The Germans paid very little attention to the Arctic trade during the war, in contrast to the Second World War, when German naval and air forces would make the Arctic a graveyard for Allied convoys to Murmansk. In 1916 mines laid by German submarines took a small toll of neutral and Entente shipping. In the Baltic Sea the Germans pursued a defensive strategy, sowing mines and attempting to protect merchant shipping from Russian cruisers and large destroyers by resorting to convoys to neutral Sweden. The Germans took the offensive once, in a destroyer raid on shipping in the Gulf of Finland in November 1916; they lost seven of eleven modern destroyers and gained no advantage. The year 1916 remained relatively quiet in the Adriatic Sea, with an occasional Austrian light cruiser and destroyer raid on the trawlers in the extremely porous Otranto barrage.

In the most important naval theater of all, the North Sea and, to a far lesser extent, the Atlantic, Britain and Germany struggled to break the stalemate that prevailed. After the "unrestricted" campaign of 1915, "restricted" submarine warfare became the order of the day for the German Navy until September 1916. Nevertheless, in this time of restrictions, U-boats could sink enemy freighters in the war zone without warning. Chief of the Admiralty Staff von Holtzendorff had become a believer in unrestricted submarine warfare, convinced by shipping experts who predicted that an enlarged submarine fleet could sink enough tonnage in supplies to bring England to its knees in six to eight months. The new commander of the High Sea Fleet, Vice Adm. Scheer, also espoused a more vigorous offensive posture in general. Falkenhayn, preoccupied with plans for Verdun, found this a welcome prospect, because he did not believe that military action alone could force the English out of the war.

In the face of American objections, in March Germany resorted not to unrestricted but to a "sharpened" submarine warfare, which entailed sinking armed enemy merchant ships even outside the war zone. Exasperated submarine commanders, barraged with a flurry of restrictive orders, had to scrutinize them to determine if a prey were legitimate, only to learn later that it was not. Naval authorities accepted Tirpitz's resignation, as Germany launched its next submarine campaign.

The navy began the offensive with fifty-two operational submarines in March. In January it had ordered thirty-one more, and in May it ordered twenty-two large long-range submarines and another twenty-four medium-range boats. The campaign quickly took a toll on neutral Dutch shipping, but Dutch protests mattered little. When the UB.29 sank the steamer *Sussex* off Dieppe with some American fatalities on 24 March, however, an American ultimatum threatening to sever diplomatic relations prompted the civilian government to pressure the navy into ceasing the campaign late in April. Monthly submarine sinkings during this short operation rose as high as nearly 190,000 tons. This figure fell far short of German desired projections of more than 600,000 tons, although it sufficed to worry the British. A disappointed Scheer reassigned the submarines in northern waters to joint operations with the High Sea Fleet.

Scheer planned to force part of the British Grand Fleet out to sea through attacks on ships by submarines and mines, and attacks on British coastal towns and installations by sea and air. He then hoped to destroy that part of it and whittle down the British advantage. The British, perfectly well aware of their advantage and intent on preserving it, were trying to lure the High Sea Fleet into a snare of their own. They answered with seaplane raids on Zeppelin aerodromes to provoke Scheer. This cat-and-mouse game continued through the spring, punctuated by occasional clashes between smaller vessels, and more often encounters with mines or collisions with one another in fog. The squadrons kept missing one another, as when Scheer sent his battlecruisers on a "tip and run" raid on the coastal towns of Lowestoft and Yarmouth timed on 24 to 25 April to coincide with the Easter Sunday Irish Rebellion. The major forces never came close.

Then, on 31 May, German battlecruisers, under Adm. Hipper's command, sortied to show themselves off the Norwegian coast and attack British patrols and shipping. Scheer calculated that the British would rise to the bait, and he followed with the bulk of the High Sea Fleet to spring the trap. The Grand Fleet, which had access to German codes and knew the Germans were putting to sea, had already set sail. Some 250 ships were at sea, and the British held a decisive preponderance over the Germans: 28 to 16 dreadnoughts; 9 to 5 battlecruisers; 8 to 0 armored cruisers; 26 to 11 cruisers; and 78 to 61 destroyers. Historian Paul Halpern terms Jutland "the largest encounter between surface ships of modern times."[30]

German and British battlecruisers, the latter under the command of Rear Adm. Beatty, were on a converging course, and Hipper, upon sighting the British ships, immediately turned and ran to the south, drawing Beatty toward Scheer's High Sea Fleet. The British outnumbered the Germans six to five, but the Germans fired faster and more accurately. Within a half hour their 11– and 12–inch shells had blasted the *Lion*'s midship turret, and sunk the *Indefatigable* and the *Queen Mary*, with total losses of 2,283 officers and men. Twenty men survived. Beatty commented, "There is something wrong with our bloody ships today."[31]

To make matters worse for the British battlecruisers, the German High Sea Fleet arrived, and Beatty began a "run to the north" to draw the German forces toward Jellicoe and the Grand Fleet, who were rapidly approaching. Now the British began to score hits, some disabling, on the German cruisers, but none blew up. Rear Adm. Hood's Third Battlecruiser Squadron entered the fray, firing effectively at the German cruisers. Then Hood's flagship *Invincible* took a direct hit on the midship's turret. The turret roof blew off, and the flash from the explosion ignited the ammunition and powder in the magazine deep inside the ship. The ship exploded, split in two parts, and 1,026 officers and men, including Hood, perished. Six men survived.

By then Scheer's battleships were taking fire from British dreadnoughts, so he turned about and fled to the southwest. The British did not pursue but steamed east and south in an attempt to block the Germans' retreat. Scheer then suddenly turned back to the northeast, and steamed right into the rear of the British. In desperation he ordered his cruisers and destroyers to cover his turn away. Ironically, Jellicoe also turned away to avoid torpedoes from the German destroyers, just as his ships were beginning to pound the Germans. By this time night was falling, and the Germans were better trained and equipped for night fighting than the Grand Fleet. In a series of sharp clashes during the night, the Germans took a greater toll of British ships from cruisers to destroyers than the British took of German. The Germans did have to abandon and torpedo their seriously damaged battlecruiser *Lützow*.

Losses on both sides amounted to 3 British battlecruisers to 1 German; 1 German predreadnought battleship; 3 British armored cruisers; 4 German light cruisers; 8 British destroyers to 5 German. The British suffered 6,945 total casualties, including 6,094 dead, to 3,058 German, including 2,551 dead. The Germans celebrated the Battle of the Skaggerak as a victory, as they had clearly inflicted heavier losses on the British. The British battlecruisers in particular suffered from inferior armor and shells, and more dangerous powder charges and handling practices of the powder, than their German counterparts. Germany built its ships better and stronger, in part because it designed them for shorter range operations and thus they carried less fuel than their British counterparts, built to police the oceans of the world.

On the British side, Jutland appeared full of missed opportunities, culminating in the failure of the Admiralty to inform Jellicoe of Scheer's position that night, information that might have enabled Jellicoe to intercept the retreating Germans at dawn. Nevertheless, the British still controlled the oceans of the world, because "The German fleet had assaulted its jailer and was back in jail."[32] As Scheer admitted to the Kaiser on 4 July, no high–sea battle, however successful, would force England to make peace. That would require unrestricted submarine warfare to strangle English commerce.

Scheer's High Sea Fleet did sortie again in mid–August, in an attempt to lure Jellicoe's Grand Fleet across a school of submarines. Although both sides lost ships to mines or torpedoes, neither side, leery of any risk, fired a shot. Afterward, the British decided to risk no more capital ships, as submarines and mines posed a prohibitive danger in the southern part of the North Sea. Beatty, a most aggressive battlecruiser commander, succeeded Jellicoe as commander of the Grand Fleet on 28 November, and assumed his predecessor's cautious policy. Lighter vessels, in particular destroyers and submarines, would now bear the offensive and defensive burdens of the war. On the German side, the high command (OHL) decided to resume restricted submarine warfare over Scheer's opposition and reassigned the submarines of the High Sea Fleet to commerce raiding.

Stalemate resumed in the North Sea, and the German High Sea Fleet essentially spent the rest of the war in port, its ships and the morale of its sailors rotting. It did not sortie again until April 1918. The submarine became the focus of German naval warfare, and in the fall of 1916 Scheer actually sent a battle squadron to cover the attempted rescue of a U-boat grounded on the Danish coast. When the Kaiser reproached him, Scheer replied that the future of German naval strategy resided in the submarine campaign, and that the Fleet's sole task lay in protecting their departure and return.

As Halpern notes, "the role of capital ships and submarines had been reversed."[33] This role reversal proved ironic because the prewar Anglo–German naval race had revolved around the building of dreadnoughts, monstrous battleships, and battlecruisers. Now, in 1916, both powers hesitated to risk these expensive, powerful giants in waters where mines abounded and submarines lurked, and for good reason. On 5 June the cruiser *Hampshire*, on the way to Russia with Secretary of State for War Lord Kitchener aboard, fell prey to a mine laid by a German submarine off the Orkney Islands. Kitchener, stalwart to the end, stood impassively on deck as the cruiser sank. Historians have made much of the eclipse of the battleship by the aircraft carrier in the Second World War. That eclipse had begun, to some extent, with the arrival of the submarine in the war of 1914–18, as a threat to merchant shipping which only smaller, lighter vessels could protect, and to the capital ships themselves.

Submarine sinkings rose rapidly in 1916 to more than 200,000 tons monthly. Even after the German Navy launched its restricted campaign in October under the "cruiser rules," which required advance warning of merchant ships before attack, submarines took an average toll of 175,000 tons of shipping. The British had compensated for earlier losses by commandeering a million tons of enemy shipping for their own use, but their production of merchant ships had declined to half a million tons in 1916 because of the priority given to naval vessels and war munitions. An average of ninety U-boats were at sea during these months, and they suffered very few losses, although, observing the rules of cruiser warfare, they sank three-quarters of their prey with gunfire. The U.S. government protested when

American citizens perished; the Germans replied with excuses, and grew bolder.

The German *Deutschland*, a long-range and supposedly merchant vessel, made two round trips to the United States in the second half of 1916. U.53, under its commander Hans Rose, visited Newport, Rhode Island, in October, and hosted American naval officers from the Atlantic Fleet's destroyer force. Incredibly, Rose sank five ships in international waters off the Nantucket coast, while his erstwhile visitors watched and rescued survivors. Rose, after nearly colliding with a destroyer, then had the temerity to ask another to move away from a Dutch freighter so that he could torpedo it![34]

By the end of 1916, German naval and military commanders increasingly contemplated the resumption of unrestricted submarine warfare. A German naval memorandum of 22 December by Chief of the Admiralty Staff Adm. von Holtzendorff summarized the reasons. Germany needed to win the war by the fall of 1917 to avoid exhaustion, and England held the key to victory. Victory on land seemed unlikely, but five months of unrestricted submarine warfare would bring England to its knees. The navy based its calculations on detailed statistical analysis of England's vital imports, shipping tonnage, even international wheat harvests, by economic experts. Ultimately, their calculations would prove erroneous, but at the time they provided final justification for the navy and the German High Command to take the ultimate gamble, and risk United States' entry into the war against Germany. Germany would have to begin the unrestricted campaign no later than 1 February, in order to achieve a victorious peace by 1 August, before the next harvest. The government would have to make the crucial decision – one on which the very outcome of the war would depend – early in the new year.

THE HOME FRONTS. "TOTAL" MOBILIZATION FOR "TOTAL WAR"

Great Britain. "To a knock-out"

As the British Army assumed a major role on the Western Front in 1916, at home the mobilization of British society and economy accelerated rapidly. The promulgation of the Military Service Bill on 27 January 1916 introduced conscription of single men between 18 and 41 years of age to Great Britain, with the exception of Ireland. It allowed exemptions for ministers, the unfit, essential war-workers, and conscientious objectors. Exemption for the last group proved rather remarkable in the atmosphere of xenophobia that reigned in England in 1916, where the press encouraged rabid anti-German sentiments and the police searched everywhere for spies and enemy aliens, often equating dens of moral laxity and vice, such as cafés and houses of prostitution, with havens of evil subversion. What had initially appeared to be an impossible infringement upon personal liberty in Britain now proceeded virtually unopposed. A second conscription act in April applied to married men.

As men were called up, women replaced them in the factories, another significant indication of wartime mobilization. In 1916 the Home Office ordered all munitions factories to appoint a welfare supervisor, a woman of the middle or upper-middle class. The employer and his middle-class supervisor tended to view working-class women as children, lacking discipline and self-control. The supervisor strove to inculcate middle-class and feminine virtues in her lower-class charges, and to improve discipline and increase output. However, these supervisors clashed with the craftsmen in control of the plant; consequently British employers declined to institute the supervisors on a long-term basis.

Employment in munitions factories entailed hard and dangerous work. Female munitions workers contended with the toxic chemicals tetryl and TNT. Although less toxic than TNT, tetryl turned the skin yellow, an early symptom of toxic jaundice, a disease that killed hundreds of workers during and after the war and could lead to fatal disorders of the digestive, circulatory, and nervous systems.[35] Prolonged exposure to TNT, black powder, cordite, acid fumes, varnish or aircraft "dope," and asbestos could produce potentially deadly conditions, especially given the long hours and exhausting work. Common on-the-job hazards included nasal bleeding, burnt throats, skin rashes, blood-poisoning, severe abdominal pains and nausea, which doctors dismissed because they had no cure for toxic jaundice in any case.

Many of these working-class women had previously toiled as household domestics or in textile factories. Now, in return for their new and important contribution to the war effort, they earned higher wages and the satisfaction of a job well done. Governmental officials also recognized women's contribution to the war effort. Minister of Munitions Edwin Montagu proclaimed in August 1916 "our Armies have been saved and victory assured by women in the munition factories."[36] Yet the rewards in no way compensated for the dangers which women bravely encountered daily in their often abysmal working conditions, in an England under siege by sea and air.

German submarines sank British shipping, while cruisers raided British coastal towns. England in 1916 no longer remained an island immune to war on its soil, and nothing brought this fact home more than the aerial menace. Early in the year German airships reached beyond London to the west of England and then to Scotland with impunity given the inadequate state of Britain's anti-aircraft defenses. The casualties of 200 or 300 civilians they produced appear modest compared to what was occurring on the war fronts or what would occur in the Second World War, yet these unprecedented direct attacks on civilians from the air engendered sentiments of fear and awe in their targets. English cities and towns and their civilian inhabitants, like their continental counterparts, became direct targets of military airpower. The military resented the diversion of anti-aircraft guns and aviation squadrons from the Western Front to protect the homeland from German depredations. At the same time unrest exploded within the empire, and very close to home.

The war provided the time and the opportunity for the Easter Rising of the Irish Republican revolutionaries in Dublin. As early as the fall of 1914 nationalists plotted an uprising, perhaps with German aid. The raising of three Irish divisions for Kitchener's New Army – the 10th, which fought at Gallipoli, the 16th, a Nationalist and Catholic brigade, and the 36th (Ulster) Division of Unionist Protestants—left the most militant Republicans at home.

By early 1916, the militants had decided to stage their rebellion at Easter. The Military Service Bill on 27 January 1916, which excluded Ireland from conscription, appeased the Irish Nationalists but angered the Ulster Unionists, loyal to king and country. It did not affect the rebels' plans. Rather than conduct guerrilla operations, they chose to fight an orthodox military battle in Dublin with uniformed troops in order to make a symbolic statement as a properly sovereign and belligerent state. The rebels planned on the substantial support of German arms, military officers, and a submarine. Sir Roger Casement had gone to Germany at the beginning of the war to enlist German support for an Irish Brigade to fight the British, followed by another Irish emissary in 1915.

Although the German High Command had supported the idea of an Irish rebellion since 1914, the Germans sent only a small shipment of arms by boat. They returned the disappointed Casement, who now determined to prevent the uprising in the absence of adequate German support, by submarine. The British intercepted Casement and the arms before the uprising and, caring little for fine distinctions of belligerency in a world war, blamed the Germans for fomenting the uprising. The army crushed the rebels in a week, ultimately using artillery to shell them into submission. Civilians constituted most of the killed and wounded. A military governor imposed martial law, court-martialed the leaders and executed fifteen of them in ten days, a deed that alienated further the Irish nationalist population.

Ironically, in Easter week the 16th Division suffered more casualties on the Western Front than rebels and British forces in Dublin combined. Then, on 1 July, the first day of the Somme, the Ulster Division went over the top to cries of "No Surrender," and lost one-third of its 15,000 men in two days. This attack and the severe losses in the Ulster community marked the Ulstermen as unswervingly loyal to the empire, in contrast to the disloyal and rebellious Nationalists. Thomas Hennessey believed that the Somme "symbolised the psychological partition of Ulster Unionism from the rest of the island" and its union with Britain.[37] Although the Irish Rebellion ranks

as a major event in Irish history, it proved less so to an England venturing
further into the maelstrom of world war.

In Britain the Somme offensive yielded monstrous casualty lists, but not
the great advances that initial reports heralded, as the struggle continued
unabated into the fall. In 1916 the slaughter of young men at the front
awakened male fears that the proportion of the sexes would be altered for a
generation, that the gains of women came at the expense of men. Front
soldiers' writings reflected a stark division between the fighting and home
fronts and their anger and hostility toward the latter, epitomized by women
in the poetry of, for example, Siegfried Sassoon.[38]

The romantic poetry of the early war exemplified by Rupert Brooke
yielded after the Somme to the disillusioned rage of young junior officers
such as Sassoon, Wilfred Owen, Robert Graves, and the young Jewish
working-class soldier Isaac Rosenberg. Owen and Rosenberg would die at the
front in 1918, Owen on 4 November, seven days before the armistice. Graves
and Sassoon, the leader and hero of the young war poets, suffered wounds
during their wartime service. Their poetry depicted graphically the execrable
conditions and wasteful slaughter in which they and their men lived and died.
They condemned their incompetent generals and staff officers who remained
distant from the trenches and whose fatuous plans of attack sentenced a
generation of youth to death. "Fat old men" and "harlots" called the young
men of England to defend them, and lured them to their deaths, but at least
the recruits would "learn/To live and die with honest men" in
"martyrdom" and "gallant sacrifice."[39] In Sassoon's poem 'Blighters,' he
wishes that a tank would clear out the audience and "the prancing ranks of
harlots" of a London music-hall whose choruses about tanks "mock the
riddled corpses round Bapaume."[40]

Yet, for those women who served as nurses or ambulance drivers in close
proximity to the front, the appreciation they gained of the horrors of warfare
overcame the disjunction between front and rear and the home front's lack
of true knowledge of conditions in the lines. Vera Brittain's service as a nurse
brought her into contact with horribly wounded soldiers, and such experience
erased some of the experiential differences separating soldiers and women
civilians, as soldiers and nurses felt equally estranged from home.

The condition of their wounded charges left nurses with no illusions about
the glory of war or man as savage predator, only the reality of its searing
effect on men's bodies. Their recollections stand unsurpassed in the graphic
nature of their depictions of the human wreckage war left in its wake. Brittain
described "the man with the hand blown off & the stump untrimmed up, &
the other man with the arm off, & a great hole in his back one could get one's
hand into, . . ." and later, "men without faces, without eyes, without limbs,
men almost disembowelled, men with hideous truncated stumps of bodies."[41]

Nurses witnessed and handled "limbs which shrapnel had torn about and swollen into abnormal shapes, from which yellow pus poured when the bandages were removed, which were caked with brown blood, and in whose gangrenous flesh loose bits of bone had to be sought for painfully with probes." One recalled "the jaw-case, who, when his innumerable and complicated bandages were removed, revealed flat holes plugged with gauze where a nose had been, and pendulous, shapeless lips." An ambulance driver noted the "stench" of her ambulance each morning as she cleaned out "the pools of stale vomit," the "blood and mud and vermin," and the excreta of the previous day's passengers.[42]

For these women, just as for the soldiers they nursed, the atrocious became the norm, and callousness necessarily blunted their sensibilities to endure such trauma. As Mary Borden recalled of a patient whose brain came off in her hands when she removed a bandage from his head: "When the dresser came back I said: 'His brain came off on the bandage.' 'Where have you put it?' 'I put it in the pail under the table.' 'It's only half his brain,' he said, looking into the skull. 'The rest is here.'"[43] Borden continued, "There are no men here. . . . There are heads and knees and mangled testicles. There are chests with holes as big as your fist, and pulpy thighs, shapeless; and stumps where legs once were fastened."[44]

Women in these circumstances existed in a different world from civilians who saw war represented in propaganda as the violation of women by barbaric men. They saw at first hand the mutilation of men in mass industrial warfare, and men as vulnerable and violated victims of war. In the process they became more relaxed about men's physicality and sex, as they developed a sense of shared participation in the war at the front.[45] Nevertheless, the closest most civilians came to such horrors were the maimed returning veterans or the German air raids that began again in the longer darkness of the fall after a summer's hiatus.

German airships returned to encounter much improved anti-aircraft defenses, particularly more powerful airplanes armed with machine-guns loaded with explosive bullets to ignite the Zeppelin's gasbags of inflammable hydrogen. German raiders from September through November claimed fewer victims and lost six Zeppelins, whose flaming descents buoyed British onlookers' morale with what the magazine *Punch* termed "the most thrilling aerial spectacle ever witnessed."[46]

The British now rejected peace for victory, as Britain prepared for, as Lloyd George intoned in September, a fight to the finish – "to a knock-out."[47] For a short time in the fall the government sent parties of soldiers to "round up" likely inductees from male haunts, and later it occasionally "combed out" fit men from occupations other than munitions and mining. In this atmosphere Herbert Asquith, detached and dispassionate except for his daily two hours of bridge, began to appear a less well-suited leader for the harsh and difficult times ahead. The Irish Rebellion, the investigations of parliamentary committees of inquiry into the abortive military campaigns at Gallipoli and in Mesopotamia – the latter leading to a Conservative political slogan "Mesopotamia and Mess-up-at-home-here" – all underscored Asquith's waning power.

One politician had certainly approached the problems of wartime vigorously and successfully – David Lloyd George. Lloyd George's reference to a "knock-out" epitomized his ability to capture the public sentiment in his utterances, while his success as Minister of Munitions and in other roles demonstrated his combination of ruthless determination and decisiveness and clever, even wily abilities of negotiation. Lloyd George certainly objected to the way Haig and Robertson squandered men on the Western Front and said so in the fall, at which time press lord Northcliffe attacked Lloyd George and warned him that he would "break" him if he got out of line again.[48]

Yet the mounting problems – inflation and shortages at home, submarines at sea, Russian and Rumanian defeats in the east, and stalemate in the west – did not abate. At the end of the first week in December 1916, various political machinations indicated that Asquith no longer had parliamentary backing and Lloyd George had gained the support of a majority coalition. The Welsh dynamo, the man of the hour, became prime minister.

France. Politics with a vengeance, and social turmoil

Politics as usual, but now with a vengeance engendered by the seriousness of wartime crisis, returned to French government by 1916. The French Parliament used its commissions to extract information from the governing Cabinet. In particular Georges Clemenceau's Senate Commission of the Army demanded that Prime Minister Briand and Minister of War Galliéni appear before it constantly. The elderly Gen. Galliéni, quite ill by the spring, resigned as Minister of War in March and died in May. Parliament worried about the prosecution of the war at the front and about the government's close links to the munitions industry in the rear.

The Undersecretariat of State for Munitions under socialist Albert Thomas collaborated with the *comité des forges*, a private consortium or metals trust controlled by industrialists but financed by the state, to control the flow of all metals to French factories. Already by mid-1916 Thomas had officially charged the *comité* as the sole purchasing agent for metals in response to British insistence upon a stronger internal organization of the French economy to facilitate their trade partnership. This unity of ministry and *comité* originated in the prewar affiliation of civil servants in the Ministry of War with the *comité*. This close relationship occasioned criticism and opposition from the government and independent producers. The Senate Finance Commission took umbrage at Thomas's decision to advance money to the armaments firm Schneider to restart a German-owned metallurgical plant at Caen early in 1916. Nevertheless, the *comité*'s position remained unassailable, because it fulfilled crucial and indispensable functions in France's government-industrial structure.

Louis Loucheur, a private munitions manufacturer, emerged as another key figure in government–industrial relations in France in 1916. To combat the critical shortage of heavy artillery in early 1916, the dynamic and innovative Loucheur proposed a bold plan using American equipment and unskilled labor, in particular untapped female labor, to increase production, despite the opposition of skilled labor. Women who entered the labor force came from the working class, were usually married and older than their British counterparts, and had been working in the textile industry or domestic service. Their factory work was "heavy, dirty . . . laborious" and potentially "quite dangerous." When the Billaud grenade factory blew up in 1916, workers at a neighboring factory counted 125 corpses and horribly wounded women and children who were certain to die.[49] From 1914 through 1917 workers in war industry worked thirteen days on rotating shifts of eleven or twelve hours with a rest on the fourteenth day. The long shifts contributed to high accident rates, typically crushed or severed fingers and hands.[50] Strict discipline reigned in war industry, and the plants ranged from Citroen's modern Javel plant to dark and dingy buildings. Women workers received less pay than their male counterparts for the same work and their male supervisors harassed them frequently.

By 1916 the workforce in France's rapidly expanding war industry comprised 30 percent mobilized men, 30 percent civilian men, 30 percent new workers, mainly women, and 10 percent foreign or colonial labor. Colonial workers performed the most arduous and worst paid jobs, and the government segregated them from the other workers in order to prevent sexual contact between the women and colonials, anathema to the colonial ethos. Despite such separation, increasing numbers of marriages between French women and colonial workers confirmed the government's fears of interracial relationships.[51]

The government prevented contact between French women and Senegalese soldiers wintering behind the lines in the south of France by segregating the soldiers from the French population. The increasing numbers of Senegalese arriving in France had just endured an arduous, often terrifying, and literally sickening voyage from Dakar, during which some died from dehydration caused by seasickness. Some French officers confined the soldiers to the ships' sweltering holds and occasionally chained them like slaves. Once, Blaise Diagne himself, accompanied by two commandants, met a ship in Bordeaux, learned of the soldiers' plight, confined their lieutenant to the hold where he had imprisoned his men for six days, and then arrested him. The Africans had never seen an African dispense justice to a white man before.[52]

Once the Senegalese *tirailleurs* arrived in France, they remained confined to their camps, segregated even from other Africans whom the French did not consider "warrior races." The more daring individuals who attempted to visit the brothels of towns and cities often never returned. Even marching through towns to cheering crowds, white officers often slapped their charges hard to keep them facing forward. Isolated, far from home, the *tirailleurs*, the great majority of Senegalese, found that they had come for one purpose alone, to fight and die for France, often without ever seeing any of the country, much less the glittering lights of Paris, God's city.[53] In contrast, the Senegalese *originaires* joined predominantly French units, often with Martiniquais, Guadeloupeans, and some North Africans, enjoyed more liberal leave policies, and counted French soldiers, families, and women among their friends.

While the government restricted African contact with the French, it also attempted to counter widespread prejudices about Africans that stemmed from imperialist attitudes with a flood of positive propaganda. Now the *tirailleurs* appeared as brave and loyal overgrown children, although the military segregated them in camps and hospitals, taught them only pidgin French, which reinforced the childlike image, and made every effort to keep them away from French women, even the *marraines de guerre* that every soldier had on the home front. Yet *tirailleur* noncommissioned officers or soldiers decorated for bravery often developed the same relationships with French women and families as the *originaires*. Such experiences contrasted greatly with their prior lives in the colonies. The Senegalese soldiers observed that Frenchmen from the south and from Paris accepted them more readily, but that Corsicans responded to them in openly racist and hostile fashion and occasionally shot Africans whom they saw accompanying French women.[54]

In the midst of this social turmoil, by June Verdun preoccupied Parliament, which monitored and criticized the government in secret sessions, as the press gained access to increasing information about the course of the war. The Chamber of Deputies voted to subject the war industries to direct parliamentary control. Briand refused, and in July the Senate voted that the government would collaborate with the commissions and Parliament in its control of industry. Thomas also began to rely on Loucheur for increased production of artillery and the formulation of a heavy artillery production program in July 1916. The crisis over Verdun prompted secret sessions of the Chamber of Deputies, which met as a committee of the whole to interpellate the government about its wartime policies, a process which historian John Godfrey labeled an "extreme form of the pre-war parliamentary method of controlling governments through harassment."[55]

As 1916 drew to a close, parliamentary discontent with the prosecution of the war led to further meetings and changes in the cabinet. Socialist propaganda from the April 1916 international conference at Kienthal, whose manifesto demanded that socialists cease participation in governments, voting war credits and take direct action, had had no effect in any country, including France. However, the notion of a peace without victory had some appeal, and despite governmental efforts to repress "defeatist" propaganda, President Poincaré believed in November that the defeatists were gaining ground every day.[56] Briand's government was under attack for its policies in the Balkans and discontent with Joffre as commander-in-chief. Other issues, such as high munitions industry profits, transportation crisis, and raw materials shortages, led to the war's longest closed door session of the Chamber of Deputies, from 28 November to 7 December 1916. These secret sessions forced the resignation of the Briand Cabinet in November 1916, but Briand received a vote of confidence with the proviso that he reform his Cabinet. He selected a smaller Cabinet, with Gen. Lyautey as Minister of War, and created a new Ministry of Supply to deal with the increasing difficulties of provisioning the cities, in particular with coal, as a harsh winter approached.

Certain key individuals, such as Albert Thomas, continued in the new Cabinet. Thomas headed the new Ministry of Armament and War Production created from the former Under-Secretariat of State for Artillery and Munitions on 31 December 1916. Loucheur became Thomas's under-secretary in charge of artillery production. In December Thomas formally proposed the appointment of Gen. Robert Nivelle as French army commander to replace Joffre, a suggestion that Briand approved and that both would live to regret.

Significant developments in the cultural realm at the end of the year exerted a longer lasting impact than the shifts in parliamentary power. French author Romain Rolland, writing from Switzerland, maintained a pacifist stance in a series of articles collected under the title *Au-dessus de la Mêlée* (*Above the Strife*), and despite French hostility toward his work, he received the Nobel Prize for Literature in 1916. Yet a novel that received the *Prix Goncourt* that same year and would become one of the most enduring war novels of all time overshadowed Rolland's work.

Henri Barbusse's famed novel *Le Feu* (The Fire), sometimes described as the war's greatest novel, presented the war from the perspective of a squad of soldiers. The work appeared first in serial form in the journal *L'Oeuvre* between August and November, and then as a book in December. Its tremendous success then and after the war rendered it a significant event in wartime culture. It was particularly unusual in that other great novels and memoirs of the war did not appear until several years after the end of the conflict.

A leftist in 1914, Barbusse conceived of the conflict as a "social war" against monarchy, militarism, and imperialism, a struggle for the emancipation of the world. The 41-year-old journalist and novelist served at the front during 1915 and received two citations for bravery before illness invalided him to the rear. His optimism in early 1915 gave way to hostility toward the command and a sense of a stupid war fought for vague reasons. He carried with him an indelible experience of the horror of war, in particular in his last tour of duty as a sick stretcher-bearer. Barbusse spent 1916 as a secretary on the army staff and as a patient in hospital, where he wrote *Le Feu* in six months. He received a medical discharge early in 1917.

Although the message of the book, clear in its final chapter, appears anti-militarist, internationalist, and revolutionary, neither the censors nor the reading public seemed to care. What they did notice and appreciate was the realism of the work, of the violence and brutality of the war, which enabled civilians to believe that for the first time they were witnessing the suffering of the soldiers.[57] Barbusse's soldiers feel marginalized, on the outside; so they experience the home front as "alienating and upsetting"; and deem women on the inside, often unfaithful.

Wartime male commentators considered *la femme moderne* "a creation of the war" which had "an enormous influence on young girls and young women.[58] Wartime memoirs and fiction showed that the soldiers tended to view the world in terms of dichotomies and polarization, opposing a "male" battle front to a "female" home front. Trench journals from 1915 to 1918 depicted a home front populated by civilians "indifferent" to and even "scornful" of the soldiers' existence, leading a life of luxury and corruption in Paris in contrast to their heroic existence of deprivation and death, and epitomized by war profiteers and loose women.

Ironically, men, who had always been the "insiders" in society, as soldiers now felt "outside," confined to the mud of a trench line on the edge of civilization, while women were now "inside" assuming their jobs and responsibilities. These soldiers responded anxiously to what they perceived as changing gender roles and the war's liberation of women. Confronted with the emasculating effect of the war, they believed female recognition of their sacrifice essential to their self-respect and sense of power.[59] Thus the image of the "good" woman became so crucial to them and that of the "bad" so threatening. Images of wife and mother superseded all others in trench literature. The traditional woman, obedient and submissive, reaffirmed the soldiers' manhood and thereby "sustained both conventional notions of femininity *and* the war effort."[60]

Sexual infidelity epitomized female betrayal, as liberated, promiscuous women assumed the prewar role of men, while their men suffered and died in the trenches. Such wartime notions would survive into the postwar era and influence later cultural and social attitudes.

Italy. Industrialization, unrest, and the state

In Italy the war accelerated industrial growth and led to a transformation from small- to large-scale industry, as major companies expanded enormously. The workforce at Fiat, for example, rose from 4,000 to 40,500 workers. The direction of industrial mobilization by the military resembled German direction of the domestic war effort, but mobilization stressed the organization of groups of industrialists in a fashion similar to France as well as Germany. The military bureaucracy presided over mobilization with the consultation of regional committees of representatives of industry and labor, and focussed primarily on disciplining labor to prevent disturbances.

Despite discontent among the workers, the absence of major strikes and unrest of 1915 continued through 1916. Short, small strikes occurred, but the harsh discipline imposed through the military penal code, which conflated negligence and sabotage or defiance and insubordination, certainly helped quell any outbursts. The number of military workers rose to 40 percent of male workers by the end of 1916, and even women workers endured some military discipline. Although limited to their job site, they could strike without the severe punishments that military workers received. The labor market's demands also exceeded supply starting in mid-1916, necessitating the employment of increasing numbers of women, regardless of the general antipathy toward female industrial labor and specific fears, evident in other countries, of lowering labor costs and enabling the induction of more males into the army.

The intervention of the state did benefit the workers, because in 1916 it regulated overtime and night wages, established the ten-hour day as a normal work day, and prevented industrialists from arbitrarily reducing "job-work rates," which they invariably did when introducing new work processes. Nevertheless, wartime legislation against individual and civil liberties, including freedom of speech, and the military control of large areas of the country, beyond control in the factories, rendered Italy one of the most repressive wartime regimes.[61]

The stalemate on the Isonzo, compounded by the shock of the Austrian offensive in May, proved the Salandra government's undoing. Although Salandra and army commander Cadorna agreed on an authoritarian and repressive approach to the war, they disagreed on which of them, civilian or military, should be directing the war effort. Salandra openly criticized Cadorna after the Austrian Trentino offensive, but the open rift backfired, and Salandra lost a parliamentary vote of confidence on 10 June and resigned two days later. His successor, 78-year-old Paolo Boselli, formed a coalition government that excluded only revolutionary socialists, but the very reason for his choice – that he posed no challenge to other political leaders – ensured that he could bring no unity or direction to the Italian government. Cadorna, meanwhile, rabidly attacked Interior Minister Vittorio Orlando's refusal to crush internal opposition.

Germany. "Hold on"

The Battle of Verdun affected not only the German Army that fought it, but the German home front as well, a change often summarized in the shift from the "Spirit of 1914" to the slogan *"Durchhalten,"* or "See it through." The atmosphere on the home front became more depressed, as people became increasingly weary of the interminable war.[62]

By 1916 German urban consumers clamored for centralized control of food supplies to assure equitable distribution, and in early spring the Prussian War Ministry responded with the creation of a civilian War Food Office. The public looked to the military administration, whose first concern lay with supply for the army, to meet civilian needs. The Food Office, however, lacked the power to enforce any regulations it established, and by the summer urban working- and lower-middle-class consumers, suffering from malnutrition, demonstrated for food and peace. For reasons of social status and custom of in-house dining, urban women refused to patronize public soup kitchens, despite worsening conditions after the failure of the potato harvest in 1916. In this atmosphere, the public viewed the rise to power of Hindenburg and Ludendorff as an answer to their prayers for a "military food dictatorship" that would feed them as well as the army.

It proved ironic that Hindenburg, whose government depended on the very interests – powerful conservative industrial and agrarian forces – that profited most from the war and demanded a victory of conquest and annexations, now of necessity sought to institute "war socialism," or measures to ensure more equity for the poor. The urban poor condemned the urban rich, whose money and status gave them superior access to food; the urban population damned the rural, which still received more food even under the ration system; and many began to attack "the Jew," the middleman, the shirker, as the source of all their woes.

This resort to the age-old scapegoat, stoked by radical right-wing propaganda, led to the infamous "Jew Count" in the fall of 1916, in which the government and army undertook to determine if Jews were serving nation and army. They were, but the very fact of the "count" indicated the depth of the problem, which posed unanticipated issues for the legitimacy of the state. After all, if the state did not solve the food problem, then was it not an "inner enemy" like the Jews?

With Col. Max Bauer as an *éminence grise* in the realm of mobilization, the new high command, or OHL (*Oberste Heeresleitung*), promised total mobilization to win the war. In August the Hindenburg Program demanded a doubling and trebling of war production, with the belief, as Bauer stated, that the war would be over by mid-1917, presumably as a result of unrestricted submarine warfare. The OHL sought to pre-empt the Prussian War Ministry's control of budget and procurement through the formation of a War Office on 1 November under the command of Gen. Wilhelm Groener. The War Ministry had sought to husband Germany's scarce resources, but now the radical militarists in charge of Germany, in alliance with powerful industrialists who had longed for even more profits, threw caution to the winds and discarded all restraints.

In order to achieve this concentration on munitions production, compulsory civilian mobilization, as embodied in the Auxiliary Service Law of 5 December, became the order of the day. To achieve this mobilization of all males between the ages of 17 and 60, Groener, much to the dismay of conservatives and industrialists, conciliated labor and center-left parliamentary forces. The monarchist Groener, a realist who understood that Germany could still lose the war, wanted union support for the monarchical state in case of defeat. Consequently, the government for the first time recognized the unions and their right to negotiate with employers, and acknowledged the importance of Parliament, the Reichstag, in passing the law.

The call of the Hindenburg Program in the fall of 1916 for "total mobilization" temporarily salvaged the urban food situation because of the consequent demand for women workers, who could then eat in factory canteens, which carried none of the social stigma of food kitchens. Workers in the armaments industry received special rations, which catapulted munitions workers, including the hundreds of thousands of women in their ranks, to a more privileged position than the lower-middle class, which complained of these "unfair" circumstances. Yet those who could not work, namely the sick, the old, infants and children, and pregnant women, now slowly starved, as photographs of emaciated and stunted children attest. English and French governments valued women as mothers; Germany's new military government valued them as workers. As Hindenburg opined in a private memorandum of September 1916, "Whoever does not work shall not eat."[63]

As the end of the year approached, the system of rationing encompassed all essential foods and fuels, and those who could not afford black market prices had to survive on a fraction of their prewar diet. A severe coal shortage meant that homes went unheated or inadequately so at best. What housing existed fell into increasing disrepair, and shortages of building materials precluded constructing new homes. People sported clothing of "natural silk," a combination of paper, cardboard, and cotton. Juvenile delinquency sky-rocketed, as the family structure collapsed in the absence of older brothers, fathers, and working mothers. Youth gained independence by earning money in the factories and often spending it in mischievous ways.

Christmas became ever grimmer and dimmer, as losses struck home to more and more families in drearily lit and poorly heated homes on darkened streets. Of course, on "Sunday excursions" urban consumers with sufficient money ventured into the country to buy goods directly from farmers, while the wealthy could purchase illicit goods on the black market, retreat to their country estates, or even vacation in Switzerland. Despite these latter exceptions, total war had come to Germany with a vengeance, and with it an abysmally cold and unforgiving winter.

Austria-Hungary. Death in Vienna

By 1916 exhaustion reigned as the dominant sentiment in Austria-Hungary, with "polarization, radicalization, and totalization" the dominant trends, according to historian Manfried Rauchensteiner.[64] The elites believed the situation hopeless, while the hungry and angry masses demonstrated and struck over food shortages. Growing privation and its effects in Austria in 1916 did not escape the notice of government officials. The railroad minister termed the situation "anarchic"; the labor minister, "dangerous"; while the finance minister wanted the army to suppress the unrest and strikes.[65] The harvest in late summer 1916 boded ill for the food situation in Austria and ensured that dependence on Hungary would increase. Farmland lay uncultivated in various areas of the monarchy with the induction of peasants into the army and the flight of populations from the war in regions such as Galicia. Imports of grain and animals from Hungary continued their stark annual decline, and in the winter of 1916–17 Austrians had to slaughter horses to save fodder. The cities had exhausted their food reserves. The situation had become critical by September, as the government resorted to commandeering food. Food riots erupted throughout Austria in November.

German dominance in military matters and dependence upon Hungary for food supplies threatened Austria equally, as its government confronted an internal polity riven with dissent. The Austrians blamed Hungarian Minister President Tisza for his determined protection of Hungary's interests, rather than the dualistic governmental structure engendering the monarchy's difficulties. Tisza and the Hungarian Parliament had certainly preserved Hungarian unity and erected customs barriers to safeguard a disproportionate amount of Hungary's farm products. However, Tisza also defended Stürgkh and Conrad and the AOK against Hungarian accusations of discriminating against Hungarian soldiers.

In contrast, Conrad condemned Stürgkh for his closeness to the traitorous Czechs and blamed him almost exclusively for the difficult conditions. German ambassador Tschirsky expressed Germany's vital interest in establishing a stronger government in Austria-Hungary. Demands from the Germans and his own military, from representatives of the various nationalities and of a hungry population, pressured Stürgkh to recall the Austrian Parliament. He resisted, fearing that Parliament might provide the stage for the disintegration of the monarchy, and knowing that the Emperor opposed it. All clamored for Stürgkh's head.

In these increasingly desperate circumstances, two calamitous events marked the waning months of 1916. On Sunday, 20 October, the Austrian Minister President dined at noon at his usual Viennese hotel. Friedrich Adler, a German Austrian who believed in international socialism and the son of the Social Democratic leader Viktor Adler, had contemplated committing a political murder for a year and a half, to protest the war's limits upon freedom and the deaths of millions. Mental illness ran in the family, yet for Adler political motives alone sufficed to explain his impending deed. He watched Stürgkh dine for nearly two hours, then walked over to his table and shot him three times. The near-sighted Stürgkh undoubtedly never recognized his assailant, and the war had claimed, however indirectly, another victim.

The assassination of the Minister President depressed an already ailing Emperor Franz Josef. However, everyone else worried more about his successor. The army command desired someone from their ranks, but two days after the assassination the Emperor turned to another civilian, his finance minister, to form a Cabinet of administrators. The AOK expected the new government to take radical measures to improve food supplies, but a new Food Office lacked authority. Emperors Wilhelm and Franz Josef announced the postwar creation of a Polish monarchy, primarily to lure Polish troops to their side in the fight against Russia. Then, on 21 November, Emperor Franz Josef, after sixty-eight years on the throne, died. The vilified Minister President and the beloved Emperor, who had reigned longer than most people lived, died within two months of one another.

In the midst of crisis, a new Emperor, Karl Franz Josef, ascended the throne. Not particularly intelligent or industrious, this shallow, immature young man impressed those around him as unaware of the difficulty and danger of the circumstances.[66] The old emperor had delegated political and military responsibility and reigned above the fray. In contrast, Karl planned to intervene in political matters and exercise his personal authority in Austria and Hungary, reminiscent of the fashion in which a young Emperor Wilhelm II had ruled Germany in the 1890s after dismissing his Chancellor, Otto von Bismarck. Karl sought to accomplish three things: to fight for peace; to lead a reformed and consolidated empire out of the war; and to cast off the German yoke. He acted hastily and imprudently. He forbade further negotiations for military and commercial treaties with Germany, although Austria-Hungary could not survive long without German support.

As of November, the Hindenburg Program had just included Austria-Hungary in German full-scale mobilization. Ironically, Austro-Hungarian armaments production had finally sufficed to meet its needs in 1916, and now the Hindenburg Program sought to double that output. Austria-Hungary would have to allocate iron and steel to munitions production and away from transport, where severe shortages already threatened to derail the entire economy, and in general to exhaust its raw materials rapidly. As in Germany, the Hindenburg Program's goals remained unrealistic and uncoordinated. By the beginning of 1917 the Austro-Hungarian government realized that the program would not only fail, but would also end in chaos.[67]

The Central Powers had decided to deliver a peace offer, but only after launching total mobilization in the Hindenburg Program in order to demonstrate their will to undertake total war. After the fall of Rumania enabled them to bargain from a position of apparent strength, they sent a peace note on 12 December, which the Entente rejected on 7 January 1917. The Central Powers insisted upon the current status quo; the Entente, viewing the Germans as aggressors, insisted upon the status quo *ante bellum*. The blood-bath would continue.

Meanwhile, Karl replaced the old regime with his own, selecting a new Minister President in late December. However, this made little difference, as the new Emperor's wife Zita assumed the role of his closest advisor. The German OHL responded by increasing its leverage directly over the AOK. On 30 December Karl was crowned Emperor in Budapest, irrefutable evidence that the war had shifted the balance in the Austro-Hungarian monarchy to Hungary, as the Dual Monarchy staggered into the new year.

Russia. Anarchy

W. Bruce Lincoln described the mood in the Russian capital Petrograd in February and March 1916 as a "pall of depressed indifference."[68] If a pall hung over the capital, the condition in the overwhelmingly rural empire in spring proved worse. The army had inducted about 50 percent of males between the ages of 19 and 45, while many others had left to work in mines or urban factories. Fewer than one man in ten remained to work the fields, leaving women of all ages to shoulder the burden.

Inductions through early 1915 had reduced rural overpopulation; now a serious agrarian labor shortage threatened the food supply at its very root. Refugees, prisoners-of-war, and even soldiers on temporary leave had to help with the spring sowing. In 1915 peasants had hoarded their bountiful grain harvests until agents from municipalities and the army competed to buy and stock grain at exorbitant prices, actually creating an urban food shortage. Now the peasants became increasingly restless, rioting and looting shops because whatever money they made did not suffice to buy goods in short supply at inflationary prices.

In urban Russia factory workers, many of them straight from rural life, demonstrated for better pay and working conditions in the midst of inflation. Factory owners compensated for the comparatively low productivity of their unskilled male and female laborers by hiring many more workers. Shortages of plant foremen meant that these workers, particularly in armaments factories, performed dangerous work under at best indirect supervision.

Gigantic munitions factories employed tens of thousands of workers –
Putilov, the largest, 30,000 – in conditions that made the factories a more
dangerous breeding ground for radicalism and revolution than they had been
in the revolution of 1905. The metalworkers, the labor elite for their high
wages, were also the most literate and the most radical.

Although many workers banded together to form food cooperatives, they
lived in abysmally crowded and unsanitary conditions, especially the coal-
miners. Hunger, disease, and accidents plagued workers and their families,
exacerbated by high rates of drunkenness among adults and youth. Although
the government had banned the sale of liquor in wartime, plentiful vodka
supplies in the cities precluded any competition from moonshine. Similar to
other countries, workers in Russian industries deemed non-essential to the
war effort suffered a serious decline in their real wages, but in Russia even the
metalworkers' wage increases did not offset rising prices, and longer and
longer lines outside shops attested to the shortages of essential goods.

Strikers in 1915 had frequently confronted police and soldiers in bloody
riots, but in the fall of 1916 soldiers began to join the strikers. Although the
labor party, the Russian Social Democrats, suffered from fragmentation and
the exile of such dynamic leaders as Lenin and Trotsky, the workers grew
more revolutionary and ready to confront the government. The Russian
government had survived the Revolution of 1905 because of the support of
the army, especially the Cossack regiments stationed in major cities like the
capital. The bodies of these loyal soldiers now littered the battlefields of
Russia's fronts. The fact that soldiers assigned to subdue riots had begun to
join the demonstrators in 1916 signaled clearly the decay of the tsar's
supporting institutions.

Nicholas and his wife Alexandra did nothing to restore faith in their rule.
The tsar resided at army headquarters, although he did return in February
to visit the State Duma. This imperial first occurred upon the occasion of the
Russian victory over the Turks at Erzerum and the retirement of Prime
Minister Goremykin. Previously the tsar had summoned the Duma to the
palace; now he went to them. This gesture might have eased some of the
tension between tsar and Parliament, except that he left the deputies with the
new prime minister, Boris Stürmer, a man even more corrupt and hated than
his predecessor.

The tsar's new selection pleased Alexandra, because Rasputin, whom she
worshipped, supported Stürmer. The heads of the few competent
government ministers would continue to roll with this triumvirate in charge
in Petrograd. The Duma languished in disarray as the Progressive Bloc
disintegrated, and more deputies began to fear a possible revolution. In June
Nicholas prorogued the representative assembly until November, as inflation,
shortages, and unrest gained the attention even of *Stavka* Chief-of-Staff
Alekseev at headquarters and prompted him to recommend to Nicholas the

appointment of a "dictator" for the home front, comparable to a supreme military commander. The tsar consequently appointed Stürmer to all the major positions in the civilian government, enraging all about him without solving any of Russia's mounting crises.

Diminishing food supplies to the cities loomed as the government's largest problem by midsummer, primarily because the peasants refused to sell their grain at government prices that did not provide them with sufficient return to purchase their needs. Stürmer's failure to solve this crisis, combined with his implication in a major bank scandal, lost him the confidence of Tsarina Alexandra, who had found an even better agent for her purposes. She suggested as Minister of Internal Affairs Aleksandr Protopopov, Vice-president of the Duma, whose appointment pleased his former associates, until they discovered that he belonged to Rasputin's inner circle and planned to repress any opposition to the rule of the Empress and her *éminence grise*. Aleksandra and Rasputin now essentially ruled Russia, in the name of the tsar, whose autocratic powers his wife vigorously defended.

These circumstances proved too much even for monarchists, however reactionary, and one of Russia's wealthiest princes, Feliks Iusupov, vowed to assassinate Rasputin, the source of all evil, the corrupter of the monarchy. With him were Grand Duke Dmitrii Pavlovich, Vladimir Purishkevich, leader of the reactionary deputies in the Duma, and two other associates. They lured Rasputin to Iusupov's palace on the pretext of introducing the lascivious monk to Iusupov's dazzling wife. Instead, they poisoned him with cyanide, shot him five times, and ultimately dumped the hardy victim under the ice of the Neva River, where he drowned.

The news of the assassination brought Nicholas back to the capital, where Alexandra and he dismissed another set of ministers, exiled the two aristocratic assassins, and then retreated into seclusion to console each other over Rasputin's death. Protopopov focussed exclusively on writing letters to petitioners. French ambassador Maurice Paleologue deplored the "anarchy" that reigned in Russia.[69]

Japan. A war of opportunity

In 1916 within the Japanese government Field Marshal Yamagata's faction of "German admirers" moved beyond the imperialist Twenty-One Demands in its relationship with China. It planned to depose President Yuan in order to establish a significant Japanese presence in China. The Russo-Japanese convention of July 1916 sought to replace Britain with Russia as Japan's key partner in diplomatic relations, in hopes that the Russians would recognize Japan's expansion of its interests in northeast Asia and support Japan against the potential opposition of the United States. The Japanese actually secured indirectly the Russian government's guarantee of support if the United States challenged Japan's growing influence in China. The Russians reciprocated and sought to forestall any German peace initiatives toward the Japanese, but they failed to secure a written commitment from Japan to fight Germany.

Divisions within the Japanese government assured that Yamagata's interest in Russia conflicted with the continued influence of former foreign minister Kato, an "Anglo-Saxon admirer," in the Okuma Cabinet to preserve undiluted ties with Britain. On 23 September the Cabinet decided to adhere to the London Declaration, in which Britain, France, and Russia in September 1914 pledged their solidarity in the war against Germany. The decision reaffirmed Japan's commitment to Britain and undercut any desires of admirers of Germany for closer ties. The Cabinet also proposed to avoid stronger commitments to Russia.

Despite the Kato government's conclusion in 1915 of the agreement that acknowledged Japan as the pre-eminent power in East Asia, now the Okuma Cabinet confronted the Chinese government's demands to reduce Japanese privileges in Manchuria and Mongolia as well as challenges to Japanese authority in Korea. Okuma warned Yuan Shikai against imperious acts and in March 1916 decided to aid opposition movements against the Chinese president. The Japanese government was now supporting Yuan symbolically while inciting opposition against him, as it attempted to make him more dependent upon Japan and secure great power recognition of Japan's pre-eminence in Asia. The Japanese Army command, led by Vice Chief of the Army General Staff Tanaka, however, was growing impatient with diplomacy, and yearned for an excuse, such as civil war, to deploy Japanese troops both to catalyze unrest and then to subdue it in China.[70]

On the domestic economic front, Japan had emerged from the severe depression in business and industry that had lasted until early 1915. Now industrial expansion accelerated, as the war increased demand for certain commodities such as iron, steel, and ships while disrupting established trade patterns and domination. Due to embargoes and blockade, Japan's prewar dependence on British and German iron and steel now gave way to domestic production and an emphasis on heavy industry which the Japanese government welcomed. The manufacturing firms also grew larger. The war clearly presented Japan with unprecedented opportunities for both industrial and territorial expansion. The preoccupation of the European powers with the growing conflict left Britain's ally in Asia as the most powerful state in that part of the world.

The United States. Colossus in disarray

Although international trade tied the United States to the Entente powers, the American colossus played no role in the war beyond words of warning. Woodrow Wilson's trusted emissary Col. House came to Europe in February to discuss peace with the combatant powers and found them all intransigent. The German sinking of the liner *Sussex* caused Wilson in April to warn Germany sternly that either they restrain their submarines or the United States would sever diplomatic relations. The Germans refrained.

Meanwhile, the United States was demonstrating how woefully prepared it was for any conflict. Pancho Villa's murderous raids across the border into Texas and New Mexico prompted Wilson to mobilize 100,000 National Guardsmen and to order a 12,000-man punitive expedition to Mexico under the command of Brig. Gen. John J. Pershing in March. Although Pershing's force failed to vanquish Villa, it did clash with Mexican soldiers late in June and brought the United States and Mexico to the brink of war. Wilson, now convinced that any conflict with Mexico would play into German hands, stepped away from the brink, as did Mexican President Carranza.

Woodrow Wilson, Theodore Roosevelt, and others did undertake a campaign for American preparedness in 1915 and 1916, in which they attacked any "hyphen-mentality" of ethnic or national heritage. In this paranoid atmosphere, recent immigrants, aliens, African Americans, any people readily identified as "other," as well as pacifists, socialists, and anarchists, because of their opposition to American involvement in the war, allegedly posed significant security risks. Rumors of German conspiracies to incite black Americans against the government circulated widely, indicating white awareness of their unjust treatment of African Americans as much as evidence of any such plots. German intrigues, propaganda, and sabotage heightened suspicions.[71]

In June, the United States government took steps toward mobilization, as a series of acts concerning national defense and the army increased the size of the regular army and the National Guard, the latter in order to satisfy those Congressmen who feared any increase in federal power. The National Defense Act established a Council of National Defense, a first step in the gradual development of a governmental bureaucracy for wartime mobilization. The Council lacked legal power and played only an advisory role through a plethora of uncoordinated committees. The Council represented a beginning, however unimpressive, but it would take much more to mobilize American industry. The rising number of strikes, from under 1,000 in 1914 to more than 3,600 in 1916, indicated the poor wages and working and living conditions of the American workforce at the time.

Overall, conditions in the United States seemed inauspicious for any participation in the war, a circumstance that did not escape the notice of ruling circles in Germany. British propagandists continued their onslaught in the United States. After the British Army's suppression of the Irish Easter Rebellion, which attracted the sympathies of Irish Americans, the British sought to keep the war with Germany in the forefront of the American press.

The approach of British propagandists attacking the Germans for their atrocities entailed downplaying the British blockade of Germany, justified on the grounds that modern war recognized no distinctions between combatant and noncombatant.

The atrocity propaganda proved particularly effective in the United States, as German attempts to deny the accusations or to justify their deeds foundered. The British published documents on the German deportation of women and girls from Lille in 1916, continuing their tradition of reporting German violations of women and the family, just as the "brutalization of Belgium" served as a "physical symbol of the violation of international law."[72] Nevertheless, German deeds, in particular submarine warfare, not British propaganda, would ultimately determine the stance of the United States toward the war, regardless of the state of American preparedness.

CONCLUSION. WAR UNENDING

The year 1916 stands as a watershed in the First World War, as Verdun and the Somme, as well as the Brusilov offensive, dashed both sides' hopes for imminent victory. The battles of Verdun and the Somme remain today among the most momentous and deadly battles in history. The German term *blutmühle*, or "blood mill," captures the essence of these long and deadly encounters. Verdun haunted the populations of France and Germany, and German soldiers at Stalingrad in 1942 recalled Verdun, either because their fathers, or, in a few incredible cases, they themselves had fought there. The first day of the Somme remains the single deadliest day in British military history. It initiated not only a four-month battle of attrition, but also an ongoing and bitter historiographical discussion of Douglas Haig's capability as a commanding general. Finally, the Brusilov offensive, less well remembered, demonstrated, as did other offensives in the First World War, that the offensive *à outrance*, pursued relentlessly and extensively, could destroy the army of the aggressor as well as the defender. The conflict seemed likely to continue to the exhaustion of one or all of the combatants, or, as some soldiers predicted, forever. As the war of attrition proved as much an industrial as a military enterprise, and the productive capacity of all the combatants increased, prospects of an ever longer war loomed.

In a sense the war reached maturity in 1916. On the various fronts the armies had the weapons to fight the conflict to the end, from airplanes and submarines to tanks. The Germans had introduced innovations in offensive tactics, with the employment of artillery firepower to prepare the way for specialized infantry with light automatic weapons, grenades, and flame-throwers operating in small units, with the support of airplanes. The British and French had introduced tanks. Defensively the Germans extended the depth of the battlefield, reducing front-line troops in favor of counter-attack units positioned further back in deep concrete bunkers to shield them from shell-fire, studding the ground with machine-gun nests, trench mortars, and pillboxes, and placing artillery sufficiently to the rear, often interspersed with the positions for counter-attacking infantry, so that they would be difficult to reach. At sea the submarine had demonstrated its effectiveness as a predator of merchant shipping, much to the horror of the British and neutral powers, and the Germans planned to unleash their undersea force upon their enemies in 1917. The conflict had evolved into a full-scale war of attrition.

The changed nature of warfare was reflected in changing images of its warriors. The ideal German soldier had evolved from the singing, sacrificial lamb of the slaughter at Langemarck to the *Verdunkämpfer*, the Verdun soldier. The *Stahlhelm*, the steel helmet shaped like a coal scuttle that German soldiers wore, symbolized the new ideal. Dark figures, whose heads and bodies merged at the top into the distinctive helmet, steely faces with staring eyes – such images conveyed the battle-hardened dealers of death and destruction that populated the European battlefield. The French soldier of 1914, attired in his red and blue uniform, had become the *poilu*, determined eyes deep set in his mustachioed and bearded face, clad in his horizon blue greatcoat and *casque Adrian*. No longer the amateurs and conscripts of 1914, these men were steely professionals, who went to industrial war as the worker went to the factory. In comparison, the British soldier of 1916 remained an amateur, but the Somme taught harsh and indelible lessons to the survivors. By the end of 1916 Bavarian soldier Reinhold Spengler exemplified the ranks of soldiers who had become inured to the "brutality and inhumanity of war." Old friends greeted one another, "Well, are you still alive?" and he had "got used to the idea of dying young."[73] The peasant armies of the fronts to the east, lacking the supplies, equipment, and logistical and medical support of their western counterparts, leave the ill-defined image of a poorly equipped mass, whose few veterans had survived amid enormous losses.

The prose and poetic literature indicates that the longer soldiers, particularly literate, middle-class, young men, spent on the Western Front, the more alienated they grew from civilian society – the men and particularly the women, who profited or appeared to gain from the war. Male civilians, the profiteers and the draft dodgers, reaped obvious benefits of wealth and security. Resentment of women, however, stemmed more from the soldiers' marginalization and fears than the mostly impermanent gains women registered. These soldiers constituted the privileged heirs of the ruling classes, whom the war now thrust to the margins of civilization in the trench lines, whom the generals wantonly expended with the rest of their conscript armies, without regard to class or intellect.

The mass of peasant soldiers, who formed the backbone of all armies, recognized and tired of their role as cannon-fodder, but evidence does not indicate that their resentment included the wives, families, farms, and villages from which the war had torn them. These men possessed little or no power and formal education, and they expected only a hard and monotonous life on the land. But they had entrusted their wives with their families and few possessions, for which they fought to return. Their counterparts from the urban working class probably resembled them more than their middle- and upper-class officers or the very few middle-class common soldiers at the front.

On the home front, the mobilization of society to fight the ever expanding war necessitated not only drafting all young and middle-aged men for the front and industry, but also recruiting women and youth for work in war industry. The combatant powers steadily concentrated their manufacturing capacity on war materiel, sucking workers from and closing down the manufacture of non-essential goods, or consumer goods that had nothing to do with fighting the war. Metal and munitions factories grew larger in size and adapted their plant to employ more semi-skilled and unskilled labor.

In all the combatant countries women filled the ranks of the new labor in 1916, thereby posing a clear threat to the traditional social and cultural order. In some countries, such as Russia or Italy, they, like their male counterparts, often migrated from rural areas to join the ranks of urban factory workers. In others, such as England, France, and Germany, working-class women seized the opportunity to transfer from domestic work to higher paying, if far more dangerous, jobs in munitions factories. Their work allegedly brought them more freedom; in fact, long, exhausting hours and supervision on and off the job render that claim suspect. The very departure of men for the army seems to have provided what independence women claimed. In England a few middle-class women worked in munitions, but primarily as welfare supervisors, and the women's work week was usually fifty-four to sixty hours, or some ten hours fewer than in France. The employer and his middle-class supervisor tended to view the working-class woman as a child, just as French employers did not consider women workers as rational beings. Women workers in other countries fared worse than their British and French counterparts, because of greater malnutrition or more primitive working conditions. The war affected and enveloped everyone, male and female, young and old, as 1916 drew to a close.

On the home fronts, civilian government controlled the war effort in Britain and France, a control implicit in democracies, but one which the French government had initially abdicated to the army command during the German invasion of 1914 and which it regained in 1916 only during and after Verdun. In the German, Austro-Hungarian, and Russian Empires, the army under the Emperor essentially dominated the war effort and steadily usurped the powers of what civilian government existed. Military control inhered in these more authoritarian systems, where the rulers' power rested ultimately upon the military, whose bureaucratic infrastructure exceeded that of the civilian government. Italy, the late arrival, presented a curious admixture of both systems, a democracy in which the army essentially intruded its repressive system into domestic affairs to mobilize Italian society.

—

Within the two alliances the balance of power shifted as the war continued. Within the Entente the French continued to bear the military burden of the conflict on the Western Front, although Verdun and the Somme indicated that the British would assume more of the bloody burden in the coming year. British insistence upon stronger governmental coordination of the French economy in 1916 indicated Britain's predominant position in Entente trade. In order to deal with serious shortages of wheat and sugar, the Entente powers in the west joined together to form an inter-allied purchasing organization, the wheat executive. Early in 1916 the British and French combined their purchasing of sugar, and later the French Ministry of Commerce bought the entire 1916 sugar crop from foreign suppliers, although it left distribution in the hands of private syndicates. French reliance on the British for wheat, sugar, and coal imports prompted the British government to force the French government to increase its internal economic controls of the French market when they had to compensate for French shortages. Submarine sinkings caused shortages of shipping that frayed Anglo-French relations. Ultimately an inter-allied economic conference in November and December resolved upon a common policy on shipping and wheat and the proportionate sharing of shortages among the Entente. In the east the Russians depended upon the French and British for financial assistance and supplies of certain armaments, such as aircraft, to supplement their domestic industrial production.

Britain and France suffered no serious food shortages as of 1916, and they negotiated the distribution of supplies. In contrast, the three eastern empires were confronting shortages of food, fuel, and transport. In Germany the OHL took command of the economy and attempted to order it about like an army in a leap toward "total mobilization" to fight "total war." The results of this effort would become apparent in the near future. The shortages exacerbated relations between the two halves of the Austro-Hungarian Dual Monarchy and rendered it more dependent upon Germany. In Russia, incompetence at the top of the government ensured anarchic disarray throughout the system.

Within the Central Powers, German predominance in the military and economic realms simply continued to increase, as Austria-Hungary became more dependent upon Germany with every passing year. The Ottoman Empire, which essentially possessed no industrial infrastructure and consequently did not present a home front as it appeared in the other major combatants, depended upon its two stronger allies, and Germany in particular, for funding and munitions. Overall, German military and industrial power formed the nucleus of the Central Powers, as Austria-Hungary contributed manpower and weaponry to a lesser extent, and the Ottoman Empire primarily manpower, in their war effort.

The Anglo-French relationship was more balanced than the German-Austro-Hungarian one, as both Entente powers contributed military and industrial strength to the alliance. The newest member of the Entente, Italy, though clearly a power of lesser rank, compared favorably in military and industrial strength to Austria-Hungary, an indication that the overall strength of the Entente potentially exceeded that of the Central Powers. Britain and France had the industrial capacity and potential, combined with ultimate superiority in manpower, to overwhelm Germany on the Western Front. With these circumstances in mind, the BEF and the French Army pursued an offensive military strategy, the British now even more relentlessly and inflexibly than the French.

The French, however, had bled themselves dry in two years of unceasing offensives, culminating in their determined resistance at Verdun. By the end of 1916 the French Army had lost 950,000 men, half of them in combat, another 19 percent dead of wounds, 13 percent of illness, and 17 percent missing in action and presumed dead. Some 400,000 French soldiers survived as prisoners-of-war. From the end of October, President Poincaré's liaison officers detected a "*mauvais esprit*," or low morale, among the troops. When soldiers received the papers to subscribe to a new war loan, some returned their sheets, cursing the loan and hoping that those who underwrote it died like dogs. As winter approached, even soldiers in units noted for their role as shock troops fell prey to exhaustion and frozen feet, as food and wine froze. The losses they had suffered during Verdun and the Somme often remained unreplaced, although some men who had not yet recovered fully from their wounds returned to their units. The Briand government's refusal even to contemplate negotiations with the Germans in September caused some to despair of an end to the war as its third Christmas approached.

In 1917 the British would have to shoulder the offensive burden on the Western Front. In 1914 Kitchener had counted on the arrival of Britain's Army on the Western Front to win the war in 1917. He had not foreseen, however, the necessity of committing his army before 1917. Kitchener drowned in June 1916 when the cruiser *Hampshire* sank after hitting a German mine, but the British government had already marginalized him, although he remained a symbol of authority to the masses. The BEF prepared to launch its offensive on the Somme, a half year earlier than the Secretary of War had planned. Despite the losses that the BEF suffered in 1915 and, on a much greater scale, in 1916, Britain had played a secondary role to that point. Its troops constituted relatively fresh fodder, compared to their French, German, Russian, and Austro-Hungarian counterparts.

In November 1916, the Entente generals convened at French GHQ as they had eleven months before, this time to plan and coordinate the campaigns for 1917. Once again the major focus would be the Western Front, with a joint Anglo-French effort on the Somme and another in Flanders to seize the Belgian coast and the U-boat bases there. The Russians would prepare a spring offensive, while the Italians would continue their offensives on the Isonzo. On 13 December Gen. Robert Nivelle, the victor of Verdun, became French Commander-in-Chief, replacing Joffre, whom the government promoted to marshal and out of command. The outgoing and confident Nivelle, whose political skills and command of the English language endeared him to the politicians, particularly the English, shared Joffre's belief in the offensive. He vaulted over the pessimist Pétain, the savior of Verdun, who did not share their conviction in the efficacy of the offensive.

The Germans husbanded their human and material resources, fought defensively, and concentrated their forces to secure an occasional mastery limited in time and space. The new German High Command of Hindenburg and Ludendorff, well aware of the Entente's potential, took steps to mobilize their industry to the fullest in the Hindenburg Program of the fall of 1916. This was now total war, and the two soldiers planned to militarize German society in order to wage it, from their perspective, more efficiently. German society felt the pinch of the blockade, and with the end of 1916 the war had already continued longer than Moltke had considered possible in 1914. The OHL perceived no prospects of victory on the all-important Western Front, and, in order to cut their losses, were preparing new defensive fortifications to straighten and shorten their lines. With these dismal circumstances in mind, the German military establishment found unrestricted submarine warfare increasingly attractive.

5

1917. Climax

"I am obliged to report that, at the present moment, the Russian Empire is run by lunatics."

French ambassador Paléologue to the French
Minister of Foreign Affairs, 14 January 1917[1]

"The war is a struggle between two *Weltanschauungen*: the Germanic . . . against the Anglo-Saxon. . . . One must *win*, the other must *perish*."

Kaiser Wilhelm II to Houston Stewart Chamberlain,
9 January 1917[2]

"It's typical of the French army. [The officers] command but they don't question whether their orders are possible. No one can challenge them. It seems to me that if no one can discuss the orders, either they should be possible or those who receive them must be much less intelligent than those who give them."

Corporal A. Bavour, 370th Regt, 170th Co, 170th Div,
10 January 1917[3]

"Only one thing is certain: Europe will either come to an understanding or it will go under. The first is impossible, and so the second follows."

German Foreign Office Councillor Kurt Riezler,
secretary to Chancellor Bethmann Hollweg,
diary entry of 3 October 1917[4]

By the end of 1916, all the combatants revealed the strains of war. However, the determination of Britain, France, and Germany to secure, not a compromise peace, but a victorious one, would render any attempts at negotiation moot in 1917.

THE WESTERN FRONT. "THE GREAT
SAUSAGE MACHINE"

Champagne. Nivelle squanders the French Army

Joffre had advised the British at the Chantilly Conference of November 1916 that they would have to assume the brunt of the war on the Western Front. Joffre and Haig sought to continue carrying the war to the Germans, and Joffre proposed another attempt to eliminate the German salient from south of Arras to east of Soissons. At the beginning of February, the British would attack from the north; the French, from the south. Subsequently the British would stage a major offensive in Flanders to seize the German submarine bases at Ostend and Zeebrugge.

British Prime Minister Lloyd George, convinced that this plan would simply launch a bloody repetition of the 1916 campaign, attempted to deflect these intentions at a conference in Rome in January 1917. He proposed a joint Entente offensive from Italy against Austria-Hungary to drive the latter from the war. Lloyd George's "Eastern Strategy" entailed seeking resolution of the war on any front other than the bloody trenches in France and Belgium. The British and French generals, however, rejected Lloyd George's effort to suborn their plans, which rested on their equally firm conviction that victory lay on the Western Front alone.

Joffre's successor, Gen. Robert Nivelle, discarded Joffre's plan and proposed that the French once again stage the major offensive, this time along the Aisne River between Soissons and Reims, and up a steep ridge known since monarchical times as the Chemin des Dames, the path of the ladies. The British would launch only a diversionary attack near Arras.

The French assault, as Nivelle emphasized, would prove quick, powerful, violent, and brutal. It would shatter the German lines within two days at most, after which French forces would pursue the beaten enemy. If extravagant language uttered with absolute confidence could win wars, then Nivelle would end the war on the Western Front. Nevertheless, if the offensive failed, Nivelle promised to call off the operation within two days, to avoid the prolonged blood-baths of 1916.

The French Army had adopted German innovations in preparation for 1917. Now three companies formed a battalion, three battalions a regiment, three regiments a division. After a devastating preliminary bombardment to smash German positions, Nivelle's soldiers, moving in small groups and well armed with grenades and light machine-guns, would follow a creeping barrage through the German lines. The infantry carried Hotchkiss machine-guns, although their eight machine-guns per battalion lagged behind the Germans' twelve. The trench mortar squads' improved weapons included the British

Stokes mortar and portable 37 mm. cannon with a range of 1,300 yards. The supply of 155-mm. heavy artillery lagged behind production quotas, but Nivelle now had tractors to pull both his 75-mm. and 155-mm. cannon.

Nivelle proposed a larger scale version of his successful reconquest of Verdun. He won support among some French circles, but, more crucially, from Lloyd George. After all, Nivelle's willingness to continue bearing the major burden on the Western Front would benefit the English. Nivelle failed to convince everyone. Among the doubters remained French Premier Aristide Briand and the general over whom Nivelle had vaulted to assume command – Philippe Pétain. Briand, similar to Lloyd George in his negotiations with his generals, refused to give Nivelle the numbers of troops he requested. Briand's government came under increasing attack in Parliament, and his Minister of War Gen. Lyautey resigned rather than discuss military matters with the representatives. Lyautey believed the offensive unfeasible. His resignation brought down the Briand government in March. Pétain, the perennial pessimist, the proponent of the defense in an army command wed to the offense, predicted disaster. BEF commander Douglas Haig, recently promoted to Field Marshal, also remained dubious of the plan's prospects of success. Haig worried further that Nivelle's intention to attack on 1 April might interfere with his own scheme to attack in Flanders in early April.

Ironically, Nivelle's offensive targeted a region where the Germans were finishing a new belt of fortifications. Ludendorff had planned to evacuate a forty-five-mile front between Arras and Soissons and retreat to this fortified line to straighten and shorten his line of defense. He could then place thirteen front-line divisions in strategic reserve. The Germans began withdrawing to the "Siegfried Line," or Hindenburg Line as the Entente labeled it, in February, and they fully occupied it by mid-March.

During the severe winter of 1916–17, malnutrition, inflation, and desperate living conditions in general plagued the people of occupied France and Belgium. Although international conventions forbade civilian work in the front lines for enemy forces, the German Army used gangs of forced labor, including French and Belgian men from the occupied territories, to build the Hindenburg Line. Many died in the severe weather and poor living conditions, although they fared better than Russian and Rumanian prisoners-of-war working there, whom the Germans wantonly abused. With the German declaration of unrestricted submarine warfare, subs sank a number of supply ships. In April, the U.S. government called Herbert Hoover home to manage food supplies for the United States. What might have signaled the demise of the CRB instead provided its salvation, as Hoover, in his new position, secured American financial support for the CRB for the rest of the war, at the rate of $7.5 million for Belgium and $5 million for northern France per month.[5]

The retreating German Army scorched the earth in that part of France, herding the population with it and returning them to France later by way of Switzerland, so that the Germans would not have to feed these French refugees. The Germans destroyed factories, towns, and villages and often booby-trapped those buildings they left standing. They blew up or blocked roads, ruined fruit orchards, and poisoned wells. Ludendorff had ordered these ruthless measures, over the protests of the German Army group commander in the region, Prince Rupprecht of Bavaria. The OHL waged total war with a vengeance.

British troops became aware of the retreat early on 25 February, while the French realized the Germans had evacuated the area on 13 March. French advance guards moved slowly across the wasteland. As they approached the new German defensive line, they confronted a virtually impregnable system of three and sometimes four belts of concrete blockhouses up to a depth of nearly two miles, interspersed with machine-gun nests, dug-in artillery and mortar batteries, and deep shelters for infantry.

The German troop withdrawal did not alter Nivelle's plans. It made no difference that the salient he planned to attack had disappeared. He had absolute faith in the ability of his artillery and troops to rupture the German front. But the front had in fact retreated from his soldiers, who would now have to advance over more exposed and ravaged territory to assault the strongest fortifications yet built on any front during the war. Although the press greeted the withdrawal as a German defeat, French soldiers recognized a strategic move to impede an attack. Jaded veterans calculated that their generals would find a pretext for another useless slaughter and they would pay the price.[6]

Nivelle's soldiers seemed imbued with a certain confidence, or perhaps desperation for an end to the war. They had suffered several changes of position during an abysmally cold winter, the third winter of the war, when temperatures reached −25 degrees Centigrade, and the weather in early April improved little. The veterans in their thirties and early forties focussed monolithically on their families, their wives and children left behind, who symbolized their once peaceful existence. They hated civilians in general, the draft dodgers, the men with easy jobs, munitions workers making three or four times a soldier's pay and leading a safe life, the press that printed lies and absurd descriptions of combat. Soldiers returned from leave with the impression that "people in the rear consider the *poilus* suckers, imbeciles. They salute us to our faces; behind our backs they don't give a damn about us."[7]

Soldiers acknowledged and feared the loss of sensitivity that the daily atrocities of trench life caused. They rejected their devaluation, the loss of individuality, the inequalities between officers and men. One soldier advised his wife to "teach him [his son] to detest the army, tell him when he's big that his father suffered a thousand miseries from officers, who are all "swine," and to be strong enough to avenge the sufferings of his father."[8] They despised their generals and the French government, which some now believed had started the war to eliminate the lower classes and exhaust any survivors to the advantage of the wealthy. The more they despised their superiors, the more they identified with the situation of enemy soldiers, as all either followed orders or risked death by firing squad. Some preferred a bullet in the head to another winter in the lines, to the continued stupid slaughter. They hoped for peace, despite their cynicism, and Nivelle promised them a relatively cheap victory, not another blood-bath. The vaunted *élan* of the French *poilu* would rise to the task.

French elite units would spearhead the attack, the French XX Corps and Mangin's colonial soldiers – Senegalese, Algerians, Moroccans. Very few men who had begun the war in the XX Corps remained. The few old veterans would lead young recruits. Mangin's Africans had retaken Douaumont. They believed that Nivelle and Mangin had the *baraka*, that fortune smiled upon them. The Africans did not divine their commanders' intention to sacrifice them to spare French lives. Nivelle demanded as many Senegalese soldiers as possible for his coming attack, to "increase the power of our projected strength and permit the sparing – to the extent possible – of French blood."[9] The French commander of a Senegalese regiment declared in April that the Senegalese were "finally and above all superb attack troops permitting the saving of the lives of whites, who exploit their success *behind them* and organize the positions they conquer."[10] A battalion commander later voiced similar sentiments, advocating the use of the *Force noire* "to save, in future offensive actions, the blood – more and precious – of our [French] soldiers."[11]

In the new Cabinet of Premier Alexandre Ribot, his Minister of War, mathematician Paul Painlevé, the first civilian war minister after three generals, believed in neither Nivelle nor his plan. Even Gen. Alfred Micheler, whom Nivelle had selected to command the offensive, doubted the wisdom of a plan of attack against such redoubtable fortifications. Painlevé called a Council of War at Compiègne on 6 April. Russian Tsar Nicholas had abdicated on 15 March, and nothing guaranteed Russia's continued participation in the war effort. However, the U.S. Congress voted to enter the war on 6 April. Should France wait for the Americans? Painlevé, supported by Pétain, endorsed the attack, but not an exploitation of a breakthrough that would destroy the reserves of the army. Painlevé rejected Nivelle's offer to resign, as he feared that removal of Nivelle from command before the general had the chance to fulfill his promises would devastate morale. In March, German trench raids had captured detailed documents of the coming offensive. Nivelle prepared to attack; Ludendorff, to defend. French and German troops knew what awaited them at the beginning of April.

Nivelle began his preliminary bombardment, intended to last for a week, on 5 April. However, snow and rainy weather, with wind currents above the battlefield so violent that they actually threw French aerial observers from their airplanes, forced postponement of the actual attack until 16 April. Some 7,000 French guns shelled a thirty-mile front, making rugged terrain even more pockmarked with muddy shell holes for assault troops.

The Germans, operating according to a new scheme of defense in depth, manned their advance trenches lightly with observers. Machine-gunners in pillboxes or shell holes dotted the intermediate zone; behind them, artillery batteries; and finally, 10 to 20,000 yards back and out of French artillery range, the reserve or counter-attack troops. The French shelling did not dent the well-fortified German positions, although it did cause severe losses among German troops caught in the open while moving into position.

Immediately prior to the attack, German fighter squadrons seized control of the air to prevent French reconnaissance planes from directing the creeping barrage and to protect German observation balloons monitoring the French advance. Elite Prussian Guards and Bavarians, supported by reinforced artillery batteries, awaited. Although French artillery observers estimated that they had disabled perhaps half of the German artillery, in fact their bombardment had affected only fifty-three of 392 German batteries.

On 16 April French assault troops awoke at 3.30 a.m. in their partially flooded and often frozen trenches. They armed themselves, drank wine and coffee, and rose to the attack at 6.00 a.m. They had to cover 8,000 yards in the next eight hours, which, nevertheless, would leave them 2,000 yards short of the heart of the German defense.

The soldiers advanced over the broken ground to occupy the first line of German trenches, but the additional territory they had to cover robbed them of momentum. When they attempted to assault up the ridge, the creeping barrage sped on beyond them, enabling German machine-gunners to rush up from their dug-outs and open fire on the French ranks. The intense machine-gun fire from undetected nests massacred the first wave.

Some 25,000 Senegalese, the core of Mangin's assault force, advanced in a half-frozen state. They had just returned from the south of France to spearhead the offensive. Thirty-five of the forty-one battalions of Senegalese on the Western Front participated in the ranks of the 2nd Corps of Mangin's Colonial Army. They attacked, armed only with Lebel rifles and their large knives, and without machine-guns or supporting artillery, as they too could not keep pace with the advancing barrage. Where they caught Germans, they massacred them. The Senegalese units numbered among the few to penetrate the German lines. German fire carved them into small groups. The survivors found, much to their dismay, that Germans, armed with portable machine-guns, emerged from caves in the ground *behind* them, ground they thought they had cleared, to fire into them. They suffered grave losses: 6,000 casualties of the 10,000 *tirailleurs* in the first wave.

Both French and German sources emphasized the savagery of the black troops, the former delighting in their black charges' use of their large combat knives, or "*coupe-coupes,*" to slice and dice the foe, the latter lamenting the uncivilized use of black savages against white troops to the rest of the world. Even France's allies protested, fearing that encouraging the slaughter of whites would lower white prestige in colonial territories.

When the infantry clashed, brutal hand-to-hand combat ensued. French soldiers, enraged by the slaughter they had suffered, beat to death German soldiers who attempted to surrender. The French pressed forward determinedly, abandoning their wounded where they fell in the snow. French artillery, blinded by fog and snow, fired on French troops.

One hundred and twenty-eight heavy French St. Chamond and Schneider tanks, armed with 75-mm. cannon, their tracks protected with hull armor, lurched to the attack at 3 mph. German heavy artillery set many of them aflame; some broke down; others could not traverse the wide trenches. German machine-gunners cut to ribbons any infantry attempting to accompany the tanks. Only forty-seven tanks survived, their commander burned to death in his flaming funeral pyre. Ludendorff concluded that artillery could neutralize tanks; French Gen. Estienne, the creator of the tank in France, decided to concentrate on the construction of light, mobile Renault tanks.[12]

By the end of the day the French had advanced fewer than 1,000 yards. Overall the attack had failed dismally, but Nivelle refused to abandon it; after all, he had two days. Two days passed. The exhaustion of the troops finally delayed the attack from 19 to 22 April; then the generals ordered their men forward again. The attacking waves met the same fate as their predecessors – slaughter – although they did penetrate four miles on a sixteen-mile front.

Wounded soldiers scheduled for evacuation often spent hours on stretchers and then in ambulances, brutally jostled on their way to battlefield hospitals. The most severely wounded did not survive long enough to undergo operations, hemorrhaging to death on the way. French military surgeons operated around the clock, sometimes performing more than thirty operations, primarily amputations, in twenty-four hours. Gangrene would kill more than one-fifth of those men suffering leg or shoulder wounds. Men nearly cut in half by German machine-gunfire, their intestines ripped to shreds, could not survive.

Still, the French divisions fought on until 9 May, gaining ground at tremendous cost, but failing to rupture the German lines. Their great expectations shattered, their total casualties approaching nearly 140,000 men, including at least 30,000 dead, twenty-four French divisions, a quarter of the army, became *hors de combat*. Even Nivelle's subordinate generals refused to continue the attack – Micheler had screamed his refusal at his chief.

In late April French units declined to attack or even to return to the lines.

Soldiers in the front lines lived surrounded by body parts of the dead, the smell of death permeating their nostrils. If they moved, German machine-gunners and snipers ensured they did not again. Segments of fifty-four divisions proclaimed that they had had enough of the senseless slaughter. No cowards, these battle-scarred veterans had survived several wounds and composed some of France's most highly decorated units, units that had fought bravely from August 1914.

Nivelle had promised the French and colonial soldiers a certain victory, and they had sacrificed for nothing more than another bloody, abortive assault on sophisticated defenses manned by equally determined and better armed men. Twenty thousand men deserted, but the great majority of soldiers remained prepared to defend France, if not to commit suicide in their generals' offensives. French generals used Senegalese units, which remained among the most reliable of troops, to maintain order. The French army "mutinied," engaged in "collective indiscipline" or a "strike," depending upon the source. Because order did not collapse nor did soldiers attack their officers, the latter two terms describe the events more accurately.[13]

The search for scapegoats began. Some attributed the collapse to pacifist and defeatist propaganda from the rear that had poisoned the troops' morale. Nivelle himself attempted to blame the failure on his favorites Micheler and Mangin. Nivelle relieved Mangin of command for his sacrifice of his African soldiers – an ironic deed in light of Nivelle's sentiments about saving French lives. The Army Commission of the National Assembly branded Mangin a "butcher" in an angry meeting. Nothing, however, could prevent Nivelle's demotion to command forces in north Africa.

Philippe Pétain succeeded Nivelle as commander-in-chief of the French Army on 15 May. As at Verdun, when the French Army faced grave danger, Pétain, apostle of the defense and truly concerned for the welfare of his soldiers, saved the situation once again. The collective indiscipline that had begun in April reached its height in May and June, but Pétain's response to the circumstances effected their progressive disappearance by the end of the year.

Pétain complained about defeatism in the rear, but concentrated on restoring morale and discipline to an army in disarray. Officers and NCOs selected members of their units for trial, and 3,427 courts-martial took place. Although the army passed more than 554 death sentences on the ringleaders, Pétain evidently limited the actual executions to forty-nine. Others received life sentences and deportation to penal colonies. The army had to restore discipline in the ranks.

More critically, Pétain visited about 100 French divisions to talk personally to the soldiers. He took their numerous complaints, ranging from inadequate time for leave, abysmal living conditions in general, and poor food and wine in particular, seriously. Although some officers blamed the disorders on propaganda from the rear, they had pushed the soldiers until the men found defeatist propaganda convincing. Troops knew that their sacrifices had proven worthless, that their commanders were "asses," as one observed, and their morale sank to an all-time low. Some 2,000 French soldiers stoned a general and stripped him of his stars, while leaving their colonel in peace, clearly distinguishing between the "blood-suckers" who had "massacred" them and the commanders whom they respected.[14]

Pétain promised to ameliorate the soldiers' conditions and kept his word. Their living quarters and recreational facilities improved, as did the quality and preparation of their food and drink in the canteens, and their leave time became more regular and adequate for them to visit their homes. In his first order of 19 May and later before Parliament, Pétain promised to cease the large-scale offensives in favor of smaller attacks with limited objectives and substantial artillery and air support in order to reduce French infantry losses to supportable levels. He also limited the number of soldiers in the front lines in favor of placing them in the second and third lines, somewhat like the German defense in depth.

Pétain demanded substantial increases in the army's numbers of heavy cannon, airplanes, and tanks. French factories strove to produce and deliver more 155-mm. cannon and munitions for all its artillery. The French air service received a new fighter long in development, the SPAD, powered by the revolutionary Hispano Suiza water-cooled V8 engine, which would become the mainstay of the French fighter force to the end of the war. Fast, sturdy, with outstanding dive and zoom characteristics, the SPAD provided famed French fighter pilots such as Georges Guynemer, René Fonck, and Charles Nungesser with a capable and reliable mount. Finally, Renault light tanks armed with 37-mm. cannon or machine-guns arrived in greater numbers as the year proceeded.

Most crucially, Pétain promised to wait for the Americans before the French returned to major offensives. Once again, the general kept his word. In August and October he undertook two limited offensives – the first at Verdun and the second on the Chemin des Dames battlefield. At Verdun he fielded thirty-two infantry divisions with overwhelming artillery support, including new French 400-mm. artillery pieces. After a six-day bombardment, French infantry literally had only to occupy the pulverized territory. At Malmaison at the Chemin des Dames, Pétain launched a tank attack coordinated with infantry and artillery. Both offensives enjoyed overwhelming aerial support from tactical bombers and fighter aircraft.

The French Army had successfully tested its mettle, thanks to extensive preparation, coordinated combined arms support from artillery, tanks, and airplanes, and to limited and attainable objectives. Pétain restored the French Army for participation in the Entente operations of 1918 in anticipation of victory in 1919 with the help of the United States. He fully understood that the French Army would have to play a significant role in the final struggle. Otherwise, France would not receive its just due and others would forget its primary role through 1916. Although French combat strength on the Western Front declined from 2.23 million troops on 1 July 1916 to 1.89 million on 1 October 1917, Pétain prevented the marginalization of France.[15]

Incredibly, the Germans did not learn of the condition of the French Army in spring 1917 until it was too late to exploit it. The French infantry's valiant if abortive assaults had taken sufficient toll of German soldiers for Ludendorff to note in his memoirs that he received only "weak echoes" of the French mutinies. Even the government's rigid press censorship could not have prevented the enemy from learning of the French Army's condition had either deserters divulged the truth or had French soldiers in the line indicated a willingness to capitulate. The French Army, however dismal its condition and morale, remained prepared to defend France.

Although the German Army had blunted a French offensive once again, it had not emerged unscathed. New army recruits in 1917 did not equal the quality of previous classes, and the army, however capable and innovative, suffered from the exhaustion of the three-year blood-bath. Entente intelligence services learned that desertions in some German units rose in 1917 under the pressure of combat on the Aisne River. Furthermore, the British had launched their offensives, which now preoccupied the German Army.

In Flanders Fields. Haig dissipates the British Army

With the failure of the Nivelle offensive and the French Army in distress, the British assumed the burden of the war on the Western Front in summer 1917. The BEF had actually begun its spring offensive slightly before the French, staging a minor attack east of Arras. The British had clearly learned from the Somme in 1916. Their seven-day bombardment, heavier than earlier ones, fired much improved shells, both high explosive and gas. At Arras the British introduced the Livens gas mortar which lobbed gas canisters into the German trenches, creating a dense and concentrated gas cloud.

Their troops advanced undetected through tunnels to the forward lines, and they attacked on 9 April behind a well-executed creeping barrage. The Canadian Corps of four divisions at the northern end of the attack stormed Vimy Ridge, a key strong point for any future defense of Arras, paying for the gain with 20 percent casualties of their 40,000 infantry. Meanwhile, British units, including ANZAC brigades, advanced one to three miles to the north of the Hindenburg lines and seized 9,000 German prisoners. The ANZACs actually breached the Hindenburg Line but could not hold against a determined German counter-attack. By 23 April the attack had dissipated, although the British continued their pressure until 23 May in order to help the French on the Aisne. The successful offensive cost the British 84,000 casualties, the Germans, 75,000.

Above the Arras battlefield, the Royal Flying Corps fought the German air service at a serious disadvantage. By April 1917 the German twin-gun Albatros fighter peaked in its D3 version, and the sleek, sturdy killer, powered by its Mercedes six-cylinder inline engine, ruled the sky. Regardless of this circumstance, RFC commander Hugh "Boom" Trenchard, very much a "thruster," an aggressive, offensive-minded leader, like Haig, demanded of his men that they undertake distant offensive patrols far over German lines. Just as British infantry commanders insisted their men stage night-time trench raids to assert British control over "no-man's land," in a sense an oxymoronic undertaking, so Trenchard insisted that the RFC establish aerial mastery not only over its own lines, but over no-man's land and far into enemy territory. If infantry sacrificed themselves daily on the ground, Trenchard expected his aircrew to do no less.

Consequently British fliers performed their assignments stalwartly in aircraft far inferior to the Albatros. German pilots, led by Boelcke's successor Rittmeister Manfred von Richthofen, known to his opponents as the "Red Baron" for the color of his personal airplane, shot down so many British aircraft that the RFC named the month "Bloody April." It ended on a particularly sour note when Capt. W. Leefe Robinson, who had won the Victoria Cross for downing a German Zeppelin over England, and his entire flight of six new Bristol Fighters all fell victim to German interceptors.

Despite this dismal debut, the appearance of the Bristol Fighter heralded better days for the RFC. In the next months British manufacturers delivered two new planes – the Sopwith Camel and the SE5 – that with the Bristol would serve as mainstays of the RFC's much improved fighter force to the end of the war. The rotary-engined Camel, although its instability posed a grave danger to novice pilots, offered unsurpassed maneuverability to its aviators. The SE5, sometimes referred to as the British SPAD because it used the Hispano Suiza eight-cylinder V8 engine, possessed speed and higher altitude performance and offered a steadier gun platform than the Camel. The Bristol Fighter, powered by a Rolls Royce Falcon engine, not only equaled the performance of single-seat fighters, a fact which Leefe Robinson did not realize, but also carried an observer firing a Lewis gun rearward. The battle for aerial supremacy over the Western Front attained new levels in quality and quantity of airplanes engaged, as both sides fought to observe the other's movements on land.

Haig now targeted Flanders, where he wanted to burst from the Ypres salient using artillery, infantry, and ultimately his beloved cavalry, to seize the German submarine bases at Ostend and Zeebrugge in Belgium and thus outflank the Germans from the north. Haig's colleague, Chief of the Imperial General Staff Robertson, urged him to pursue limited objectives in attritional warfare which, when combined with Germany's growing privations, would force Germany to make peace without squandering British manpower. Haig, however, vowed to destroy the German Army. In early June Haig confided to Gen. Sir Henry Wilson that Germany would soon run out of manpower and that he could break the heart of the "Bosche" army in another six weeks of fighting.[16]

First, Haig needed to take the German high ground at Messines Ridge to secure the southern end of the salient. The British Second Army, under Gen. Sir Hubert Plumer, known to his men as "Daddy" for his concern for them and his grandfatherly appearance, confronted Messines. Plumer had long prepared for this task. His engineers dug twenty tunnels deep under the ridge and packed high explosives at the end. This feat represented the "tunneling" war at its most sophisticated: although German tunnelers found one of the tunnels and blew it up, the Germans never detected most of them nor suspected Plumer's grand design. Plumer's artillery shelled the area from 30 May to 7 June.

At 3.10 a.m. Plumer's engineers detonated nearly a million pounds of explosives in mines at the end of the nineteen tunnels. The blast reverberated in London. The ridge rose into the air, erupting in flames, and then fell, collapsing and swallowing German defenses and defenders. Pvt. J. Bowles, exhausted from tunneling and marching through "liquid mud" up to his knees by day and attempting to sleep while swarms of rats crawled over him at night searching for food, concluded of the use of mines, "It is not war, it is wholesale butchery."[17] British and ANZAC troops followed a creeping barrage up the slope of the remains of the ridge, to find the surviving defenders in no condition to resist. After seizing the crest, they repulsed determined German counter-attacks for the next week.

With the southern flank secured, Haig prepared his offensive in Flanders, but not without opposition. Prime Minister Lloyd George feared a repeat of the Somme, as did other members of the War Cabinet and even Chief of the Imperial General Staff Robertson, who usually supported his fellow Scotsman Haig. Ultimately the War Cabinet approved the offensive, capitulating before Haig's strong political connections, including King George V.

Flanders Fields posed one potential problem. The clay soil proved impervious to water, which collected on the surface forming puddles and swamps. Invariably heavy rains fell in August. Haig insisted that Gen. Hubert Gough's Fifth Army change positions with Plumer's Second to execute the attack. Although Gough did not know the region and the logistics of the exchange delayed the assault for weeks, the Field Marshal reasoned that the dashing cavalryman Gough would effect the breakthrough better than the methodical Plumer. Haig scheduled the offensive to begin on 31 July.

Meanwhile the Germans, fully aware of the coming onslaught,

strengthened their defenses to some nine layers in depth – a forward three layers for dispersed defenders of the division in line, then a middle segment of pillboxes and machine-gun nests, and in the rear counter-attack divisions in concrete bunkers interspersed with artillery batteries. On 17 July, the day before the British preliminary bombardment began, the Germans attacked the Ypres salient with shells marked with a yellow cross containing a new and deadlier gas – dichloroethylsulfide – mustard gas to the British, and "Yperite" to the French because of the place of its introduction. They also introduced blue cross shells, whose arsenic penetrated gas mask filters, causing the soldiers to tear off their masks and expose themselves to the phosgene and mustard gases that the Germans had fired simultaneously. The BEF suffered 26,000 gas casualties in July alone.[18]

Gough's preliminary bombardment began on 18 July, and continued for two weeks, thoroughly cratering the battlefield. On 31 July the third battle of Ypres began, as the attacking infantry advanced nearly two miles before a German counter-attack threw them back. Starting on 1 August rain fell for two weeks, turning the battlefield into a muddy quagmire some ten feet deep with the consistency of porridge, as one British battalion commander noted.[19] In this nightmarish landscape, British and German soldiers alike struggled merely to survive. Their wounded lay in the dark crying for help as the water level steadily rose, slowly drowning them. When the rains stopped, Gough resumed the attack, only to confront German pillboxes whose machine-gunfire limited any advance.

Haig replaced Gough with Plumer, who on 20 September initiated a series of limited concentrated attacks in which his troops gained the heights overlooking Ypres from the east, before the rains began again in early October. Against the advice of Gough and Plumer, Haig resumed the attack to take the high ground near the village of Passchendaele. On 12 October he launched the II ANZAC Corps, which foundered in the mud against uncut barbed wire and German machine-gunfire.

New Zealand Pvt. Leonard Hart wrote his family that the night they relieved the British troops, cries for help from surrounding shell holes led them to "Tommies," British soldiers who had lain seriously wounded, in rain and half-frozen mud for four days and nights. ANZAC stretcher-bearers spent the next day gathering the abandoned men, while the Germans held their fire. A "sickened" Hart condemned British officers for the "unnecessary sacrifice of those lives" and a "callous brutality" that made them no better than the "Hun." In the ANZAC attack Hart's company lost 148 of 180 men, including all of its officers, to German fire, and failed to take its objective.[20]

On 26 October the Canadian Corps attacked, and by 10 November succeeded in wresting most of the high ground from the Germans. The struggle in the interim had continued under the most atrocious conditions.

Men and animals drowned in the mud, which filled the trenches and shell holes with a slippery and treacherous ooze. To reach the lines or stay above water in the trenches, men teetered on duckboards. Moving forward under full pack, if a soldier slipped off the duckboards and fell into a shell crater, he drowned in the cold slime. Stretcher-bearers often could not reach the wounded, and at least one doctor told them to stop wasting their time bringing in seriously wounded men and leave them to "die quietly."[21] Doctors and stretcher-bearers were inured to three years of witnessing horrible wounds of every description, but Sgt. W.J. Collins brought in a soldier who had walked up to him with what he described to the doctor as a "rather uncomfortable wound." "[A] shrapnel bullet right in the top of his penis" had "split it open as if it had been cut equally and *there it's lodged*."[22] The four Canadian divisions suffered nearly 16,000 killed and wounded. Because of these notorious conditions, the name *Passchendaele* often looms larger in memory than Third Ypres. British soldiers referred to the Western Front as the "Great Sausage Machine."

Haig finally relented because the Austro-German breakthrough at Caporetto on the Italian front forced the transfer of five divisions. He had expended officially some quarter of a million casualties, unofficially many more, to inflict German casualties of perhaps 50,000 fewer men. He had weakened the morale of his own soldiers, as well as the Germans, in the process. The Ypres battlefield had claimed 70,000 British dead and 170,000 British wounded, in a battle the point of which, in the judgment of John Keegan, "defies explanation."[23] The British would lose 226,450 officers and men killed in 1917; the French, 136,200. The Germans lost 121,622 officers and men on the Western Front the same year.[24]

Haig had not finished on the Western Front, as commander of the British Tank Corps Gen. Sir Hugh Elles and his Chief of Staff Lt. Col. J.F.C. Fuller desired to assault the Hindenburg Line with a combined tank-infantry force. They eyed the terrain southwest of Cambrai between Cambrai and Arras, where the rolling and relatively unscarred seven-mile-wide plain of a heretofore quiet sector offered ideal ground for the slow and ponderous behemoths. Haig and his Third Army commander Gen. Sir Julian Byng hoped that six divisions and a force of 300 Mark IV tanks, some with two 57-mm. (six-pounder) cannon and four Lewis machine-guns, the others with six Lewis guns, might actually break through the German lines. Elles and Fuller contemplated only a raid. Preparations for the assault occurred in complete secrecy. Tanks moved to the front at night while the engine noise of airplanes flying at low altitude over the front concealed the roar and clatter of the mechanical monsters.

The attack began on 20 November without preliminary bombardment, as tanks and infantry followed a rolling barrage. The German defenders panicked and fled as the tanks rolled toward them firing as they advanced, crushing the barbed wire and crossing trenches by dropping brush and wood bundles in front of them. By the end of the day the tanks had penetrated to the third enemy position, but infantry had followed them only with great difficulty. The Germans regrouped quickly, and contained the attack by 23 November. Artillery fire and light mortars proved effective against tanks, while a 12.98-mm. rifle firing an armor-piercing bullet, which the Germans used to blast snipers' armored peepholes, could penetrate tank armor and metal, and bodies inside. Finally, tank armor, when struck by machine-gun and rifle bullets, emitted shards and splinters that could blind or otherwise seriously injure the crew. In an unexpected turnabout, the inevitable German counter-attack infiltrated the new British lines so quickly and forcefully that it actually pushed the British back further than they had advanced in some places. The front settled into stalemate by 5 December.

The attack demonstrated to the British the potential of the new weapon, and the British and French planned to use tanks *en masse* in future attacks where possible. The counter-attack, however, confirmed the Germans' reliance on their new infantry infiltration tactics, which had worked well earlier on the Eastern and Southwestern Fronts. The Germans would have to do without tanks in any case, as severe metal shortages precluded their production.

The aerial struggle raged to new levels of ferocity over the Western Front during the summer and into the fall, as both sides fought to gain aerial superiority. The French Army's difficulties did not affect its air service, and its fighter pilots fought grimly over the Somme and Flanders along with the British. As the air services of all three countries grew, the air war evolved into a mass struggle of attrition in 1917, similar to the war below in the trenches. In the fall two of the great lone hunters, English ace Albert Ball and French ace Georges Guynemer, would disappear over Flanders. Legend maintained that the frail Guynemer, idolized throughout France as a symbol of its will to endure, flew so high that he could not descend. In fact, unless man and plane vaporized in a mid-air explosion in the same fashion that falling shells vaporized men at the center of the blast, they all fell to earth in an aerial war every bit as casualty ridden as the land war.

The air war now stretched from hundreds of feet above the ground to 20,000 feet into the heavens. The British mounted high-altitude daylight raids over the German lines with DH4 single-engine day bombers accompanied by fighter escort. The Germans concentrated on perfecting a concept they had introduced late in 1916, namely highly maneuverable and even armored two-seat attack planes for ground-strafing missions. These Halberstadt and Hannoverana biplanes, their pilot and observer sharing the same cockpit for close communication, flew in weather that grounded other aircraft. Coming in low over the trenches, they descended in squadron strength into an imaginary tunnel delineated by the trajectory of arcing shells in order to machine-gun and grenade enemy troops and tanks. Junkers armored all-metal planes, known as *Möbelwagen,* or furniture vans, for their slow, lumbering performance, proved practically impervious to ground fire. The aircrew of these ground attack squadrons, with the exception of the commanding officer, comprised non-commissioned officers, often former infantrymen, who considered it their responsibility to protect their comrades on the ground. These aircrew fought the air war at its grittiest, on what the German crews called "*la rue de merde,*" or "shit street."

After a bruising year on the Western Front, Haig, supported largely by Robinson, still sought all available manpower for the Western Front, and only Lloyd George's refusal to give it to Haig enabled the British to balance manpower between the army and the economy. Robinson, because of the imperial nature of his general staff position, granted more importance to other fronts while accepting the primacy of the Western Front. Furthermore, by 1917 he had accepted Kitchener's earlier belief that only a war of attrition and blockade could defeat Germany. Unlike Haig, he ceased to believe in a *percée,* or breakthrough battle, that would destroy the German army. Haig concluded that only a complete victory would justify the appalling losses, and considered "for the future of our race to fall in the next year's offensive" preferable to compromise.[25]

THE EASTERN FRONT. RUSSIA QUITS THE WAR

The Provisional Government's Minister of War Alexander Kerensky and his Chief of Staff Gen. Brusilov launched the "Kerensky Offensive" on 18 June, an unmitigated disaster. After two days the army "voted with its feet," as the men deserted toward the rear, looting and raping as they retreated. The German and Austrian counter-attack simply drove the Russian Army and its Rumanian ally further back. The collapse of Russian morale enabled a German offensive against Riga, the key port on the Baltic coast.

In September German Eighth Army commander Gen. Oskar von Hutier seized Riga, which had resisted German conquest for two years. He used shock troops, trained to probe for and exploit gaps in enemy defenses, and armed with light machine-guns, portable mortars, and flame-throwers. The attack followed a short, ferocious, preliminary artillery barrage, in which artillery Gen. Bruchmüller, hereafter nicknamed "*Durchbruchmüller*" or "Breakthrough-Muller," had his batteries register their targets prior to the assault but wait until the moment of attack to fire. Riga fell in two days. The position of the Provisional Government grew more precarious, as the Germans on the Baltic front began to threaten Petrograd from the Gulf of Riga.

In late October, in the second Russian Revolution of 1917, the Bolsheviks seized power in Petrograd. They immediately decreed peace and requested a three-month armistice. The Russian war effort as a member of the Entente against Germany expired. The Bolsheviks appealed again for peace on 15 November, and a Soviet delegation met German, Austrian, Turkish, and Bulgarian representatives on 3 December at the Polish fortress city of Brest-Litovsk. The Bolsheviks and Central Powers argued and debated terms there for three months, through the start of the new year.

Meanwhile, behind the front in *Ober Ost*, the German military administration continued its colonization of occupied territory. *Ober Ost*'s byzantine bureaucracy requisitioned, levied direct and indirect taxes and tolls, and formed monopolies in order to milk the territory for the German Army. In the face of a relentless and arbitrary regime, popular resistance mounted. Farmers withheld their produce, and urban populations starved. In the midst of the chaos, the army's officials dreamed of creating a "new land," a bread basket, imposing their superior *Kultur* on the primitive peoples of the east. Early in 1917 they proposed to settle depopulated areas with German soldier-farmers, creating a military preserve for the next decisive war that Hindenburg envisaged. The army and its settlers would clear this *"Ostraum,"* or "East Space," of its "vermin," the "dirty" and primitive peoples. To begin creation of this new land the army press-ganged inhabitants into forced labor battalions. Resistance and growing national consciousness directed against the Germans' arbitary rule led inhabitants to join gangs of bandits and smugglers, who soon ruled the night, if the police ruled by day.

The developing peace movement in Germany and the Russian Provisional Government's concessions to the subordinate nationalities of eastern Europe prompted German Chancellor Bethmann Hollweg in May to moderate the army's insistence on outright annexation and order civilian officials to present the appearance of national autonomy. The OHL agreed to create client states, with indirect domination of the conquered nationalities, who would appear to ratify German rule. However, the high command's tendency to grant official posts to the Baltic Germans, who hated the region's Latvians and Estonians and preferred to remain a privileged caste in a German-dominated state, convinced the subordinate nationalities that German occupation exceeded Russian rule in severity.

Simultaneously, German soldiers began to "go native," fraternizing with women, who prostituted themselves to survive deprivation. The soldiers, increasingly undisciplined and brutalized, stole from army stores and inhabitants and traded on the black market. Class conflict arose within the army, as the officers enjoyed their special brothels and prospects as future despots, while the men, suffering in miserable conditions, became attracted to socialist propaganda. The military occupation of *Ober Ost* dispelled any notion of a *Frontgemeinschaft*, a special bond between officers and men that postwar German ideologs later touted.[26]

THE SOUTHWESTERN FRONT. CAPORETTO AND THE NEAR COLLAPSE OF THE ITALIAN ARMY

Italian Army commander Gen. Cadorna, adhering to the agreements of the Chantilly conference, launched the Tenth Battle of the Isonzo on 12 May. At its conclusion on 6 June, the Italian Army once again had registered small gains and large casualties. Cadorna attacked again in the Eleventh Battle of the Isonzo on 18 August. This time the Italian Second Army under Gen. Luigi Capello crossed the Isonzo River, climbed the face of the Bainsizza plateau, and beat the Austro-Hungarian forces back five miles. The Italian troops outran their artillery support and supply lines and concluded the offensive on 15 September. Once again, they suffered high casualties – 100,000 men – but their success had surprised Austro-Hungarian Emperor Karl and his advisors.

With the collapse of the Russian summer offensive on the Eastern Front, Karl moved forces to counter the Italian offensive with one of his own. He requested Ludendorff's permission to transfer Austro-Hungarian forces from the Eastern Front as well as German artillery support. Ludendorff offered seven German divisions, including ski troops, the famed Bavarian mountain division *Alpenkorps*, and Gen. Otto von Below to command a new joint Austro-German 14th Army to spearhead the offensive. Below would use German shock troops to infiltrate the rugged terrain of the Julian Alps to the rear of Italian units in the mountains. His infantry planned to cross the Isonzo near the town of Caporetto, advance twenty-five miles to the Tagliamento River, and halt, because Ludendorff had no intention of becoming bogged down in an Italian campaign. The Austro-German force outnumbered the Italian by fourteen to four divisions at the point of attack.

The Italians learned of enemy preparations, and Austro-Hungarian deserters had provided details. But the rigid Cadorna, accustomed to staging offensives and uncertain of the locus of the coming attack, simply left his front lines full of troops and his reserves too far back to help in a crisis. He planned to hold all ground gained in past offensives, and his forces actually outnumbered the enemy by forty-one to thirty-three divisions on the entire Isonzo front. Capello, confident after his success in the Eleventh Isonzo, positioned his weakest troops at the point of attack, intending to strike the attackers in the flank.

Fog, rain, and snow concealed the offensive's beginning on 24 October, and within twelve hours the Central Powers' combined forces had advanced ten miles through the Italian lines. In the Julian Alps, a young company commander in the Württemberg Battalion of the *Alpenkorps*, Erwin Rommel, led Schwabian companies in a spectacular and daring infiltration through the peaks deep into the Italian rear. His units ensnared thousands of Italian prisoners, including an entire regiment of 1,500 men, who surrendered to the lone Rommel standing in the road in front of them waving a white handkerchief, after he pointed to the machine-gun positions he had established on the hills above them. His daring tactics, which foreshadowed his methods as a famed tank commander in France and North Africa in the Second World War, gained him Germany's highest award for valor, the *Pour le Mérite*.

All along the line, other German and Austrian units cut deep into the Italian rear, bypassing strong points and sowing panic and demoralization among Italian troops they surprised. Cadorna ordered the Italian Army to withdraw to the Tagliamento River, Ludendorff's final goal, but the Austro-German forces' rapid advance and the collapse of Capello's Second Army at the focal point of the attack forced the Italian Army to flee. Cadorna consequently ordered a retreat behind the Piave River, seventy or eighty miles from the start of the offensive and twenty miles from Venice. He ruthlessly demanded the summary execution of stragglers, which only increased Italian casualties. By 9 November the Italians had stabilized the front along the Piave River. Ludendorff, more than content with the results, now returned German troops to the Western Front. Continued Austrian attacks through January 1918 failed to gain further ground.

American author Ernest Hemingway described the Italian rout at Caporetto in his famous novel *A Farewell to Arms*. The Italian Army had broken and run, not merely because of German skill and Italian errors, but because Italian soldiers had fought under abysmal conditions and subject to Cadorna's severe discipline for two years. Many of the soldiers, with the exception of elite troops such as *Alpini* had lost all will to fight. Consequently, 265,000 Italian soldiers surrendered and 300,000 deserted, while they suffered only 40,000 casualties.

The new Italian Premier, Vittorio Orlando, removed Cadorna as commander in chief in favor of a younger general, Armando Diaz, who, like his French counterpart Pétain, improved conditions for the Italian troops. His efforts, like Pétain's, would yield results in 1918. Caporetto prompted the Entente leaders to meet in the Italian city of Rapallo and to enact Lloyd George's proposal to form a Supreme War Council to coordinate the war effort against the Central Powers. Six French and five British divisions, along with aviation units, arrived from the Western Front after the Italian Army had contained the offensive.

OTTOMAN FRONTS. BRITISH AND ARABS IN THE MIDDLE EAST

Unlike 1916, when the Russian Army pummeled the Turks in the Caucasus, in 1917 the Russian Army slowly began to disintegrate in the summer. The

Turks could not exploit the decay, so in 1917 the Caucasus front became inactive. The Ottoman leaders could use their reserves either to stand on the defensive on all fronts, in Palestine, Mesopotamia, and the Caucasus, or to launch an offensive or offensives and expend their last strength.

As the Russian presence waned, British interests waxed. New Prime Minister David Lloyd George believed in the value of the Middle East, for its own sake and as a route to India, and sought to establish British hegemony there. Kitchener had placed no value on Palestine and the Middle East. Lloyd George's war aims, however, included the destruction of the Ottoman Empire, and he ordered British imperial forces in Egypt to attack. Furthermore, he planned to ignore the Sykes–Picot Treaty and to establish British power in Mesopotamia and Palestine. These new intentions represented a dramatic shift in British policy.[27]

Late in March 1917 the British imperial forces in Egypt launched an offensive against the Turks' twenty-mile-long Gaza–Beersheba defensive line. The Ottoman forces repulsed them then and again in April in the First and Second Battles of Gaza. In June 1917 Gen. Sir Edmund Allenby arrived from the Western Front to command the British forces, with the commission from Lloyd George that he deliver Jerusalem as a Christmas present for the people at home. "Bull" Allenby spent the rest of the summer preparing an offensive to break the Turkish line.

In Mesopotamia British Gen. Sir Stanley Maude commanded greatly strengthened forces against a Turkish Army in decline. Maude attacked up the Tigris River in December 1916, and on 11 March 1917 his troops entered Baghdad, which the Turks had abandoned to retreat upriver. Although Maude had a five-to-one advantage in manpower over the Ottomans, he chose to wait the summer in Baghdad, both in order to strengthen his supply lines and to avoid fighting the summer heat and disease. In the fall Maude resumed his offensive to capture as much of Mesopotamia as possible, although he himself died of cholera in November 1917.

The British advance in Mesopotamia forced the Turks to retreat from Persia, leaving it to the British and Russians, in order to reinforce their forces in Mesopotamia. Nevertheless, Enver Pasha determined to retake the strategic initiative by seizing Baghdad, the rest of Mesopotamia, and perhaps even Persia, with a new army group, the *Yildirim*, or Thunderbolt. In June his army commanders feared such grandiose schemes and preferred to husband their reserves to defend the empire. Gen. Falkenhayn, who discussed the options with the Turkish general staff, preferred to use the new army to push the British out of Palestine. Enver resolved the matter by placing Falkenhayn in command of the *Yildirim* and other forces in the region in July. Mustafa Kemal appreciated neither Falkenhayn's assumption of command over him and his army nor the offensive plans. In September he wrote Enver advocating a strictly defensive policy against the superior British forces and complained about Turkey becoming a German colony.[28] Kemal had to resign his army command several weeks later.

On 31 October Allenby rendered all Turkish discussions moot with a crushing offensive against the Gaza–Beersheba line, culminating in a charge by the Australian Light Horse straight through the Turkish defenses. Falkenhayn ordered a fighting retreat toward Jerusalem, as Allenby's forces advanced relentlessly. On 9 December Allenby entered Jerusalem, and Lloyd George secured his Christmas present for the British people. Allenby then proceeded to push the Turks further up the coast. The Turks finally held the line north of Jaffa, and Allenby's troops, exhausted from their victories, their logistical lines stretched to the limit, ceased offensive operations in late December. In the intervening three months, his forces, for the loss of 18,000 men, had inflicted 25,000 casualties on the Turks, who had held their defensive positions in the hilly, rocky country reasonably well against Allenby's two-to-one superiority in infantry and eight-to-one advantage in cavalry.

Throughout the year the Ottomans also contended with the Arab Revolt, which emerged full-blown in 1917 with British advice and financial aid totaling £11 million. Large-scale raids of four bands of 3 or 4,000 Arab horsemen repeatedly attacked Turkish garrisons and cut communications and transport lines, forcing the Turks to divert troops to protect them. The military significance of the Arab Revolt paled before the brute force of Allenby's army, but its political implications proved significant.

In January Feisal's force captured Wejh on the Red Sea, positioning them to strike Turkish troops in northern Arabia. Then, in the summer, Feisal and Lawrence secured the services of the tribes of northern Arabia. Lawrence accompanied 2,500 of them led by Auda abu Tayi, sheikh of the eastern Howeitat tribe, through arid desert to seize the small port of Aqaba at the southern point of Palestine. Aqaba's fixed defenses faced the sea, because approach from the desert posed minimal threat. Catching the Turkish garrison by surprise, Auda's force captured Aqaba on 6 July.

The epic march and striking victory made Lawrence a national hero in Britain, although in the final charge he accidentally shot his own camel in the head and fell unconscious. Auda had planned and led the strike, but Lawrence crossed enemy territory and the Sinai desert and appeared in Arab dress at British headquarters in Suez to report the victory, immediately after Allenby arrived to assume command. His participation in the epic exploit and his sensational arrival in Suez would have sufficed to catapult Lawrence into the public eye. Yet Lawrence coveted fame. His propensity to exaggerate led his listeners to believe that he had engineered the Aqaba campaign. They concluded that "Lawrence took Aqaba," creating the legend of Lawrence of Arabia.[29] From the new base at Aqaba, the Arabs could raid the Hejaz railway between Damascus and Medina and the Turkish left flank in Palestine.

Consequently, when Allenby launched his offensive in October, the Arab forces of Feisal and Lawrence protected Allenby's right flank and staged raids on the railway in the north while besieging the city of Medina in the south.

In March, the Imperial War Cabinet in London plotted the postwar reconfiguration of the British Empire. Not only did it entail the independence of the "white" dominions of South Africa, Canada, Australia, and New Zealand, it also sought to connect the empire in Africa and Asia. Palestine and Mesopotamia provided Britain with the land bridge connecting the two continents and ultimately creating a continuous empire from the Atlantic to the mid-Pacific Oceans.

Lloyd George also sought Palestine for a Jewish homeland. He stated nothing openly, but biblical indoctrination from his youth had inculcated in the Welshman a desire to restore the Holy Land to the Jews, an aim which coincided with the new political Zionist movement's desire for a Jewish homeland. The assistant secretaries in Lloyd George's War Cabinet, Leo Amery and Mark Sykes, who operated upon these assumptions of empire and a Jewish homeland, naively discerned no inherent conflict in their pro-Arab and pro-Zionist stances. A Jewish Palestine became a "bridge between Africa, Asia and Europe." The British Foreign Office more cynically believed that it would win powerful and wealthy Jewish communities, in the United States, for example, to their side.

On 2 November Foreign Secretary Balfour wrote Lord Rothschild conveying the government's sympathy toward Jewish Zionist aspirations and their intention to facilitate the establishment of a Jewish homeland in Palestine. The Balfour Declaration, with the later approval of the United States and France, would have a far greater effect on the peace settlement than anyone could have anticipated in 1917. Furthermore, what had begun in 1915 as a sideshow, namely the war against the Ottoman Empire, had now become the main theater of Lloyd George's imperial policy.[30]

THE WAR IN EAST AFRICA. THE PURSUIT CONTINUES

On 20 January 1917 Gen. Smuts relinquished his command to Maj. Gen. Reginald Hoskins, and within the week proclaimed the defeat of German resistance and the imminent end of the campaign. On 20 March Lloyd George invited Smuts to London to participate in the Imperial War Cabinet conference, where the Prime Minister introduced the South African as "One of the most brilliant generals in this war."[31] Hoskins, Lettow-Vorbeck, and the soldiers still in East Africa would have taken issue on all counts.

Hoskins accepted the fact that black Africans soldiered better than white Africans, Europeans, or Indians, and trebled the numbers of the King's

African Rifles (KAR), but always with European officers and additional European non-commissioned officers. He also improved the men's equipment and conscripted large numbers of Africans as porters. In May the Afrikaaner Gen. van Deventer replaced Hoskins, who went to command a division in Mesopotamia.

Meanwhile Lettow-Vorbeck stripped his columns of noncombatants, leaving European women for the British to intern and tend. The wives of the African *askaris*, however, defied the General's orders to remain behind and refused to leave their men. In February Capt. Max Wintgens took a force of some 700 *askaris* and without orders set off to wage his own little war against the British. Sick with typhus, Wintgens surrendered to the Belgians, but his force, under the command of Lieut. Heinrich Naumann, continued its depredations, pursued by 4,000 Belgian, KAR, and South African soldiers. The Entente forces finally corraled Naumann in early October, after a pursuit of eight months and 2,000 miles. His force had shrunk to fourteen Europeans, 165 *askaris*, and 250 porters.

In mid-July the KAR confronted a force of perhaps one-third its size under Capt. Eberhard von Liebermann, only to lose most of its British officers. The KAR troops under the command of African NCOs stood firm, however, and repulsed the attacks of the *askaris*, who disappeared into the bush. In early August Lettow-Vorbeck defeated an attacking Indian Army force, then slipped behind them to attack their supply column and disappeared. The Kaiser promoted Lettow-Vorbeck to Major General later that month. At the end of September, Deventer announced his readiness to advance, now that he had sufficient trucks. The opposing forces clashed in the bush on 17 October. The clash became a pitched battle much like the Western Front, as the forces attacked and counter-attacked, using bayonets and grenades with machine-gun and artillery support. They fought on the next day, until both sides pulled back and Lettow-Vorbeck withdrew. The British had lost 2,700 out of 4,900 men engaged, the Germans 500 out of 1,500.

Lettow-Vorbeck, short of supplies and ammunition, abandoned his sick and wounded for the British to tender, and forged ahead with some 200 Europeans and 2,000 *askaris* to unite with a force of 1,300 men under a subordinate, Capt. Theodor Tafel. Tafel, however, after repeatedly defeating British forces, ran out of food and believed that Lettow-Vorbeck had abandoned him. He consequently surrendered to Indian forces that he had ambushed in November. In fact, the two German forces had passed within a mile of one another in the bush. Later in November Lettow-Vorbeck crossed into Portuguese territory, promptly annihilated a 1,000-man Portuguese force, and seized supplies, weapons, and ammunition. King George V congratulated Gen. van Deventer on driving the *Schutztruppe* from German East Africa, but Lettow-Vorbeck and his troops still eluded their grasp.

By the end of 1917 the British withdrew all Indian troops from East Africa and would begin the campaign in 1918 with a force that was more than 90 percent black, with the addition of troops from West and South Africa and the West Indies. Now one black army officered by Europeans pursued another in Portuguese East Africa.

THE NAVAL WAR. SUBMARINE OFFENSIVE

British shipping losses to submarines fell to only 110,000 tons in January 1917, although the German submarine fleet had available 103 of 148 operational boats. Adm. von Holtzendorff's memorandum of 22 December 1916 stipulated breaking Britain's back by fall 1917 by sinking 600,000 tons of shipping monthly. He dismissed the possibility of war with the United States, and on 9 January 1917, the conference at Schloss Pless authorized unrestricted submarine warfare on 1 February, to win the war before the next harvest, by 1 August.

Chancellor Bethmann Hollweg labeled the judgment "a second decision for war," and viewed the undertaking as a dangerous military gamble, yet he could offer no alternative and capitulated to the military. Bethmann Hollweg's secretary Kurt Riezler further recognized the significance of the decision for the German monarchy, noting that the Kaiser would be "Wilhelm the Very Great or Wilhelm the Last."[32] Historian Avner Offer considered the decision "Germany's most critical action during the course of the war."[33] After the conference Hindenburg and Crown Prince Wilhelm denounced Bethmann Hollweg as a weakling and demanded that the Kaiser fire the chancellor.[34] In Britain Adm. David Beatty observed on 27 January, "[T]he real crux lies in whether we blockade the enemy to his knees, or whether he does the same to us."[35]

One hundred and five German submarines stood ready for action on 1 February: 46 in the High Sea Fleet; 23 in Flanders; 23 in the Mediterranean; 10 in the Baltic; and 3 at Constantinople. New construction, despite losses, ensured that the Germans had at least 120 boats available monthly for the rest of 1917. Unrestricted submarine warfare proved catastrophic for the British. German submarines blockaded the British Isles and the Mediterranean, sinking nearly half a million tons monthly in February and March, and then more than 860,000 tons in April. The number of merchant ships reaching Britain plummeted. By the end of April British wheat supplies had dwindled to six weeks. April would prove the zenith of the campaign, but in May losses exceeded 600,000 tons and in June rose to nearly 700,000. In the first three months of the campaign the Germans lost only nine subs, two to their own mines. At that rate Britain would face disaster and the prospect of a forced peace by late fall.

The United States replied to the German resumption of unrestricted warfare by severing diplomatic relations with Germany on 3 February and declaring war on Germany on 6 April. In contrast, the British Admiralty failed to respond effectively to the submarine offensive. First Sea Lord Jellicoe, and the older naval commanders, exhibiting the preoccupation with the offensive common to all British forces, proposed to undertake hunting patrols of *U-Boote*. The Admiralty refused initially to consider convoy or escort, which they deemed a defensive measure. They conveniently ignored the success of imperial troop convoys early in the war, the Dutch, French, and Scandinavian convoys that plied the European coast, and finally channel convoys between England and France. Junior naval officers and Maurice Hankey, secretary of the War Cabinet, believed in the potential of convoys, and on 27 April the Admiralty endorsed the convoy system, as did Lloyd George on 30 April. The first convoy sailed from Gibraltar on 10 May.

In early April Rear Adm. William Sims arrived in London as United States naval liaison. The Admiralty informed him, much to his dismay, that Germany would win the war if its submarines remained unchecked. Sims cabled Washington to send American destroyers to base at Queenstown and patrol west of Ireland. In May and June 1917 the British and Americans established a regular system of convoys across the Atlantic. After July, the monthly losses to submarines never again exceeded half a million tons, although they remained above 300,000 tons for the rest of the year. The Germans lost between five and ten submarines monthly, and their initial sense of imminent victory gave way by early June to the realization of the need to produce as many submarines as possible through to the end of 1918, even at the expense of further construction of battleships and battlecruisers. Labor and material shortages, however, delayed production.

Even as late as summer 1917 the British Admiralty accepted convoys only reluctantly, and launched an abortive sub-hunting operation with destroyers and submarines in June. However, hunting subs without first luring them toward a target such as a convoy offered limited prospects of success. German submarines sank more than sixteen British Q-ships, no longer the predator but the prey, in 1917. Mine-laying, once the British replaced their unreliable mines with copies of the proven German one, did account for eleven German subs in 1917; British submarines, another six in three and a half months after August. But these losses barely dented the German submarine force and fell well within the bounds of acceptable attrition.

The convoy system narrowly averted a disaster that the Admiralty's stubbornness had allowed. In convoy, destroyers and smaller escort craft could protect the merchant ships using the hydrophone to detect the submarines and depth charges to attack them. Merchant ships traveled in fast or slow convoys, and escorts prowled the seas around them searching for German predators. These escorts sank ten submarines in September. First the submarine had supplanted the battleship; now the construction of escort vessels further deflected Entente construction from the behemoths.

The submarine war in the Atlantic became the focal point of the naval war in 1917, but other naval struggles continued on the high seas and on the northern and southern seas around Europe.

German surface raiders – the *Moewe*, *Wolf (II)*, *Seeadler*, and the *Leopard* – sailed late in 1916 or early in 1917 on cruises ranging from eighteen months for the *Wolf* to ten days for the *Leopard*. The *Moewe*, the most successful of the raiders, sank or captured twenty-five ships totaling slightly more than 120,000 tons during a four-month cruise. The *Wolf* sank 114,000 tons in eighteen months, while the *Seeadler*, a sailing-ship whose exploits American correspondent Lowell Thomas romanticized, sank only 30,000 tons. A British cruiser sank the *Leopard* before she could prey on a single ship. These surface raiders recalled an earlier era of naval warfare. The ships and their commanders became popular topics in the 1920s, perhaps because of the romantic contrast they offered to the submarine war. But these 1917 cruisers failed to best the records of their predecessors *Emden* and *Karlsruhe*. Furthermore, the nearly 270,000 tons of shipping that they sank or captured paled before the depredations of the submarines.

In northern waters German destroyer flotillas staged raids in the Straits of Dover to facilitate the passage of submarines through the Channel, while the High Sea Fleet supported minesweepers that cleared passage of submarines. The war had resulted in a complete reversal of naval priorities, as the submarine and destroyer played more crucial roles than did capital ships. The German submarine service lured the best and most experienced junior officers from the fleet and rendered its surface ships more vulnerable to internal disturbances caused by disgruntled sailors, which began in August 1917.

German light cruisers successfully attacked Scandinavian convoys in the fall of 1917, and the British retaliated, unsuccessfully, with a battlecruiser and destroyer raid into the Helgoland Bight against German minesweepers. The Scandinavian convoys, nevertheless, proved highly satisfactory overall. The German raid, however, did stoke the fire of growing dissatisfaction in Britain with the Admiralty, which removed Jellicoe as First Sea Lord in December.

In the Baltic, the revolution administered a final blow to the Russian fleet. Sailors murdered their officers and formed revolutionary committees to share command of the ships. The larger the vessel, the worse the relationships between officers and men. Discipline collapsed, and the Baltic Fleet lost its effectiveness. Russian submarines did sortie, but with no results, while German submarines sowed mines and attacked shipping.

In October the Germans undertook the major naval operation of the Baltic war in concert with the army's advance on Riga. They planned to control the Gulf of Riga and enlisted the participation of the High Sea Fleet, whose commander Scheer hoped that action might raise the morale of his idle and restless sailors. The operation, code-named Albion, entailed the seizure of two islands by an amphibious landing of nearly 25,000 soldiers supported by a powerful German task force. The landing succeeded on 12 October, although German ships suffered some damage from mines. By 20 October the Germans commanded the islands. The Russian Navy retreated from the gulf, ending the Baltic Fleet's war. The German Navy did not pursue.

By mid-1917 the British had assumed the predominant role in the anti-submarine war in the Mediterranean from the French and Italians. The Japanese played the predominant naval role in the Indian Ocean and sent at British request three destroyer flotillas totaling fourteen new destroyers to assist the British in escorting troop-ships through the Mediterranean. In the fall the U.S. Navy, having assigned its newest vessels to the North Atlantic, sent a few cruisers, its four oldest destroyers, and a motley collection of Spanish-American war gunboats and cutters to Gibraltar. The Entente navies ran individual convoys, but lacked the escort vessels to establish systematic escort for all convoys. In any case, the Central Powers mustered under twenty German and a few Austrian submarines in the Mediterranean.

In the Adriatic Sea action focussed on the Otranto barrage, which amounted to a patrol by trawlers with nets. Nevertheless, severely inadequate numbers of trawlers rendered the barrage porous. In mid-May an Austrian cruiser squadron attacked the trawlers at night while destroyers and submarines hunted any transports. The cruisers sank or disabled eighteen trawlers, but then found their escape blocked by a superior Entente cruiser force under Italian command. As night turned to day, additional Entente and Austrian forces raced to join the fray, but the Austrian ships eluded their pursuers in a running fight. The Austrians considered the encounter the high point of the war for their navy, because their ships had engaged a superior enemy force, inflicted more damage than they suffered, and escaped. The battle, however, did not alter the naval stalemate in the Adriatic.

The Russian Navy continued to dominate the Black Sea even after the revolution, as it continued its blockade of Turkish merchant traffic and undertook mining and coastal bombardment operations well into the summer. Turkish and German ships dared enter the Black Sea only on raids. The Bolshevik Revolution and the armistice of 16 December signaled the abrupt end of Russian naval operations in the Black Sea. Naval combat ceased in the Baltic and Black Seas. Stalemate reigned in the Adriatic and the Mediterranean. The key to victory remained in the North Atlantic.

German unrestricted submarine warfare failed to drive Britain from the war, and drew America into it. Historians' analysis of the supposedly rational economic calculations supporting the entire venture demonstrates the Germans' incredibly optimistic wishful thinking. Germany never had sufficient submarines to drive Britain from the war. The Germans' desperate strategy proved so successful and threatening only because of the initial British failure to react.

Ultimately, the British and American navies' adoption of the convoy system and their naval manufacturing capacity meant that Germany faced 1918 with its submarines still dangerous, but no longer as effective, and fighting mounting odds. Germany now had to win the war before the United States could bring its potential might to bear on the European continent, or face likely defeat by the mightier coalition that German strategy had instigated.

THE HOME FRONTS

Russia. Revolutions

By 1917 the Russian economy was collapsing. The industrial mobilization had drawn people to factories and mines from the fields to the detriment of agricultural production. Those left on the land suffered reduced incomes and often simply retreated from the market economy in order to survive. The urban population's wages, even those of metalworkers, fell far behind the rate of inflation, plunging them into a poverty and despair reflected in the sky-rocketing numbers of suicides. The secret police reported the growing embitterment of the masses, but Tsar Nicholas refused to hear of the worsening conditions.[36] Declining railway stock could no longer supply food and fuel to the cities as well as to the armies.

A series of strikes commemorating "Bloody Sunday," 9 January 1905, when the Tsar's Cossacks had crushed the revolution of 1905, evolved into huge demonstrations. Banners demanded bread and decried the war and the autocracy. Cossacks responded lackadaisically. On 25 February 200,000 workers smashed shops and fought with police. The tsarist government responded as it had in 1905, summoning the Guards, the elite of the Russian Army, to crush the mob. With 180,000 soldiers in the Petrograd garrison, and another 150,000 in the area, the fate of the workers seemed sealed. But war had transformed the Guards. Reserve battalions comprised new recruits or wounded veterans commanded by young, inexperienced officers.

Working women, fed up with their long hours, low wages, and inability to secure the necessities of life for their families, led the demonstrators, fearlessly confronting Cossacks and elite Guards, urging the soldiers to let them pass. The soldiers relented, and when the police opened fire on the crowd, the Cossacks charged the police, not the demonstrators. A few of the tsar's troops remained loyal to the government, and found themselves fighting other soldiers and the crowd. Violent demonstrations on 27 February continued the next day, when the Petrograd garrison joined the crowd. The bulwark of tsarist authority in the capital had essentially revolted against tsarist rule.

The Russian Duma, or Parliament, established a Provisional Committee, but the Duma represented at most one-eighth of the Russian people, those of means, who voted in its elections. Soviets, or committees of workers, peasants, and soldiers, arose spontaneously around the country to represent the seven-eighths of the Russian people previously without political voice.

At military headquarters Tsar Nicholas, now that the demonstrators had his attention, resolved to send the army to restore order, but Gen. Alekseev cautioned that they risked a clash between military units and the desertion of more troops to the revolution. Nicholas refused to consider the appointment of a ministry responsible to the Duma, because that would violate his autocratic prerogatives. Alekseev advised him that revolution meant a "disgraceful termination" of the war, since the army at the front was "intimately connected" to life and events in the rear.[37] Nicholas solemnly concluded, "I shall renounce the throne."[38] Later he abdicated, and his only likely successor, his brother Grand Duke Michael, wanted no part of the throne. The tsar's abdication on 2 March thus concluded some 300 years of Romanov rule in Russia. Nicholas Romanov and his family became the prisoners of the Provisional Government and the Petrograd Soviet, while the crowd in the capital destroyed all symbols of the autocracy.

The new Provisional Government of the Duma, led by the liberal P.N. Miliukov as Foreign Minister and the Executive Committee of the Petrograd Soviet, agreed on a number of reforms, from equality of civil rights, such as trial by jury, to the granting of independence to Poland and autonomy to the Ukraine. Only the dynamic socialist Alexander Kerensky sat in both the Provisional Government and the Petrograd Soviet. The Provisional Government did nothing to stem inflation or to enact land reform by distributing fields to the peasants. Most fatally, Miliukov's government and Soviet agreed to continue the war: the former, to pursue Russian war aims and honor obligations to the Entente; the latter, to defend the revolution and seek a peace without annexations. Law and order disappeared along with the police, but the Petrograd military garrison formed committees of soldiers and sailors and swore allegiance to the Soviet. Furthermore, not only workers' factory committees but also revolutionary workers' militia arose, the latter annointed the "Red Guard of the Proletariat," to protect the revolution.

April marked the German Army's return of Vladimir Ilyich Lenin to Russia from exile in Europe, most recently Switzerland, since 1907. Lenin, a brilliant and dedicated Marxist revolutionary, asserted that the party constitute the vanguard of revolution. Since 1903 he had led the Bolshevik faction of the Russian Social Democratic Party, which became the Bolshevik Party in 1912. Lenin believed that the long, savage war weakened its participants and made them ripe for revolution.

The German OHL, which would use any means necessary to drive its opponents from the war, sought to foment revolution in the empires of the Entente. To increase the chaos in Russia, they shipped Lenin and associates, like germs, in a sealed train across Germany to the Baltic, where the Russian *émigrés* sailed for Sweden and entered Russia by train at the Finland Station in Petrograd on 16 April.

Lenin immediately broached to the Bolsheviks and then the Soviet his April Theses advocating land, bread, and peace for the people, and all power to the Soviets. The slogan initially surprised the Bolsheviks and the Petrograd Soviet, but Lenin, undaunted, pressed on. Soon Petrograd workers were calling for peace and Miliukov's resignation. In May Prince Lvov formed a coalition Cabinet without Miliukov, in which Kerensky became Minister of War and Navy and emerged as its most charismatic figure.

Shortages still plagued Russia, and continued inflation meant that Russians could afford neither sufficient food nor adequate shelter. Workers sought higher wages and an eight-hour working day, although the former simply exacerbated the inflationary spiral. Urban strikes became violent again, while the peasants, who understood little about the politics occurring in the cities, insisted on their demands for land and peace.

In May another socialist exile, Leon Trotsky, returned to Russia from New York. Brilliant intellectual, peerless organizer, and spellbinding orator, Trotsky had played a key role in the revolution of 1905 before being exiled to Siberia, where he escaped to western Europe. He joined the Bolsheviks in July and quickly rose to prominence in the party and the Soviet.

The First All-Russian Congress of Soviets of Workers' and Soldiers' Deputies convened in Petrograd in June. The mass demonstration of nearly half a million marchers indicated that although the Bolsheviks formed a distinct minority in governmental institutions, the masses in the capital shared their sentiments about peace and power to the Soviets.

Kerensky proved the man of choice of the Duma and Soviet to lead Russia at this crucial time. As Minister of War, he selected Brusilov as his chief of staff and ordered an offensive at the front for June 1917. Soldiers deserted, threatened the transport authorities, threw passengers off trains and boarded them for home. Female soldier Maria Bochkareva, supported by the Provisional Government, formed the volunteer First Russian Women's Battalion of Death in early July in an attempt to shame the men to fight. The women suffered 80 percent casualties, while 12,000 soldiers deserted weekly. Even in early Russian advances, commanders watched their men turn and walk away from the battlefield.[39]

The collapse of the Kerensky offensive and worsening economic conditions led to a spontaneous uprising against the government in Petrograd on 16 July. Government troops crushed the uprising in three days, arrested some Bolsheviks and ransacked their party headquarters and press, but Lenin escaped to Finland and the government did not root out the party for fear of alienating other socialists. After the July uprising, Kerensky became Prime Minister, and removed Brusilov for a Cossack general risen from the ranks, Lavr Kornilov. Kerensky, who had promised to protect Nicholas Romanov and his family, sent them to Siberia.

Kornilov attracted the support of a newly arisen counter-revolutionary movement of generals and industrialists seeking to overthrow Kerensky. Kerensky initially sought Kornilov's help in restoring the military and crushing the Bolsheviks. The general ordered reliable troops to Petrograd late in August to protect the Provisional Government and crush the Soviets and their supporters. Kerensky, however, suspected that Kornilov in fact planned to overthrow the government and responded by dismissing the general and ordering his troops to desist. Kornilov ordered his forces to advance on the capital. Kerensky threw in his lot with the Soviet and even opened the armory in Petrograd so that the Red Guards could better arm themselves.

Kornilov's army "melted away" in September on the way to Petrograd. Railroad and telegraph workers refused to cooperate, while people, including Bolshevik agents, encouraged his men to desert rather than attack. In the aftermath Kerensky acquired dictatorial powers as prime minister and supreme commander. But the "Kornilov Affair" undermined the authority of the Provisional Government, and Kerensky had alienated the right and armed the Bolsheviks.

As the Russian Army disintegrated at the front, the Germans advanced toward Petrograd in September and October. The Provisional Government proposed to transfer the government to Moscow; the Bolsheviks insisted on the defense of the capital at all costs. Among the various parties, the Bolsheviks had the strongest connections to the workers and soldiers in Petrograd and Moscow. This mass support enabled them to win majorities in the Petrograd and Moscow Soviets.

Lenin returned from Finland for a party meeting on 23 October, and insisted on seizing power immediately. Because Lenin had to remain in hiding, Trotsky directed the coup. He chaired the Petrograd Soviet and its military committee in charge of the Petrograd garrison, the Red Guards, and the sailors of the Kronstadt naval base. On the night of 24/25 October, the Red Guards, the Petrograd garrison, and the sailors from the Kronstadt naval base seized communications, transport, and financial agencies and the tsar's former Winter Palace where the Provisional Government convened. They accomplished their mission so discreetly that few people realized what had occurred.

When the Second All-Russian Congress of Soviets convened the following day, many representatives seceded in protest against the developments of the preceding night, leaving the Bolsheviks firmly in charge. The Bolsheviks announced a new government of the Council of People's Commissars, with

Lenin as Chair and Trotsky in charge of foreign affairs, and proclaimed an end to the war and the abolition of private ownership of land. They decreed the expropriation of the wealthy. After a week of violent struggle, led by the Red Guards, the Bolsheviks completed the seizure of power in Moscow, which gave them control of the critical central Petrograd–Moscow axis of Russia.

On 25 November the Bolsheviks allowed a free and open election for a constituent assembly, and won fewer than a quarter of the seats. The Socialist Revolutionaries, an amorphous party comprising a spectrum from peasants to assassins, won more than half of the assembly's seats. The assembly would convene on 18 January 1918.

Austria-Hungary. Near exhaustion

The Austrian and Hungarian governments had to renegotiate the *Ausgleich*, their agreement establishing the Dual Monarchy in 1867, as its twenty-year term would end on 31 December. The Cabinets signed a preliminary agreement on 27 February, but events precluded further negotiations. Kaiser Karl planned to remove Tisza from office as soon as possible. Karl sought to enter history as a prince of peace and wanted to end the war as quickly as possible. Consequently, he planned to purge his government of any statesman or general who had been involved in the origins of the war. Conrad suggested that if the Central Powers could not resolve the war to their advantage early in 1917, conditions would only worsen.[40] Karl removed Conrad from the AOK on 28 February, replacing him with the apolitical, unobtrusive, and obedient Gen. Arthur Arz von Straussenburg. With the removal of the generals around Conrad, the new AOK fell even further under the influence of the German high command.

In the winter of 1916–17 Austrian civilians experienced severe coal and food shortages that left them cold, hungry, exhausted, and discouraged. Hungary enjoyed better fuel and food supply, and the army, but not the Austrian civilian population, received Hungarian food supplies. Exploiting the conquered territories did little to alleviate the shortages. Inflation and food shortages reached crisis proportions in spring 1917. Even the government judged the monarchy to be "at the end of its endurance."[41] Habsburg Foreign Minister Czernin, noting that soldiers had recently killed more than twenty men and women in a hunger demonstration, believed that Austria-Hungary stood on the brink of revolution.[42]

By Easter 1917, Austro-Hungarian and Russian troops were fraternizing at the front. The Petrograd Soviet's call for the working masses of the world to unite prompted the AOK to consider moving troops of questionable reliability, such as the Czechs, Serbs, and Rumanians, from the Russian to the Italian front. By the end of May 1917 the Czechs had already begun to reject autonomy within the Habsburg monarchy in favor of an independent existence.

Karl insisted that Tisza introduce a voting system into Hungary that would grant equal voting rights to all nationalities. When Tisza refused, Karl demanded and obtained Tisza's resignation on 22 May. The emperor also summoned the Austrian Parliament, as the collapse of autocracy in Russia catapulted Austria into the position of the most repressive of regimes. On 30 May the Austrian *Reichsrat* convened for the first time since 1914. Embittered debates about the relationship of the nations to the state and about the future of the empire immediately dominated the proceedings. Austrian Prime Minister Clam-Martinic resigned in June, an indication of dwindling hopes for a favorable future for the monarchy.

The dismal internal political and economic circumstances boded ill for the future of the Dual Monarchy. The peasants' anger about requisitions of their crops made a further decline in the food supply likely. Even the occupation and exploitation of Poland, Serbia, and Montenegro did not enable the government to improve the food supply to the monarchy's population. Polarization between town and country, conflicts among nationalities, and the radicalization of political parties, which adopted the slogans of the Russian Revolution, plagued the monarchy. After May strike followed strike, as metal and railway workers vented their rage at long hours, inflation, and food shortages. Early in July the government militarized all factories, subjecting all workers to military discipline and penalities, and introduced a shorter work week of slightly over fifty hours. The war for civilians focussed no longer on the front, but on securing the basic necessities of life. Listlessness, apathy, anger, and resignation reigned.[43]

Austria-Hungary used prisoners-of-war to compensate for manpower losses, and by 1917 more than a million prisoners labored on agricultural estates and built roads. Most of them lacked the skills to work in industry, but Austrian and Hungarian employers still preferred to use prisoners-of-war rather than women in industry and mining. Women wanted to work like their counterparts in other countries, but industry employed far lower percentages of female labor than in other countries. Industrialists remained convinced that women should remain at home and that their presence in industry would cause unrest. Women who did join the industrial workforce received abysmal wages and housing.[44]

In the spring Kaiser Karl formed a commission to prepare for postwar demobilization as he broached unsuccessful peace initiatives with the French government. The army began to plan its postwar force as well, although in the fall the Hungarian government demanded separate postwar Austrian and Hungarian armies. The emperor postponed a final decision on the matter until after the war.

The War Minister informed the Kaiser in August of their bleak prospects for survival through the coming winter. Poorly fed and clothed troops, malnourished and inadequately trained conscripts, and substandard officers began the litany of problems. The army lacked adequate transport, fuel, and essential materials. In contrast, a surfeit of generals, some of whom profited from the war by selling farm produce from their estates to the army, acting as middlemen to war industry, and serving on boards in industry and banking, plagued the army. The monarchy had to husband its humanpower by avoiding offensives at the front, incorporating women in the industrial workforce at home, and, above all, ensuring adequate supplies of food and coal. With the approach of winter, Austria-Hungary teetered on the brink of collapse.

The defeat of Russia and the successful offensive at Caporetto did cause some officials to change their minds about the survivability of Austria-Hungary. Foreign Minister Count Czernin, who in April had predicted the collapse of the monarchy in the fall, concluded by the fall that the Dual Monarchy had sufficient soldiers, armaments, and food to continue the war.[45] Austria-Hungary had little choice. On 7 December the monarchy acquired another enemy. The United States, answering the request of the Italian government for assistance after Caporetto, declared war on Austria-Hungary.

Germany. "Total war" and the "infinite screw"

The OHL's Hindenburg Program sought to mobilize Germany "totally" to fight a "total" war. Hindenburg, conceiving of war production as an "infinite screw," expected to command industry through the War Office as he and Ludendorff commanded the German Army. The entire German population would exist to serve the Fatherland, either as warriors or as workers. Soldiers at the front had become workers of war, hardened infantrymen who strode the battlefields, or aviator aristocrats who mastered the new technology and products of industry to kill mercilessly and efficiently. Industrial labor, worker bees in the gigantic hives of German factories, would provide the warriors with the weapons they required. A program of patriotic instruction initiated in July 1917 would educate the population – women, youth, crippled soldiers – about the importance of mobilization, and they would all be trained to work in war industries.

Not only did the Program foresee the mobilization and regimentation of the population, but the War Office under Gen. Groener infringed the powers of the Chancellor and the Prussian War Ministry. It presumed further to centralize a federal state whose civilian bureaucracies jealously guarded their states' prerogatives.

The infringement of its powers infuriated the Prussian War Ministry, which labeled the new production quotas "impossible" and the Auxiliary Service Law mobilizing the population "a wild-goose chase." The War Ministry damned Groener for "moving too far to the left" in his encouragement of better wages for labor and his acknowledgment of the unions' right to collective bargaining and to establish mediation committees in factories. Nevertheless, Groener recognized the necessity of concessions to the workers to secure their loyalty to the monarchy after the war, especially if it did not end victoriously. Neither his superiors Hindenburg and Ludendorff nor the leaders of heavy industry, however, could conceive an end other than a victorious peace of conquest and annexations, and the OHL removed Groener from office in July 1917.

The War Ministry experienced righteous anger, because it had attempted to coordinate and increase its targets for the production of powder, cannon, rifles, machine-guns, and ammunition judiciously. Now the War Office's targets, although often not significantly greater, claimed to double and triple the previous ones. These new production targets further lacked comprehensive coordination, so that powder production did not correspond to ammunition and shell production, nor did weapons production accord with the army's actual manpower. The army consequently had more powder and more weapons than it could use by the end of the year.

In July 1917 the OHL still had to release 1.9 million more workers from the military to meet production quotas, while the transportation system was collapsing under the weight of the additional demands. The Reichstag's adjustments to the Auxiliary Service Law did not secure new workers in the already tight German labor market. Workers who were already employed exploited the law to increase their rights, much to the dismay of the industrialists.

The "turnip winter" of 1916–17 ushered in a most difficult year for the German home front. In this unusually bitterly cold winter temperatures plunged to 25 degrees below zero Fahrenheit. Women froze in lengthy food lines for minimal foodstuffs, and began to battle with police in food riots or in their attempts to loot food stores. News of the Russian Revolution and later the United States' declaration of war did not displace urban workers' concerns about food. Police noted that many people simply did not care about the war and had lost faith in the government. Georg Michaelis, former head of the Prussian Grain Authority, became head of the Prussian Commissariat for Provisions on 21 March because he seemed a forceful proponent of government control of food to equalize distribution.[46]

Hunger strikes turned into food riots with political overtones, as workers demanded equal votes in Prussia. Public anger at the government's failure to ensure equal distribution of food and curtail the black market as well as a decrease in bread and potato rations spawned strikes in April 1917 that spread from Berlin throughout Germany. Strikers often numbered in the hundreds of thousands, bringing entire industries to a standstill. Government officials committed themselves to improving the distribution of food and prosecuting profiteers, but Michaelis could do nothing to rectify the food shortages.

In the cities only industrialists and highly skilled workers in war industry earned enough to keep pace with the increasing inflation, which eroded the income and the savings of salaried employees and impoverished the petty bourgeoisie and other workers. Those on government relief, from wives and children of servicemen to the elderly, simply could not afford the higher prices of the basic necessities of life. People were slowly starving. They collapsed in food lines, in the streets, in front of posted casualty lists. In Berlin a starving horse collapsed in the street, and hordes of women brandishing kitchen knives instantly rushed from apartments, screaming and fighting as they stripped the carcass, even collecting the blood in cups. Afterward they disappeared as quickly as they had appeared.[47] Prescribed rations fell below subsistence level, as ration coupons became worthless scraps of paper apportioning non-existent food.

Government promises notwithstanding, the black market boomed, as by spring 1917 farmers cared little about the war or the government and refused to accept price ceilings. They either ate their produce or sold it to the wealthy on the black market. Even when the police actually confiscated food trains, the government often failed to dispense the goods, guarding the train while the food rotted. By the summer people had become thoroughly fed up with substitute, or ersatz foods, some of which proved patently toxic. A woman in Leipzig commented that she did not mind eating rat, but she objected to rat substitute.[48] Demonstrations that summer became increasingly violent, because police did not intervene to halt the depredations of women attacking stores and government offices. Poorer women did not concern themselves about the vote as did their bourgeois counterparts; food and the state's obligation to supply it preoccupied the poor.

The OHL's concern on the home front focussed on urban workers who produced weapons and munitions. Military agencies pushed industrialists to redesign large factories to use women's labor, and the War Office established a Women's Bureau that collaborated with bourgeois women's organizations such as the National Committee for Women's Work in the War. Middle-class women "exhibit[ed] their patriotism predominantly by pressing working-class women into war factories."[49] By mid-1917 some 3.5 million women labored in munitions factories, comprising perhaps 50 percent of the armaments industry's workforce and reaping the benefit of extra rations the War Office accorded these highly valued workers.

Employers and the government reminded the growing numbers of women in industry that they were replacing men only temporarily until the end of the war, when they should return to their families. This bromide ignored the reality that working-class women had invariably worked before the war, but in other jobs. Perhaps a million women toiled in machine shops and ammunition plants under difficult circumstances. Long hours working with poisonous chemicals in ammunition factories, night work, and lower pay than men meant that they left their children for long periods of time for work that undermined their health. Perhaps a quarter of a million youths aged 14 to 17 also worked in the factories, missing formal schooling and often falling into delinquent ways with money in their pockets and no family structure to constrain them. Finally, all except the wealthy and the farmers suffered from malnutrition. "Food edema" – swelling of arms and legs – appeared in spring 1917 and the wartime mortality rate among civilians increased, certainly in substantial part because of the British "hunger blockade."

The stress of wartime was eroding the fabled German unity of 1914, as the deprivations and losses drove resentments between rural and urban dwellers, farmers and consumers, industrialists and workers, rich and poor to boiling point. Perched above this cauldron, Hindenburg, Ludendorff, and the leaders of heavy industry pursued extensive war aims of conquest and annexation, counting on a victorious war to preserve the social and political structure of Germany and placate the German masses.

The OHL looked forward to annexing territory in western and eastern Europe, in the west for industry, iron, and coal, in the east as a buffer against Russia and for colonization. The Admiralty planned to annex the Belgian and Baltic coasts and gain naval bases around the globe. Furthermore, the OHL publicized war aims for public debate to rally the right-wing conservatives, Pan-Germans, nationalists, and industrialists against the "weak" and "defeatist" Chancellor Bethmann Hollweg and against the German left's advocacy of a "peace without annexations and indemnities" in mid-April 1917. That same month the German left fractured under the influence of the Russian Revolution, when the radicals seceded from the Social Democratic Party, formed the Independent Social Democratic Party, and opposed the war. The split compounded the unrest within the working class. Some conservatives contemplated replacing not only the Chancellor but also the Kaiser with a military dictatorship under the High Command.

Bethmann, in fact, supported substantial annexations, but sought to bridge the chasm between right and left in Parliament to ensure passage of loans to finance the war effort. Confronted with the direct challenge of the OHL, in April 1917 Bethmann Hollweg announced his plan to replace the current Prussian three-class voting system – in which the weight of the male vote depended upon wealth – with direct, secret, and equal male suffrage. Horrified Prussian Conservatives opposed the idea unequivocally, and the Kaiser's Easter message of 7 April promised to study, not to reform, the Prussian suffrage after the war. The OHL and its right-wing minions now targeted Bethmann Hollweg, who had once played Hindenburg and Ludendorff against Falkenhayn, but who now stood alone with no recourse. Ludendorff now alleged that the Chancellor was catering to the forces responsible for revolution in Russia.

Events in the German Parliament, the Reichstag, reached a climax on

7 July, when Matthias Erzberger, leader of the Catholic Center Party, insisted that Germany needed to sue for peace abroad and prepare to introduce democracy at home. A parliamentary committee of Progressives, Catholic Centrists, and Social Democrats called for a peace "without annexations and indemnities." The debate over the "peace resolution," which the Reichstag passed 214 to 116 on 19 July, catalyzed the OHL into action, and on 12 July they threatened to resign, demanding the Kaiser choose between them or the Chancellor. Bethmann Hollweg, whose "policy of the diagonal," or zigzag between right and left, had satisfied no one, resigned on 13 July. That same month the OHL removed Groener from the War Office and introduced patriotic instruction in an attempt to restore order in Germany.

The OHL suggested as their candidate for chancellor Georg Michaelis, whom the Kaiser endorsed. Michaelis's reputation as an expert on and champion of food distribution to the cities justified his appointment. He promptly quashed the peace resolution and later refused Pope Benedict XV's offer of mediation in September. Yet Michaelis could not bring order to the increasingly chaotic circumstances in Germany. A despondent population feared the future, particularly a fourth winter of war. Disgruntled sailors in Kiel commented that they would merely like to eat their turnips like officers, with lots of meat.[50] On 2 August in the naval port of Wilhelmshaven, restless sailors from an idle fleet mutinied. Naval authorities, informed that many sailors had recently joined the Independent Socialist Party (USPD), acted forcefully, and executed two sailors and imprisoned another three in early September.

On 2 September Grand Adm. (ret.) von Tirpitz and Prussian bureaucrat Wolfgang Kapp founded the right-wing German Fatherland Party. Funded by wealthy industrialists, it sought a victorious and annexationist peace and opposed any reform of the Prussian three-class voting system. Industrialists such as Emil Kirdorf and Hugo Stinnes, much agitated by the Peace Resolution in July, regarded the party as essential to German security. Stinnes fanatically supported the introduction of unrestricted submarine warfare in the cause of shortening the war, however great the risk. Here, he differed from Walther Rathenau, who had confronted Ludendorff in February and July with negative assessments of the potential of submarine warfare. Questioning the wisdom of risking war with the United States, Rathenau advocated the necessity of ending the war quickly, based on a peace without annexations and political reforms at home.[51] Rathenau's sense of Germany's vulnerability had led him to conclusions diametrically opposed to those of most major German industrialists, who, like the OHL, became more extreme in their annexationist demands and absolute resistance to change at home.

In October Michaelis attempted to use the naval mutinies to censure the USPD in the Reichstag, but his plan backfired as the deputies interpreted this as a step to revoke parliamentary immunity. The opposition of a center–left coalition forced Michaelis's resignation on 31 October. The aged Bavarian Catholic Count Georg von Hertling replaced him as Chancellor. By winter the Fatherland Party, representing the OHL and industry on the right, and the SPD and USPD, representing labor on the left, completely polarized German politics. Meanwhile, government food scandals proliferated around Germany, including promises of jam in Berlin in the fall that never materialized. Jam commanded attention equal to the Bolshevik Revolution, and neither boded well for future popular trust in the legitimacy of the monarchy.[52]

Italy. Riot and repression

In the winter of 1916–17 women and youth began to flock to industry, as Dallolio's government undersecretariat promoted rationalization and mass production and the consequent employment of unskilled, low wage labor. Fiat's workforce expanded from 4,000 in 1915 to 40,150 in 1918; Ansaldo, from 6,000 in 1916 to 111,000 in 1918. Food shortages resulted in inadequate nutrition for workers, while the imposition of the military penal code, which soldiers enforced in factories, led to exploitation of the workers – low wages with increases that failed to keep pace with the cost of living, and hours, including overtime, up to sixteen or eighteen per day. The state reduced taxes on entrepreneurs, provided them with advances on payments and raw materials, and bought their products at prices granting them high profits.

As the war continued, these conditions led to rural and urban popular rebellion. The outbursts began in the winter of 1916–17. Peasants demonstrated and workers struck, as social protest spread throughout the country. They had much to protest: declining living standards and working conditions; food shortages; bitterness about social inequality as the long war benefited the privileged minority in society at the expense of the masses; and resentment at the state's inefficient distribution of food and inadequate welfare.

Upon news of the Russian Revolution, the mass demonstrations gained in intensity in the spring, abated in the summer, and intensified again in the fall. In the south peasant crowds invaded government buildings, trashed offices, burned induction and requisition orders, and openly cursed the war and class injustice. The urban workplace did not escape the spread of violent demonstrations, as workers ripped up trolley tracks, cut communications lines, and attacked town halls.

Women predominated in the workers' ranks of Milan who started demonstrations in Lombardy in May. Factory disciplinary legislation late in 1916 rendered male workers liable to charges of military insubordination for even a small argument with a factory superior. Consequently women, members of the "new" working class, or a new segment of a more complex working class, comprised more than 60 percent of strikers. The lowest paid workers, dissatisfied consumers, and the focus of appeals to demonstrate against the war from soldiers at the front, women played key roles in the demonstrations.

The elevation of Dallolio's undersecretariat to a Ministry of Arms and Munitions in June 1917 demonstrated the increasing importance of industrial mobilization in the midst of growing unrest. Already in the fall of 1916 Dallolio had counseled his subordinate agencies that in industrial disputes they should take more impartial stands independent of employers and incorporating workers' demands. In part he hoped to secure the workers' acceptance of the government's industrial mobilization in the postwar era. In this respect Dallolio's pursuit of postwar worker loyalty through his agency's policies replicated Gen. Wilhelm Groener's conduct of the War Office in Germany.

The main strikes of 1917 occurred in industrial centers of the metal and mechanical industries. In Turin in August what began as a protest of women workers over the absence of bread exploded into a popular insurrection of riots and barricades. Police and soldiers intervened, killed or wounded some demonstrators and arrested a thousand others. In the metalworking centers of Liguria strikes that began in the summer evolved into a general strike in October. Police designated the entire province of Liguria, including Turin and Genoa, a war zone.

The state responded by dissolving the most militant labor organizations and sending militants either to the front or to island penal colonies. The defeat at Caporetto also enabled the state to extend the war zone, and military control, to much of northern Italy. Consequently the Munitions Ministry asked the Interior Ministry to move even suspected radicals away from industrial zones, while its agencies sent militant workers to the military authorities for punishment. The Italian government's fear of a general strike and insurrection also prompted it to ameliorate living conditions, increase subsidies to soldiers' families, improve leave for soldiers, increase food supplies by compensating farmers more for requisitions and importing food, and control food prices. Dallolio's ministry intervened with industry to ensure the improvement of wages, hours, and sanitary conditions. It also included workers' representatives on all of its committees.

The rout at Caporetto, and the high level of unrest and agitation throughout Italy, made 1917 a year of crisis on the home and fighting fronts. Socialists and Catholics criticized the continuation of the war and demanded peace. In the summer Pope Benedict XV condemned the war's "useless carnage" and offered to mediate, in vain, among the warring powers. Interventionists, on the other hand, urged the martinet Cadorna to establish a military dictatorship to crush the "defeatists."

Domestic political events climaxed as the Caporetto battle began. The

Boselli government fell, replaced by one led by Boselli's Interior Minister, Vittorio Orlando, the focus of attacks from the right wing and Gen. Cadorna for leniency toward dissenters. An excellent orator, Orlando proved much stronger than his predecessor, and removed Cadorna as commander in favor of the younger Gen. Armando Diaz. Yet morale at home and at the front remained dismal. The Austrian enemy had seized the northeastern provinces; Italy's very existence hung in the balance. Orlando summoned all their power to resist. The Entente could help in bolstering the army at the front and in routing more supplies to Italy, but would that suffice to sustain the Italian war effort in the coming year?

France. Collapse, or Clemenceau

In January 1917 Minister of Armaments Albert Thomas imposed a uniform standard of wages in war industry and raised the minimum wage for all workers, thereby decreasing the gap between men's and women's wages. He also outlawed strikes and imposed government arbitration of disputes. The rising number of women workers required further measures.

Natalist concerns, stoked by the slaughter at Verdun in 1916, prompted the introduction of female superintendents in the war factories in France in spring 1917. In Britain the female supervisors were responsible to government. In France the employers, now concerned for the health of their women workers, instituted the superintendents to create a harmonious matriarchal order in the plants.[53] The creature of the employer, the institution of welfare supervision spread quickly in France in the postwar years.

In spring 1917, Thomas's prohibition of strikes notwithstanding, a massive strike of 43,000 mostly women workers struck the Parisian war industry, the most widespread eruption since 1914 and hard on the heels of the mutiny of the French Army at the front. Workers protested their low wages, long hours, and poor working conditions. The strike of May and June 1917 began with the dismissal of a few female "troublemakers" at the Salmson aircraft factory in Boulogne-Billancourt and spread to other factories in the area. Friction between women and their male foremen usually entailed the foreman's brutality, although in at least one case, that of "La Boxeuse," the woman became the aggressor, knocking the foreman flat. The women composed one-sixth of the metalworkers and rejected their inequality. A combination of concessions and arrests of ringleaders restored order in June. Officials, employers, and male trade unionists all categorized the strikes as "unpolitical"; employers deemed only male workers capable of motivation for "political" reasons, i.e., only men could be political activists. These "unpolitical" women would play a prominent role in the near revolutionary workers movement a year later.[54] The *Union Sacrée* was disintegrating under wartime pressure.

In 1917 race also became an issue in the factories of the French home front. As France had drawn on colonial soldiers to compensate for a shortage of military manpower, labor shortages prompted the French to import workers. During the war over half a million foreigners came to work in French factories and on French farms, most of them, some 330,000, from Europe, particularly Spain. Yet others came from overseas – 78,556 Algerians, 48,995 Indochinese, 36,941 Chinese, 35,506 Moroccans, 18,249 Tunisians, and 4,546 Malagasy – a total of 222,793 colonial laborers. Although some prewar hostility had been evident toward European immigrant workers, wartime antagonism focussed on the colonial workers at the bottom of the socio-economic hierarchy, thereby racializing xenophobia.[55]

The government had begun to import large numbers of non-white workers in 1916. The indifference or acceptance that greeted them in 1916 gave way to racial hostility and violence in spring 1917, when French morale sank to its lowest point during the war. In the crisis of wartime morale in 1917–18, people of color symbolized the war's deleterious impact on French workers.

The French government recruited colonial workers in their home countries, and the War Ministry's Colonial Labor Organization Service (SOTC) regimented them. They constituted the poorest paid laborers in France, and industrialists used them to lower wage demands from other workers. Organized into labor battalions, they worked and lived in isolation like prisoners-of-war. This attempt to transplant colonial conditions to France in order to exploit the workers to the maximum and prevent their "corruption" by the temptations of French society fomented racial antagonisms. The SOTC feared that the colonial laborers would gain a "taste for strong drink and white women," as well as experience with strikes and unions, all of which would upset established hierarchies in the empire by returning a seasoned body of radicals to the colonies.[56] Ironically, the French government created what it feared most – large concentrations of white women and men of color together in the absence of white men and non-white women – because it imported no women of color. Working side by side, French women and colonial workers naturally became acquainted and engaged in sexual relations, thus reinforcing the French authorities' determination to isolate the non-white workers for fear of miscegenation.

French labor unions grew hostile to the non-white workers, as workers believed colonial propaganda advocating white racial superiority. Even union leaders who emphasized the equality of all workers, such as Léon Jouhaux, worried about "the survival of the French race."[57] In these circumstances colonial workers, whom many civilians viewed with fear and mistrust as "outsiders in the national community," usually became the victims of racial violence.

Such violence in the spring and summer of 1917 proved brief and small scale. North Africans, particularly Algerians, cleaned Parisian streets, and thus became the most frequent targets of individual incidents of violence. Collective violence did occur, often incited or abetted by French soldiers, such as in Dijon and le Havre in June and Brest in August. The French authorities responded not by bringing the French perpetrators to justice but by concentrating on re-establishing control and preventing further violence.

The violence assumed a pattern – French men, including soldiers home on leave, attacked colonial workers. French officials disapproved of interracial relationships, so they threatened the workers with prison terms. Censors feared that the flow of pornographic postcards featuring nude French women to the colonies threatened to undermine established sexual and racial hierarchies in the empire. The perceptions that colonial workers, who were exempt from conscription, served as strike-breakers and that the government used them to induct more Frenchmen into military service stoked the hostility toward them.

This widespread antagonism toward colonial workers contrasted sharply with the reception accorded some 600,000 colonial soldiers who fought in France during the war. African soldiers received no leave to return home to Africa, and European soldiers who served with them in mixed units also had to forgo leave, often for eight months at a time. Such deprivation led to problems of morale with the white troops, although not with the black. African soldiers who were interviewed nearly half a century after the war remembered fondly the packages they received from their *marraines de guerre*, those godmothers whom all French soldiers had to reassure them that those at home had not forgotten them. Those same soldiers recalled that French women never refused intimate relations on account of color. Others recalled going on leave with French comrades.

African-American soldiers later contrasted the friendly treatment they experienced from the French to the racism of their own white officers. This striking difference underscores the contextual nature of racism and racial violence, for the use of colonial soldiers, "good savages," remained popular in France. Nevertheless, the racial violence that occurred in 1917 and 1918 countered the myth of French racial egalitarianism that the war enhanced.

Despite the demise of social peace and the army's difficulties in 1917, French President Poincaré adamantly opposed any compromise peace or offer of mediation, because he remained determined to regain Alsace and Lorraine. By the fall he faced a critical decision, for in the midst of the rising "defeatism," plummeting national morale, and the disintegration of the *Union Sacrée,* Poincaré would appoint the next prime minister. Poincaré considered his options unappealing. Since 1915 he had worried about politician Joseph Caillaux's campaign for a negotiated peace. Now Caillaux's movement seemed to be gaining momentum, positioning him as a prime contender for the position of premier.

Poincaré considered the alternative candidate "a devil of a man." *Le Tigre*, Senator Georges Clemenceau, outspoken, tenacious, and obstinate, had denounced Minister of Interior Malvy for weakness toward defeatists and forced Malvy's resignation in June. Clemenceau remained popular with the public and troops for his denunciations of shirkers, irresponsible commanders, and incompetent politicians. Ultimately, despite their personal antipathy, he and Poincaré shared two essential aims – utter opposition to defeatism and resolute commitment to total victory. Poincaré understood further that Clemenceau's "legendary strength" would undermine the Cabinet of any other politician.[58]

On 15 November 1917 Poincaré summoned the 76-year-old *enfant terrible* of French politics to form his government. The following day the Clemenceau government took power, Clemenceau became his own Minister of War, and in his speech of 20 November clearly stated his purpose: "I make war." He promptly pushed through a decision to try Malvy before the Senate and then initiated legal proceedings against Caillaux on 11 December. Clemenceau vowed that France would fight to the finish, and he refused to allow small issues of parliamentary immunity to stand in the way of rooting out defeatists and resurrecting France from the jaws of looming defeat in 1917.

On 17 December, Clemenceau, urged by Mangin, ordered the formation of a recruiting mission comprising 300 decorated veteran West African officers and men to draft more African soldiers for the war in France. He ignored the vehement opposition of the French colonial governor, who feared the "political and economic bankruptcy" of French West Africa from the drain of young men.[59] On 8 January 1918 the Council of Ministers voted to renew recruitment in West Africa.

President Poincaré agreed to offer knowledge and advice; Clemenceau agreed to inform Poincaré of his decisions in advance. Alone together before the first Cabinet meeting, the older Clemenceau jokingly enquired of his former antagonist, "Well, Raymond old chum, is this love?" Love, it most certainly was not. They were declaring war to the knife against France's enemies, internal as well as external.[60]

Britain. "No longer merry but not downhearted"[61]

The numbers of disabled war veterans at home, as in other countries, reflected the long and wearing conflict. The German aerial bombing campaign, now waged by Gotha and R-plane giant bombers, brought the war home to England. The twin-engined Gothas struck first in daylight, and then, in the fall, joined by the multi-engined giants, they raided England at night. The raids disrupted life and work in London. Some families attempted to crowd into the tube, or subway, stations, as many in London would do during the Blitz in the Second World War. Others simply left London. The limited range of German bombers over England meant that they posed no threat to most people.

By 1917 the war inconvenienced inhabitants of the British Isles in many ways, from lighting restrictions to limits on train travel. With the introduction of coal rationing in London by October, allocations actually granted working-class families more coal than they could have afforded before the war. Shortages in food supplies and rising food prices occurred in the spring, and sugar and butter proved particularly scarce during the year. The addition of wheat husks and potatoes rendered bread less palatable, but war bread, if darker than prewar, was readily available and nutritious. Bread consumption actually rose beyond prewar levels in 1917.

The British response on the home front to the grave submarine threat demonstrated the capacities of a democracy. The government's establishment of a Ministry of Shipping, a Food Production Department, and ultimately a Food Controller to monitor imports and then buy and sell food – all indicated the elasticity of democracy under threat in the resort to "war socialism."

The Food Production Department, acting according to new regulations in DORA (Defence of the Realm Act), ordered farmers to increase their land devoted to cereal grain production at the expense of grassland for livestock, a measure which reduced livestock by perhaps a quarter but greatly increased net food output. It could guarantee prices and supervise farming to produce designated crops, and allocate labor and other factors of production to ensure their production. Increased output of cereals and potatoes occurred at the expense of meat, milk, butter, and cheese.[62]

Labor unrest increased in Britain in 1917 as it did in all the combatant powers due to the rising cost and decreased availability of certain food supplies. The masses protested the inefficient distribution and the hoarding of food, and they particularly resented war profiteers who controlled the markets of certain foods and then forced up the prices. The working class also noticed the conspicuous consumption of the wealthy and the shorter food lines in bourgeois neighborhoods. Such social inequities and the unequal burden of wartime deprivations increased the hostility of the workers toward the upper classes. Strikers consequently protested rising food prices and sometimes raided food shops.

Despite the disruptive strikes, which indicated the workers' anger and exhaustion at the length of the war, the example of the Russian Revolution and its workers' and soldiers' councils appealed to only a small minority of British labor. The government refused to issue passports to the British delegation to the international socialist conference in Stockholm, but most of the working class opposed the conference in any case. Some workers struck as they faced potential induction into the army. Skilled engineers of the ASE

(Amalgamated Society of Engineers) and coal-miners resented the "comb-outs," or retraction of exemptions and induction into the armed forces, among their ranks. Both groups insisted that the most recent workers, specifically those hired since the outbreak of the war, should go first. The enthusiasm for war evident among volunteers in 1914 and 1915 had long since disappeared by 1917.

The increased employment of women and youth, or dilution, enabled the government to "comb-out" male workers. The government and press continued to praise women for their contribution to the war effort. Winston Churchill declared: "without the work of women it would have been impossible to win the war," while former prime minister Herbert Asquith, a convert to the cause of women's suffrage, observed in 1917: "How could we have carried on the War without them [women]?"[63] The war had arrested efforts for the vote, but parliamentary fears of postwar revolution, disorder, and renewed war between the sexes made female suffrage imperative.

Feminists would accept a compromise, abandoning their principle of equality of the sexes to accept the age qualification of women aged over 30, as they feared the impermanence of wartime gains. Furthermore, objecting to compromise and destroying the nation's apparent wartime unity might make them appear unpatriotic. Finally, feminists, like many others, believed that after the enormous struggle, Britain could not tolerate further conflict, and they believed in Britain's racial and moral superiority and "the white man's burden."[64]

Ireland, after the Easter Uprising, remained quieter on the surface. The ideal of separation from Britain had added another rebellion to the myths of Irish Nationalism. The Irish Party's attempt to enroll Nationalists in Irish regiments in the British Army foundered after the British Army's brutal suppression of the rebellion. A larger and more diverse Sinn Fein movement drew support from the Irish Party, which appeared to have little influence with the British government. Sinn Fein refused to send its elected representatives to Parliament and planned to appeal for Irish sovereign independence at a postwar peace conference. Sinn Feiners, however, included monarchists and republicans. Meanwhile, Ulster Unionists could not conceive of an Irish nation separate from Great Britain. The Nationalists' touchstone had become the Easter Rising, an act of rebellion from Britain; the Unionists', the loss of 5,000 men of the Ulster Division in the first two days of the Battle of the Somme, an act of sacrifice for Great Britain.[65]

Across the Atlantic, Canada, in the midst of industrial mobilization, inflation, shortages, and increasing turmoil from French Canadians' refusal to commit to the war effort, introduced conscription in August 1917. On 6 December the ship *Mount Blanc*, carrying a cargo of 3,000 tons of TNT, blew up in Halifax Harbor, killing 1,630 and injuring thousands, mostly working-class Canadians, many of whom were black residents of the slums near the harbor.[66] The war had come home to Canada with a vengeance.

The Canadian Expeditionary Force departing for Europe included individual black soldiers among its ranks. British and Canadian recruiting offices in the United States also enlisted recruits from the Caribbean, stamping their papers "coloured." These individuals, like individual black Frenchmen and the French *originaires* from Senegal serving in French metropolitan units, fought in British regiments. Walter Tull, a black footballer who had played for Tottenham Hotspur, had fought and died at the Somme in 1916, but recently released documents from the Public Record Office indicate that hitherto unknown others from the Caribbean would follow Tull.[67]

Prime Minister David Lloyd George governed with a smaller War Cabinet that acted more decisively. *Ad hoc* subcommittees on air policy and war priorities produced important reports and forwarded recommendations for the action of the War Cabinet, whose Secretariat under Maurice Hankey assiduously recorded the meetings and decisions. New ministries of shipping, food, labor, and national service responded to the crises of an expanding war and increased the state's role in the economy, and in matters of manpower and communal welfare. The government had to mesh the army's manpower demands with those of the munitions industry. Consequently it raised the age for certain exemptions from 26 to 31. The Ministry of National Service, where Auckland Geddes replaced Neville Chamberlain, sought to secure more fit men for the army. However, the government did not impose national service on all adult males, in particular after the May strikes by engineers upset at dilution.

The Ministry of Shipping required more merchant ships in 1917, partially to replace ships sunk by submarines, but also to transport the cargo and troops of Britain's allies. The Minister, shipowner Sir Joseph Maclay, advocated state direction of the merchant marine and undertook an ambitious policy of construction of new ships to keep pace with the exponentially increasing demand, which reached crisis proportions in 1917.

While the government acted firmly in the above realms, it hesitated to take strong measures to control the allocation and prices of food. The Food Controller Lord Rhondda established a bureaucracy that would enable such control by the end of the year, but the government seemed reluctant to act in the absence of a crisis. Disorder in bread lines prompted public demand for the control of food distribution through compulsory rationing and food lines threatened "to undermine public order."[68] Nevertheless, Britain, unlike the Central Powers, did not confront famine; in fact, its citizens did not even go hungry.

The United States. A troubled associate

The German government's declaration of unrestricted submarine warfare on 31 January 1917 precipitated American entry into the war. The United States government severed diplomatic relations with Germany on 3 February. Although Congress would not approve arming American merchant ships, Woodrow Wilson used his executive power to arm them. On 1 March Wilson made public the Zimmermann telegram, in which German Secretary of State Arthur Zimmermann proposed a German–Mexican alliance which would reward the Mexican government with territories lost in the Mexican–American War of 1846–8. British intelligence had transmitted the note to Wilson. Zimmermann, who considered himself an expert on the United States on the basis of a transcontinental railway excursion earlier in the century, arrogantly and openly admitted his authorship of the note. German submarines now sank American ships. On 2 April 1917, Woodrow Wilson declared war on Germany, in a crusade to make the world safe for democracy. Although small but significant minorities in both the Senate and the House opposed ratification, the United States now entered the great conflict as an Associated Power of the Entente.

American credits and loans had kept the Entente afloat, because the United States had manufactured and delivered nearly a quarter of Entente munitions between 1915 and 1917. The Wilson administration planned to exploit this Anglo-French dependence on American loans in its conduct of the war and preparations for peace. Wilson and his Secretary of the Treasury William Gibbs McAdoo intended to play the predominant role in the Entente economic war effort and war finance, with the United States coordinating Entente purchases and spending by controlling the distribution of American money and resources.[69]

Culturally, east coast elites supported the British. American volunteers already serving in Entente armies included wealthy, college-educated, young men imbued with a mission to protect western culture and civilization from the Germans. As the Lafayette Escadrille epitomized, they had received the bulk of the publicity in efforts to draw the United States into the war. Conversely, most American volunteers, especially the thousands who crossed the Canadian border to serve in the Canadian Expeditionary Force, and the hundreds who joined the Royal Flying Corps, did not come from the American elite and fought and died in obscurity, their motives for joining and fighting lost to history.

The government quickly mobilized popular sentiment through a mixture of propaganda and repression. The Committee on Public Information, established on 14 April under the direction of George Creel, promoted a national ideology in the crusade for peace and freedom, while the Espionage Act of June empowered Postmaster General Albert Burleson to censor any recalcitrant publications. The Justice Department formed a Bureau (later Federal) of Investigation under a young J. Edgar Hoover to enforce the law. Volunteer organizations encouraged vigilante-ism against anarchists and, in particular, leaders of the Industrial Workers of the World (IWW). The

Federal government ignored these blatant violations of civil liberty and the hysterical intolerance sweeping the United States, which reflected the fear of the immense and unbridgeable diversity in the American populace. In the war for freedom and democracy, German *Kultur* became synonymous with barbarism, militarism, authoritarianism, and a drive for world domination. Such propaganda encouraged the demonization of, and consequent hysterical and mob violence against, all things German, and by extension those whom society identified as different, including aliens and African Americans.[70]

The Wilson government proceeded with mobilization, but always with the premise of minimal governmental interference in accord with *laissez-faire* ideals. Military procurement among various army agencies proved chaotic, because the Council of National Defense lacked the authority to coordinate and organize the war effort. The Council consequently gave way in August to the War Industries Board, to mobilize industry and provide it with "fair" profits while controlling prices. Herbert Hoover expected to repeat the success he had enjoyed as Director of the Belgian Relief Fund in his appointment as Food Administrator in May, and he eschewed mandatory controls in favor of voluntarism and patriotic exhortations.

In two realms, however, voluntarism did not suffice to solve the enormous difficulties. In the winter of 1917–18 transport and fuel crises brought the national transportation network to the brink of collapse. Secretary of the Treasury William Gibbs McAdoo ruthlessly intervened, took control of most railroads, and rendered the rail system more efficient if still regulated by the companies themselves. The Lever Food and Fuel Control Act of August granted sweeping powers to administrator Harry A. Garfield, who managed to increase the inadequate coal supply.

Labor shortages loomed immediately with the mobilization of industrial production, the introduction of the draft, and the reduction in immigration. Ultimately one million women, half a million blacks, and 150,000 workers imported from Mexico and Puerto Rico would fill the demand. The conditions for American labor resembled those of other wartime countries – their real wages fell in any inflationary wartime economy. Consequently, the number of strikes rose to 4,200, its highest level to that time. The government coopted the more conservative AFL (American Federation of Labor) in its campaign against radical workers such as the IWW. In September Wilson appointed a mediation commission, which included Harvard Law professor Felix Frankfurter, that actually negotiated with the unions for the first time.

The black migration north, which the war accelerated, caused alarm among southern and northern whites: the former fearing the loss of cheap labor; the latter, the presence of blacks in their midst. Participation in the war effort seemed to offer African Americans an opportunity to improve their conditions and secure fairer treatment and less injustice from white America. Most black citizens consequently prepared to defend their country.

To raise an army, the proposed draft bill on 5 April was passed on 17 May as the Selective Service Act. Despite the initial outbursts of patriotic fervor, the draft proved unpopular: between 2.4 and 3.6 million men never registered for it; a further 12 percent of the 2.8 million men drafted deserted.[71] Congressmen from the rural South and Midwest opposed entry into the war and, more vehemently, the draft. Many considered it a rich man's war, a Wall Street plot, which had no connection to their existence. Conscription and the draft seemed steps on the road to "Prussianization," as they had to many Britons in 1916, and some Americans questioned the merit of fighting the Germans if the United States had to emulate them to win. Others preferred to finance and supply the Entente powers and even to enter the naval war against the submarines, but not to send American youth to die in Europe. The United States in 1917, unlike the European populations in August 1914, experienced no outpouring of unity about entering the war.

Nor did the United States speak with one voice about who should wage the war. At every step whites resisted black involvement in all aspects of the war effort. Fear of black soldiers pervaded society, predicated on southern white fears of arming a people they had so viciously persecuted and of armed black males preying on defenseless southern white womanhood. Southerners vigorously opposed a black draft, as Mississippi Senator Vardaman could conceive of no greater menace to the South than armed Negroes.[72]

Lynchings rose, from fifty-four in 1916 to seventy in 1917, as did racial violence, culminating in the race riot in East St. Louis, Illinois in May and June. In Houston, Texas, in late August 1917, members of the 25th Infantry Regiment, after the usual racist provocations, marched into the city, exchanged fire with whites, and then drifted back to camp after killing seventeen at the cost of two of their own men. The army summarily condemned thirteen soldiers to death and hanged them in December. The army and white America demanded from black soldiers faithful service and unquestioning obedience to the rules and mores of white society.

The valiant performance of black individuals and units in the American Army, whether in the American Revolution, the Civil War, Spanish American War, on the Western Front, or in the Philippines, did not alter white racist opinions. White historical memory of black accomplishments remained incredibly short and riven with denial. White American officers, including those who would command black soldiers, like the broader white public, adamantly persisted in their unfounded belief that blacks would be useless in combat. In August Army Chief of Staff Gen. Tasker Bliss endorsed a plan first delaying the call-up of the black draft and then, after minimal training, sending them to France for use exclusively as "service" troops, i.e., labor battalions.[73] Secretary of War Newton Baker promised W.E.B. DuBois in December 1917 that more than 35 percent of the black troops would engage in combat. In fact, 20 percent would fight, while 80 percent would serve in labor battalions. Ironically, immediately after the United States severed diplomatic relations with Germany, the government mobilized the Colored Battalion of the District of Columbia National Guard to guard federal buildings. The army reasoned that no German agent could disguise himself as black. For once, whites appreciated the presence of armed and uniformed African Americans.

The government decided not to send regular army units to France but to divide its officer cadres among newly formed divisions. The training that all American units received in the United States proved inadequate, and British and French instructors provided remedial training in Europe. The British emphasized the use of the bayonet, while the French focussed on grenades and small unit operations. Neither method corresponded to Pershing's adherence to a war of movement in which American troops could use their skills of open field fighting and riflery. Pershing's ideas, however, bore little relation to the actual conditions on the Western Front, to modern warfare, and to the U.S. Army.

Black troops received substandard training in substandard facilities, and served under few black officers, because the army allowed no black officer to command a white soldier. For this reason the army command had forced cavalry officer Col. Charles Young, the third black graduate of West Point and the army's highest ranking black officer, into retirement. The white military did not intend for black officers to succeed. Trained to fail, the black officers found themselves, like their men, in a hostile environment in the United States Army. For black soldiers, the war – the one to prove themselves equal – began at home, in the army.

The army's new divisions included two black ones – the 92nd Division and the 93rd Division (provisional). The army sent these units south for training, despite the protests of some southerners that the presence of black soldiers would lead to racial incidents. New York's white guard division, the 42nd or "Rainbow" Division, had rejected the 15th New York Guard, which became the 369th Regiment, 93rd Division, with the comment that "black was not one of the colors of the rainbow."[74] The 369th shipped to Spartanburg, South Carolina for training that racial incidents aborted, and prematurely sailed for France in the middle of the winter, to remove it from the United States. The 8th Illinois National Guard, which became the 370th Regiment, the 371st and the 372nd regiments formed the 93rd. All sailed before completing even rudimentary training in the United States, and the 370th's full complement of black officers would find themselves under constant threat of removal from their superiors, who automatically deemed them unsuitable for command.

All American divisions would require French artillery, transport, and aircraft, as American industry proved incapable of supplying its country's army. France, not the United States, became the arsenal of democracy in the war of 1914–18. The 92nd Division's artillery regiments had fewer guns than a comparable white American division and no signal or fire-control equipment. The division received even less training than comparable white divisions, and its General, Ballou, warned the men that "white men had made the division and could break it just as easily" if it became a troublemaker, i.e., if they stood up for their rights.[75] It departed for France in June 1918.

The 92nd and 93rd served at the front, but at least 160,000 black men toiled as army laborers, comprising one-third of all labor troops, the military equivalent of chain-gangs. So-called black pioneer infantry units did exist, but did not receive the training necessary for usual pioneer or engineering duties immediately behind the front, and ultimately became laborers. Their white officers sometimes lined their own pockets by hiring them out to work for civilians in the United States, and their non-commissioned officers included former overseers of black work gangs. The first labor units sailed for France in June 1917, to pack and unpack the AEF, build military facilities, roads, and railways, tasks which they accomplished with unparalleled speed. Nevertheless, they endured abysmal living conditions, frequent abuse from their officers and military police, and denial of social contact, particularly with French women. These men, who formed the Services of Supply (SOS), performed the most arduous and indispensable labor for the military. Along with small complements of white soldiers, they formed the vanguard of the American Expeditionary Force in Europe.

Japan. Asia beckons, America threatens

The war produced a new Cabinet under General Terauchi Masatake in the fall of 1916, a "bid for national unity at a time of crisis,"[76] similar to the Lloyd George and Clemenceau governments in Britain and France. The European governments fought for national survival; the Japanese government, for the power to guide Japan's future. The Terauchi Cabinet's initiatives included the Nishihara loans, the Sino-Japanese Military Agreement, and the Siberian Intervention in 1918. It focussed on the Sino-Japanese relationship and sought to increase Japanese presence in the Pacific in expectation of an eventual conflict with the United States. The imperial army and navy insisted on increases in the Japanese military establishment to keep pace with the United States.[77]

Terauchi preferred financial diplomacy to armed intervention in dealing with China, in order to strengthen the Japanese position on the Asian mainland and ultimately to achieve Japanese economic hegemony in Asia. The Chinese government accepted the loans, used them for its purposes, and then evaded repaying the loans for the next twenty years. In January 1917 Terauchi formally launched his "new" China policy, stipulating no interference in China's internal political unrest. By March the Chinese government, encouraged by Japanese negotiators, severed ties with Germany. This step indicated Japan's growing influence in China, although the Chinese declaration of war with Germany exacerbated internal unrest in China and threatened the government's position. Meanwhile, the Japanese General Staff pursued its own foreign policy to control China and contemplated expansion in the South Pacific.

Japan had sponsored China's diplomatic break with Germany in order to gain European recognition of its dominion over former German territories at a future peace conference. Wilson's aims to make the world safe for democracy and destroy German militarism implicitly threatened a Japanese state modeled after imperial Germany, and Wilson's appeal to democracy and internationalism aroused internal Japanese opposition to the Terauchi Cabinet. The Russian Revolution's toppling of another imperial government heightened the dismay of Japanese imperial elites.[78]

The wartime economic boom led to the growth and expansion of Japanese industry and enabled Japan to participate in international finance, as in 1916 it achieved its largest balance of payments surplus in history. Agriculture remained the largest single occupation in Japan, but it was declining in significance compared to industry. Farmers profited from record high food prices in 1917 and later in 1918 as domestic and world need for rice rose. The war occasioned domestic political competition for control of the Japanese government, but it also opened new vistas of imperial and economic achievement in Japan.

CONCLUSION. A MOST DIFFICULT YEAR

By 1917 the conflict had become total war, as states mobilized all the resources, human and material, at their command to continue the struggle. With the introduction of unrestricted submarine warfare, Germany, according to historian Holger Herwig, "crossed the threshold into total war" to achieve "total victory."[79] Total war had evolved steadily since the start of the conflict. Certainly the German unrestricted submarine warfare represented a major escalation of the war, but both sides engaged in the escalation.

The OHL, for example, had refused to support the Easter Rising in Ireland in 1916, leaving Sir Roger Casement twisting in the wind, rushing home in a vain attempt to prevent the rebellion. Germany lacked the desperation in early 1916 to resort to such subversive measures, although German war aims from the start had entailed striking at the British Empire. In 1917, however, the OHL shipped Lenin and company to Russia to exacerbate conditions after the first revolution. Capitalizing on a revolution by sending human cargo posed fewer risks and expenses than helping to foment a rebellion from scratch with a substantial arms shipment. Furthermore, sending a small group of revolutionaries to Russia in early 1917 undoubtedly paled before the momentous submarine campaign.

If total war entails targeting civilian populations on the home front as well as the fighting front, then Great Britain, by blockading the Central Powers, began in 1914 with a strategy entailing total war. By 1917 the blockade starved the home and fighting fronts of food and materials in Germany and Austria-Hungary. Grass was not growing in the streets of Hamburg, as a British naval officer earlier predicted. Yet neither Central Power could compensate effectively for the drastic reduction in imports or evolve a fair and comprehensive system of food distribution to equalize the suffering, failings which undermined their citizens' confidence in their governments. The German and Austrian populations suffered far more than their French and British counterparts from shortages of food and other basic necessities of life. Here the advantage over the long term militated in favor of the Entente, which enjoyed access to world markets that it severed from the Central Powers. Shortages of transport, food, and fuel that plagued all the powers in the winter of 1917–18 consequently proved soluble in the Entente powers and the United States, and insoluble in the Central Powers.

Furthermore, American entry into the war closed the noose around Germany, as the Entente blockade now became total. The United States' presence as a powerful neutral had forced the British to show some respect for the rights of other neutrals, such as Holland, in their blockade. Now the Entente and the United States imposed comprehensive control over neutral trade, culminating in an embargo against the Netherlands in October 1917, the seizure of Dutch ships in British and American ports, and insistence that the Dutch halt all exports to Germany.[80]

Finally, the powers' use of embryonic strategic air power entailed the intention to "totalize" the war from the start. As early as August 1914 various German officials contemplated "systematically working on the nerves of British towns" or "breaking British resistance" through air warfare. However inflated a perception of the Zeppelin's capabilities they held, they recognized the potential of the aerial weapon to strike directly at Britain and even to counter British naval power. By 1917 a "vicious circle of reprisals and counterreprisals" of air raids that had begun in 1914 struck civilian targets rather than military or industrial installations. The air raids constituted a new phenomenon that contributed to the war's total nature by blurring or erasing the boundary between military and civilian targets. The British and Germans, in particular, deflected war materiel and men from the front to defend against the raids. The military could not completely protect the population from the enemy raids, and some inhabitants, whether in London or in Freiburg im Breisgau in western Germany, unimpressed with the military anti-aircraft defense, took the initiatives of turning cellars and pubs into shelters or even moving out of town.[81]

The demands of fighting a great and "total" conflict challenged the combatant societies' traditional inequalities of class, gender, and race. The civil peace, or *Burgfriede*, in Germany, and the sacred union, or *Union Sacrée*, in France had evaporated, as lower class resentments of the unequal burdens they bore surfaced. Social unrest rocked Austria-Hungary and Italy. The working class and the peasantry provided the ranks of soldiers and labor, while they endured shortages and inflation. They observed that the wealthy continued to purchase luxury items, if necessary through a black market, and to live well. In peacetime a few radicals questioned such inequities, but wartime privations and losses rendered them increasingly unbearable and unacceptable to the masses. Although the lower middle class, civil servants, and those dependent on government assistance suffered even more during the war, they lacked the weight and mass to influence politics.

Fighting an increasingly "total" war with no foreseeable end was rending the social fabric of the European countries. Russia's disintegration into revolution epitomized these circumstances, but developments in Austria-Hungary, Germany, France, and Italy demonstrated the vulnerability of all to this fragmentation and disintegration. This class unrest affected Britain less than its continental counterparts. Britain enjoyed a superior supply of foodstuffs and materials, and its well-established working class, a longer history, stronger unions, and more effective representation in the parliamentary political system. In 1917 French workers condemned the "gross inequalities in fortune, suffering, and sacrifice" they experienced and the war engendered deeper social divisions in France than in England.[82] Everywhere, working-class dissatisfaction and unrest could disrupt the war effort. Consequently, even when governments resorted to repression to maintain order, such as in Italy, they also ameliorated working conditions to ease the plight of the working class.

The necessity of mobilizing female labor to free men for military service also threatened to upset traditional social and cultural norms. Working-class women played key roles in the industrial strikes, food riots, and political demonstrations of 1917, to the extent that the greater and more violent the unrest, as in Russia and Italy, the larger the female role in it. Women also fomented unrest in Germany, France, and Austria-Hungary. In the Dual Monarchy industry employed female labor less than in other countries, but women remained significant participants in unrest. Everywhere their roles as workers, consumers, family providers, and increasingly heads of households in the absence of males placed them at the vortex of all the ills besetting the working class. They consequently instigated and led strikes, food riots, and demonstrations.

These working-class women had invariably worked before the war, but either in household handicrafts such as textile manufacture or in domestic service. Now the war launched many of them, at least temporarily, into more dangerous and better paid munitions and metalwork. Middle-class women, who usually had not worked before the war, filled supervisory and clerical jobs, or, if sufficiently wealthy, did charity work. Working-class women often did not share the bourgeois aim of female suffrage, because securing the basic necessities of life directly and immediately preoccupied them.

Women's new "freedom" aroused the concerns of males, those in power as well as those at the front, whose marginalization from society greatly troubled them. The greater the freedom and independence that women seemed to achieve, the greater the determination of politicians and union leaders to restore males to their "rightful" supremacy after the war. Often the women viewed their positions as temporary, but some would not relinquish their new-found positions so easily.

Racial issues arose primarily in France and the United States with the raising and deployment of black combat soldiers. Britain's refusal to bring black colonial fighting men to the Western Front precluded this problem, although Liverpool, England, which as a port city had a black community, did experience a race riot in 1917. France imported colonial manpower as soldiers and factory workers, duties that African Americans, who comprised 10 percent of the population of the United States, sought. Concerns that the French use of African troops in Europe accustomed Africans to kill whites and would undermine the colonial system paralleled the dilemma that now confronted white Americans, who feared that African American participation as combat troops would threaten the system of segregation. The African American migration north to secure factory work stoked further the fears of southern and northern whites.

The French, however, considered their West African soldiers "warrior races," and employed them as shock troops, often with the aim of husbanding French lives. They segregated many of them behind the lines, although a few enjoyed equal status with French soldiers. Indeed, French officers punished French soldiers who did not acknowledge or obey African non-commissioned officers. In contrast, white America considered its black soldiers, despite their service in every war America had fought, suitable for labor only. The American Army segregated all African American soldiers and never required its white soldiers to acknowledge, salute, or obey a black officer, commissioned or non-commissioned.

African American hopes that participation in the war effort would gain them improved conditions in the United States echoed the sentiments expressed by the more informed colored peoples inhabiting or representing inhabitants of the European colonies. The similarity of aims reflected the oppressive conditions that American blacks and colonized people of color shared, although white Americans constantly congratulated themselves on their moral superiority to the "Old World." From the very beginning the Wilsonian crusade for freedom and democracy posed the implicit question:

Freedom and democracy for whom? Racist that he was, Wilson never intended to free the "inferior peoples" of the world from the yoke of white domination. The war, and in particular the peace afterwards, would clarify whom he had in mind.

———

In 1917 the Entente survived its most difficult year of the war up to that point. First and most significantly, two revolutions had not only removed the Russian Empire from the war, but also brought about its demise. In leading to the fall of the Romanov dynasty and the Bolshevik rise to power, the war had catalyzed events of "world historical" importance. The inability of the tsarist autocracy to meet the demands that an all-encompassing conflict posed at home and at the front, personified in the ineffective rule of the autocrat himself, led to its demise. The crux of its problems centered on the supply of food and necessities of life to the industrial, urban centers, and of weaponry and ammunition to soldiers at the front. Ultimately, a tsarist government riven with incompetence and corruption could not deliver the necessary goods.

At the same time, conducting the war had necessitated the mobilization of millions of men in the army and men and women at home to manufacture war materiel. Developments on the fighting and home fronts proved inextricably intertwined, as Gen. Alekseev at *Stavka* stated during the first revolution. Consequently, when the women and men of the industrial working class took to the streets for bread and peace, they deflected the army's attention from the front and affected its ability to continue the war. However, after the tsar's abdication, the Provisional Government failed to meet the needs of the mobilized and dissatisfied urban masses and did nothing to allay rising peasant demands for land. Most critically, it not only continued to wage war, but even honored its international commitment to the Entente by staging an ill-fated offensive in the summer. The masses revolted and the army disintegrated. The Bolsheviks, endowed with the most astute and decisive leaders and the strongest ties to the urban masses and representatives in the Soviets, seized power in Petrograd and Moscow and removed Russia from the war.

The "collective indiscipline" of the French Army at the front resulting from Nivelle's disastrous offensive at Chemin des Dames, and rising industrial unrest and the disintegration of the *Union Sacrée* on the home front lowered French morale and fighting ability for the rest of the year. Nevertheless, the army under Petain's leadership and the home front endured, and Poincaré's appointment of Clemenceau as prime minister in November brought a dynamic, decisive, and domineering leader to power.

The collapse and rout of the Italian Army at Caporetto and the urban and rural unrest in Italy seemed to herald the collapse of another Entente power in the fall. But the Italian Army regrouped and held once the Germans returned to the Western Front, and the change in government and high command, with military and material assistance from its allies, enabled Italian survival into the new year.

Finally, Great Britain now bore the major brunt of fighting on the Western Front for the first full year, with bloody and inconclusive results. Great Britain turned to Canada, Australia, and New Zealand for manpower reserves and shock troops on the Western Front, as France resorted to North and West Africa. The imperatives differed, however, as the French had drained themselves bearing the brunt of the fighting against Germany, while the British, in pursuit of far-flung imperial goals, dispersed imperial troops in the Middle East and Africa. After disastrous beginnings in the Middle East, British forces in 1917 beat back their Ottoman opponent, while in East Africa their forces hotly pursued the last vestige of German colonial dominion, namely Lettow-Vorbeck's small guerrilla army.

At home, however, the British Isles contended with their most serious threat of the war: the German submarine campaign. With the great battle fleets stalemated and eyeing one another warily across the North Sea, the submarine took center stage in the naval war, its ascendancy both indicating and requiring a shift in naval priorities from behemoths to barracudas. A German submarine fleet of some 120 boats nearly brought Britain to its knees, in part because of the Admiralty's dilatory response to the undersea threat. Britain survived, but even at the end of the year German submarines still sank hundreds of thousands of tons of shipping monthly.

The German submarine offensive led directly to a development second in importance only to the Russian Revolutions – the entry of the United States into the war. The "new" world would save the "old," but at a price, namely the imposition of Woodrow Wilson's agenda on international politics and economics. The events of 1917 demonstrated that the Entente badly needed more than American finances and munitions, but neither Lloyd George nor Clemenceau would likely or easily concede world leadership to Wilson. In any case, the ability of any Entente power to influence peace terms depended, first, upon their ability to defeat the Germans, no certainty in 1917, and, second, on the relative weight of each power's contribution to the defeat of the German war machine.

The British and French Armies' mastery of new offensive tactics coordinating infantry attacks with artillery, aviation, and armor support at the end of the year offset German superiority in that realm since the start of the war. The prospect of millions of fresh American troops arriving on the continent, their officers intoning "Lafayette, we are here," as the United States prepared to pay a debt owed for French support in the American Revolution that it had renounced long before, could only buoy the spirits of the Entente and pressure the Central Powers. The Entente had to hold until

American forces could intervene, but not so overwhelmingly that Wilson could dictate peace terms in case of victory. The Central Powers had to seek victory before the United States could bring the weight of its forces to bear.

On 11 November 1917 Hindenburg and Ludendorff convened a staff conference at Mons, Belgium. There they announced their plans to launch an offensive no later than March 1918. Russia's collapse enabled them to transfer their fifty best divisions in the east to the Western Front. They had no tanks, but they staked their plan on infantry and artillery, based on their experience on the Eastern and Southwestern Front. Ludendorff planned to attack on a fifty-mile front against the British, the stronger of the two western opponents, and he rejected any proposals of a reprise of Verdun to break the French. To win the war, he had to beat the British before America's arrival in force and before German exhaustion.

He planned to amass nearly 6,500 artillery pieces and 3,500 mortars, with more than a million shells in preparation for the heaviest bombardment yet unleashed. Artillery would range immediately on to their targets with a mixture of explosive and gas shells. The preliminary bombardment would last for only five hours, but the weight of shell fired in such a short time would literally crush, while the variety of gas shells would first irritate and then kill enemy soldiers.

German storm battalions of elite troops specially trained and husbanded for the attack, armed with light machine-guns, carbines, and grenades, would infiltrate quickly through the enemy lines, leaving strong points for regular infantry to dispatch. They would advance as far and as fast as possible, supported only by their own light mortars and ground attack aircraft once they had moved beyond the range of their own artillery.

For the offensive's target Ludendorff selected the old Somme battlefield abandoned for the Hindenburg Line in 1917. Three German armies totaling seventy divisions, of which thirty-two would strike the initial blow, would attack along a seventy-mile front. The three German army commanders included von Hutier, the victor at Riga, and von Below, the victor at Caporetto. They planned to punch a hole in the enemy defenses, strike up the River Somme in an attempt to roll up the British front, and see what happened. Ludendorff lacked a strategic objective, probably because the Somme region, unlike Flanders with its Channel ports, offered none. But the Flanders mud through April sufficed to deter consideration. Operation "Michael's" goals remained open-ended; its schedule, tight.

6

1918. Denouement

"All of Russia is nothing but a great pile of maggots."

Gen. Max Hoffmann, Brest Litovsk, February 1918[1]

"Come on, you sons-of-bitches. Do you want to live forever?"

Gunnery Sgt. Daniel J. Daley, U.S. Marine Corps, Belleau Wood, 6 June 1918[2]

"My men never retire; they go forward or they die."

William Hayward, Colonel commanding the 369th Infantry Regiment, 93rd Division, near Belleau Wood, 6 June 1918[3]

"[I am like] a captain of industry who is working with his plant at full capacity."

Gen. Philippe Pétain, October 1918[4]

The German High Command knew that it had to win the war in early 1918, or face defeat. Britain and France, preoccupied with the near future, hoped to survive the imminent German offensive. As fighting continued on many fronts, the combatants approached exhaustion. Nevertheless, western observers expected the war to last into 1919, or even 1920.

THE WESTERN FRONT

Germany attacks

On 21 January 1918 Ludendorff issued final orders for Operation Michael. On 10 March the detailed plan stipulated 21 March as the day of the attack.

Gough's Fifth Army, the weakest of the British armies at fourteen divisions, held the line opposite the attacking divisions along a forty-two-mile front. To the north Julian Byng's Third Army of seventeen divisions defended a twenty-eight-mile front. The Fifth Army of Cavalryman Gough had suffered severe casualties at Passchendaele because of Gough's superficial administration and excessive aims. Now Gough contended with a major reorganization of the British Army as it took charge of more front from the French.

Following the German example in 1915 and that of the French in 1917, the British Army reduced its regimental strength from four battalions to three, in order to increase artillery and machine-gun support and to compensate for a shortage of manpower. Some 145 battalions of the most recently formed nine-battalion divisions, many of which belonged to the new Fifth Army, would disband to reinforce the remaining divisions. The reorganization began in January and supposedly ended in early March, but the Fifth Army, in fact reduced to little more than a headquarters, could not constitute a well-knit entity so quickly after such far-reaching change.

The semi-autonomous status of the Canadian Corps under its commander Lt. Gen. Sir Arthur Currie meant that its divisions did not conform to this new rule. A British division totaled 15,000 men, including 8,100 infantry; each of the four Canadian divisions in the Corps, 21,000 men, including 12,000 infantry. A Canadian division contained more and larger infantry battalions, which had an automatic weapon for every thirteen men, compared to one for every sixty-one soldiers in British battalions. Canadian divisions possessed substantially more powerful support organizations of machine-guns, artillery, trench mortars, engineers, and transport. The awesome striking power of the Corps, combined with the circumstance that "In the stark terms of political capital, Canadian lives were, for Haig, far cheaper than British lives," to ensure that the Canadian Corps would become the spearhead of British offensives later in 1918.[5] By June the British recognized Canada as "an ally, not a colony," as befitted the strength of the Canadian contingent and their future plans for it.[6]

Improving the French trenches to British standards required more labor than Gough could draft; consequently his army had completed only two of three planned defensive lines by March. The German buildup prompted Gough's demand for reinforcements, but Haig had none because Lloyd George feared he would squander them in another pointless offensive. Upon request, Pétain moved his reserves closer to the British, but he anticipated another attack against Verdun.

At 4.40 a.m. on 21 March, the Germans unleashed a ferocious barrage, trench mortars shelling forward positions while high explosive and gas shells fell on the rear. Gen. Georg Bruchmüller's barrage was intended to disrupt and disorientate the British defenders so that German storm troops could infiltrate their lines. At 9.40 a.m., German shock troops filtered through gas and dense fog into the British lines. Some British defenders and artillery survived to contest the German offensive. In most cases, however, the storm troops penetrated the British lines before they realized it. A British machine-gunner thought they had stopped the German attack, when a German officer appeared behind him and said, "Come along, Tommy. You've done enough." The British soldier, knowing full well that in the German's place he would have shot a gunner, complied thankfully.[7]

Within an hour German infantry had overrun the forward defensive zone to a width of twelve miles. By noon, when the fog lifted, the penetration reached a depth of three miles. With clearer weather German ground attack squadrons strafed and bombed retreating British infantry from low altitude. Above them German fighter aircraft fended off British fighters and bombers. In the afternoon, the Germans punched through the second, or main defensive line. By evening they had advanced seven miles, flanking British positions, killing 7,000 and capturing 21,000 British soldiers in the process. Keegan considered this "the first true defeat" the British had suffered since the onset of trench warfare.[8] The Germans suffered 78,000 casualties, including the death of Ludendorff's son, a fighter pilot. This amounted to their highest single day loss of the war, about twice the casualties of the British. Nevertheless, the number of British prisoners and the loss of infantry commanders indicated that British cohesion and morale had collapsed. That night German bombers struck ammunition dumps and railway junctions behind the British lines. In some parts of the front new British troops, many of them boys, ran away, turning the retreat into a rout. At other places these youth fought, and the Germans quickly annihilated them.

Since Hutier's army in the south had advanced further than the others, Ludendorff reinforced him in an attempt to drive a wedge between the British and French armies in the next four days. The British withdrew all along the front, although still holding the high ground of Vimy Ridge and preventing a German advance on Arras and Amiens. Pétain held fast instead of committing his reserves to attack the German flank. His top priority remained blocking any avenue toward Paris, even at the risk of a total rupture of the Franco-British front.

On 26 March, Poincaré, Clemenceau, Lloyd George, his War Minister Lord Milner and Chief of Staff Robertson, Pétain, Haig, and French Chief of Staff Foch met in the midst of the debacle at Doullens, a town between Arras and Amiens. The desperate situation required desperate measures. Until now both Haig and Pétain had refused to commit their reserves to a general reserve force, but a shaken Haig angrily accused Pétain of defeatism, while Pétain compared the Fifth Army to the Italians at Caporetto. Foch, a proponent of the offensive who had spent some time out of favor after earlier French disasters, insisted upon no retreat, no surrender, specifically of

Amiens. His aggressiveness prompted Haig to concede to serve under Foch's command. Foch would now coordinate the Entente Armies on the Western Front, while Haig commanded the British and Pétain the French. Later, on 14 April, the U.S. Army would ratify Foch's appointment to Supreme Allied Commander, or Generalissimo. Foch authorized the transfer of French reserves to bolster the British line; however, on 27 March the Germans captured the main rail center of Montdidier, opening a ten-mile wedge between the British and French. The British fought doggedly to protect Amiens and Arras, but by 5 April the Germans had advanced within five miles.

In Germany Kaiser Wilhelm had already proclaimed 23 March a victory holiday. That same day the Germans opened fire on Paris with a giant artillery piece capable of firing a shell an incredible seventy-five miles. Ultimately six such guns shelled Paris over the next three months, killing 256 people, 156 in a church on Good Friday, 29 March. This random shelling of Paris foreshadowed the Germans' use of terror weapons, the V1 and V2 rocket, against London in the final stages of the Second World War. The Kaiser celebrated prematurely, as the Paris guns could only sow terror among the civilian population, not force a peace. The Germans, stalled in front of Amiens and Arras in the center and north, pushed further in the southern sector of the salient attempting to separate the British and French. But by 1 April the French had managed to re-establish a tenuous link with the British, as they fought to form a new defensive boundary.

The Germans could bring supplies or artillery through the wilderness of the old Somme battlefield only with difficulty. Their exhausted infantry had advanced forty miles in the greatest breakthrough on the Western Front since 1914. In the British rear areas they found materiel and luxuries of food and drink that the blockade had rendered unavailable in Germany. These temptations proved too much, as divisions "gorged themselves on food and liquor," and plundered the rest, including an estimated two million bottles of whiskey.[9]

Some soldiers, burdened with plunder, pulling livestock behind them, began to turn toward Germany. They replicated the behavior of their ancestors, the German *Landesknechte*, or freebooters, who plundered central Europe during the Thirty Years' War. Forged in the fire and deprivation of the war, these soldiers had degenerated into *Landesknechte*, as their discipline eroded. Later, on 15 April, Australian troops took Villers-Brettoneux at night and found a winery full of German soldiers, "drunk as owls." Soon Germans and Australians were "drunk as owls together." The former ended in prisoner-of-war camps; the latter, back at their units; and the winery, under police guard.[10]

On 4 April the Australian Corps counter-attacked outside Amiens; the following day the German High Command conceded the end of Operation

Michael. German casualties of over 300,000 men narrowly exceeded those of the British and French, although the Germans had captured 70,000 British prisoners. In killed and missing men, the BEF lost 150,000; the French, 60,000; and the Germans, 105,000.[11] But the Germans had exhausted more than ninety divisions, including their irreplaceable elite assault divisions, some of them reduced to 2,000 men after losing four-fifths to five-sixths of their initial complement.

Ludendorff now focussed on several offensive alternatives he had devised by early in January. He turned north to Flanders to strike for the channel coast behind Ypres sixty miles away, although the British heavily defended Ypres. On 9 April another Bruchmüller bombardment led German infantry right through a Portuguese division, one of two on the Western Front since Portugal declared war on Germany in 1916. The Germans pursued the terrified Portuguese as they ran.

The following day the Germans repelled Plumer's Second Army, seizing the high ground southeast of Ypres including Messines Ridge, which the British had taken in 1917. In conference with Haig, Foch commissioned the British to hold and refused to commit French reserves. On 11 April, a shaken Haig issued his famous "Backs to the Wall" order to the First and Second Armies, ordering "To All Ranks of the British Forces in France": "Every position must be held to the last man: there must be no retirement. With our backs to the wall, and believing in the justice of our cause, each one of us must fight on until the end."[12]

Yet retreat the men did if they could, as Plumer abandoned Passchendaele Ridge, so expensively acquired in 1917. The Germans forged ahead to capture Mount Kemmel southwest of Ypres, which French defenders simply relinquished. Foch relented and committed four French divisions to aid the British. On 29 April, when the Germans attacked again, the French and British held them short of Ypres. The Germans had lost another 120,000 men of 800,000 in the Fourth and Sixth Armies.

The German casualties included the Red Baron, Manfred von Richthofen. On 20 April the Baron, flying his red Fokker triplane, had shot down two airplanes, bringing his total to eighty. But Richthofen now suffered from exhaustion and the residual effects of a head wound of summer 1917. The following day, in pursuit of a British Sopwith Camel low over the lines, the Red Baron, under fire from machine-gunners on the ground, fell prey to another Camel. The air service, its ace of aces gone, continued the fight against increasingly overwhelming numbers of Entente aircraft. At the end of April, the service took delivery of a new fighter aircraft, the Fokker D7 biplane. The D7's superb maneuverability at high altitude made it the best production fighter of the war and ensured that the German fighter force remained a deadly opponent to the war's end.

The Entente strained to defend against these repeated German offensives.

Foch's stinginess with French reserves angered Haig. Foch considered Haig's request for reserves annoyingly premature. All resented Gen. John J. Pershing, commander of the AEF, for insisting at the Supreme War Council of 1–2 May on an independent American force rather than assigning his troops to the British and French armies. Pershing did allow the U.S. First Division to help the Entente at Cantigny late in May.

American units had been filtering into the lines since February, primarily with French units, to complete their baptisms of fire. The Germans would occasionally test the novices. The 26th Division, the New England National Guard, moved into the lines around the village of Seicheprey on 4 April. Small German patrols probed the 26th's front almost nightly. Then, on the night of 20 April, the Germans shelled them heavily. At 5 a.m. in heavy fog, German infantry in battalion strength seized Seicheprey and inflicted 570 American casualties. Having administered this bloody nose to the green American troops, the Germans withdrew after repulsing an American counter-attack.

Pershing had already released the 93rd Division for training and service with the French, who welcomed the black soldiers of its four regiments. Upon the arrival of the 369th Regiment in France in January 1918, Pershing, in an outright breach of the promise to use the 93rd as combat infantry, proposed to reduce them to pioneers or labor units. Instead, he uncharacteristically complied with French requests for American soldiers by transferring the 93rd to the French Army, though they technically remained under ultimate American military authority. The 93rd Division consequently became the only American unit completely integrated into another army for the duration of the hostilities.

The four regiments retained only their American uniforms; they received French standard issue helmets, gear, and weaponry. Maj. Arthur Little of the 369th described his regiment as a "black orphan" that Pershing had left on the French doorstep, to which a French colonel replied, "Welcome leetle black babbie."[13] French troops accommodated their African American peers too well for white American tastes. Later, in August 1918, Col. Linard, the French Military Attaché at AEF HQ, issued a memorandum from the American High Command warning the French Army and civilian officials not to treat African Americans in friendly fashion or praise them, but to segregate them and prevent any intimacy between them and French women. Linard relayed the arrogant and presumptious attitudes typical of white toward black Americans. The AEF Command discarded the 93rd to the French, and then presumed to advise them to prevent French "corruption," or equal treatment, of the black troops. The French allegedly rescinded the memorandum after two or three days, but issued no counter or comment, although the French National Assembly condemned the memorandum in July 1919.

In mid-April the 369th moved into the Argonne Forest as part of the French Army and took over a nearly three-mile sector of the line. Fewer than 1 percent of the American soldiers in France, the 369th held 20 percent of all territory assigned to American troops at the time.[14] In late May, in an encounter that brought fame to the 369th, a German raiding party attacked Sgt. Henry Johnson and Pvt. Neadom Roberts in their sentry post in no-man's land. The Germans wounded both men early in the fight, but, with grenades, rifles, and Johnson's adept use of his bolo knife, the two soldiers beat the Germans off, killing four and wounding a large number in the process. Both men received the *Croix de Guerre*.

In contrast to the French, the British adamantly refused to accept any black American troops for training and service with their army when Pershing offered them the 92nd Division. The transfer of the 92nd would have left American combat units lily white, but even British desperation had its limits, specifically racial. The British employed colored forces, either African or Asian, only as labor troops behind the front in France.

While the Entente quarreled, Ludendorff mustered his forces for his next attack against the French Army from the Chemin des Dames Ridge toward Paris, seventy miles away. With this thrust he intended to divert Foch from assisting the British, whom he planned to attack again later. On 27 May, after a four-hour bombardment of 6,000 guns with two million shells, forty German divisions would descend upon sixteen French and British divisions. Ludendorff initially ordered an advance of only twelve miles, in order to husband his troops for the later strike against the British in Flanders. The Germans, however, seized the Aisne River bridges before the French could destroy them and opened a salient thirteen miles deep and twenty-five miles wide the first day.

The intended German diversion became a full-fledged offensive. The following day the Germans captured the city of Soissons and advanced toward Reims, and by 30 May they had returned to the Marne, fifty-five miles from Paris. Despite Foch's reluctance to commit reserves, the Entente forces gradually allotted twenty-seven divisions from 28 May to 3 June, including the U.S. Third Division at Chateau-Thierry and the U.S. Second Division, which included the U.S. Marine Corps Brigade, at Belleau Wood on 2 June. Ludendorff halted the offensive on 3 June because of overextended supply lines and losses of another 100,000 men in creating a salient forty miles deep.

Still, it took the 2nd Division twenty days of savage fighting to clear Belleau Wood with some help from the 3rd Division. The Marines prepared to counter-attack. They moved forward in waves right into the teeth of the German defenses. On 6 June, in rising to the initial assault, bullets striking all around him and his men, 5-foot-4-inch, 49-year-old Gunnery Sgt. Daniel J. Daley shouted, "Come on, you sons-of-bitches. Do you want to live forever?" With those words, the two-time Medal of Honor winner led his men toward Belleau Wood. German machine-gunners mowed down entire platoons as the Marines doggedly advanced in waves. The Marines attacked three times, on 6, 9, and 12 June. Army units relieved them on 17 June, but they returned on 21 June to complete the seizure of the Wood in the next four days. In hand-to-hand combat, the Marines resorted to the bayonet, brass knuckles, and "toad-stickers" (knuckles with an 8-inch blade), punching and slashing their way into the Germans, who resisted determinedly with bayonet, blade, and shovel. During those twenty days the Marines suffered 5,600 casualties of their 13,500 men. German soldier Emil Amann observed that "the Yankees paid dearly" for their inexperience, as they "bunched together" in the attack and made excellent targets at close range for German machine gunners and riflemen.[15]

On 6 June the 369th fought near Belleau Wood. The extremely heavy fire prompted a French officer to suggest to Col. Hayward that he pull his men back, to which Hayward replied, "My men never retire; they go forward or they die." Hayward had informed the French early on that the 369th would become elite troops. He believed it, the men believed it, and their deeds convinced the French. In mid-August, after 130 days in the lines, the 369th earned a week's rest. The aggressive ardor of the American soldiers buoyed the spirits and confidence of their tired and battered French comrades. The soldiers of the two nations established good relations with one another, and the French praised African American soldiers as "well-trained . . . well-disciplined . . . [and] above all very dedicated."[16]

Ludendorff now struck yet a fourth time, on 9 June, in a limited and hastily prepared attack to connect his salients against the British and French armies. The French initially retreated, but Mangin, back in favor and commanding the French Tenth Army, counter-attacked with 144 tanks and halted the German offensive by 14 June. The French Army also rained mustard gas shells on the attackers. Nearly half a million German troops fell sick in June in the first outbreak of the Spanish influenza, as their poor diet rendered them less resistant than the allies opposite them.

Despite the German threat to Paris, the government did not evacuate the city as it had done in September 1914. Clemenceau, spoiling for a fight at 76 years of age, rallied the people with promises to fight before, in, and behind Paris until victory. In late June, the Entente launched two successful minor attacks which exemplified the effectiveness of combined arms tactics. Mangin's Tenth Army and Gen. Sir John Monash's Australian Corps coordinated all arms from artillery to aviation in limited offensives, presaging future Entente operations.

Nevertheless, Ludendorff seized the initiative once again, and on 15 July launched fifty-two German divisions toward Reims and ultimately Paris. His forces outnumbered the French by fifty-two to thirty-four divisions, but allied intelligence and observation aircraft detected the German buildup in

Champagne and Flanders. The French even learned the time and details in advance from German deserters and prisoners. Pétain prepared to defend; Foch, to counter-attack when the opportunity arose.

Pétain ordered an elastic defense entailing only lightly manned forward positions, which one of his generals, Henri Gouraud, executed perfectly. Bruchmüller's preliminary bombardment on 15 July consequently smashed positions, not men, while Gouraud greeted the barrage with a counter-barrage of his own. German infantry seized Gouraud's first line, but his infantry and artillery in the second stopped the German drive in its tracks in the eastern sector of the offensive. In the west, however, the Germans cracked the defense, crossed the Marne River, and advanced a few miles, only to come under concentrated ground attack from Entente airplanes and to find that the French had quickly re-established a front.

On 18 July Foch struck back. Mangin mounted a ferocious strike of eighteen divisions, spearheaded by his Moroccans in the middle, with the American 1st and 2nd divisions, each double the size of a European division, on either side. In a coordinated storm of infantry, artillery, tanks, and aviation, Mangin's forces pushed the Germans back across the Marne, although German artillery fire slowed their progress the following day.

The Entente had done the necessary damage. The German Army's fifth offensive, which the French called Second Marne, had clearly failed, precluding any further offensive plans which Ludendorff contemplated. On 22 July Ludendorff ordered a general retreat, and by 4 August the Marne salient ceased to exist. Ludendorff had exhausted his own armies in five offensives which netted much more territory to defend, but no decisive victory. The German Army had expended some 900,000 irreplaceable men since the start of the year, and now had to reduce its number of divisions, disbanding weak ones and funneling the units into the remaining divisions.

German infantry, supported by artillery and aviation, had demonstrated remarkable offensive power, breaking the Entente front in several places and reintroducing open warfare to the Western Front after a stalemate of more than three years. However, sheer exhaustion, hastened by overextended supply lines and the ravages of malnutrition in even the best of the German units, halted their advances. In the process the German soldiers had seen the incredible material and numerical wealth of the Entente.

German generals had promised their troops a decisive victory, in a sense reminiscent of Nivelle's promises to the French Army in April 1917. Pétain could await the Americans; Ludendorff could turn to no one. The German Army had pushed its opponents to breaking point early in the offensives. But the OHL, by keeping its end goals flexible in order to exploit operational gains, secured no concrete set of significant objectives. In the absence of ultimate victory, exhausted German soldiers, faced with the defense of more territory with fewer men, evacuated the salient.

Ludendorff had striven mightily to achieve total victory and a victorious peace of annexations by military means before the arrival of the U.S. Army. His forces had certainly taken a grave toll on the British Army, which had declined by more than 200,000 men by June 1918. Yet Ludendorff's armies had exhausted their resources, and now the Americans were arriving at the rate of 250,000 men a month. Twenty-five divisions had already arrived in France in various stages of readiness and another fifty-five were forming across the Atlantic. Individuals on the German General Staff urged a retreat to the Siegfried Line and the immediate initiation of negotiations with the Entente. Ludendorff contended that the Entente could not break the German lines.

The western powers had evolved new combined arms offensive tactics that relied on their advantages in quantity of artillery and aviation and their absolute advantage in tanks. In the air, Entente fighter planes now ranged low over the lines to strafe German troops. Fighter aircraft operating at low altitudes often fell prey to fire from the ground. British ace of aces, Irishman Edward Mannock, fell to ground fire on 26 July after following his seventy-third victim down to 200 feet. At high altitude two-seat single-engine bombers such as the fast and powerful French Breguet 14s struck targets forty miles behind the German front in daylight. At night multi-engined bombers such as the British Handley Page 0400 lumbered over German lines at low altitude to bomb targets of opportunity.

In tanks the Germans could muster only 170 captured Entente specimens and a few dozen of their own monster A7Vs, crewed by twelve men. The British and French Armies each had several hundred tanks. French armor ranged from the thirteen-ton Schneider-Creusot giant armed with a 75-mm. gun to the seven-ton two-man Renault tank with a 37-mm. gun mounted in a turret that could traverse 360 degrees. British armor included 500 Mark IV and V medium tanks, armed with cannon and machine-guns and capable of speeds of up to five miles per hour, and "whippets" with a road speed of eight mph.

The combination of the sheer weight of materiel, and the sheer numbers of American soldiers, although they required training, portended ultimate victory for the Entente, as Ludendorff had acknowledged when he planned his 1918 offensives. His worst fears had materialized, but he refused to relent. The Entente would have to pound the Germans into submission on the Western Front.

The Entente attacks

Foch prepared to preside over the pounding. Under severe political pressure at the height of the German offensives, Clemenceau had contemplated sacking Foch. Instead, the victory at Second Marne gained Foch promotion to Field Marshal. Now Foch would reap the fruits of his policy of hoarding reserves for future attacks, as he coordinated a series of Entente counter-attacks by his three main armies, the British, French, and American. He hoped to exert constant, intense pressure on the German defenses, so that once one force lost its momentum, another would attack elsewhere on the front to test German endurance and resolve.

The BEF struck first. Haig attacked the western side of the Amiens salient and re-entered the old Somme battlefield with 400 tanks and 800 planes. Foch ordered a French attack on Haig's right flank supported by 1,100 airplanes. The Entente mustered twenty-seven divisions against twenty understrength German divisions and 1,500 planes to fewer than 400 German. At 4.20 a.m. on 8 August, a creeping barrage swept over the German trenches. Behind it, out of the early morning fog, came tanks and troops of the spearhead Canadian and Australian Corps. They routed the German defenders, opened an eleven-mile gap in the German lines and advanced eight miles. However, the German defenses stiffened and the British lost most of their tanks. Haig ended the offensive on 12 August, having retaken most of the old Somme battlefield. After three years of battering the Germans, heedless of human losses and territorial gains, Haig found himself in the unusual position of terminating an offensive over Foch's objections.

Ludendorff later termed 8 August "the black day of the German Army," as a number of German troops surrendered to smaller Entente units and even individual soldiers. Others fled, cursing reinforcements for prolonging the war by attempting to stop the Entente advance. In attributing the unrest and insubordination of the soldiers to the home front, Ludendorff initiated the later popular myth of the *Dolchstoss*, the "stab in the back," blaming the loss of the war on a home front that stabbed the army in the back. On 11 August Ludendorff attributed the breakdown of morale to Bolshevik agitators in units transferred from the east, asserted that he could no longer win the war, and tendered his resignation. Although he urged a negotiated peace, he insisted on territorial annexations that would prevent such a peace. He further demanded that the army defend every inch of conquered territory. Hindenburg and Kaiser Wilhelm refused his resignation.

At the Battle of Amiens, the Canadian and Australian infantry assaulted a weaker German opponent than they had confronted in earlier years. Understrength and overextended German units relied on machine-guns to offset their deficiencies in manpower and artillery. The Canadians relied on artillery, first to crush their German counterpart in an artillery duel and then to prepare the way for the attack. Then the coordinated and synergistic use of artillery, air power, and armor supported the infantry assault. Their success heralded the "beginning of the end for the German Army on the Western Front." Historian Shane Schreiber echoed J.F.C. Fuller's description of the Battle of Amiens as a "decisive battle of the Western World" because it "would be the first and last truly combined arms battle of the Great War," foreshadowing "the development of modern mechanized warfare."[17]

On 18 August Mangin's army assaulted the southern end of the Amiens salient, while the British forces attacked toward Bapaume on the northern end of the salient. By 29 August the British captured Bapaume, and two days later the Australians captured the height of Mont St. Quentin on the east bank of the Somme, rendering any German stand in the region impossible. Haig selected the Canadian Corps to spearhead the attack toward the Hindenburg Line by striking along the heavily defended road from Arras to the rail and communications center of Cambrai, because the elite force could sustain the "hard pounding" of his relentless offensive operations. Foch concurred, describing the Canadians as "the ram with which we will break up the last line of resistance of the German Army." The Canadians launched the four-day Battle of Arras with a daring night attack on 26 August, and broke the crucial German defensive Drocourt–Quéant line, their final objective, on 2 September. While the Entente offensives continued elsewhere, the Canadians would spend the next three weeks refitting and replenishing for their next major attack.

In August the Entente had pushed the Germans back on an eighty-mile front from Arras to Soissons, forcing German withdrawal to the Hindenburg Line, a step Ludendorff had refused to take a month before. The Germans destroyed the region as they retreated, but now the German salients at Amiens, on the Marne, and in Flanders created by their attacks in 1918 had disappeared. In September the Germans consolidated their positions on the Hindenburg Line.

One German salient remained – St. Mihiel – which dated from 1914 and bulged to the southeast of Verdun between the Meuse River in the west and the Moselle River in the east. The First Army, the nucleus of an independent AEF, became operational on 10 August, as the French supplied all of its tanks and most of its artillery, aircraft, and munitions. For the debut of the independent American force, Pershing intended to reduce the St. Mihiel salient. Pershing and Foch agreed on the offensive on 17 August.

Haig then proposed a major British offensive between Cambrai and St. Quentin to Foch, with a supporting Franco-American offensive. Foch consequently advised Pershing to split the U.S. forces in two Franco-American attacks, one in Champagne to support the British, the other in the Argonne Forest west of Verdun. Their meeting degenerated into an angry argument, as Pershing refused to divide his force. Later Foch relented, and Pershing agreed to attack in the Argonne after he had finished at St. Mihiel. The St. Mihiel offensive would begin on 12 September, with French colonial troops in support of American units. The French air service also supplied half the aircraft for the operation, so that American Gen. "Billy" Mitchell commanded more than 1,500 aircraft, the largest aerial armada of the war.

Ironically, Ludendorff had ordered the evacuation of the St. Mihiel salient on 8 September, so the attack surprised the Germans in the act of withdrawing. The Americans captured 450 guns and 13,000 German prisoners. Foch praised the Americans' morale, and President Poincaré and Prime Minister Clemenceau visited the army to congratulate it. Ludendorff acknowledged that the sheer number of American soldiers depressed and undermined German morale.

On 23 September the allied commanders agreed to attack at points along the German line, from the Americans in the Argonne Forest on the Meuse River on 26 September, to the British in Flanders two days later. The Entente amassed 220 divisions – 102 French, 60 British, 42 American, 12 Belgian, 2 Italian, and 2 Portuguese – of which 120 would attack, to 197 German, but only 50 German divisions remained combat-worthy. The Entente possessed overwhelming superiority in manpower and materiel – artillery, airplanes, and tanks. As of September the AEF now held a hundred miles of front to the BEF's ninety miles, with the French holding the rest. French soldiers had grown confident of victory, their morale restored as they fought alongside American troops. French factories supplied the Americans with essential weapons.

The American forces faced the daunting task of rooting the Germans from the dark wilderness of the Argonne Forest and heavily wooded ridges beyond. They also had only ten days to move from St. Mihiel to the Meuse-Argonne sector on three inadequate roads. The time necessary for some experienced divisions to disengage at St. Mihiel and move to the Argonne meant that four of the nine attacking divisions had seen no combat.

French light Renault or heavy Schneider tanks with French and American crews supported the attacking infantry. The tanks proved effective, though vulnerable to artillery fire and to the German M-98 Mauser anti-tank rifle. According to an American tank lieutenant, "this thing throws an armor-piercing bullet the size of your thumb, went through my front plate [¾-inch armor], the driver, the rear bulkhead, and smashed hell outa the engine."[18]

Lieut. Col. George S. Patton, who had trained American tank units, led the AEF tank brigade supporting the attack of the novice 35th Division. In the confusion and fog of 26 September, Patton's tanks advanced beyond most of the infantry, whom the fog and fire rendered reluctant to advance. Patton found himself on foot in front of his tanks, with six runners for communication. As the flamboyant officer attempted to rally infantry and tanks, German machine-gunners mowed down his runners, and then hit Patton in the upper left thigh, the bullet exiting, in Patton's words, " at the crack of my bottom about two inches to the left of my rectum."[19] Patton's batman, the last man untouched, bandaged his fallen commander and ensured his evacuation for medical aid, thereby ending Patton's war.

Among the artillerymen supporting the attack, Capt. Harry S. Truman commanded the four 75-mm. cannon of Battery D, 2nd Battalion, 129th

Field Artillery Regiment. When Truman's battery reached the crossroads at Cheppy, where Patton had fallen, they found the bodies of nearly thirty dead American infantry in a pile or lying end to end. Patton had barely escaped their fate.[20]

In two days American forces advanced seven miles; then the attack became bogged down. Pershing halted to bring up his experienced divisions, including the First, the "Big Red One" of First and later Second World War fame. They advanced again on 4 October, but staff inexperience compounded the problems of coordinating movement through a dense forest nearly impenetrable to sunlight in the snow and rain.

The 1st Battalion, 308th Regiment, 77th Division, totally lost its way, and German troops surrounded and attacked it. It lost more than two-thirds of its original complement of 600 men before its rescue on 7 October. Its commander, Maj. Charles Whittlesey, received the Medal of Honor for the valiant stand, but, troubled by the loss of his men, he committed suicide after the war. On 8 October Corp. Alvin York, a Tennessee mountaineer and marksman, killed twenty-five German soldiers and captured 132 prisoners, a feat which, unimaginable earlier in the war, made him America's greatest hero of the war.

The fighting in the Meuse-Argonne campaign proved a difficult and grim test for inexperienced American troops. William S. Triplet's platoon started the offensive on 26 September with fifty-one men. By 30 September only seven remained. Triplet recalled that the Germans were "artists with machine guns, used them at two thousand yards or more, placing them well back where the trajectory of the bullets would follow the curve of our reverse slopes. . . . It was a good substitute for the field artillery they seemed to be short of."[21] German gunners could thus hit men more than a mile away on the other side of a hill. He marveled that a gunner more than 1,000 yards away could fire a ten-round burst in such "tight shooting" that he could have caught the bullets in a helmet.[22]

Triplet's fellow soldiers received terrible wounds. He recalled, "I found Segram wounded . . . it was bloody awful. . . . [T]he shell burst and a chunk of iron the size of a saucer had hit him dead center in the tail. Made a hole you could put a fist through and shoved everything including six inches of his spine right up through his tattered guts. . . . He was dead. Unfortunately he was still breathing and conscious and in pain.[23] Later, in combat, another soldier "overtook us. He was holding one blood-dripping hand over, his face. . . . He was a shocking sight. Looked like a bullet had hit him on the right cheek and taken several molars out the hole on the left. Probably hadn't done his tongue any good either . . . bleeding like a stuck pig."[24]

Triplet recalled that their British instructors had emphasized the bayonet. Instead of shooting retreating German soldiers, the men occasionally chased and confronted them. A prewar coal-miner, transformed into an "enthusiastic bayonet expert," challenged a retreating German. The German parried his thrust, then struck his arm so hard with the butt of his rifle that the miner dropped his gun. With two more strokes the German drove the miner's head down between his shoulders and broke his ribs. The German was strangling him until a friend who had watched the entire match casually strolled over and shot the German in the head, blowing his brains all over the miner. The miner, now cured of his enthusiasm for the bayonet, readily admitted his fear, but volunteered that working in a coal-mine frightened him more.[25]

The Americans emerged from the Argonne on 12 October, seized the heights above the Meuse, and crossed the river. They pushed grimly ahead. By late October their slow progress so dissatisfied French Premier Clemenceau that he almost asked Woodrow Wilson to remove Pershing from command. Foch intervened on Pershing's behalf.

Fighting in the French Army in Champagne, black American units acquitted themselves well. The 369th returned from a week's rest to fight the rest of the war as part of the French 161st Division. In September it fought in support of the American offensive in the Meuse-Argonne. Advancing some eight miles against stubborn German resistance, the 369th's battalions, which began the attack with some 700 men each, lost most of their officers and 400 to 600 men. In particular, the 369th stormed through the town of Séchault after an advance across nearly a mile of open ground studded with German pillboxes and machine-gun nests. Some 800 men, half of the regiment, fell in the assault, and their French division commander praised their élan. They left no German alive in Séchault.

The French withdrew the 369th from the line and in mid-October assigned it to a quiet sector, where it remained at the armistice. It had been in combat 191 days, longer than any regiment in the AEF, after the shortest combat training of any regiment.[26] The other three regiments of the 93rd Division also fought well, and the division suffered 32 percent casualties – 584 men killed and 2,582 wounded.

In the AEF, the 92nd Division comprised black draftees and some black officers of company rank. Its commander, Gen. Ballou, feuded with its army commander, Gen. Robert Bullard, although both considered blacks inferior.[27] The division enjoyed no social freedom, and black and white officers ate separately. The 92nd moved to the front in late August. German planes dropped leaflets about lynching and unequal rights in the black lines, but the pamphlets provoked no desertions.

For the big push in the Argonne, Pershing assigned the 368th Regiment of the 92nd to the gap between the French and American Armies. The unit lacked heavy-duty wire cutters, signal flares, grenade launchers, or American artillery support. Under these circumstances, despite hard fighting at Binarville and casualties of some 250 men, the regiment failed to keep contact between the armies. The AEF command condemned the entire division, although the 92nd's other three regiments had not entered combat. Significantly, when three white divisions retreated with their morale shattered, no one suggested that their poor performance proved that white soldiers could not withstand modern warfare.

Despite continued slurs, the 92nd Division fought to the war's end. Some white officers at company and battalion level grew to respect their black troops, and twenty-one of the division's soldiers won the Distinguished Service Cross, a greater number than in the 35th, 6th, 81st, or 88th Divisions of white soldiers. John Keegan notes "the poor record of black American troops on the Western Front in 1918" and attributes it to "self-fulfilling prophecy: little being expected of them, little was given."[28] The AEF command certainly expected little of black soldiers and gave them less equipment and training, but the soldiers performed not only above expectation, but better than some white divisions.

In general, the AEF's inexperienced, large divisions proved difficult to manage and supply. If a division's four large regiments provided lots of manpower for trench warfare, it proved too cumbersome and unwieldy for a war of maneuver. In the fall, nearly 100,000 "stragglers," allegedly searching for their units, wandered behind the front. Although Pershing constantly proclaimed the value of open warfare, he himself had no idea how to achieve it.[29] The European armies in 1918 outperformed the inexperienced doughboys in open warfare, because they had mastered combined arms operations of skilled specialists.

Pershing grew more impatient to prove the value of the AEF as Entente forces liberated most of France and the western part of Belgium by November. Foch reserved for the French Army the "liberation" of the fortress city of Sedan, where Emperor Napoleon III had surrendered to the Prussian Army at the end of the Franco-Prussian War forty-eight years earlier. Pershing, ignoring Foch's orders, sent the 1st Division across the path of the 42nd Division in an unseemly and impolitic move to seize Sedan and the glory. Units of the 1st did capture Brig. Gen. Douglas MacArthur of the 42nd, whom they mistook for a German officer because he persisted in wearing a soft cap similar to the enemy's. Before Franco–American and AEF inter-divisional relationships deteriorated further, the French approached Gen. Hunter Liggett, commander of the First Army AEF, which comprised the 1st and 42nd divisions and whom Pershing had not informed of the plan. Liggett canceled the operation.

Early in November German resistance weakened, and the French and Americans advanced more rapidly in Champagne and in the Meuse-Argonne. In 1918 Pétain commanded a smaller army than Joffre had in 1914, but this army had more than 2,500 airplanes, 3,000 tanks, and 13,000 artillery pieces. Pétain described himself in October as "a captain of industry who is working with his plant at full capacity."

Such observations did not mean that the war had grown less costly in men, however. In June French casualties for the year peaked at 81,000, and casualties for the two-month period of June and July of 133,000 men took second place only to those of August and September 1914 of 329,000 men.[30] Materiel proved no substitute for men; the war consumed both to the very end.

In Flanders British and Belgian forces retook Ypres, eliminated the salient south of Ypres by 2 October. Haig's forces assaulted the strongest sector of the Hindenburg Line. On 27 September the Canadian Corps crossed and bridged the Canal du Nord, a major obstacle, and seized the heights overlooking Cambrai in a daring and well-coordinated assault relying on artillery, engineers, and the skill of commanders and troops at maneuver and combat. The British Fourth Army crossed the St. Quentin Canal in another bold attack, then advanced into the first defensive positions of the Hindenburg Line. On 4 October they broke the line.

The Germans, hammered constantly, retreated everywhere through October and into November, destroying the region and leaving tenacious teams of machine-gunners to delay the Entente advance. The failure of the spring offensives gradually demoralized the German soldiers. Desertions and disciplinary offenses rose. The number of "*Drückeberger*" or shirkers, who did not desert but avoided any duties, especially combat, reached between three-quarters of a million and a million men in the final months of the war. The soldiers sometimes staged a "covert military strike," similar to their French counterparts in 1917, in order to end the war. Military units in the rear mutinied or sometimes just disbanded.[31]

Yet, even in this demoralized state, vastly outnumbered and with no hope of victory, reliable German units could still mount determined opposition. In the last five months of the war the BEF lost more than 100,000 men killed; the French Army, 161,000; and the AEF, some 60,000.[32] The Royal Air Force suffered its worst losses of the war on 30 October. Death remained constant on the Western Front to the very end.

THE EASTERN FRONT. RUSSIA QUITS THE WAR

The negotiations at Brest-Litovsk between the Bolshevik government and the Central Powers continued in 1918, as the Bolsheviks stalled in anticipation of world or at least European revolution. Lenin sent Foreign Commissar Leon Trotsky, whose novel suggestion of a state of "No war, no peace" prolonged debate for a time. Finally, German military representative Gen. Max von Hoffmann, planner of Tannenberg, lost patience on 16 February and ordered the advance of German forces. Proclaiming that "All of Russia is nothing but a great pile of maggots," Hoffmann laughed at the "comical war"[33] as the German Army raced relentlessly eastward in trains and automobiles at a pace of 150 miles a week.

The Bolsheviks returned to Brest-Litovsk at the end of February. In March the peace of Brest-Litovsk demolished the empire, recognizing Finland and Ukraine as independent, and ceding Estonia, Latvia, Lithuania, Russian Poland, and Belarus as client states of Germany, and districts in the south to Turkey. Russia lost a million square miles, 50 million inhabitants, 90 percent of its coal mines, 54 percent of its industry, 32 percent of its agricultural land, and most of its oil and cotton production.[34] In additional treaties the Central Powers divided Ukrainian grain production and demanded reparations from the Bolsheviks. In May, at the Treaty of Bucharest, Germany reduced Rumania to a vassal state and divided Rumanian oilfields with Austria–Hungary.[35]

The German military administration of *Ober Ost* extended into Latvia and Estonia, creating a territory called "Baltikum." German Foreign Secretary Richard von Kühlmann attempted to persuade the OHL to allow the subject nationalities a semblance of self-determination. When he announced in the Reichstag that military force would not suffice to end the war, the High Command had him dismissed in July.[36] The OHL envisaged a colossal new order in the east where Hindenburg would maneuver his left wing in the next war. But the inhabitants did not provide the food supplies demanded, and the morale of the German troops declined. From more than a million men in March 1918, German troop strength in the east declined to half a million in October. Some of the men transported west for the offensives used the opportunity to desert.

Kaiser Wilhelm ended *Ober Ost* on 3 November by establishing a civilian government in the east. After the armistice on 11 November that government collapsed, and authority and discipline in many German units disintegrated as officers fled to Germany. Their men "melted away" and left for home, as Russian soldiers had done the previous year. Client states declared their independence. The Bolsheviks annulled the treaty of Brest-Litovsk on 13 November and began to move their army west, while the Entente demanded that German troops remain in the east as a bulwark against Bolshevism. Chaos reigned in the east.

THE CENTRAL POWERS SURRENDER

On the Southeastern Front in Europe the Allied army in the "internment camp" of Salonika numbered more than 500,000 men by 1918. In the spring Gen. Franchet D'Esperey, known to British soldiers as "Desperate Frankie," took command of the force. On 14 September he attacked north through the mountains in Macedonia, breaking the Bulgarian Line with two French divisions and exploiting the breakthrough with Serb troops. The exhausted and disillusioned Bulgarian Army and population, short of food and other essential supplies, faced the Entente Army alone. Their initial resistance quickly collapsed. Entente forces split the Bulgarian Army on 19 September; British and Greek troops entered southern Bulgaria. On 26 September Bulgaria requested an armistice based on the Fourteen Points; the fighting ended four days later. Bulgaria's collapse isolated the Turks as the Entente Army moved through Bulgaria east into Turkey toward Constantinople, and threatened the Austro-Hungarian Empire as they moved north through Serbia.

On the Southwestern Front in Europe, the Italian Army recovered from Caporetto and enjoyed the support of British and French aerial and ground forces. In spring 1918 Kaiser Karl ordered another offensive, disregarding the exhausted and starved state of the Habsburg Army. Conrad and Gen. Borojevich von Bojna disagreed on the location of the attack, and Karl allowed both army groups to attack simultaneously. The Italians knew of both offensives. Consequently, within five days of the start of the attack on 15 June, the Habsburg Army retreated, after losing 140,000 casualties. Karl promptly removed Field Marshal Conrad from command in July, and the army gradually collapsed in a welter of desertions and mutinies. Underfed men and animals collapsed from inadequate diet; uniforms sufficed to clothe only a small minority of soldiers. In mid-September Karl and his Foreign Minister Stephan Burian failed to persuade the Germans to apply for an armistice, and Burian approached the Entente alone. National units in the army deserted and went home.

On 24 October Italian Army commander Gen. Armando Diaz launched fifty-seven divisions, including three French, two British, and a Czech division of deserters from the Austro-Hungarian Army, in a three-pronged attack in the mountains and along the Piave River. An equal number of Austro-Hungarian divisions opposed the Italian attack for two days, then divisions broke, fled, or mutinied as the Italians crossed the Piave, pierced the front at Vittorio Veneto, the village which gave its name to the battle, and reached Austrian territory within a week. On 28 October the Habsburg generals demanded that the AOK negotiate an armistice. With Diaz approaching from Italy and Franchet D'Esperey from Serbia, the monarchy collapsed on 30 October. On 1 November the Austro-Hungarian government requested an armistice, which the Italians accepted on 4 November. By that time Austro-Hungarian soldiers were returning home as fast as possible, jettisoning their weapons, crowding into and on the roofs of trains, and disappearing when they neared their homes.

Turkey, confronted at long last with the collapse of the Russian enemy, found itself under siege from every other direction. The Russian Army in the Caucasus withdrew and disintegrated with the revolution, leaving their equipment to an emerging Armenian National Army. The Turks seized the fortress of Erzerum from the Armenians in March, crossed the Russian frontier of 1914 later that month, and advanced to the frontier of 1877 by the end of April. Enver's grandiose plans for a Pan-Turanian empire prompted the Turks in peace negotiations with the Bolsheviks in May to demand Georgia and access to Baku and its oil depot on the Caspian Sea. The German Army coveted the Caucasus for Germany and engineered the creation of a Georgian state as a German protectorate. In this confrontation of the two allies, the German government threatened to withdraw its support from the Ottoman Empire. Enver ceased expansion into Georgia and aimed instead at Azerbaijan and Persia with an "Army of Islam" as of July 1918.

The British, concerned already about a Turkish threat to Persia, assigned Maj. Gen. L.C. Dunsterville to lead a military mission named "Dunsterforce" into the Caucasus. The "Army of Islam" and a "Dunsterforce" reinforced with Cossacks confronted one another at Baku in July. Dunsterforce evacuated by sea on 14 September, and the Turks stormed the city the following day. Turkish forces advanced into the Caucasus Mountains and into northern Persia by the end of the war. While the Turks advanced east, the British advanced through Mesopotamia and Palestine against them. In Mesopotamia, British imperial cavalry flanked the Turkish forces and forced their surrender on 30 October, and the British occupied the oil-rich city of Mosul on 1 November, ending the war in Mesopotamia.

Allenby sought to conquer the rest of Palestine, advance toward Damascus, Syria, and force the Ottoman Empire from the war. However, the necessity of sending two divisions to the Western Front during the German spring offensives undermined his planned offensive. He decided to wait until September to stage another major offensive while he trained new Indian troops. On 19 September Allenby's infantry proceeded north up the coast while his ANZAC cavalry moved east to outflank the Turks. Allenby's Fourth Cavalry Division galloped through a breach in the lines and covered seventy miles in thirty-four hours, encircling thousands of Turkish troops. As the Turkish forces fled, Royal Air Force airplanes bombed and strafed the defenseless troops.

Allenby named the battle after a small town in the region, Megiddo, site of the first recorded battle in history, also predicted to be the site of Armageddon, the final struggle between good and evil, in the Bible. Feisal's and Lawrence's Arab forces seized the railway junction at Deraa, severing the Haifa and Hejaz railways, on 27 September. Allenby entered Damascus on 2 October. His troops had broken three Turkish armies and resistance, taken 75,000 prisoners, and were sweeping north unopposed, at the cost of only 5,600 casualties. By 26 October they reached Aleppo, 200 miles beyond Damascus, ending the Syrian campaign. Allenby's successful offensive had crippled the Turks in the Middle East, and Franchet D'Esperey's advance from Salonika through Bulgaria directly threatened Constantinople. On 30 October the Ottoman government's armistice with the British left the Turkish Army in possession of the Anatolian heartland and much of the Russian Caucasus.

Finally, only Paul von Lettow-Vorbeck in East Africa continued to elude his Entente pursuers. Lettow-Vorbeck's invasion of Portuguese East Africa in late 1917 presented his *Schutztruppe* with numerous supply depots to plunder. They pursued overmatched Portuguese troops while British forces chased them. After occasional clashes with British KAR forces, and now struck by the influenza pandemic, Lettow-Vorbeck's force re-entered German East Africa in September, leaving behind their sick and wounded. Some of his *askaris* deserted as they approached home, while his force marched north, then west into Northern Rhodesia, and then south, dogged by his KAR pursuers. On 12 November he fought a last skirmish, then learned the next day of the armistice and Germany's defeat. On 25 November he surrendered his troops – 154 Europeans, 1,156 askaris, 1,600 porters, and women and children. The British lionized their former enemy and transported the officers to Dar-es-Salaam by 8 December. On 17 January 1919, five years after landing in East Africa, Lettow-Vorbeck and 302 German troops, women, and children sailed for Rotterdam, where they received a hero's welcome. They traveled to Berlin by special train to receive further accolades, as the undefeated general returned to his defeated country.

THE NAVAL WAR. GERMANY SINKS

The naval war continued in the Adriatic and Mediterranean Seas, but its focus remained the North Sea, the English Channel, and the North Atlantic. In the Adriatic Sea the Habsburg Navy began the year with a mutiny in February at the naval base at Cattaro, after which Kaiser Karl attempted to rejuvenate the navy with the promotion of Capt. Nikolaus Horthy to rear-admiral and his appointment to command the fleet. Horthy had commanded his cruisers aggressively, and now planned to attack the Otranto barrage in June. He aborted it when an Italian motor torpedo boat sank one of his new dreadnoughts. The Habsburg Navy had sortied in strength for the last time. On 31 October Horthy turned the fleet over to the Yugoslavs, and that night two Italian officers attached mines that blew up another dreadnought. The naval war in the Adriatic had ended with a bang.

In the Mediterranean Sea in 1918, the Germans added ten new U-boats, but a shortage of skilled labor to maintain them offset the reinforcements. Through May 1918 German submarines sank between 75,000 and 113,000 tons of shipping monthly, but totals subsequently declined steadily from 77,000 in July to 10,000 tons in November. The Allies dispersed their merchant shipping more efficiently, and actually sank four subs in May, including UB.68, commanded by Karl Doenitz, the future commander of German submarines in the Second World War and Hitler's successor in 1945. The German submarine campaign essentially dwindled to nothing, although UB.50 sank an old British battleship on 9 November, the last British warship sunk during the war.

Meanwhile, the Entente powers, particularly the British and French, clashed over command of the Mediterranean, a struggle that the British won and eliminated the French from armistice negotiations with the Turks on board a British battleship. British ships led the Allied fleet into the Dardanelles on 12 November to anchor off Constantinople.

On the major naval front of the war, late in December 1917 First Lord of the Admiralty Eric Geddes replaced an exhausted Jellicoe with Adm. Sir Rosslyn Wemyss as First Sea Lord. Adm. Beatty then proposed a new strategy for the Grand Fleet, containing the German fleet in its bases rather than seeking to bring it to battle. He acknowledged superior German battleship and shell construction and the Grand Fleet's inadequate margin of superiority over the German High Sea Fleet in light cruisers and destroyers.

American battleships formed the Grand Fleet's Sixth Battle Squadron, and although they had much to learn, Beatty worked to incorporate them successfully and to keep the morale of the Grand Fleet high despite its inactivity and the harsh conditions of North Sea bases. The U.S. Navy also attempted to lay a gigantic minefield between the Orkney Islands and Norwegian waters to block German submarines from exiting the North Sea into the North Atlantic. This Northern Barrage, at enormous effort and cost, claimed perhaps six submarines in the waning months of the war.

Roger Keyes, chairman of the Channel Barrage Committee in the Admiralty, focussed on preventing German submarines from passing through the Dover Straits to sink channel shipping. He replaced Vice Adm. Bacon, with whom he had disagreed, as commander of the Dover Patrol. He laid deep minefields, and trawlers and minesweepers equipped with searchlights lit the channel from Folkestone in England to Cape Gris Nez in France. The barrage forced the U-boats to dive, enabling the minefield to claim six submarines from January through April, compared to two submarines throughout the entire war before the barrage. The British succeeded in forcing most German submarines to sail north around the British Isles, thus reducing their hunting time.

German destroyers did stage a raid on the barrage vessels in mid-February. Later the German Flanders flotilla of destroyers and torpedo boats accompanied Ludendorff's offensive with an attack on Entente coastal communications during the night of 20–21 March. Neither raid met with success, and by summer 1918 the Royal Navy sank more submarines off the east coast of Britain and in the Straits of Dover.

The aggressive Keyes now focussed on blocking Zeebrugge and Ostend, as both led by canal to the German submarine pens at Bruges. Keyes's plan of 24 February stipulated sinking blockships, obsolete cruisers, in the entrances to the Zeebrugge–Bruges Canal and Ostend harbor with a force of 165 ships, and 700 Royal Marines and 200 sailors to attack German artillery batteries on the mole, or stonewall breakwater, at Zeebrugge.

After several postponements, Keyes's force attacked during the night of 22–23 April. In an assault marked by violent encounters and heroic deeds, and marred by error, the British partially blocked the Zeebrugge Canal entrance and failed at Ostend. British sailors and marines suffered casualties of 505 men and won eleven VCs, and the gallant raid buoyed the spirits of the navy, the British public, and the allies. In fact, the Germans had the canal back in partial use in two days and in full use three weeks later, but the raid had given the British a valuable psychological boost during the German offensives. Keyes failed again to block Ostend on 10–11 May, and the Admiralty canceled a third attempt planned for June.

On the night of 23–24 April the German High Sea Fleet sortied to attack a Scandinavian convoy, but missed any contact because of faulty intelligence and returned, one battlecruiser in tow after an engine breakdown. The Grand Fleet sailed when the Germans broke radio silence after the battlecruiser accident, but the fleets missed each other. The German High Sea Fleet had sortied for the last time in the war; the Grand Fleet, for the last time in strength. Subsequently, the German fleet gradually descended into decay as the morale of its sailors declined.

The British and Germans also contested the air over the Channel and North Sea, the Germans using high-performance Hansa Brandenburg floatplanes designed by Ernst Heinkel, the British patrolling with powerful multi-engine flying boats of modified Glenn Curtiss design. The British also developed aircraft carriers by the end of the war. A Sopwith Camel flying from a large barge shot down a Zeppelin in August, while German floatplanes sank three and disabled three British motor torpedo boats intent on attacking German minesweepers.

The main naval war lay in the North Atlantic, where the submarines of the High Sea Fleet prowled. By 1918 strikes and shortages of labor and materials prevented German industry from delivering submarine orders to the navy. Nevertheless, as of September 1918 the navy optimistically expected to receive hundreds of submarines in 1919 and 1920. Through August the U-boats sank an average of 300,000 tons of shipping monthly, far below the losses they inflicted in 1917. Afterward their sinkings plummeted below 200,000 tons in September and to slightly above 100,000 tons in October. Submarine commanders could find fewer vulnerable targets, as convoys, aircraft, and blimps protected merchant shipping. The Germans resorted to night attacks on the surface, and large U-cruisers and merchant submarines even entered American waters. Nothing could affect the convoy traffic across the Atlantic. American troops in their hundreds of thousands crossed monthly in British and American ships, the latter including converted German passenger liners long interned in American ports, with insignificant loss.

In accord with armistice negotiations, the German Navy recalled its submarines on 21 October, but Admirals Scheer and Hipper planned a final sortie of the High Sea Fleet, a "death battle," while Beatty yearned to strike a final blow against the German fleet. The German ships never sortied, because their crews, learning of the suicidal plans, mutinied. The armistice terms stipulated the surrender of all German submarines, the internment of significant numbers of surface ships, and the maintenance of the allied blockade until the Germans signed the peace treaty. The German Navy surrendered 176 submarines after the war. On 21 November, nine German dreadnoughts, five battle cruisers, seven light cruisers, and forty-nine destroyers sailed into the Firth of Forth to surrender, escorted by the Grand Fleet and representatives of the Allied Navies.

HOME FRONTS

Russia. Internal war, external intervention

The authority of the Russian central government over the provinces and rural areas in general collapsed, while the Treaty of Brest-Litovsk removed the periphery of the empire. At the beginning of 1918 the Bolsheviks controlled Moscow and St. Petersburg, but in some local soviets the Mensheviks or the Socialist Revolutionaries dominated. In the midst of the collapse and chaos, civil war began in the summer of 1918, pitting the Reds, or Bolsheviks, against a number of White (monarchist or anti–Bolshevik) armies. The Whites enjoyed the support of foreign powers, particularly Britain, France, Japan, and the United States.

More than half a million Communists served in the Red Army during the Civil War, and 33 percent of the Bolshevik Party members in 1927 had joined during the Civil War. To them, the party constituted a "fighting brotherhood," and this military experience left a tradition of coercion, summary justice, and rule by centralized administrative fiat.

The workers of Petrograd proved belligerent at the end of 1917, and the Bolshevik Party members preferred to wage a guerrilla war against the Germans rather than sign a peace agreement. Trotsky, who became War Commissar in spring 1918, had to build the Red Army using the Red Guards and pro–Bolshevik units of the army and navy as a nucleus. From the start he organized it as a regular army, with appointed officers and military discipline.

Volunteers and then drafted workers and Bolsheviks expanded the ranks. Both the Bolsheviks and White forces conscripted peasants, but the former attracted peasants more easily than the latter because they had seized land and distributed it to the village mir, while the counter-revolutionary White armies upheld the claims of large landowners. Lenin and Trotsky also conscripted officers from the imperial army and paired them with political commissars. Some junior officers from the old army joined willingly and rose rapidly in the new army.

In addition to the army, the Bolsheviks also relied on their new secret police, the Cheka, which they organized in December 1917. The Cheka evolved from an agency to combat banditry into a security police force and finally an agency to use terror and dispense summary justice to ensure loyalty to the Soviet regime. In order to generate a war economy from the collapsing economy of the tsarist era, the Bolsheviks nationalized all large-scale industry. They, and the white opposition, requisitioned grain and foodstuffs from the peasants.

The Communists faced a host of opponents. Imperial army officers in the south and Adm. Alexander Kolchak in Siberia prepared to fight the Bolsheviks. The Bolsheviks had the advantage of controlling the crucial Petrograd–Moscow axis of communications and transportation, while the White forces lacked a single leader and did not coordinate their assaults on the Bolshevik center from the periphery. To ensure that the White forces could not rally to the Romanovs, the Ural regional Soviet sent agents to execute Nicholas, Alexandra, and their entire family in Ekaterinburg in Siberia, on 18 July 1918. A Czech legion of some 30,000 men was fighting its way east along the Trans-Siberian Railway to Vladivostok to ship to the Western Front to continue the fight against the Central Powers.

In February the Entente Supreme War Council recommended occupation of the Trans-Siberian Railway from Harbin to Vladivostok by British, French, American, and Japanese troops. Allegedly these troops, including the Americans, would guard the tons of munitions and war materiel in Russian ports that various countries had sent the imperial Russian government. In fact, Woodrow Wilson and advisors such as Robert Lansing and the State Department sought to "Make the world safe for Democracy by destroying Bolshevism." While proclaiming to the American public that the United States would not interfere or intervene in Russian internal affairs, Wilson in fact did everything he could covertly to undermine the Bolshevik regime.

U.S. Army officers, including the American military attaché in Moscow, who counseled coming to terms with and supporting the Bolsheviks,[37] considered the undertaking misguided and dangerous. It sent American soldiers into a snake pit, in which the Bolsheviks constituted the least of the vipers. Extreme climate and living conditions, indistinguishable friends and foes, and shifting alliances complicated the situation further.

Joint Entente expeditions under British command landed at the ports of

Archangel and Murmansk in the north. The 4,500 American infantry of the 339th Regiment landed in Archangel in August with little training and inadequate equipment to find, according to one, "269,831 inhabitants, of which 61,329 are human beings and 208,502 are dogs."[38] They would soon find themselves clashing with Bolshevik forces in the region in small, deadly encounters.

The 9,000 soldiers of the U.S. 27th and 31st Infantry regiments assigned to Vladivostok arrived in August without proper uniforms and training along with French, British, Italian, Rumanian, Serbian, Polish, Canadian, and Japanese troops. Although each country had agreed to send no more than 10,000 troops, the Japanese sent 72,000 men to Siberia, a reflection of their interest in the Asian continent. All had come to support the authoritarian Adm. Kolchak, who would declare himself "Supreme Ruler" of Russia in November.

Kolchak's thuggish generals, whom the British, French, and Japanese paid, supplied, and protected, treated the population savagely. Allegedly attempting to exterminate the Bolsheviks, they terrorized the area with armored trains, murdering and robbing the population, kidnapping and enslaving women. Maj. Gen. William S. Graves, the American commander in Vladivostok, considered Kolchak's forces to be far worse than the Bolsheviks. He calculated they killed a hundred people for every one the Bolsheviks killed and believed the Japanese allowed them to run amok in order to have an excuse to intervene in Siberia later.[39] Ultimately, allying with such despicable figures would discredit the Entente forces, as their depredations would drive the people into the arms of the Bolsheviks. American soldiers, while fighting the Bolsheviks, occasionally had to defend themselves against Kolchak's men and the Japanese.

The Bolsheviks would forge the Soviet Union in the flames of the Civil War, which polarized society, devastated the economy, shaped the future development of the party and the Soviet government, and left the Bolsheviks with a lasting fear of "capitalist encirclement."

Austria-Hungary and Germany. Starvation and disintegration

Austria-Hungary barely survived the winter of 1917–18. The population teetered on the brink of starvation and possible revolt. In Vienna food, at best scarce, had become unavailable, and tens of thousands of desperate women and children froze in food lines to no avail. A flourishing black market sold only to those few who could afford the prices. The government's reduction of the flour ration in mid-January provoked industrial strikes and riots, some lasting for a week, in the cities of the Dual Monarchy. The demonstrators' slogans included revolutionary and nationalist demands, and expectations of peace from the negotiations with the Bolsheviks at Brest-Litovsk combined with hunger to fuel the unrest. The people blamed the circumstances on the government or Jewish middlemen, and complained about shortages, inflation, and requisitions. As in other countries, the poor disproportionately bore the burden of war and increasingly resented the inequity. The government rescinded the new flour ration, and the army, contemplating a military dictatorship, substituted for an impotent police and arrested the leaders of the unrest. By this time the command had stationed large numbers of soldiers at home, not at the front, to keep order.

The return of some 2.1 million Habsburg prisoners-of-war from Russia in the spring added to domestic problems. They needed supplies and food as the army processed them, sent them on leave, and then on to depots for the Italian front. In the midst of this domestic chaos, Karl ruined his reputation at home and abroad, with ally and enemy, by denying that he knew about his Foreign Minister's diplomatic approach to France through Prince Sixtus of Bourbon-Parma in 1917. Within the monarchy it tempted the German ally and the various nationalities to fill the political vacuum, while the Entente powers decided to recognize fully the monarchy's nationalities' right to self-determination.

Industrial production plummeted from late spring, as factories ran out of coal and metal in May, and workers, concerned only with an end to the war, refused to report to their jobs. In May Karl met Kaiser Wilhelm at OHL at Spa, agreed to a unified army command, standardization of weapons, an officers' exchange – Ludendorff insisted on the exclusion of Jewish officers – and later discussions about a customs union between the two monarchies. The Entente powers concluded that the pact bound the two indissolubly, and decided to support the resolutions for independence that a Congress of the "suppressed peoples" of the Dual Monarchy proclaimed in Rome in April.[40]

By the fall the home front had descended into disorder; the people, soldier and civilian alike ragged skeletons, scrounged for food. The transport system and food supply had very nearly collapsed in the winter of 1917–18; they did in 1918. Austria-Hungary fragmented, wracked by ethnic claims for independence. In mid-October Karl issued a manifesto transforming Austria into a federal state, with autonomy for Czechoslovaks and South Slavs. The people ignored the monarch and the manifesto, while Woodrow Wilson demanded independence, not autonomy, for the subject nationalities.

Hungary, hoping to conciliate the western powers, declared its independence and dissolved its union with Austria. Count Mihely Karolyi, an opponent of Tisza who had opposed the Dual Monarchy's entry into the war, took power. An admirer of democratic ideas and Wilson's principles, he allowed the distribution of his own landholdings of more than 50,000 acres among his peasants, then initiated land reform to dissolve all the large estates. He also hoped to convoke a constitutional assembly elected by universal suffrage after the war.

Beginning on 28 October, the subject nationalities began to declare their independence and to secede from the Habsburg monarchy, while the Hungarian government recalled its troops. On 31 October the Swiss ambassador wrote in his last report, "Chaos reigns in the former Dual Monarchy."[41] Angry soldiers murdered Count Tisza in his house in Budapest in revenge for his responsibility for the war. Although Karl renounced power on 11 November, he refused to abdicate, and only in March 1919 did he enter exile in Switzerland.

After four years of blockade, Germany's stock of pigs had declined by 77 percent; of cattle, 32 percent; the weekly per capita consumption of meat, from 1,050 grams to 135. Women's mortality had risen 51 percent; children under 5, 50 percent; tuberculosis deaths, 72 percent. The birth rate had declined by 50 percent. The German Health Office attributed 730,000 deaths to the wartime blockade.[42]

The food scandals of late 1917 left the population apathetic and convinced of the government's irresponsibility, while soldiers and sailors complained about circumstances on the home as well as the fighting front. According to some historians, the people hated the controlled economy; according to others, they believed in the controlled economy, but not the government's ability to manage it, which raised the specter of revolution.[43]

On 28 January a national strike began in Berlin that ultimately involved perhaps as many as a million participants throughout the country before it ended on 4 February. Beyond food, the demonstrators wanted an end to the war, the restoration of civil rights abridged by the wartime state of siege, the democratization of Prussia and its three-class voting system, and the release of political prisoners. In Berlin soldiers joined police, who began to disperse the crowds. Finally, the Brandenburg Deputy General Command threatened to militarize the Berlin factories, enabling the army to treat the workers as soldiers. Later it sent a few thousand workers to the front.[44] The workers returned to their jobs, but the "Civil Peace" existed no longer. The government still refused to democratize Prussia.

An uneasy quiet followed, but by summer internal order was disintegrating. Respect for the law had disappeared. Amid demonstrations and general unrest, which the German left, the Spartakists, attempted to focus on a mass strike, women were asking their men to leave the front and come home. Men at the front occasionally complained about their inferior rations compared to officers. Urban consumers complained of the lack of food; farmers, about requisitions and low prices. The rationing system, which reduced allocations drastically, had in fact collapsed, so urbanites bought on the black market and even took trains into the countryside to buy direct from farmers. Children suffered most from the inadequate nourishment, succumbing increasingly to diseases such as tuberculosis. Supplies of all necessities disappeared. Members of the middle classes, dependent upon salaries that inflation eroded, exhausted their savings and fell into poverty.[45]

The people had long ceased to believe the press, which trumpeted German victories, in favor of rumors of defeats; they fell prey to apathy and depression.[46] Food problems led to the collapse of morale on the home front in October and November. In early November, when sailors at Kiel revolted and marched on Berlin, the government in Berlin had already collapsed by their arrival in the midst of strikes and demonstrations that the police refused to disperse. Women played a major role in this final collapse, as food remained a major issue to the very end of the monarchy.

Italy. Resistance and repression

Orlando's attempt to conjure patriotic unity after Caporetto failed given the disasters and divisions of the Italian wartime experience. Labor militancy did not diminish, although it became less violent. Of course, rescinding the exemptions of the most militant workers and a massive induction of new troops at the beginning of 1918 helped to diminish open conflict. Simultaneously, early in 1918 Dallolio recognized the unions and also pushed industrialists to concede wage increases and to accept workers' commissions in the factories.

However, the employers also insisted on greater worker productivity and higher levels of exploitation. Furthermore, they refused to acknowledge the workers' commissions and arbitrarily sent workers' representatives and militants to the front. Consequently, by late spring strikes increased in centers of metal, mechanical, and textile industries, as strikers demanded higher wages, the eight-hour day, and the right to organize both within and outside the factory. Exempted skilled workers and military workers now reasserted their leadership in the working class, with a consequent increase in political awareness and trade union consciousness.

Because the government controlled industrial mobilization, regulating disputes and exercising military discipline over the workers, the working class associated the government with the employers. Contrary to Dallolio's hopes that the workers would appreciate the role of his ministry in mobilization, the workers linked the state and his agency to the difficult conditions they experienced. The industrialists forced Dallolio's resignation as minister in April 1918 and replaced him with a minister more loyal to the supreme command and the industrialists' interests. At the end of the war, Commissar for Arms and Munitions Ettore Conti, an industrialist and financier, dismantled the industrial mobilization organization within a few months and returned to *laissez-faire* practices.

The workers perceived the state ambivalently. An anti-authoritarian challenge to the abuse of state power, with the aim of fighting and defeating the state as enemy, coexisted with demands for the state as the locus of power to compensate the population for their sacrifice, to correct injustices, and to recognize their rights. Politicians such as Orlando furthered millenarian aspirations by proclaiming the war "the greatest social and political revolution recorded in history, surpassing even the French Revolution."[47]

The workers had also gained an appreciation of their power, the essential value of their labor to society and state. This sense that they played the key role in the new industrial society, whose evolution the war had certainly necessitated, would affect their postwar conduct. The peasants, who had fought the war at the front and suffered at home, not only became more aware of their importance, but also expected redistribution of land as a reward for their service. If neither land redistribution nor recognition of the value of industrial labor occurred, the laboring classes, rural and urban, would view Italian landowners and industrialists as the enemy.

France. Father Victory

Clemenceau monopolized control of governmental affairs in order to achieve total victory. He used his own Cabinet council for decisions which the full Cabinet would sanction. A law of 10 February gave the government the power to legislate by decree in such realms as production, distribution, and sale of products, and Clemenceau concentrated all power in the hands of his few close associates and himself. His popularity enabled him to govern firmly, and neither Parliament nor President dared challenge the Tiger. At a sign of parliamentary opposition, Clemenceau proposed a vote of confidence and won. As Prime Minister, he presided over the War Council and the War Ministry. The French High Command recognized his authority, which he used to impose governmental control, his control, on the military. While he defended his generals against Parliament after the German attack late in May, he authorized parliamentary commissions to visit the front as he often did. Clemenceau clearly restored the executive power of the state in 1918.

Clemenceau invited the socialists to join his government, but they chose to become the official opposition to his government. They also suffered from increasing internal dissension, as the minority socialists, propelled by the Bolshevik Revolution, gained strength within the party. Neither segment, with the exception of a small fringe, desired to yield to the Germans.

Clemenceau's Minister of Armaments Louis Loucheur negotiated cost-of-living bonuses for the lowest paid munitions workers and arranged for a week's leave for mobilized workers whose assignments took them away from home. However, when Paris shop delegates announced a resolution demanding peace without annexations in February, he strongly warned them that their purview concerned internal factory matters, not foreign policy.[48]

Strikes had the potential to disrupt production in 1918. Employment in war industries had risen from 50,000 in 1914 to 1.7 million in 1918. By spring 1918 the number of women metalworkers in Paris had risen to 100,000 from

44,000 in 1915. In 1917–18 they comprised 30 percent of metalworkers in the Paris region and 25 percent of the national metalwork force, five to six times their prewar percentage. In fact the war accelerated the long-term trend of rising female participation in paid work, as their proportion of the paid labor force rose from some 38 percent in 1911 to 46 percent in 1918.[49]

In mid-May a mass strike erupted in Paris, as shop delegates proclaimed an immediate general strike. Women played a prominent role in the May strike, even as part of the elite shop stewards who galvanized the workers to strike to end the war.[50] The movement, which included some 200,000 workers, protested the induction of young conscripts assigned to the munitions factories, and demanded to know the government's conditions for peace. After warning the shop delegates in February, Loucheur expected a German offensive against Paris later in May, conceded nothing, and began inducting shop delegates who held military deferments. He did not resort to the right wing's proposed solution of militarizing the workforce. Union and socialist officials, who feared a defeatist and revolutionary movement at this crucial moment in the war, did not support the strike, and workers had resumed their jobs by 20 May, a week before the Germans attacked.[51] Even pacifist trade union leaders refused to contemplate or to aid in France's defeat.

The French Army required ever more men to replenish its ranks and looked to Africa for manpower reserves in 1918. After the French Council of Ministers voted to renew recruitment in Africa early in January, Blaise Diagne, as Commissioner of the Republic in West Africa with a rank equivalent to governor-general, received plenary powers of recruitment. The governor of the region, who had opposed further recruitment in Africa, resigned, to die at the front as a captain. Colonel Eugene Petitdemange, commander of the Senegalese training camp at Fréjus, planned to use his "brave Senegalese" increasingly "to spare the blood of French servicemen," and he opposed dilution of his force by interspersing them with French units because they had recruited these warriors "to replace the French, to be used as cannon fodder to spare the whites." Clemenceau, convinced of the debt that Africans owed France for its "civilization" and of the necessity to avoid further French sacrifice, told French senators on 18 February 1918, "Although I have infinite respect for these brave blacks, I would much prefer to have ten blacks killed than a single Frenchman."[52]

Diagne bargained with Clemenceau for better schools and health facilities in Africa, and rewards for soldiers, including exemptions from the worst obligations of colonial servitude, preferred status for postwar government jobs, and French citizenship upon request for distinguished soldiers. These concessions, the first that an African extracted from the French government, offered the opportunity for equality: "Those who fall under fire, fall neither as whites nor as blacks; they fall as Frenchmen and for the same flag."[53] Diagne faced a recruitment quota of 47,000 men, but in under ten months he succeeded in recruiting 63,208 soldiers, as the Senegalese responded to one of their own in power most positively. Diagne had realized Mangin's conception of a black force. African front-line soldiers took pride in Diagne, and interpreted the agreement to mean that if they prevented the Germans from entering Paris, that same paradise forbidden to them, they would gain equality. On 14 October Clemenceau commissioned Diagne to prepare to have a million Senegalese troops in spring 1919,[54] as Mangin planned to form a shock army which would amalgamate French and Senegalese troops for 1919. The defeat of Germany, however, precluded such measures.

As the year progressed, Clemenceau wore gloves to relieve and conceal a severe case of eczema. He kept Pétain and Foch working in tandem, presided over the rehabilitation of Mangin, and drove his government to supply the army with the implements of victory. Minister of Armaments Loucheur worked with factories to raise the production of artillery, tanks, and airplanes. The manufacture of heavy artillery and tanks rose steadily, and France had the most powerful air service in the world in 1918. Although technically inferior to the German, French heavy artillery outnumbered it. By summer French factories were producing 600 light tanks monthly, while French aero-engine companies outproduced Germany and England combined.

The German advance in March threatened French coal supply, disrupted Allied transport, and forced Loucheur to prepare for the possibility of relocating industry away from Paris. The British, French, and Italians negotiated a tripartite coal agreement to ensure French and Italian coal supply, but British and French coal production flagged in 1918. By fall France lacked coal, iron, and steel, while the transport system teetered on the brink of collapse. Such difficult circumstances forced Loucheur to continue his efforts to centralize production and supply to the very end of the war, as he still had to increase the supply of munitions to the army.

To meet the demand for shells, Loucheur commissioned André Citroën to expand the state arsenal production. During the German offensives from March through July the army fired 250,000 shells on average *daily*. At the start of the German attacks the French had stockpiled thirty-four million shells for the French and American Armies. At the end of July they still had 22.5 million, and in September 1919 Loucheur planned to produce 350,000 shells daily. Such incredible exertions enabled the French to equip not only their army with artillery, tanks, and airplanes, but the American Army as well.

In September a German shell felled two parliamentary deputies visiting the front. One, Gaston Dumesnil, died quickly of a ruptured femoral artery. Clemenceau, who was already visiting Mangin's headquarters, arrived in time to comfort a bloody and dying Abel Ferry. A month later, when he received the news from Foch that the German plenipotentiaries had accepted the armistice conditions, his eyes filled with tears and he wept silently.[55] At the signing of the armistice on 11 November, Parliament lionized Clemenceau, who became *Père-la-victoire*, Father Victory. He would preside at the Peace Conference.

Britain and the United States. Triumph and intolerance

Until 1918 the British government had attempted to concentrate men, supplies, and munitions on the Western Front. By 1918 the government concerned itself with "proportionate" dividends for its investment of all the factors of war, including manpower. After March the government concentrated on the expansion of food, shipping, and coal production and on the need to limit recruitment. In August Lloyd George, aware that out of 9.5 million men available in Britain, 6.1 were serving in the armed forces, attempted to convince the French that Britain had stretched its manpower to the limit and needed more men in industry. Instead, the French government remained convinced that Britain was withholding men from the Western Front and could send more, just as BEF commander Haig claimed. Lloyd George still refused to release men to Haig. As of September the British government prioritized naval personnel first, supply second, and the army and air force third, in order for the army's size to accord with their ability to supply it.

The shadow of the German spring offensive hung over Britain from the start of the year, and its onset and early successes thrust upon an anxious country the recognition of the continued threat that a determined and skillful foe posed. In April the government called more men to the colors, "combing-out" industrial workers and schoolteachers, and raising the age of conscription from 41 to 50. Men aged over 40 served uselessly in home garrisons, while many received exemptions because of the importance of their work. It conscripted the clergy to serve as noncombatants. Although the government declared the conscription of the Irish, it desisted because any attempt to induct the Irish would have provoked a violent response.

The government raised taxes and attracted substantial funds through campaigns for war bonds and loans, a stark contrast to declining subscriptions to war loans in Germany and Austria-Hungary after 1916. In February the government also passed the Representation of the People Act, which increased the electorate from 8 million to 21 million people. It enfranchised women over 30 years of age, reduced the qualifications for male voters and consequently enabled universal suffrage for male voters over 21, and allowed men on active service aged 19 to 20 to vote. Late in 1918 women would gain the right to candidate for Parliament.

By granting the vote to women, the government pre-empted the renewal of the "sex war" that it perceived in prewar British society. However, the requirements for women ensured their minority status as voters, limited the suffrage to property-owning wives and mothers, and excluded single, working-class women. The suffragists, in their compromise with Parliament, had sacrificed the principle of sex equality and the votes of many of the very women whose sacrifice of their health in the factories had done so much to secure the vote.[56]

By May the Germans had ceased their bomber offensive against England after six raids and some 400 casualties, because they required the bombers for raids over the front. The German Navy's Zeppelins persisted in abortive raids until a British pilot shot the airship L.70 down in flames, and with it Capt. Peter Strasser, the driving force behind the Zeppelin bombing raids. At least by the summer and clearly by the fall, in October, the Entente had not only survived the German onslaught but also taken the offensive, arousing hopes that the war might end by Christmas.

The navy surmounted the worst of the submarine threat in 1917 and the food situation began to improve in February. That same month the Ministry of Food introduced rationing and by mid-July had established a national system. Food lines disappeared. Lord Rhondda, the Food Controller, collapsed from overwork and died in July, but the system ensured more equity between rich and poor and applied to all the inhabitants of Great Britain. Britain did not suffer the shortages of foodstuffs racking the Central Powers. Rationing and national kitchens in poor districts ensured that the population ate adequately and, in some cases, more nutritiously than it had done before the war. If food supply sufficed, fuel – coal, gas, and electricity – did not, restricting travel and heating during the entire year.

The serious industrial unrest of 1917 declined in early 1918, as equitable food rationing and higher wages combined with a heightened German threat and the capitulation of the Bolsheviks on the Eastern Front to keep labor loyal to the war effort. The German offensive prompted many workers who had previously resisted recruitment to join. Strikes effectively disappeared in April, only to emerge again in July, after the German tide receded. The government's attempt to tie skilled workers to their jobs occasioned a series of strikes; the government countered with both the threatened induction of strikers and the abandonment of the attempt to curtail labor mobility. A police strike in London in August secured them higher wages, while railway workers and miners prepared to strike in the future over wages and hours. Nevertheless, labor, like the rest of Britain, pledged to support the war effort until the defeat of Germany.

The British staged a rabidly xenophobic campaign against anything German. The British government had interned or deported any dangerous aliens early in the war, but now the crowd targeted enemy aliens in a "Hate the Hun" campaign. Unfortunately the crowd did not discriminate between foreigners in Britain, French and Belgian refugees, or the many German aliens who had lived in England for years. City councils changed German street names. Lloyd George himself contributed to this hysteria by declaring before the House of Commons in July that he had received anonymous letters from Germans postmarked within Britain gloating over every German success. Two days later, on 13 July, mobs gathered in London to demand sanctions against aliens, and late in August a crowd delivered a two-mile-long petition from 1.25 million people to the Prime Minister's residence at 10 Downing Street.

In May and June Pemberton Billing, a right-wing Member of Parliament, won notoriety for the second time during the war. In 1916 he had exposed an alleged scandal in British aviation, attributing the RFC's inferiority to the German air service to the purportedly villainous practices of the government's Royal Aircraft Factory. Now Pemberton Billing declared that the Germans possessed a Black Book with the names of 47,000 corrupt and perverted Britons, in particular homosexuals, in high positions and high society. He found the root of Britain's failures and Germany's successes in British sexual misconduct and perversion, as they engaged in sexual activities "all decent men thought had perished in Sodom and Lesbia." A jury acquitted the outrageous Pemberton Billing of libel, an indication of the extent to which hysteria had permeated public attitudes in 1918.[57]

The worsening war also stimulated more virulent assaults on women. Attacks on women and homosexuals, or men acting like women in then current opinion, had occurred throughout the war, but peaked in 1917 and 1918, as did women's war work. The number of women in private engineering firms rose from 170,000 in 1914 to 518,000 in summer 1917 and 597,000 by 1918, of whom 363,000 directly replaced men.[58] Writers such as Arthur Conan Doyle, the press, and the government portrayed women indiscriminately as predators and vampires stalking the land in search of innocent young soldiers to infect with venereal disease. They included women factory workers and the recently formed Women's Auxiliary Army Corps (WAAC) among the prostitutes undoing pure young soldiers. An amended Defence of the Realm Act (DORA) in March 1918 forbade women suffering from venereal disease from having sexual intercourse with servicemen. As Susan Kingsley Kent concluded, "such images threatened traditional gender and sexual arrangements . . . [and] challenged the system of separate spheres and heterosexuality."[59] In the midst of this epidemic of hysteria, the Spanish influenza struck Britain, as other countries, for the first time in June, abated after July, and then raged throughout Britain starting in the fall through the spring of 1919, claiming 150,000 to 200,000 lives. It felled the old and young, rich and poor, indiscriminately.

In June Lloyd George, after Canadian Prime Minister Currie had warned that he would withhold Canadian soldiers if a Passchendaele recurred, granted the Dominions a "direct voice in the conduct of the war," a voice which Lloyd George anticipated would help him against Haig.[60] Canada supplied soldiers for the Allied intervention in Russia, as the Canadian government, beset with labor militancy and strikes as a result of the inflation in 1918, deemed their source to be Bolshevism, which became an excuse to repress aliens at home and intervene abroad.[61] In Australia, the campaign against German aliens peaked in late 1917, but it reinforced the prewar prejudice against Asians, particularly Japanese, and the government set its surveillance agencies upon any citizen who dared speak against it. Australia would be the "exclusive home" of the "British race," the Anglo-Saxons, excluding other Europeans and all colored races from abroad.[62]

After the fuel and coal crisis of the winter of 1917–18, the United States government centralized the war economy gradually. From March 1918 Wilson's unofficial War Cabinet included Bernard Baruch, under whose leadership the War Industries Board integrated the interests of business and government, set manufacturing priorities and prices, and standardized products. Although the Overman Act of May 1918 endowed the President with the power to requisition economic resources, Wilson continued to rely on the voluntary participation, cooperation, and self-regulation of industrialists and businessmen in federal and state government. The government's emphasis on engineers' and managers' increased regulation and scientific management of industry set the "precedent for state corporate capitalism" and represented the "triumph of business."[63] Under the umbrella of the government, the representatives of large corporations developed a "centralized war capitalism," a "welfare state for the American business community."[64]

In contrast to the warring nations of Europe, the United States did not have to resort to war socialism or concrete concessions to labor. The war's length forced European governments to such measures, because it destroyed segments of their economies or deflected them entirely to war production. The United States benefitted from supplying the Entente during nearly three years of warfare, while it entered markets in South America that the war closed to European competitors. The United States alone of the western combatants enjoyed an improved economy after the First World War.[65]

A National War Labor Board established in April 1918 proclaimed "a new deal for American labor" and encouraged better pay, the eight-hour day, and collective bargaining. It lacked real authority, as Congress never approved its existence, and consequently relied on propaganda. In May Felix Frankfurter headed a War Labor Policies Board that included Franklin D. Roosevelt and paid more attention to labor and its standard of living, in a foreshadowing of the New Deal during the Great Depression.

The American populace continued its migration as blacks moved north and whites moved west. Increased urbanizaton continued to lead to overcrowded, unsanitary housing conditions, which in turn led to higher rates of infant mortality and susceptibility to influenza. Abysmal housing also played a role in racial violence, as blacks invariably inhabited the poorest areas, where whites sought to contain them.

Black discontent increased by the summer of 1918, as white racial intolerance manifested itself in more violence and lynching. Much of the black press balanced deftly between pledging loyalty to America and the war effort while demanding change. However, the absence of improvement in race relations convinced some black Americans that the war constituted "a white man's war." The Sedition Act of May, the Alien Act of October, and the Espionage Act of 1917 empowered the government to deport people, to crush the Socialists by imprisoning party leader Eugene V. Debs, and to monitor closely and even to threaten the black press to keep it in line. The government did not hesitate to abridge civil liberties in wartime.

Freedom to drink liquor also went the way of civil liberties, as the temperance movement, already popular before the war, increased in connection with efforts to keep soldiers from drink, prostitution, and venereal disease. White women played prominent roles in this crusade to make America moral, as they served overseas as nurses and volunteer workers and worked stateside in clerical positions, all of them temporary. Citizens groups often razed red light districts close to army camps, while the Selective Service Act forbade the sale of liquor to servicemen. In contrast, continental military practice welcomed houses of prostitution for servicemen, with appropriately better ones for officers, and provided liquor in abundance behind the lines. Propaganda characterized German brewers in America as internal German enemies for inebriating workers. Strong drink led to crime, as black men who bought gin with pictures of naked white women on the bottle would allegedly rape them and become lynch victims.[66]

As in Britain, paranoid hysteria against all things German burgeoned in 1918. Both items with German names and Americans of German descent anglicized their names to avoid the stigma. A mob in Collinsville, Illinois lynched German American Robert Prager in April 1918. At least this deed finally elicited the condemnation of lynching from President Woodrow Wilson that blacks had long requested.

Repression became rampant as the war continued, and the armistice in November 1918 abruptly ended the war as the United States was preparing to press it to a victorious conclusion in 1919 and 1920. Ironically, the American elections in November transferred control of Congress to the Republicans, handing Wilson domestic defeat before wartime victory. The fighting at the front might have ended; however, the violence and repression at home would gain in strength.

Japan. Intervention abroad, riots at home

The Japanese decision to deploy troops to Siberia, a major initiative of the war, occurred as the Russian Revolution presented the Entente and Associated Powers with the perceived need to counter Bolshevism. The

British, French, and American Armies sent limited forces, in accord with their justification of defending against Bolshevism and the exhaustion of the first two powers after four years of war. The large size of the Japanese contingent, however, indicated their offensive intent, in accord with the government's wartime aim of strengthening Japanese presence on the continent. Japanese governmental officials had already been contemplating a major incursion into North Manchuria and Siberia, to establish an independent Siberia as a Japanese client state and to extend the Japanese empire into northern Asia.

The Japanese also negotiated a Sino–Japanese Military Agreement to increase Japanese influence in China, another wartime aim, and to obtain Chinese cooperation in Manchuria. The Chinese prepared to defend the Chinese Eastern Railway and North Manchuria against Japanese troops. The two compromised in May: the Chinese aided the Japanese Army, which in turn promised to respect Chinese sovereignty. In fact, the Japanese planned to support White Russian generals who sought to establish an independent Siberia from their base in Manchuria by seizing the Chinese Eastern Railway.

The Japanese clearly planned to fill the vacuum in the Russian Far East, and a Siberian expedition sanctioned by the Entente powers provided the perfect opportunity to display Japanese power and pursue supremacy on the Asian continent. Japan would become a great imperial master like Britain and America. They sent their troops to Vladivostok in July to achieve these long-term goals. Once Japanese troops arrived on the continent, the army used the mobilization of troops to send troops to the Russo–Chinese border, the Amur River basin, and to secure the Siberian railway.

The expedition justified a major increase in the army budget, and provided a counterweight to the Japanese Navy's expansion plans. However, the Japanese Diet granted the navy's full budgetary requests in March 1918 because it confronted an expanding American fleet in the Pacific, while it halved the army's proposal. The navy's success threatened the continental basis of empire and the army's importance.

The army thus pursued an external goal of continental expansion linked with a domestic goal of primacy in the Japanese military establishment. It hoped further to strengthen national loyalty to the militarist regime in the face of a rapidly changing Japanese society. Urbanization, prosperity, industrialization and labor unrest, the influence of western democracy – all threatened the army's position in government and society.

The day after the Japanese government announced the Siberian expedition, a demonstration by fishermen's wives over the high price of rice spread quickly around the country and ultimately involved some two million people. The wartime industrialization and urbanization of Japan and general industrial unrest provided the context for the rice riots of 1918, which stemmed from the wartime inflation. The price of rice had trebled between 1915 and 1918, rising far more rapidly than wages. The government imposed martial law and some 100,000 troops fired upon crowds and arrested 25,000 people in the three weeks they required to restore order. The riots thwarted the generals' plans to elicit a rousing display of patriotic unity from the people upon the occasion of the soldiers' departure for the continent.

Instead, the riots led to the election of the first prime minister from the common people, Hara Takashi, and a party Cabinet in September 1918, a decisive step toward democracy in Japan. The Japanese Cabinet of 1916 had arisen in response to the war in its shift to the right and its focus on national unity. The Hara Cabinet responded to demands for political and social change that stemmed from wartime domestic developments. Now the Hara Cabinet would negotiate the army's drive for power and the peace conference to end the war.

ARMISTICE

At German headquarters on 28 September, Ludendorff flew into a rage, ranting against the German home front and even the Kaiser. Later he advised Hindenburg that the exhaustion of the army and the home front necessitated an immediate armistice. The German government appealed to Woodrow Wilson on 3 October 1918. The Kaiser's selection of a liberal, Prince Max of Baden, as Chancellor and the appeal to Wilson aimed pragmatically to gain Germany better terms than the French and the British would offer.[67]

The German request for an armistice caught the western powers unprepared, as it came a year earlier than they anticipated. The French government planned to demand Alsace Lorraine, the Saar, and a guarantee of the left bank of the Rhine, whether through annexation, independence, or occupation by French troops. Clemenceau, however, had avoided any discussion of war aims, because he understood that a gravely weakened France would have to depend on its allies, in particular the United States, to secure the peace.[68]

French concerns centered on Europe, but British policy-makers focussed more on imperial territorial arrangements. In late October 1918 Haig rated the BEF "the most formidable fighting force in the world," compared to an exhausted French and an inexperienced American Army.[69] Lloyd George presciently believed that the Germans needed to "know" that they had lost or they would start another war in twenty years' time. The British Army's severe shortages of manpower, however, prompted immediate acceptance of armistice rather than a prolonged war to force unconditional surrender.[70]

Lloyd George and Haig sought to prevent the French from expending further British and American manpower to achieve their aims on the continent and to forestall any American threat to Britain's status as a world power. Of Woodrow Wilson's Fourteen Points, freedom of the seas particularly clashed with British policy; the longer the war lasted, the more Wilson's power to impose peace terms on ally and enemy alike would increase. Smuts warned the War Cabinet that by 1919 the United States would replace Britain as the leading "military, diplomatic, and financial power" in the world. Consequently, on 26 October, the British War Cabinet decided to seek an early armistice.

That same day the Kaiser sacked Ludendorff. On 24 October, Ludendorff, who had changed his mind in the intervening month, defied the German government and exhorted the army to reject the Wilson peace proposals and to continue fighting. On 26 October Hindenburg and Ludendorff reported to the Kaiser at Schloss Bellevue. There, Kaiser Wilhelm demanded and received Ludendorff's resignation. Ludendorff, alone that night with his wife in their hotel room, gloomily predicted, "in a fortnight we shall have no Empire and no Emperor left, you will see."[71] On 26 October he departed, in disguise, for Sweden.

Wilson and the AEF had also presumed the war's continuation into 1919 and even 1920, and America's subsequent ability to dictate the terms of peace to all. Wilson warned the Germans that they would have no say in the armistice terms. His attitude toward Germany had come full circle during the war. He had graduated from tirades against Germany and Prussian militarism in 1914[72] to proposals of a negotiated peace "without victory" in January 1917. But German actions the following month – demands for a victorious peace, unrestricted submarine warfare, and the Zimmermann telegram – convinced Wilson of the impossibility of negotiating with a militaristic and evil empire. Germany's treaty of Brest-Litovsk strengthened Wilson's resolve first to punish Germany in a dictated peace and then to rehabilitate it later.

In armistice negotiations Lloyd George and Clemenceau acquiesced to Wilson's Fourteen Points in return for his acceptance of their military conditions. They demanded surrender of the German fleet, weapons, and railroad stock, the evacuation of invaded countries, and the Allied occupation of the left bank of the Rhine with bridgeheads on the right bank. The British reserved two conditions – freedom of the seas and the amount of German compensation for all damage inflicted on Allied civilians and their property – for later discussion at a peace conference. Wilson's emissary Col. House pre-empted further reservations by threatening an open discussion of the prospect of continuing the war to achieve Entente war aims in front of their war-weary populations.

Final discussion of the armistice terms began in Paris on 29 October. Britain tempered its demands on Germany for fear that the latter might continue to fight rather than submit. Only on 5 November, after all had agreed on the terms, did the British and the French realize the extent of the German collapse, prompting Sir Eric Geddes to comment on 12 November,

"Had we known how bad things were in Germany, we might have got stiffer terms."[73] On 30 October Pershing defied Wilson's authority and violated the constitutional subordination of the army to civilian authority by advocating Germany's unconditional surrender.[74] The French and English ignored him. Unlike the Kaiser's response to Ludendorff's insubordination, Wilson did not sack Pershing.

On 5 November U.S. Secretary of State Robert Lansing, acting on behalf of the western powers, informed the German government that Foch would present the armistice terms to its representatives. On 8 November Mathias Erzberger and the German delegation sent the terms to Berlin. On 9 November Hindenburg and Gen. Groener, Ludendorff's successor, concluded that Kaiser Wilhelm had to abdicate. Groener informed the Kaiser that the army no longer supported him. Later that day, Prince Max prematurely announced Wilhelm's abdication and handed the government to the Socialists, who announced the creation of a German republic. Wilhelm departed for exile in Holland. The delegation of the embryonic Republican government agreed to armistice terms at 5 a.m. on 11 November. The war on the Western Front ended on the eleventh hour, of the eleventh day, of the eleventh month, of 1918, which we continue to celebrate as Armistice Day.

While people in the victors' capital cities celebrated in the days and weeks after the armistice, exhausted soldiers at the front more often simply felt relieved. Men had died to the very end. A German machine-gunner in action the entire morning of 11 November fired a thousand-round burst at five minutes to eleven, stood up, tipped his helmet to the British opposite, and walked away.[75] Later, soldiers often wandered the lines in search of souvenirs. Aviators took squadron automobiles to look for the poorly marked graves of comrades who had fallen over the lines. On 14 November American Private Arthur Yensen scavenged on the banks of the Meuse River, the battlefield littered with rotting stinking corpses. He spied a German helmet, but discarded it quickly because of the blood and brains inside. He saw, variously, "a leg with the genitals hanging to it," "a solitary head," "a stomach lost in the grass, while wound around the limbs of a nearby tree were the intestines," and finally, "an American soldier stamping a dead German's face into a pulp."[76] The war on the Western Front had ended.

CONCLUSION. A GRISLY ACCOUNTING

The greatest war in history to that date had officially ended. The Entente and Associated powers had won; the Central Powers had lost. Historical debates continue concerning such topics as the attribution of credit for the former's victory and of responsibility for the latter's loss.

In the discussion of who won the war, the crux of the debate lies in the contributions of Great Britain and the United States to victory. All agree that had the war continued into 1919 and 1920, the AEF would have swept all before it in the march to victory, enabling Woodrow Wilson and the United States to impose peace on Europe. Historians still debate whether the British led the charge to victory in 1918, with the French and Americans playing a supporting role, or American arms and men determined the outcome of the war in favor of the western powers. Proponents of the first interpretation point to the inconsistent performance of the inexperienced AEF in the battles of 1918, in contrast to steady if costly British advances to victory against German strong points on the northern part of the Western Front. Adherents of a decisive American contribution to victory point to the AEF's role in stemming the German tide in June and then its gritty struggle through the impenetrable Argonne Forest. Some even attribute the assignment of the Argonne to the AEF to the Entente Powers' conspiratorial determination to prevent the AEF from marching triumphantly to victory.

The essence of Foch's plans lay in the power of simultaneous or consecutive offensives to wear down the German Army. The British forces, whose freshest and most aggressive men came primarily from Canada, Australia, and New Zealand in 1918, performed well in the 1918 offensives. The Canadian Corps in particular could justifiably claim to be the best corps on the Western Front for its performance in the 100 Days campaign that ended the war. Its 105,000 troops had suffered 45,830 casualties, or 975 per German division defeated (forty-seven) during their advance of eighty-six miles. In comparison the AEF's 650,000 troops had suffered 100,000 casualties, or 2,170 casualties per German division defeated (forty-six) of 650,000 troops engaged, in an advance of thirty-four miles during the forty-seven days of the Meuse–Argonne offensive.[77]

Despite its youth and attendant uneven performance, the AEF still attained its objectives fighting through difficult terrain, if more slowly than desired. Probably the greatest contribution the AEF rendered was its psychological impact on the German Army and High Command. Ludendorff had pressed his spring offensives in a vain attempt to end the war before the arrival of the American Army, which portended Germany's ultimate defeat. The rapidly increasing numbers of American soldiers in summer and fall 1918 sealed Germany's doom.

Ironically, in the debate over the contribution to victory, English-speaking historians invariably omit the role of the French Army in the center of the front and the link between the British and Americans. The French Army, with its African and elite corps as spearheads, also forged steadily ahead. In the fall the French held the longest distance of the Western Front, and the British, the shortest. The French suffered the most casualties of all three armies on the Western Front in the march to victory. The French proved themselves no less adept than the British in the execution of attacks in which the combined arms of infantry, artillery, aviation, and armor coordinated to pressure the Germans.

In fact, each army waged their interlocking and interdependent offensives well, certainly to the best of its ability. The AEF had undeniably not yet attained the proficiency of its allies, and its men paid for their inexperience with their lives, as the other armies had before them. To praise or credit one army above the others, as the commanders of 1918 and historians since then have done, reflects the tensions and difficulties of coalition warfare and indicates the continuing importance of the First World War in the historical memory. The struggle among historians, however, unlike the outcome of the Entente campaign in 1918, admits no definitive answer.

The debate about military victory in 1918 focuses on military developments on the Western Front, which all agree remained the decisive theater of the war of 1914–18 from start to finish. This focus, however, contradicts the nature of the 1914–18 conflict as total and global war, in which the interaction of all the fighting and home fronts determined the outcome. Furthermore, the importance of socio-psychological factors equaled that of military/material determinants. Finally, an examination of the military events in the last five months of a fifty-one-month conflict offers at best a partial and inadequate answer to the questions of how and why the Entente and Associated powers won the war. These considerations suggest a more total approach to analysis of the war's outcome than the narrow and futile discussion of which western power "really won" the war in the offensives of 1918.

The war began and ended as a global conflict that imperial powers waged with their armies and navies in Europe, Africa, the Middle East, and Asia and on the oceans of the world. The European powers relied on their possessions for men and materials. European soldiers and soldiers from the empires fought not only in Europe but around the globe.

The balance of power from the start weighed against the Central Powers and in favor of the Entente. Germany supported two – Austria-Hungary and the Ottoman Empire – and later three, with Bulgaria, much weaker powers. Germany's army, navy, and industry had to carry its allies, who could contribute manpower, and some industry as in the case of Austria-Hungary, but little else. Finally, in the crucial realm of food and raw material supply, the strongest Central Powers, Germany and Austria-Hungary, became the most vulnerable to blockade, and thus potentially the weakest of the powers.

The Entente comprised the strongest financial, commercial, imperial, and naval power in England, the largest population in Russia, and in France the second leading imperial power with the best airplane and aero-engine industry. The Anglo-French combination endowed the Entente with a solid nucleus that could draw upon its empires as inexhaustible sources of manpower. Russia added an immense threat in the east, and Italy later contributed a diversion in the south. When Russia collapsed, the United States – the Entente's financial, commercial, and industrial reservoir – became its salvation, the ultimate source of manpower for victory.

The superlative German Army maintained Germany and its allies against a world of enemies, and although its offensives in 1914 did not result in victory, they positioned Germany advantageously in Europe for the rest of the war. The Entente offensives of 1915 did not shake those positions, nor did the great battles of 1916 and even 1917. In fact, Germany's military circumstances actually improved in 1917, with the fall of the tsarist empire.

Certain critical factors, however, undergirded military power and, with the war's continuation, offset it. Starting in 1914, when the powers realized that the war would not end in six months, much less weeks, they began haphazardly the mobilization of the home front to continue the fight. Governments secured supplies or raw materials, while industries refocussed on the manufacture of supplies for the military, or shrank and closed. Despite the concentration on war production, a temporary shell crisis occurred in most of the combatants in 1915, as the enormous wastage at the front outpaced production.

To replace the millions of men inducted into mass armies, government and industry drew on additional labor, from women and youth to prisoners-of-war and men from the colonies, to industry and agriculture. This economic and social mobilization also entailed the mobilization of culture, as many representatives of high and popular culture, from intellectuals and professors to cartoonists and poster artists, encouraged the masses to participate enthusiastically in the war effort. By 1916 the mobilization of industry bore deadly fruit, enabling the armies to wage lengthy battles of attrition.

The nature of warfare, of siege-like battles that endured for months, took its toll on the combatants. The German terms for this new warfare, "*Materialschlacht*" and "*Verwüstungsschlacht*," a battle of material and devastation, capture the nature of war predicated on the slaughter of men and the devastation of territory. Since combatants seldom declared a truce to clear the battlefields of the wounded, men died after languishing for hours or days between the lines. The use of such terms as *Materialschlacht* sometimes implies that the state of technology caused those in power to lose control of the war. Like some metal monster, or "Great Sausage Machine" as British troops referred to the Western Front, the war developed a life of its own, feeding on the bodies of men. Such implications remove responsibility from decision-makers, as if technological demands robbed them of their free will. Technology may create certain imperatives or options, but it does not possess agency. Humans do, and they develop and exploit technology. German commanders at least revised offensive and defensive tactics to adjust to and exploit firepower. Both British and French commanders, with few exceptions such as Pétain or Plumer, either made no effort to do so or did so at a snail's pace, killing large numbers of their troops in the meantime.

The demands of war certainly hastened the progress of military technology, particularly in the realms of aviation, armor, and submarines. The wartime evolution of reliable airframes, engines, and metal aircraft construction prepared the foundation for the rise of civil, commercial aviation after the war. The submarine had threatened to upset the naval balance of power during the war, while the tank, even in its rudimentary state, provided much needed support for attacking infantry. The introduction of flame-throwers, light machine-guns, mortars, and small-caliber cannon tremendously enhanced the firepower of the infantry. Gas proved an irritating and deadly but insufficiently controllable weapon; hence its disappearance from postwar battlefields. Between 1914 and 1918 the military establishment and industry combined to evolve ever deadlier and more effective weapons and then to produce them in quantity. Their further development of the airplane, the tank, and the submarine prepared the way for future warfare on land, in the air, and under the sea. The war demonstrated unequivocally that technological progress did not necessarily equate to human progress, but could instead enable greater destruction and conceivably the regression of civilization.

The brutalization of the European combatants, with attendant atrocities against soldier and civilian, began in imperial wars and accelerated in the First World War, not with the rise of totalitarian regimes and the Second World War. Combatants described enemies and their practices as barbaric and savage. The Germans attacked civilians in 1914, then deported women from the occupied zones in Belgium and France. Atrocities against civilians accompanied the invasion of Serbia. The British "Hunger Blockade" sought to starve civilians. To the east, the Turks massacred the Armenians, and Hitler queried in 1939, "After all, who today still remembers the destruction of the Armenians?"[78]

In the realm of mobilization, the western Entente powers benefitted from resources unavailable to the Central Powers. The former drew on their empires and the United States for financial loans, raw materials, agricultural products, and manpower. Meanwhile, they blockaded Germany, gradually severing it and the Central Powers from the global resources that the Entente enjoyed.

As the war continued, attrition inexorably drained the pool of manpower of all sides. The Entente possessed reserves; the Central Powers did not. The German Army maintained its tactical and even technical superiority, but the margins shrank as its opponents adapted German techniques and introduced their own technologies. By the end of 1916 the German High Command acknowledged its diminishing position by resorting to unrestricted submarine warfare. It thereby risked the entry into the war of the United States in an attempt to starve Great Britain from the war.

No greater proof of the signal importance of food supply to the war effort exists than the vaunted German Army's resort to the German Navy's submarine service. Avner Offer asserts that despite the industrial nature of the war, the western allies' resources of primary commodities such as food, raw materials, and population decided the outcome of the war. Food caused "the greatest discontent" and constituted the "weakest link" in the German war economy. Food shortages played "a critical role in Germany's collapse." In Offer's judgment, the Allied blockade and resulting food shortages played a key if indirect role in Germany's collapse.[79]

Germany sought to do unto Britain as Britain had done unto it – to gradually starve the enemy into submission. Shortages of food and fuel undermined first public morale and then health in Germany and Austria. Governmental inability to manage the shortages through rationing led to domestic unrest and undermined governmental authority, as civilian populations took to the streets, took the law into their own hands, and demanded peace from their governments in their desperate struggle against privation. The shortages disrupted production through strikes and demonstrations in all countries, but the privations and their consequences loomed largest in the Central Powers.

Finally, the shortages affected the German and Austrian Armies: indirectly, as soldiers worried about their starving families at home; and directly, as they began to suffer from malnutrition despite their priority in rations. To keep the masses engaged in the war effort, all states replaced the intellectuals' "self-mobilization" of 1914–15 with their own mobilization of culture in coordinated fashion, using mass entertainment, such as cinema, and mass kitsch.[80] People, however, could not eat propaganda, which did not suffice to sustain a freezing and starving population.

By 1918 Germany faced a do-or-die situation. It had to win the war before the United States became a significant presence on the Western Front and before it collapsed from exhaustion. Its allies – Austria-Hungary, the Ottoman Empire, and Bulgaria – were faltering, ready to fall in quick succession if Germany failed. It did. Germany, losing and collapsing, quit before the western powers conquered it.

———

The Great War cost its participants immeasurably. It devastated France's ten northeastern departments and diminished France from a creditor to a debtor nation. It reduced Great Britain from the world's leading economy, a financial and commercial center whose stable currency, the pound sterling, essentially paralleled the gold standard, to another nation in debt to the United States. Neither the gold standard nor the pound sterling would re-establish itself globally, and instead of one international economic center – London – the world now had at least three – New York, London, and Paris – none of which coordinated with the others. It had ruined German finances, although it left the German industrial infrastructure intact. It had dismantled the natural economic union of Austria-Hungary, leaving chaos in its wake, and it had destroyed the Russian economy. Only the United States, and to a lesser extent Japan, had benefitted from the conflict. The war had irretrievably fractured the global economy, like Humpty-Dumpty, and putting it back together again eluded the efforts of future generations. The statistics on war casualties vary depending upon the source, but still yield a graphic impression of the war's deadliness. Holger Herwig concludes that 9.3 million men died in the war, 3.6 million from the Central Powers and 5.7 million from the Entente and Associated powers, including 2.3 million Russians, 2 million Germans, 1.9 million French, 1 million Austro-Hungarians, 800,000 Britons, 450,000 Italians, and 126,000 Americans.[81]

The violence of the war surpassed any in previous memory: in France 16.8 percent of men mobilized were killed; in Germany, 15.4 percent. Of combatant troops, the numbers rose higher: 22 percent of French officers died, 18 percent of soldiers.[82] Historians tend to focus on the major battles of attrition, but such struggles formed only a part, albeit the most dangerous, of the individual soldier's experience. In certain areas of the front the attitude of "live and let live" reigned, which minimized hostilities and losses. Nevertheless, even on so-called quiet days, when communiqués reported "*Im Westen nichts neues*," or "All quiet on the Western Front," thousands of men fell. On average some 900 Frenchmen and 1,300 Germans died daily between August 1914 and November 1918. Although the casualties in the Second World War exceeded those in the First, only in Russia/the Soviet Union did the daily losses in 1941–5 (5,635) exceed those in 1914–18 (1,459).[83] The number of wounded totaled about 40 percent of the men mobilized in all powers, while the gravity of wounds that modern weapons inflicted offset any improvements in medical services. Probably half the survivors suffered psychological problems, and doctors' convictions that cowardice or some character flaw, instead of the stress of sustained bombardment and combat, caused nervous collapse impeded their effective treatment of the psychologically wounded.

By armistice 1918 nearly two million Frenchmen had perished, the heaviest casualties 27 to 30 percent of the youngest conscript classes of 1912–15. The infantry had lost 22 percent of its ranks. Nearly five million men suffered wounds, which disabled 1.1 million permanently, leaving some so mutilated as to prevent their re-entry into society. In the four years of war ninety-four battalions of Senegalese, or 161,250 men, served, of whom 134,310 saw combat and 29,520 died in combat.

The Germans lost nearly 770,000 killed on the Western Front, and a total of 1.6 million men were killed or died of wounds to the end of 1918. More than two million Germans died in the war or later of wounds, and men born in the years 1892–1915 lost 35 to 37 percent of their cohort. The army suffered losses of 23 percent of its officers and 14 percent of its enlisted men. Austria-Hungary had mobilized eight million men; one million had died, 1.9 million suffered wounds.

The United Kingdom lost 900,000 men killed, including 57,000 Canadians and 59,000 Australians, more than 750,000 of them on the Western Front. The AEF suffered some 50,000 deaths in battle and a total of 125,000 dead by 1 July 1919. The Belgians lost 40,000 soldiers killed.

Serbia suffered the most proportionately, as 125,000 soldiers and 650,000 civilians died, a total of 15 percent of the prewar population compared to 2 to 3 percent of the British, French, and German populations. The estimates of Ottoman casualties suggest that of over 2.8 million men mobilized, about 770,000 died or disappeared, of whom more than half succumbed to disease. An additional 300,000 men suffered permanent injury from their wounds.

Entire societies mourned, as in the major combatant countries the war touched everyone. One-third of the war dead left behind widows: 525,000 in Germany, 200,000 in Italy, 600,000 in France, and 240,000 in Britain. The numbers of war orphans reached more than a million in Germany, 760,000 in France, 350,000 in Britain, and 300,000 in Italy.

After death came the dislocation of populations, as the war set entire peoples in motion as refugees, driven from their land and homes. Then came the devastation of large areas over which the combatants had fought, the destruction of houses, plant, farms, wells, everything. The war had rendered these regions wastelands. Battlefields remained dangerous and muddy moonscapes littered with the human and material debris of war. Occupying forces had systematically looted and pillaged entire countries. Death, dislocation, and destruction occurred globally, in Africa, Asia, and the Middle East, wherever the heavy hand of European empire had extended.

In addition to the man-made calamity of war, the influenza epidemic of 1918–19 claimed 21.5 million victims globally, most of them in Asia, and particularly in India, where 12.5 million people died. In the years 1914–19 humans had wreaked a catastrophe of epidemic proportions on themselves in the First World War, the Great War, which concluded in the midst of an epidemic of catastrophic proportions.

7

The Postwar World

A "peace to end peace"?

"After 'the war to end war' they seem to have been pretty successful in Paris at making a 'Peace to end Peace.'"

Archibald Wavell, British officer (later Field Marshal Earl Wavell)[1]

"The Great War seems to have split up into a lot of little wars."

U.S. Secretary of State Robert Lansing, 22 January 1919[2]

THE WEST AND THE PARIS PEACE CONFERENCE

Versailles

The victorious allies comprehended with difficulty the suddenness of their victory. The German people now abruptly learned that they had sacrificed in vain. The new German democracy had to depend on the High Command to bring the troops home and demobilize them in an orderly fashion. Now the German republic would pay for the sins of its imperial predecessor, as it would bear the responsibility for the armistice, the coming peace, and, by extension, the loss of the war.

Germans floundered in a "dreamland," a realm of illusions, after the armistice. Famed author Thomas Mann raged against the victors, western civilization, and democracy. German communists dreamed of world revolution, armed proletarians, and a German Red Army. The German High Command denied its culpability in losing the war with *Dolchstoss*, or "stab in the back" propaganda, blaming the collapse on the home front. The fundamental facts that the OHL had demanded an armistice because it could not continue the war and that the Bolshevik threat constituted "more propaganda than reality" disappeared in a welter of illusion and denial.[3]

After the armistice, the British focussed on empire. The army, faced with mutinies of soldiers demanding immediate demobilization in January 1919, could barely man imperial garrisons, much less occupy Germany for any lengthy period. The French concentrated on Germany and the Rhine border, but depended on the support of their allies to resolve these issues. Niall Ferguson summarizes the Entente policies in the following manner: France's rational attempts to secure leverage over Germany; Britain's unrealistic effort to return to prewar economic conditions and abandon its continental commitment in favor of empire; and America's large-scale private export of capital for European economic recovery and political stability.[4]

The home fronts influenced the proceedings in Paris. During the armistice negotiations in October, a German submarine sank the liner *Leinster* in October, enraging the British public. Campaigning for the general election in December, Lloyd George pandered to a public out to "hang the Kaiser and sack Berlin," and to make the Germans pay "until the pips squeak." The so-called Khaki election returned the Lloyd George coalition's Conservatives with the largest majority in history.[5] Lloyd George went to Versailles saddled with the election pledges of harshness toward Germany. French national elections yielded similar results and encumbered Clemenceau with a similar burden, but Clemenceau had long demonstrated a penchant for independence in decision-making.

The armistice had enabled Britain to end the German naval threat and to acquire German merchant shipping – two major goals. After the armistice the allies tightened the wartime blockade by severing Scandinavia from Germany and used the food blockade as the key weapon to force Germany to sign the Treaty of Versailles. As Avner Offer wrote, "combat had ended, but the war continued."[6] Lloyd George observed on 8 March 1919 that "the Allies were sowing hatred for the future," as Germans starved while tons of food lay on the Rotterdam docks.[7] He consequently decided in April 1919 against a punitive peace, so he went to London and confronted Parliament, then returned to Paris to press for moderation. After Germany agreed to surrender its merchant fleet in spring 1919, Herbert Hoover persuaded the allies to allow Germany food shipments through his Inter-Allied Conference for Relief. In return the German government paid in gold transfers from its treasury, which provided American producers with a profit and stoked hyperinflation in Germany.

Wilson received a hero's welcome from the Entente publics when he arrived in Europe in 1919, although the Republicans had won control of the Congress in the mid-term elections immediately before his departure. He came convinced that European leaders posed the major obstacle to his peace aims, only to learn that their vindictive publics demanded vengeance. He consequently relinquished his principle of open diplomacy for obsessive security at the conference.[8]

The Big Three of Clemenceau, Lloyd George, and Wilson lacked a personal rapport with one another. Wilson considered Lloyd George "as slippery as an eel." Lloyd George thought Wilson, if a noble visionary, unscrupulous and bigoted. In Clemenceau's opinion Wilson envisaged himself "another Jesus Christ"; while Wilson lumped Clemenceau among the "mad men."[9] These three statesmen would attempt to formulate a peace in the circus-like atmosphere of the Paris Peace Conference, with all its innumerable delegations of experts and representatives of old and new countries.

Actually, five powers supposedly would determine the future – Britain, France, Italy, Japan, and the United States. The Japanese, however, confined their interests to Asia and the Pacific, most particularly to win the recognition of the great powers for Japanese gains in China. The western powers rebuffed Japanese efforts to include a clause on racial non-discrimination, which entailed the equality of nations and equal rights for aliens, in the covenant of the League of Nations. A Big Four, including Italian Prime Minister Vittorio Orlando, made the final decisions, but Orlando departed in a huff for a time because the Big Three awarded the new state of Yugoslavia territory that Italy coveted.

The western Allies formulated the most important peace treaty – Versailles – for their supreme enemy, Germany. Germany returned Alsace Lorraine to France and ceded territory, the Polish Corridor, to provide the new state of Poland with an outlet to the Baltic Sea at Danzig, now a free city. Germany also lost Upper Silesia and its coal-mines, other pieces of territory in Europe, and all its colonies. At the same time, the Allies, despite their assertion of the principle of national self-determination, forbade a union of Germany and Austria. The German Army, now limited to 100,000 men, could have no airplanes or tanks; the German Navy, only twelve ships of less than 10,000 tons and no submarines. Germany had to surrender to the Allies all artillery, armor, and aircraft; its surface fleet, which it scuttled; most of its merchant marine; a quarter of its fishing fleet; and much of its railway rolling-stock. It would have to build ships for the Allies and deliver coal to them for a specified time. To ensure German compliance with the treaty's terms, the Allies, primarily the French, would occupy three zones in a permanently demilitarized Rhineland for from five to fifteen years. France gained control of the Saar and its iron and coal-mines and industry for fifteen years. The treaty contained a war guilt clause, Article 231, which stipulated German responsibility for loss and damage in a war that their aggression had caused, and consequently entailed German payment of reparations.

The French brought the German delegation to Versailles by a very slow train through the devastated region of the Western Front on 29 April and then confined them behind barbed wire. On 7 May Clemenceau presided over the presentation of the treaty to the Germans, who could respond only in writing. On 16 June the Allies gave the Germans an ultimatum to sign the treaty in seven days or face the resumption of hostilities. The Germans agreed on 23 June, and all signed the treaty on 28 June 1919 in the Hall of Mirrors at Versailles, where the Germans had proclaimed their empire in 1871.

As presiding officer, Clemenceau had relentlessly steered a lone course between the more moderate allies and French nationalists who desired to dismember Germany. During the conference a would-be assassin shot Clemenceau point-blank in the chest. The wounded Prime Minister insisted before leaving for the hospital that his guards bring the gunman to him. Clemenceau ordered the man inducted into the army so that he could learn to shoot straight. In hospital, Clemenceau conducted negotiations from his bed. Ultimately he hoped to achieve French security through the reduction of German economic power and the establishment of an eastern barrier of states around Germany. Acknowledging French financial dependence upon Britain and the United States, Clemenceau desperately sought a permanent alliance with Britain and the United States. However, neither power honored its commitments to France under the treaties of guarantee.

Pre-armistice negotiations with Robert Lansing had required Germany to compensate the Entente for all "damage done to the civilian population . . . and their property by the aggression of Germany by land, by sea, and from the air."[10] The preamble to paragraph 19 of the armistice stated only vaguely "reparation for damage done." After the armistice Britain and France claimed recompense for their full costs of waging the war, even pensions, thereby clearly contravening the pre-armistice agreement.

The German economy exited the war intact as the continent's strongest, in contrast to the devastation of occupied France and Belgium. France sought reparations for its economic recovery and reconstruction and as compensation for its inferiority compared to Germany. Both Britain and France planned to use reparations to pay their war debts to the United States and appease their populations by avoiding new taxes. The Entente powers intended to use the Versailles Treaty to limit German economic power.[11] The clauses on reparations and war guilt reflected the demands of governments and publics at home, and, to some observers, "fatally corrupted the Versailles settlement."[12]

The Allies concluded that Germany could not afford to pay such costs, so American representatives on the Reparations Commission, Norman Davis and John Foster Dulles, proposed a compromise. It led to two articles in the Treaty: Article 231, the infamous "War Guilt" clause, which presented Germany with moral responsibility and legal liability to pay; and the lesser known Article 232, which limited actual German liability for such enormous amounts.[13] The Big Three left the explosive issue to a Reparations Commission.

The Germans had presumed a moderate peace settlement based on Wilson's Fourteen Points. When the presumption proved in error, the Weimar government contested all charges in an attempt to split the Entente.[14] The German republic had charged diplomat Count Ulrich von Brockdorff-Rantzau with the conduct of negotiations. Brockdorff-Rantzau, arrogant and uncompromising, rejected Article 231 as an insult to German honor and lodged a formal protest against war guilt. German intellectual Max Weber, an expert advisor at the negotiations, agreed with Brockdorff-Rantzau. Against the instructions of the government, Weber and other German experts challenged the Allies over German war guilt. Weber preferred rejection of the treaty to submission to a "rotten peace."[15] He consequently left Versailles embittered, hoping that the Germans would oppose the treaty, with force if necessary.

German complaints about the humiliation and injustice of war guilt and draconian reparations elicited a sympathetic response from the British delegation, most crucially from economic advisor John Maynard Keynes. Keynes disregarded the fact that Germany remained stronger than France and sought to restore British trade with Germany. His conviction that political order rested on financial stability led to his advocacy of a moderate peace to restore Germany and, by extension, Britain and Europe. Keynes concluded that reparations payments would severely damage the German economy and resigned, rather than condone what he considered a punitive treaty.[16]

Finally, the rational argument of German Catholic Center Party leader Matthias Erzberger that the Allies would invade Germany and impose an even harsher peace convinced the German government to sign the peace. Weber's stance, however, epitomized the public feeling in Germany that right-wing politicians would exploit.[17] Erzberger would pay for his participation at Versailles with his life, at the hands of right-wing assassins in 1921. In the London Schedule of Payments of May 1921, the Commission later claimed 132 milliard gold marks (U.S. $33 billion) and then stipulated a payment of 50 milliard from Germany. Regardless, the Germans had decided to use Article 231 as a pretext to oppose reparations.[18] Reparations, as historian Sally Marks observed, concerned "two fundamental and closely related questions: who won the war and who would pay for it." With the balance of power at stake, the struggle over them became "the continuation of war by other means."[19]

Historians still debate the reasonableness of the treaty toward Germany, Germany's ability to pay reparations, and the connection between reparations and the hyperinflation that plagued Germany until 1924. Some contend that the non-punitive nature of the peace, which left German industrial potential intact, meant that Germany could have paid reparations by raising taxes and pursuing a stringent fiscal policy.[20] Some historians add that with modest reductions in consumption, Germany could have paid even the 132 milliard gold marks (U.S. $33 billion) stipulated in the London Schedule.[21] In fact, "Without reparations the French and the Belgians, not the Germans, would be paying the price for the First World War."[22] Nevertheless, the German government chose to sabotage the treaty.

Other historians argue, as did German diplomats from 1919–32, that the seizures of German assets led to a "chronic balance of payments deficit" that damaged the German and by extension the world economy.[23] The excessive reparations demanded in 1921 strained Germany's state finances intolerably, formed "the lion's share of the Reich deficit in 1921 and 1922," and thus bore ultimate responsibility for the inflation. "No Weimar government could have raised taxes or cut spending sufficiently to pay reparations *and* balance the budget."[24] Even historians who consider reparations excessive acknowledge the failure of the German government's strategy of using inflation to pay reparations, which precipitated the "domestic economic disaster" of German hyperinflation.[25]

Gerald Feldman deemed the territorial and economic/financial settlements of Versailles "horrendous failures," which "produced immense insecurity." In the opinions of J.P. Morgan of June 1922 and Feldman in 1998, the Allies needed to decide "whether they wanted a weak Germany who could not pay or a strong Germany who could pay." Feldman concludes that the "perpetual blight" of reparations "undermined German democracy," promoting "inflation at the beginning of the republic and deflation at its end."[26]

John Maynard Keynes's criticism of Versailles in his treatise of December 1919, *Economic Consequences of the Peace*, influenced several U.S. Senators before the vote on the treaty. Keynes's portrait of a Wilson outfoxed by his sly European counterparts reverberated in the work in 1922 of Ray Stannard Baker, American press chief at the peace conference. Baker depicted the European Allies, particularly the French, as "avaricious, aggressive, reactionary powers no more deserving of American sympathy or support in the postwar period than the recently defeated enemy." Such works reinforced the tendency in Britain and the United States to view "Versailles as a fatally flawed peace settlement from which the United States should remain aloof and which Great Britain should seek to revise." Harold Nicolson's *Peacemaking, 1919* of 1933, another account by a disillusioned participant, condemned the attempt to impose a Carthaginian peace on a "defeated, demoralized, but staunchly democratic Germany."[27]

The peace settlement left a powerful and embittered Germany surrounded by fragile nation states containing German-speaking minorities and the French with no alternative but to try to make Germany pay. The

Weimar Republic could use American loans to pay reparations and finance its economic recovery in the mid-1920s before defaulting in the Depression. From historian William Keylor's perspective, popular mythology, based on the writings of disillusioned participants, has perpetuated the incorrect notion that vindictive and punitive peace terms and unjust and gargantuan reparations led to the rise of the Nazis and the Second World War.[28]

The ultimate resolution of all the issues of Versailles depended upon political will to enforce its conditions, yet all the participants left dissatisfied with the treaty. The Allies' formulation of a peace based on their conflicting aims after Germany's unexpected collapse had necessitated a *Diktat*, as any negotiations with Germany might unravel the entire package. The subsequent compromises and dissatisfaction rendered enforcement of the treaty a precarious proposition from the outset.

In France the right condemned the absence of guarantees in the treaty; the left, its excessive territorial demands. Nevertheless a disillusioned French government ratified the treaty overwhelmingly. Clemenceau described the treaty as "the beginning of the beginning," a framework for future negotiations, which would be what they made of it.[29] Britain, preoccupied with its global position and reluctant to enforce the treaty, became convinced of its injustice toward Germany and welcomed its revision at French expense. All parties in Germany in the 1920s viewed the treaty as a "dictate of shame" and the blame for the war as unjust.[30] Germany thus resented the treaty's stipulations and set out to revise or undo it.

The United States withdrew its forces and extended loans. Upon return to the United States, Wilson refused to acknowledge the Senate Republicans and to enlist the help of the press to ensure ratification of the treaty. He preferred to abort the treaty rather than compromise on the League of Nations. He ordered moderate Democrats to oppose "reservations" to the League Covenant, dooming ratification.[31] After the defeat over the treaty and his fall from the Presidency, the gravely ill Wilson, who had suffered a stroke campaigning for the League, withdrew into isolationism, wanting as little to do with Europe as possible.

France alone remained to enforce the treaty. After repeated German defaults, the French government under Prime Minister Raymond Poincaré occupied the Ruhr in January 1923. By this time the British and French had confronted one another in the Middle East and over enforcement of Versailles. The British desired to ease German reparations payments. Poincaré, however, already angered that the Germans had killed nearly thirty French occupation soldiers in Silesia in the previous year, insisted that Germany pay. The Americans and British condemned the French for offending the Germans by using Senegalese in the Rhineland occupation, an act which also offended their own racist proclivities.

The Germans defaulted on reparations to test French resolve. Poincaré sent French troops to occupy the Ruhr. An embittered Woodrow Wilson denounced the French occupation, assailed Poincaré as a "skunk" and a "sneak," and hoped that Germany would crush France.[32] The German government declared passive resistance and a general strike, which exacerbated hyperinflation as the government paid the striking workers. The French and Belgians responded by taking over and running the railroads and the mines. The German government, overwhelmed by hyperinflation and chaos, yielded in September 1923. The French withdrew, relinquishing confrontation with Germany in favor of conciliation. In 1924 the Dawes Plan revised the London Schedule, in effect halving German reparations payments. The plan, named after American negotiator Charles Dawes, established a vicious circle of American short-term loans to central Europe, German reparations to Britain and France, and their war debts to the United States. This house of cards collapsed in the Great Depression.

The other treaties

The Treaty of St. Germain-en-Laye with Austria, signed on 10 September 1919, confirmed the dissolution of the Austro-Hungarian empire into its ethnic components. A small Austrian republic now coexisted with and recognized Czechoslovakia, Yugoslavia, Poland, and Hungary and surrendered portions of the old empire to Poland, Italy, and Yugoslavia. Its army could number 30,000 men, and it would have no air force or navy. The treaty barred it from union with Germany, and Article 177 acknowledged its war guilt and agreement to pay reparations. In the Treaty of Trianon of 4 June 1920, Hungary lost three-quarters of its land and two-thirds of its population to Rumania and the new states of Czechoslovakia and Yugoslavia. It could maintain an army of 35,000 men and also accepted guilt and reparations.

Bulgaria lost territory to Yugoslavia, and its outlet to the Aegean Sea to Greece through the Treaty of Neuilly on 27 November 1919. The Treaty of Sèvres in August 1920 treated Turkey like a colony, stripping it the most of the losers. It lost land to Greece and all of its Arab population and territories to British and French control through mandates, while Armenia became independent.

St. Germain and Trianon essentially confirmed the collapse of the Austro-Hungarian empire, which no one missed until its demise, for it had formed a coherent economic unit now rent asunder by the rise of small independent successor states. Austria became a small Catholic, conservative state with a giant socialist capital, as Vienna's population formed one-third of Austria. Czechoslovakia also remained a democracy because of the cooperation of the Czechs and Slovaks, a balanced economy, and the wise presidency of Slovak Tomas Masaryk.

In other states, precarious democracies did not endure. In Yugoslavia the

Serbs established a greater Serbia, dominated the Croatians and Slovenes, and resorted to military dictatorship in 1928. In Bulgaria, an army resentful of the treaty staged a coup in 1923 that ended democracy. A dissatisfied Hungary reeled from communist republic to reactionary regency under Adm. Nicholas Horthy, who had commanded the Austro-Hungarian Navy in the Adriatic at the end of the war. In Poland, deadlock between upper and lower classes ended in a military coup in 1926 staged by Marshal Josef Pilsudski, commander of the Polish Legion during the war and of the Polish Army during the Russo-Polish War. Rumanian democracy floundered, torn between a liberal bourgeoisie and a conservative peasantry. The attempt of the conference to arrange the polyglot puzzle of central and eastern Europe into democratic nation states on the whole failed, proof of the limits of great powers to dictate the internal destiny of other states.

—

The Paris Peace Conference proved unique in the history of postwar summit conferences in size and complexity, and also in its diplomatic innovations of "open diplomacy," national self-determination, and reparations.[33] Versailles validated ethnically pure nation states, although none existed after the war, and required new states to accord their minorities rights.[34] Its major weaknesses stemmed in part from the absence of the Soviet Union and later the withdrawal of the United States.

The Paris Peace Conference could not have solved and thus should not bear responsibility for the problems that an unprecedented war created. Problems of the interwar era stemmed from the disillusionment of the immediate postwar period, which dashed the extreme hopes that politicians and propagandists had stirred and populations accepted to justify such massive blood-letting. A massive war, in and of itself, creates conditions, regardless of the nature of the peace, that endure. The extent of the investment of human, financial, and material resources in the great conflict bred expectations that no peace other than a victorious one, if that, could have satisfied. In the postwar world of Versailles, many intellectuals and cultural observers believed that the war signaled the death of western culture. The war to save civilization had aborted in a civilization that seemed to have gone mad, a civilization in its death throes, as Oswald Spengler's work *The Decline of the West* (1918) and others propounded. As Ezra Pound's poem *Hugh Selwyn Mauberley* intoned: "There died a myriad,/and of the best, among them,/for an old bitch gone in the teeth,/for a botched civilization."

Positivist beliefs of the prewar era in linear human progress, human rationality, and the goodness of technological and industrial progress – under challenge before the war – fell casualties to a conflict that proved conclusively their illusory, and invalid nature. The nature of war itself, a glorious undertaking before 1914, now emerged as an evil, grotesque, and unmanageable slaughter. Versailles could not repair such wounds.

THE AFTERMATH OF WAR. SEXISM,
ANTI-BOLSHEVISM, AND RACISM

Some historians have considered the war to be a revolutionary event. It effected the fall of the three eastern empires – Germany, Austria-Hungary, and Russia – and the rise of Bolshevik Russia, the Weimar and Austrian republics, and a host of smaller states in their stead. The cataclysm of the Great War led to collapse, revolution, and potential upheaval. These threats – real, exaggerated, or perceived – occasioned such violent postwar responses that the war's overall effect became reactionary. The war on the Western Front ended on 11 November 1918. But brutality, violence, and conflict reigned across Europe, the Middle East, and Asia Minor, in such struggles as the Irish Civil War, *Freikorps* operations in the Baltic against the Bolsheviks, the Russian Civil War and Allied intervention in Russia, the Russo–Polish War, and the Greco–Turkish War. Not only had the war overturned the traditional political order and left endemic war, it also appeared to threaten the traditional order in other realms such as race and gender.

In the realm of race, both domestically and internationally, the war heightened the fear of white people toward peoples of color. The enormous slaughter of Europeans and their use of colonial peoples to fight, particularly on the Western Front, aroused the specter that Europeans might lose their accustomed supremacy. This very fear exposed further the true nature of imperialism, in its insidious exploitation of peoples through division, conquest, and continued violence. The participation of African and Asian troops, and African Americans, in the slaughter of white men, their access to white women in ways heretofore only imagined, and the French use of African troops in the postwar occupation of Germany – all threatened the traditional order of racial supremacy and repression. European women appeared to threaten the traditional order as well.

Gender

The First World War resulted in neither economic equality for women nor as much progress for women as some observers initially perceived. However, it heightened fears of the disruption of the traditional order and precipitated a reaction against any change in the status of women. The image of the modern woman did not mean that the war actually liberated women, but that it unleashed fears of a destabilized society.[35]

The belief that the war upset gender relations and concepts has given way to understanding that the fundamental conceptualization of woman as mother underwent little or no change. The notion of the "new woman," the "flapper," with her new-found freedom, skimpy dress, and loose morals, stemmed from male fears arising from the war and the deprivation of large numbers of young women of potential candidates for marriage. Attempts to re-establish stability, to return to the perceived "normalcy" of the prewar era, included an attempt to reconstruct gender relations after the war.[36]

Women's work in war industry had conformed to sexist stereotypes. Male employers alleged that monotonously repetitive and rapid work suited women better than men and consequently paid women lower wages. In the industrial shift from craft to mass production, women thus functioned as lesser or unskilled workers.[37]

In England, national duty and patriotic sacrifice required women to relinquish their jobs to demobilized soldiers just as they had assumed them to replace departing men. The Restoration of Prewar Practices Act in October 1919 kept the government's prewar promise to the Amalgamated Society of Engineers (ASE) to return to the status quo *ante bellum* in the factories. Some 579,000 of 819,000 women lost their jobs in munitions work. During the recession starting in December 1920, employers increased the differential between male and female wages from 33 percent in 1919 to 50 percent by 1922, thus restoring the traditional inequities for women who remained at work.[38] Nevertheless, the percentage of women in the metalworking force rose from barely 5 percent prewar to at least 10 percent in the 1920s and 15 to 20 percent in the 1930s.

In France severe labor shortages ensured that women would continue to work. During demobilization and conversion to peacetime production, employers abruptly dismissed many women in 1918–19, only to recall some of them as peacetime production rose. France's more catastrophic losses of manpower – 10.5 percent of the active male population dead compared to 5.1 percent in England, and a further 6.6 percent so grievously wounded that they could not lead a normal life[39] – opened up opportunities for some Frenchwomen.

French employers attempted to reconcile work and home, in contrast to the British approach of throwing women out of work wholesale. The French economy expanded in the 1920s, while the British economy slumped into extended recession. Nevertheless, in both countries stereotypical assumptions about gender differences and women's natural attributes of speed, dexterity, capacity for hard work, and lack of initiative determined women's work and wages.[40]

During the war the French had represented women in two dichotomous images – the good patriotic mother and the bad promiscuous wanton.[41] An obsessive concern about issues of gender – female identity and the proper role of women – in a postwar debate focussed the larger issues of the impact of the war and of rapid social and cultural change. The war continued a long-time tendency in France to crystalize issues in discussions of the place of women. Postwar intellectuals focussed on three ideal types: the mother and her reassuring sense of continuity and domesticity; the modern woman, a threatening symbol of rapid change and cultural crisis; and the single woman, a product of the war.[42]

The image of the mother bore particular significance in a country where intellectuals and politicians had debated natalist concerns since the previous century. Demographer Paul Haury actually located "the essential cause of the war of 1914" in France's prewar demographic inferiority to Germany, which regarded France as a "dying nation."[43] Politician Henri Cheron, fearing another German invasion in fifteen to twenty years' time, proclaimed: "If France had had as many children as in Germany in 1914, you can be sure that the war would not have taken place."[44] This depopulation threatened to jeopardize France's status as a world power. After the blood-bath of 1914–18, the mother symbolized "rebirth, healing, redemption, and a restoration from the war's moral trauma."[45]

Fashions that emerged from the war – short "bobbed" hair, low-cut dresses, short skirts – symbolized the war's social upheaval and women's liberation. Women of all classes worked fastidiously to adopt the streamlined silhouette, without breasts, waist, or hips, which blurred gender boundaries and "scandalized and infuriated" many postwar Frenchmen and women.[46] Roland Dorgelès's famous novel *Les Croix de Bois* (The Wooden Crosses), published after the armistice, continued the theme of marital infidelity from wartime. The scandalous *femme moderne* symbolized change that threatened to undermine traditional French society. The war had destroyed bourgeois society's moral certainties, resulting in moral decadence, as women, their traditional moorings loosened, and returning soldiers, often emasculated by the war, sank into promiscuity and hedonism.

France's need for regeneration and repopulation confronted the fear that women might not desire children and the fact that the war's losses of men deprived an entire category of women, *la femme seule*, of domesticity and child-bearing. In 1920 physician and professor Paul Carnot recommended the importation of Canadians "to bring the sexes into equilibrium among peoples of the white race."[47] Some men advocated polygamy, others single motherhood, issues of immorality and Catholicism notwithstanding. French attempts to reassure themselves of the continued viability of domesticity thus led to a maze of contradictions.[48]

In Britain postwar feminists accepted motherhood and constraints that they had rejected in the late Victorian and Edwardian eras.[49] Prewar British feminists and suffragists had attacked the ideology of separate spheres for women and men and viewed relations between the sexes, not as complementary and cooperative, but as a state of war. They had viewed masculinity and femininity as cultural and social constructs, not as biologically determined states. The anti-suffragists believed in inherent and immutable masculine traits, which necessitated separate spheres to protect women from men. During the war feminists gradually accepted the notions of separate spheres, complementary relationships between the sexes, and psychoanalysts' and sexologists' theories of sexual difference.[50]

The riots of returning soldiers in England in January 1919, and isolated incidents of violence, including sexual attacks on women, suggested that social peace required pacifying these potentially violent men. Philip Gibbs, a war correspondent who had idealized the war as a crusade, commented in 1920 that the returning crusaders seemed queer, bitter, violent, and frightening. Gibbs concluded that "our armies established an intensive culture of brutality. They were schools of slaughter." These sex-starved front-line soldiers fell prey to "poor sluts" who infected them with venereal disease and rendered them insane. The war had unleashed primitive barbarism, the "brute," the "ape-man."[51]

Freudian theory emphasized the war's colossal brutality and mortality, the links between the instincts and lust for killing and sex. Its popularization in the 1920s made the informed wary of continuing conflict. A return to the prewar world's "traditional" gender order seemed necessary to avoid further conflict. The press that had once praised women now "vilified and excoriated" them if they did not relinquish work and demands for equality and return to domesticity and motherhood, to procreate happily in accord with biological necessity. The reassertion of sexual difference offered "a means of reestablishing order in society."[52]

Postwar laws enabled women over age 30 to vote and stand for Parliament and for the competitive civil service examinations. Nevertheless, in Susan Kent's words, an ideology of "*Kinder, Kirche, Küche* stressing traditional femininity and motherhood permeated British culture."[53] Postwar feminists accepted separate spheres as they accepted the inherent aggression and violence of returning soldiers and men in general, which women had to accommodate in order to protect themselves and society. Thus British society returned to "conservative and reactionary images of masculinity and femininity" in order to re-establish social peace.[54] The Great War had derailed prewar feminism's drive for equality of the sexes and led to the preservation of traditional modes of viewing gender.

Susan Grayzel argues that wartime rhetoric in Britain and France linked "women with mothers and men with soldiers." The emphasis on "motherhood as women's primary patriotic role and the core of their national identity" maintained "gender order" in both societies. "[A]ny transformations for western European women's gender identities over the entire course of the war years remained 'truly limited.'"[55] Each nation considered women necessary to postwar recovery through reproduction. The public acclaim accorded women for their heroism and service would not disrupt the social order. Postwar women became mourners, as the "grieving mother" expressed collective memory and sorrow. The First World War increased the importance of women to the nation and threatened to destabilize gender roles. The emphasis on motherhood offset the war's potential disruption of gender roles and served "as an anchor for stabilizing gender during this total war."[56]

The new republic in Germany granted women the right to vote and to stand for election. Nearly 90 percent of the women eligible to vote did so in 1919, and women deputies, most of them socialist, composed nearly 10 percent of the National Assembly. Once in the Reichstag, the party elites excluded them from fiscal and economic policy and the women accepted their concentration on issues concerning women and the family.

The "new," "modern," or "liberated" woman, her hair bobbed, smoking cigarettes in public, also appeared in Weimar Germany. As in other countries, males manufactured a threat where none existed, as in Germany single, young, urban, clerical workers epitomized the new. Although movies, magazines, and newspapers made much of the liberated woman, she did not threaten male predominance. In German industry as elsewhere, women filled the unskilled and semi-skilled jobs on automated production lines at lower wages than men. Immediately after the war, women had lost their wartime work in industry. In white-collar work, men served apprenticeships that prepared their way beyond clerical work, while women remained at the clerical level. All agreed that this temporary work should lead to marriage, for women truly belonged ultimately in the home.[57]

Fears of "Judeo-Bolshevism" and "lesser races"

Social conflict and fear of revolution reigned in postwar Britain. Strikes and industrial unrest, the rise of the Labour Party as the key opposition party and its adoption of socialism as a new platform in June 1918, and the specter of Bolshevism drove British Conservatives into paroxysms of fear. They tarred Labour with the brush of Bolshevism and equated Jews with Bolsheviks. The right wing believed fervently in a "Jewish Bolshevik" conspiracy, and from the end of the war until late 1921, the right-wing press waged a hysterical anti-Jewish Bolshevik campaign which made anti-Semitism respectable.[58]

Conservatives regarded Russian Bolshevism as a German–Jewish conspiracy, and made no distinction between Bolshevism in Russia and socialism in England. Lloyd George, in intemperate efforts to win the election of 1918, had lambasted Labour as Bolshevik sympathizers and a threat to Britain's security. By 1919, conservatives alleged connections between "Bolshevism and Bochedom," "the twin enemies of civilization."[59]

Continued British intervention in Russia polarized the nation further.

Labour openly opposed it as a contravention of the principle of non-intervention, while the right wing, with Winston Churchill's staunch support in the Cabinet, promoted the intensification of intervention. In April 1919, Churchill, against Lloyd George's better judgment, raised a 4,000-man volunteer army to reinforce British soldiers in north Russia.[60] The government subsequently refused to commit to further intervention.

At home, popular authors such as John Buchan feared "the threat of social disintegration" by a conspiracy to undermine civilization led by "young Bolshevik Jews."[61] In 1920, the publication of an English version of the *Protocols of the Elders of Zion* under the title *The Jewish Peril* occasioned the right-wing press's campaigns against the influence of Jews in the British government.[62]

Only the failure of a planned general strike in 1921 and the Anglo-Soviet trade agreement of 16 March 1921 calmed the atmosphere of crisis and fear, although the right-wing papers *Morning Post* and *Blackwood's* continued to attack Jews.[63] The Labour-Liberal victory of December 1923 that propelled Ramsay MacDonald into office as the first Labour prime minister once again aroused anti-Bolshevik hysteria in a "Red Scare" that brought down the government in the fall. The extent of anti-Semitic anti-Bolshevism in victorious England contextualizes the virulence of similar attitudes in postwar Germany.

In Germany, *Freikorps* units brutally crushed leftist revolution with the complicity and support of the moderate socialist government and the army. Their bloody murders of Rosa Luxemburg and Karl Liebknecht, the leaders of the German Spartakist group, epitomized the reign of terror in the various states of Germany to extirpate revolutionaries and left-wing governments. In the midst of destabilizing hyperinflation, right-wing *putsch* attempts in major cities such as Berlin and Munich – the latter in 1923 by a little-known ex-corporal named Adolf Hitler – rose and disintegrated. Political murders abounded, as right-wing assassins settled scores with Walther Rathenau and Matthias Erzerger, and hundreds of other lesser figures of the center and left in Germany.

By the end of the hyperinflation and the stabilization of the German currency in 1924, conservative governments, whose key figure was Gustav Stresemann, controlled the Weimar Republic and busily pursued clandestine rearmament in league with Soviet Russia. The army High Command arose anew in the guise of the Troop Office (*Truppenamt*) under Gen. Hans von Seeckt, who made the 100,000-man army a cadre for a future German armed force. Only in Prussia, with the introduction of universal male suffrage, did solidly social democratic governments reign throughout the Weimar Republic. Germany would enter the League of Nations in two years, no longer a pariah. It accepted its western border with France, but it would never accept its eastern border with Poland.

Postwar France, suffering from demographic and economic devastation and inflation, depended upon reparations from Germany to compensate for its material losses. After 1918 the French government sent colonial workers home as quickly as possible to preclude France becoming a multiracial society. The manpower it required came from massive immigration of other Europeans in the 1920s.[64]

A radicalized working class flocked to the *Confédération Générale du Travail* (CGT), the socialist union, which demanded not only the eight-hour working day but also a just peace toward Germany, nonintervention in the Soviet Union, and more progressive taxation. Clemenceau responded with a combination of concessions, granting the eight-hour working day, and repression, as police and troops injured several hundred demonstrators on May Day 1919. When the CGT called a general strike for May Day 1920, then Prime Minister Alexandre Millerand broke it by using soldiers to maintain transportation, arresting leaders, and firing striking state workers. At the end of the year, the Communists captured the Socialist Party and the CGT and, for a short time, the majority of active workers. Although the Socialists regained their party, the CGT, and the support of the majority of workers, the rise of the Communist Party and its union, the CGTU, signaled the irremediable schism of the left.

In 1920 Clemenceau departed the political scene, relinquishing the probability of succeeding Poincaré as President. Clemenceau did not mask his scorn for the office of President. He had commented derisively: "There are two useless organs – the prostate and the presidency" and further, that he voted "for the stupidest" in presidential elections.[65] Nevertheless, the presidential electors, senators and deputies, feared that the authoritarian Prime Minister might seek to accrue even more power as President. A preliminary ballot gave the innocuous moderate senator Paul Deschanel a narrow victory. A furious Clemenceau withdrew before a formal vote, resigned as Prime Minister, and departed from public life. Clemenceau left Paris, and in September embarked on a nine-month trip abroad.

In May 1920 Deschanel, attempting to open his compartment window during the night, fell from the slowly moving presidential train. He seemed to suffer no permanent damage from this embarrassing incident, but in September the press announced that the President had gone swimming stark-naked in a palace fountain. Deschanel resigned, Millerand became President, and the prime ministership proceeded to alternate between moderate leftist Aristide Briand and rightist ex-president Raymond Poincaré. After the occupation of the Ruhr in 1923, France would cease to play an independent role in European politics. Politicians and political pundits faced east, awaiting the rise of the German phoenix from the ashes, convinced that Germany would come again.

The postwar Red Scare in Italy provided the mythic excuse necessary to crush workers' and peasants' demands already evident in wartime. The Bolsheviks had no chance to seize power in Italy, where the leading leftist Antonio Gramsci already languished in prison. The postwar government, under the elderly Prime Minister Giovanni Giolitti, did not respond to the strikes and lock-outs occurring in urban industry or the strife between large landlords and peasants in the countryside. Nor did the government take action to curtail the Italian nationalist seizure of the city of Fiume, which the peace treaty had allocated to Yugoslavia. Governmental inactivity allowed the Blackshirt thugs, or combat squads, of Benito Mussolini's Fascist movement to fill the power vacuum. The ex-soldiers violently repressed workers and peasants, thereby gaining the favor of industrialists and landlords, and ultimately of the army, the king, and the queen mother. The conservative elite around the monarch invited Mussolini to power in 1922, in order to enlist the thuggish demagogue in the preservation of the traditional order against the lower classes.

The Red Scare in the United States, like its counterpart in Italy, occasioned government repression of "outsiders" in American society: workers, immigrants, and African Americans. The federal government quickly dismantled wartime agencies in order to cease any regulation of business. Recently mobilized industries now reconverted to peacetime production, releasing workers, in particular women, in the process. Severe inflation and dismal working conditions led to thousands of strikes, including major ones in the steel industry and coal-mines, which owners used troops and strike-breakers to repress. The military rapidly discharged soldiers, armed with their US$60 bonus, into increasingly chaotic conditions.

The federal government and much of the American public interpreted any strike or hint of radicalism as Bolshevik inspired. The press incited them to violence, judges and juries condoned it, while the Senate Judiciary Committee under Lee Overman found Bolsheviks everywhere plotting to overthrow and Bolshevize the American government. A series of anarchist bombings provided Attorney General A. Mitchell Palmer and the Justice Department's new General Intelligence Division, under J. Edgar Hoover, with the excuse to act. Invoking the Espionage and Sedition Acts, agents raided labor offices, rounded up more than 5,000 aliens at the turn of 1919–20, imprisoned them, and then began to deport them *en masse* without trial or hearing. Although Assistant Secretary of Labor Louis F. Post canceled many deportations and released many from jail and the Scare receded in 1920, it led to stricter immigration laws and stimulated the phenomenal growth of the Ku Klux Kan in the early 1920s.

The government acknowledged that the oppression of African Americans made them likely fodder for Bolshevik propaganda. Instead of working to end oppression and improve conditions for black people, the government simply increased surveillance and repression. The army, fearing the radicalization of black troops, searched for an organization among black officers to fight white ascendancy and to secure equality for African Americans. Northern cities, particularly New York, welcomed black troops home, but in the South black troops encountered hostility, as Senator Vardaman's weekly newsletter encouraged lynching of "French-women-ruined negro [sic] soldiers."[66]

In the United States lynchings and race riots bloodied the American scene from 1917 through 1921. The year after the war, whites lynched eighty African Americans, burning eleven at the stake. Twenty-five race riots, with white servicemen often leading the mobs, bloodied the American scene. In Tulsa, Oklahoma, mobs burned entire black residential and commercial sections of the city to the ground while they murdered the residents. Press and police invariably blamed black people for the violence. White mobs lynched black soldiers in uniform to disabuse African Americans of any ideas of improved, much less equal treatment they might entertain. The violence with which white Americans rewarded the wartime service of black citizens proved that the war had not made America safe for democracy. A popular American song jovially intoned "How're you gonna keep 'em down on the farm, after they've seen Paree?" With murderous violence, answered white mobs in the case of black soldiers.

The war and the rise of Bolshevism exacerbated racist fears in the United States. In the popular book of 1917, *The Passing of the Great Race*,[67] Madison Grant advocated eugenicist solutions of racial cleansing to achieve racial purity through breeding registries, stringent marriage laws, and segregation. He wanted to eliminate not just "inferior" races but also "inferior" segments of all races through forced sterilization and selective breeding. New Yorker Grant deemed immigrants from eastern and southern Europe inferior to "nordic" peoples. He further warned that "inferior" white southerners – Georgians, Alabamans, and Mississippians – presaged the downfall of the white race in America. The Great War, a "civil war" between superior Europeans, had delivered an enormous blow to European dominance and superiority by decimating the "nordic" races and allowing the rise of the "little dark man."

In 1920, Lothrop Stoddard's work *The Rising Tide of Color against White World Supremacy*[68] surveyed the appalling effect of the Great War on European supremacy. "The Great War was unquestionably the most appalling catastrophe that ever befell mankind. The racial losses were certainly as great as the material losses."[69] The racial health of the white race had suffered irreplaceable losses of genetically superior people. The flower of the superior races had fallen, leaving weaklings, the unfit, and undesirables to breed faster than the best elements in society. Other races would view the divisions of the war in Europe as a sign of weakness, and Asians – Japanese, Chinese, and Indians – might unite and assert themselves.[70] The French use in Europe of African troops, whose sense of their ability compromised European superiority, posed the worst danger to European superiority.[71]

To Stoddard, egalitarianism Jewish Bolshevism – antithetical to his notions of racial superiority – threatened nordic Europe. A chaotic Russia, racially inferior to most of Europe, had fallen prey to this philosophy of the "Under-Man." Those who plotted "the disruption of civilization and the degradation of the race" needed to be "hunted down and extirpated." Stoddard, like Grant, advocated forced sterilization, regulated breeding, and segregation.[72] Grant's work served as a model for the United States' more stringent immigration laws in the 1920s, while Presidents Warren Harding and Herbert Hoover recommended Stoddard's work.

Such mainstream American thought had much in common with Nazi ideology.[73] Grant and Stoddard strongly influenced the writing of Professor Hans Günther, who provided a "scientific" basis for Nazi thought. Günther acknowledged his reliance on their racial theories, and deemed the primary result of the First World War the "denordization" of Europe.[74] Through Günther, American racist thought filtered to Alfred Rosenberg, the philosopher of the Nazi movement, Walter Darre, Nazi Minister of Agriculture, and even Adolf Hitler, who met Stoddard in 1939 and labeled Grant's *The Passing of the Great Race* his "Bible."[75] Nazi and American racist thought agreed about the challenges the "superior" races confronted and about the solutions, as Stoddard had no qualms about the "physical elimination" of the Jews from Europe.[76]

The Great War thus heightened the racism already evident in the prewar western world. In reaction to its slaughter of Europeans, the proponents of racist theory proposed further slaughter, the annihilation of the threatening "inferior" races, in particular the Jews, who in their Bolshevik guise now posed the ultimate threat to a racist, capitalist, western society. Fears that Bolshevism would penetrate the colonial world and undermine European global power pervaded Europe, similar to fears in the United States that it would incite African Americans to violence.

THE WIDER WORLD

Soviet Russia

Imperial Russia had participated in the European balance of power and community of states for two centuries. Now the former great power found itself ostracized, unstable, and under attack by counter-revolutionary, or "White" forces, and Allied intervention troops. As of 1919, British, French, American, and Japanese forces remained around the borders of Soviet Russia, supporting the uncoordinated "White" forces of various Russian generals and admirals who sought power. Gradually, Trotsky's Red Army, grown to three million men in 1919, defeated them all. The Allied intervention forces began withdrawing in October 1919, although the Japanese remained in Siberia until October 1922. The Bolsheviks had won; Soviet Russia had survived. In the process the Allied intervention had confirmed Leninist belief that the new Soviet state existed in a hostile world of capitalist states. The origins of the Cold War lie here – in Bolshevik proclamations of world revolution and the allies' hostile reception of the Bolshevik Revolution, culminating in the Allied intervention – not after the Second World War.

A pariah in a world of capitalist great powers, Soviet Russia did not participate in the Paris Peace Conference, although the shadow of Bolshevism loomed as a backdrop to the peace negotiations. By the mid-1920s England, France, and Germany had recovered from the war's devastation and the postwar inflation, while the Soviet Union, only three years removed from the struggle to reincorporate territories such as the Ukraine, lagged behind. German diplomats played a shrewd game between Bolshevik Russia and the western powers, relying on the threat of Bolshevism to moderate the victors' policies toward it, while rearming in secret with the Soviet Union and allying with it in the Treaty of Rapallo of 1922.

The leaders of the USSR consequently realized in fact that Germany, as a revisionist power, would most likely cause a second major war. Ultimately, socialism in one country and rapid industrialization and collectivization aimed to create a military-industrial complex and a militarized Soviet society capable of fighting a modern war.[77]

Japan

Japan gained Shantung Province and control of former German possessions in the South Pacific, but Woodrow Wilson's pronouncements for democracy and against imperialism threatened the oligarchic and imperialist rulers of Japan. They feared a rising tide of democracy, and future British and American efforts to expand their influence in China. The Versailles Treaty's recognition of the rights of labor movements to organize encouraged Japanese labor to confront management, and its proclamation of the right of national self-determination aroused demonstrations in Korea and China. The war had provided an opportunity for Japan to extend its influence in East Asia and the Pacific, but it had also occasioned a domestic struggle between proponents of British-style parliamentary government and those of a more authoritarian imperial Germany. Some domestic developments hastened by the war also pointed toward democracy, such as the general unrest and rice riots and the rise of the first generation to experience mass state education.

The outcome of the war and the peace threatened to undo the militarists, who already anticipated a race war with the west and held to their imperialist and militarist faith, dissatisfied with their imperial acquisitions. At the same time, the rise to prominence of the *Zaibatsu*, powerful economic pressure groups, did not necessarily augur well for democracy. Furthermore, Japan's limited military experience of the war spared it any potential restraining influences similar to Europe's recognition of the horrors of war, in a rather similar fashion to its American counterpart.[78]

Japanese wartime intrigue and self-aggrandizement in East Asia aroused the concerns of the British and Americans. Japan's refusal to cooperate with its British ally's demands to deport Indian revolutionaries who had taken refuge in Japan further angered the British. On the other hand, the western powers' tendency to ignore the Japanese at Versailles and their rejection of the non-discrimination covenant indicated their continued perception of the Japanese as a secondary and inferior power and people, and infuriated the Japanese.

The Washington Naval Conference of 1921–2 provided the venue for potential resolution of some of these issues. Britain and the United States established parity for their navies as the strongest at 525,000 tons of capital ships, Japan second at 350,000 tons, and France and Italy third at 175,000 tons each. A Nine Power Treaty supplementing the conference guaranteed Chinese integrity and sovereignty, forcing Japan to return the former German colony of Kiaochow to China. Finally, a Four Power Treaty among the United States, Britain, Japan, and France recognized their possessions in the Pacific and provided for consultation in case of problems. The conference provided the occasion for the abrupt British cancellation of the Anglo–Japanese Treaty of 1902, which the United States distrusted. British termination of the alliance reflected the weakness of the British Empire and its fears of a rising Japanese rival in Asia.[79] Yet all of these steps – the refusal to acknowledge the Japanese as an equal naval power, the attempt to corral their expansion in Asia with multi-power pacts, and finally the very manner of abrogation of the Anglo–Japanese alliance – could only insult the Japanese. In the short term they might swallow their pride; in the long term they would press for revision and recognition of their status as a great power in Asia and the Pacific.

Entente empires

The white Dominions – Australia and New Zealand, Canada, and South Africa – became sovereign states and achieved autonomy within the British Empire as a result of the war. These states turned away from Europe and to some extent from Britain as well, although, in the case of Australia, the exploits of ANZAC soldiers had proved to Australian political leaders such as Prime Minister William "Billy" Hughes that they were worthy of being called Britons. Canada, for example, kept its distance from the League of Nations and from Britain's call for military assistance against a resurgent Turkey in 1922.

However, the Allies did not consider offering national self-determination to the colored peoples of their own empires. Smuts wanted control of Germany's former territories in Africa and designed the mandate system as a substitute for annexation to appease Woodrow Wilson.[80] The Allies divided Germany's former colonies among themselves, cloaking their imperial control in Smuts's scheme of mandates. The Europeans deemed Class A mandates, the Arab regions of Mesopotamia (Iraq), Palestine, Syria, and Lebanon, at a higher stage of development than Africa and the Pacific Islands, and thus eligible for preparation for earlier independence. These mandates, however, would have no say in the matter.

Class B and C mandates in Africa and the Pacific faced no prospect of independence. Blaise Diagne convened a three-day Pan-African Congress at the Grand Hotel in Paris on 19 February, which African American intellectual W.E.B. DuBois had helped to organize. Nearly sixty delegates, most of them from the United States, the French West Indies, and French colonies, proclaimed the right of self-determination for African peoples and called for the League to assume direct control of the former German colonies, but to no avail.[81] Although DuBois pleaded eloquently for consideration for Africa, the American colonial expert, historian George Louis Beer, whom DuBois met, opined: "The negro [sic] race has hitherto shown no capacity for progressive development except under the tutelage of other peoples."[82]

The former Ottoman Empire

The Ottoman Empire had fought the entire war at a severe disadvantage in terms of manpower, munitions, logistics, and economic and industrial bases. The Turks had begun the war with twenty-two million people inhabiting 1.5 million square miles of land; with the armistice at Mudros they ruled only ten million people and nearly 0.8 million square miles of territory. Foreign powers occupied Turkish territory, and Greece planned to take even more land. The Turkish economy lay in ruins, but a nucleus had survived. After the armistice the Turkish Army demobilized, but retained core divisions of ethnic Turks as the nucleus of the postwar army in 1919. The British occupied Constantinople and the Dardanelles; the French, the southeast; the Armenians, Kars; and the Greeks, Smyrna and its hinterland.

By 1918, even before the end of the war, the British government decided to discard the Sykes–Picot Treaty of 1916 dividing the Middle East with the French. Wilson's Fourteen Points and the Bolsheviks' publication of all secret treaties, Sykes–Picot included, embarrassed such blatantly imperialist policies. Meanwhile, along the Russo-Turkish border in Georgia, Armenia, and Azerbaijan – collectively labeled Transcaucasia – Enver Pasha endeavored to expand Ottoman influence in this oil-rich region. The British government viewed the Russian Bolsheviks and the Turks as pawns of the German government and feared a coordinated German-inspired thrust into a chaotic central Asia toward Persia, Mesopotamia, and ultimately India. The British decided to counter this thrust with one of their own for mastery of Central Asia. With the German request for armistice in October 1918, Britain sought urgently to position its troops to dominate former Ottoman holdings in the Middle East and Asia and to exclude the French from the Middle East if possible. In January 1919, the British Empire attained its zenith, with more than a million additional square miles and more than a million British imperial troops in former Ottoman domains. Lloyd George lay claim to dominance in the Middle East, just as demobilization and economic necessity at home began to undermine the strength of the British Army. By summer 1919 the army had declined by two-thirds to some 320,000 men.

Meanwhile, the Ottoman Sultan attempted to retain his tenuous control as governmental authority collapsed in the Anatolian heartland of Turkey, and appointed Gen. Mustapha Kemal to command the region in May 1919. Later that year, at Kemal's headquarters in the interior at Angora (Ankara), the deputies elected to a new Turkish Chamber of Deputies agreed to create an independent Muslim nation state, which they openly declared early in 1920. Kemal's forces were soon fighting French, British, and finally Greek invaders. The British seized Constantinople and the Sultan, Kemal's troops retreated into the interior, and Turkey collapsed in civil war.

The Syrian National Congress then defied the Entente, prompting the French to seize Damascus in July 1920 and force British puppet King Feisal into exile. The French took control of Syria, splitting Lebanon from it. The British, who had placed Feisal on the Syrian throne, later had him installed as King of Iraq.

The Treaty of Sèvres of 10 August 1920, which the Entente forced upon the Sultan, dismembered the Ottoman Empire among the British, French, and Greeks, leaving only a small part of Anatolia to the Ottoman Sultan, whose finances would be controlled by an international commission. Earlier in April 1920 at the conference of San Remo in Italy, the British and French agreed secretly to monopolize the oil supplies of the Middle East.

Even before the powers could conclude the treaty, the Middle East flared into violence – riots in Egypt and war against the Afghans on the Indian frontier in 1919, riots in Palestine and revolt in Iraq in 1920. Egypt's leaders demanded complete independence, which Britain's need for the Suez Canal precluded. During the war Egypt had become Britain's major base for African and Middle Eastern operations. Military occupation resulted. On the Indian border, the British, using the Royal Air Force to strike at the tribes, quickly subdued the Afghans. But Britain conceded complete independence to the Afghan government in Kabul, which still conspired with the Bolsheviks to create unrest on the Northwest Frontier.

In early February 1921 Reza Khan seized power in Teheran, Persia (Iran) and signed a treaty with Soviet Russia. The new governments of Persia, Turkey, and Afghanistan had now all signed treaties with Russia for protection against British imperialism. The treaty with Turkey enabled the Bolsheviks to dominate Georgia, Armenia, and Azerbaijan and retain the Russian imperial territory. The British viewed all their difficulties as a product of Bolshevik intrigues, rather than attributing agency to the aspirations of various actors such as the ardently anti-Bolshevik Mustapha Kemal.

A greedy British government had essentially overextended itself in the Middle East, while domestic concerns such as education and poor housing in Britain cried out for attention. By 1922 the British granted both Iraq and Egypt limited autonomy. During the same year the League of Nations approved a British mandate establishing a Jewish home within Palestine, west of the Jordan River, while eastern Palestine became Jordan. Feisal ruled Iraq in the east, and France ruled Syria and Lebanon.

By fall 1921 the French withdrew from Turkey, recognized Kemal's regime at Angora as a legitimate government, and began to support it against Britain and Greece. In 1922 Kemal crushed the invading Greek Army and drove it and 1.5 million Greeks from Turkey. Winston Churchill, now Colonial Secretary, prepared to fight the Turks just as he had sent troops to fight the Bolsheviks. The Dominions – Australia, Canada, and New Zealand – now sovereign entities, refused to follow Britain to war. Kemal and the British commander in Turkey negotiated an armistice in October that recognized a new and independent Turkish nation state in Asia Minor that would include Constantinople and the Dardanelles.

In November 1922 the Kemal government deposed the Sultan, and the Ottoman Empire, like the German, Austro-Hungarian, and Russian, passed into history. Kemal became President of a one-party state, and, as Kemal Attatürk, created a modern state based on the Swiss legal code and more equality for women. In 1923 the Treaty of Lausanne with the Entente ratified the existence of Turkey. In Britain David Lloyd George had fallen from power in November 1922, as the victorious Conservatives discarded him after press attacks on his Middle East policy. Colonial Secretary Churchill lost his seat in Parliament. Kemal would rule Turkey until his death in 1938.

Africa and the British West Indies

All of Africa ultimately became directly or indirectly involved in the war. The war disrupted African economies, as the declaration of war brought first depression and then boom in the demand for primary products. It also eliminated the Germans, tropical Africa's major trading partner, and replaced them with the British. Colonial governments had intervened in the economy, often to control the prices and thus the profits from primary goods sold to Europe.

Many European administrators, merchants, and mobilized soldiers left Africa, and their departure occasionally made work available for educated and trained Africans. In the Volta-Bani region of French West Africa, the departure of colonial soldiers combined with the brutality of the colonial administration to unleash a war of rebellion. Although the French colonial administration brutally crushed the insurgents, many of the latter remained "independent and fierce" despite the decimation of the ranks of their young men and the destruction of their economy.[83] Continued French fears of future flare-ups of violent opposition prompted them repeatedly to punish and seize any arms from the former rebel villages. In 1919 the colonial administration divided the vast Haut-Sénégal-Niger territory into two colonies with the creation of Upper Volta, which led ultimately to the current nation states of Mali and Burkina Faso.

More than a million African soldiers had fought on various fronts, and even more served as bearers or porters. Some 150,000 soldiers and bearers died, and many more suffered wounds. African soldiers played key roles in suppressing revolt in Africa. Only the Senussi persisted in their revolt in Libya, forcing the Italians in 1919 to recognize the Tripolitanian Republic and the Emirate of Cyrenaica. African soldiers fought in Africa, Europe, and in the Balkans and Middle East. Some Africans, such as Senegalese and Madagascans, volunteered for service, but most entered as conscripts.

More than 135,000 West African conscripts, ranging from aristocrats to the low-born, had fought in the French armies on the Western Front during the First World War. Their systematic conscription from 1915, combined with the flight of some men to other colonies to avoid conscription, had caused famine in their homeland for want of men to work the fields. Some had fought for family honor; others had fought because the French had promised to make slaves chiefs. Senegalese had fought in West Africa, where they had conquered the German colonies of Togo and the Cameroons, on the Western Front, and at the Dardanelles and on the Balkan front, where they participated in the final offensives against the Austro-Hungarian Army. With the armistice of 11 November, demobilization and return to West Africa awaited the Senegalese soldiers.

The wartime experience of fighting with and against Europeans, as well as killing them, provided a new experience for African soldiers. African soldiers considered the war terrible, evil, and futile, and concluded that the French had exploited them – a belief that French statements about shedding African blood instead of French corroborated. From the war experience, however, the soldiers returned self-confident, assertive, and aware of a wider world. They insisted on the respect from the Europeans that they had earned. Although this new self-assurance and fearlessness threatened the French colonial authorities, the returning soldiers essentially sought to resume their normal lives. In Senegal they formed veterans' associations and helped re-elect Blaise Diagne with an overwhelming majority, but the French governor general and the French government thwarted plans for African control over Senegal's policies by 1922. Diagne, acknowledging defeat, became a spokesman for French commercial interests, which prompted some veterans to denounce him for accommodating the French. Despite the postwar defeat of the African drive for political equality, they would eventually reach that goal, which originated in the "War to Obtain Rights," after a second world war. Many veterans of the first war judged their service a crucial step on the road from conquest by the French to independence from the French.[84]

In Nyasaland, later Malawi, the government had requisitioned rice and cattle starting in 1916, while labor shortages resulted in less land under cultivation, a consequent decline in agricultural production, and ultimately famine. Many demobilized soldiers died of disease on their way home, as venereal disease and influenza compounded the ravages of smallpox and bubonic plague in 1919. The war in East Africa had dominated their lives for years, as it became Malawi's "first national experience." Many people had lost their wealth, especially livestock, and suffered the effects of inflation, although the ex-servicemen's pay and their exploits earned them new respect in their villages. As with their West African counterparts, Malawian veterans no longer feared Europeans, as some concluded that Europeans "were all fools." Some Malawians respected Europeans; more undoubtedly loathed them for their cruelty and failure to acknowledge and recompense the Africans for their sacrifices.[85]

Nigerian veterans often returned with better fluency in English and assumed non-commissioned officer rank, replacing British non-coms. They did not contemplate revolution, but, after their first national experience, Nigerians lost respect for Britain's power and prestige. The educated elite and veterans felt cheated, the former of opportunities for participation in government, the latter of back pay and medals, and the opportunity to participate in the London Peace Parade.[86]

The war in general, and conflict in Africa in particular, had led to famine, disease, destruction, and depopulation. But it had also imparted a new sense of black African nationalism, often in response to increased white nationalism in South Africa and Kenya. White settlers in Kenya, for example, prospered during the war at the same time that the colonial state exploited African labor, stock, and wealth. Conditions for Africans by and large did not improve. Imperialism, if shaken, remained, and the war had redrawn the map of Africa as it would remain in the twentieth century. But the war had sown the "ideas concerning the self-determination of peoples and the accountability of colonial powers" which would influence events later in the century.[87]

West Indian soldiers' wartime experience in Africa and the Middle East stimulated the rise of black nationalism in the British West Indies. The West Indies, beyond raising 15,000 soldiers to serve in the West Indian Regiment, had donated some £60 million in today's money for the war effort. Although some islanders had rejected the "white man's war," others served to prove their loyalty and to earn equal treatment.

In December 1918 black soldiers of the British West Indies Regiment revolted at their base at Taranto, Italy, to protest against the racism they had encountered. Relegated to loading ammunition and cleaning the latrines of British soldiers, who referred to them as "West Indian 'Niggers'," the West Indian soldiers did not receive pay raises accorded other imperial troops because the War Office considered them "Natives." Their repeated requests for transfer to European battlefields elicited the answer that it was "against British tradition to employ aboriginal troops against a European enemy." Protests against such treatment accompanied the mutiny, which led to the arrest of fifty men and the disarming of some eight thousand men in eight West Indian battalions. The ringleaders went to prison, and the War Office repatriated the battalions. When other battalions of the West Indian Regiment arrived from the Middle East at Taranto in 1919, they also complained about their segregation and assignment as laborers to other units. None of them marched among the British forces in the 1919 victory parade in Paris.

Upon return home, demobilized soldiers led an insurrection in Belize, British Honduras, in July 1919 and a severe strike in Port-of-Spain, Trinidad, in December. Jamaican authorities remained apprehensive about unrest because non-commissioned officers from Taranto who had formed a "Caribbean League" to press for self-determination came from Jamaica. The government encouraged politicized soldiers to emigrate to Cuba, Colombia, and Venezuela. A secret colonial memorandum in 1919 acknowledged that "nothing we can do will alter the fact that the black man has begun to think and feel himself as good as the white." W.F. Elkins concluded that "The soldiers of the British West Indies Regiment began the national liberation struggle that eventually led to the demise of open colonial rule in most of the British Caribbean."[88] In 1962 former gunner Norman Manley, who had seen his brother blown to bits before his eyes, would lead Jamaica to independence and become its first prime minister.[89]

India

Although Australia, New Zealand, and Canada secured their independence from Great Britain as dominions within the Empire, India did not. Before the war the British ruled India and its population of more than 300 million people by a combination of divide and rule between various groups such as Hindus and Muslims, support for moderate politicians, and repression of any revolutionary or terrorist movements. The war had reduced the number of white soldiers, who defended the Northwest Frontier against warring tribes and Afghans, from more than 70,000 to 15,000 and provided an opportunity for revolutionaries such as Hindu nationalists and Muslim Pan-Islamists, the latter of whom held strong pro-Turkish sympathies.[90] The British government, which could already intern suspects without trial, responded with the repressive Defence of India Act in March 1915, with special courts meting out severe sentences of execution and life imprisonment and lengthy detention of suspects without trial in Bengal and Punjab, the sites of the strongest movements.

In 1917 Secretary of State Montagu proclaimed the "gradual development of self-governing institutions" as the objective of British policy in India. In the Government of India Act of 1919, the British government of India retained the key powers and offered little to Indian politicians, while enlarging the electorate to give the semblance of power.

Yet the war had drawn some 1.5 million Indians into service for the Empire, and brought heavy taxes, war loans, requisitions of grain and raw materials, and inflation. A very few entrepreneurs reaped huge profits by supplying the army with uniforms, for example, while most Indians suffered misery and declining living standards. Strikes of an embryonic trade union movement and food riots dotted the Indian landscape in 1918–19, along with near famine and the influenza epidemic in some regions. Although Bolshevism gained some adherents in India, internal developments in 1919 and 1920 propelled the rise of Mahatma Gandhi.

The Rowlatt Act of March 1919 attempted to make permanent the wartime system of special courts and detention and restrictions on civil rights. Gandhi organized a mass urban protest unifying Hindus, Muslims, and Sikhs that provoked a frightened British administration to excessive repression. In Amritsar, in the Punjab, Lieutenant Governor Brig. Gen. Reginald Dyer, already noted for brutality, opened fire on a peaceful unarmed demonstration, killing 379 and wounding some 1,200 people. He regretted only running out of ammunition and not employing an armored car for "moral" effect. Dyer then resorted to a reign of arrests, torture, public whippings, and humiliation. Sporadic violence by Indians elicited extreme violence from the British, with the final tally four whites killed, and at least 1,200 Indians killed and 3,600 wounded.

Prior to the massacre, Gandhi had hoped to cooperate with the British in constitutional reform. Now, the combination of Britain's disregard for Muslim concerns in its postwar treatment of Turkey, the Rowlatt Act, and Dyer's recourse to violence precluded cooperation with such an evil regime and launched Gandhi's first Non-Cooperation Movement with the backing of the moderate Indian National Congress.[91] Gandhi, however, the sole leader who might have capitalized on the revolutionary potential of the

situation, preferred non-violence. After outbreaks of violence, he called off
the campaign of non-cooperation early in 1922 after a year and a half. The
British crushed the movement and, in March 1922, carted Gandhi off to jail
to serve a six-year sentence.[92]

———

Thus did the war, fought to make the world safe for democracy, protect the
global rule of whites over other races. In this context the race riots in the
United States and the Amritsar massacre emerge as repressive measures that
attempted, but failed, to drown aspirations of emancipation and equality that
participation in the Great War evoked in blood. Ho Chi Minh, a waiter in
Paris during the Paris Peace Conference, found his petitions for the freedom
of Indo-China ignored, although the French had sent his countrymen to fight
in the Balkans and to labor in France. He and the Indo-Chinese, and the
colored peoples of the world, would realize their aspirations only after the
Second World War.

THE REIGN OF MYTH. THE GREAT WAR IN
LITERATURE AND ART

In the wake of war, defenders of the traditional order much exaggerated the
threat that Bolshevism, women, and oppressed races posed to their position.
These dangers assumed mythic proportions in their minds. But then, war
involves myth and fear, and a cataclysmic war, arousal of monstrous myths and
fears. Representations of the peace treaties, of mutilated victory on the part of
the Italians who did not gain all the territory they sought, of unfair burdens
placed upon Germany, rest more upon the interpretation of disillusioned
participants than a realistic assessment of the circumstances and limitations of
any unenforced peace after such a war. Fears and resultant myths of Bolshevik
threats to governments as secure as that of the United States, and the violent
responses to such fears, indicated the inability of forces of the traditional order
to place such threats in perspective after the upheaval of war.

The Novelists' and poets' depiction of women as unfaithful betrayers
enshrined a myth that the letters of peasant soldiers to their wives, which
express their love and trust to care for the children and farm, do not reflect.
The myth probably did not reflect the attitudes of soldiers from the lower
classes in general, yet such men formed the overwhelming majority of front
soldiers.

The rapid return of most soldiers to hearth and home, their perception of
class boundaries intact or at best blurred, also does not accord with the myth
of the violent front fighter incapable of demobilization and imbued with the
spirit of a unifying community. In Britain such men did fight in Russia or fill

the ranks of the Royal Irish Constabulary, the so-called Blacks and Tans, who waged a brutal war in Ireland against the IRA. The similar minority of German soldiers joined with youth, often university students, who regretted missing the Great War and yearned to prove themselves men by crushing Bolshevism and revolution, either within Germany or in the Baltic. In Italy they became fascist Arditi, the Blackshirts, who smashed the heads and aspirations of workers and peasants.

Once again the myth enshrines as gospel the attitudes and actions of the minority of middle- or lower-middle-class junior officers, whom the war's end robbed of status and position. The literary and intellectual predilections of the few, not the actions of the many, have formed the basis of much of the history and legacy of the war. Most postwar veterans' associations fought, not in the streets as paramilitaries, but as interest groups for better benefits for soldiers and their families. Ironically, when the London police, most of whom were veterans, went on strike for better wages after the war, the press reviled them as unpatriotic.

The experience of Adolf Hitler and the Nazis in Germany exemplifies the pervasive power of myths from 1914–18, as historian Peter Fritzsche shows. Hitler, a decorated *Frontsoldat*, firmly believed the myths that lenient military justice led to the decline of the German Army and that the collapse of the home front had caused Germany's loss of the war. He resolved to re-create the *Volksgemeinschaft*, the mythical classless, unified society proclaimed in the civil peace of 1914.[93]

The front experience, or *Fronterlebnis*, that writers such as Ernst Jünger exalted, allegedly created a new man, a "technological warrior," "willful, amoral, cool, functional, and hardened." These men, forged in struggle, would form a new *Gemeinschaft*, or community. Popularized ideas of Jünger's works influenced many German soldiers of the Second World War. Raised in the Nazi era, soldiers' letters home from the front and their cold-blooded conduct demonstrated this influence. Nazi propaganda played on such themes, linking the trench fighters of 1918 to the soldiers of 1939–45.[94]

The myth of the *Volksgemeinschaft* of the First World War attracted the next generation despite the disintegration in 1918. "The secret of Nazi popularity lay in . . . reviving the passions of 1914. National Socialism, based on the model of 'trench socialism' that Hitler held so dear,"[95] would forge a national community, beyond all classes, like the community of the front soldier, where death recognized no distinction. "Both Hitler and the army leaders thus shared a vision in which the revered *Frontgemeinschaft* of World War I would be transformed into a permanent state of affairs."[96] The front community became the basis for a national community in Nazi Germany, as young German males served in the Hitler Youth, then the Labor Service, and ultimately the armed forces, adhering to the values of "camaraderie, sacrifice, loyalty, duty, endurance, courage, obedience."[97]

Concentration on the myths linking the two wars may misrepresent the actual experience of many front soldiers. Benjamin Ziemann's study of Bavarian peasant soldiers from 1914 to 1923 suggests that the cohesion of the troops lay not in a mythicized sense of front unity but primarily in the military structure.[98] The alleged *Frontkameradschaft* did not overcome rank and class. Peasant soldiers loathed the war, which made them feel impotent to affect its course. They fought in the expectation of the nearest time of relief, either food, rest, or leave, and not for some metaphysical justification that a small minority of educated middle-class soldiers required. Their hard, monotonous life on the land led them to expect nothing positive from a war that their hardiness enabled them to endure. After 1916, however, the annexationist propaganda of powerful interest groups convinced them that prosecution of the war opposed their own interests, and the determination of the monarchy and officer corps to continue disillusioned them. Facing a hopeless situation in the fall of 1918, they simply refused to fight and deserted for home.

Peasant soldiers did not lose their identity, their attachment to farm and family, and they desired to return to this life. Once the armistice enabled them to do so, they returned to their villages and the Catholicism of their prewar life. Postwar paramilitary organizations such as the *Freikorps* and the *Stahlhelm*, which connected the front experience (*Fronterlebnis*) and political power, nationalism, and anti-Semitism in the Weimar Republic, held little attraction for the great majority of such former soldiers. During the Weimar Republic the radical right created the image of an enduring and dominant front experience, but this had less to do with the actual wartime experience than with contemporary political aims. Ziemann concludes that in fact, Nazi propaganda led to a considerable radicalization of militarism, racism, and brutalization that differentiated and distanced the first from the second conflict.

In many respects the myth of the "Lost Generation," those future leaders of Europe who fell on the battlefields of the war, proved among the most potent and debilitating beliefs to emerge from the war. The young intellectuals who believed and lamented this slaughter were referring, of course, to the fallen members of their group and class, and not to the millions who had died for the same causes. The long lists of the dead in the chapels of Oxford and Cambridge attest to the appropriate and necessary sacrifice of the youth of the ruling elite in the random slaughter of war. To dwell upon the dead as the best of the generation, and the living as less, posed serious problems for those who elevated the dead to mythical proportions. It attested to the sense of guilt of the survivors and their inability to comprehend why war had spared them. It also alienated these survivors from the world about them, deprived them of the will to act constructively, or provided an excuse for their aimlessness and anomie.

Finally, the portrayal of the war by the so-called angry young men, such as Siegfried Sassoon and Robert Graves in Britain, left an indelible and formative sense of the war for later generations. Bitterness and alienation, the recollections of idyllic times past never to return, the sense of a generation duped by its elders into heedless sacrifice – all infuse the work of Sassoon, Graves, Erich Maria Remarque, and others. On the other hand, Ernst Jünger's exaltation of war and the modern warrior provided a cold-blooded antidote to condemnations of the slaughter.

Yet, first of all these portrayals reflect their individual experience and the personalities of their authors. Jünger, a particularly cold and distant individual, steeped himself in the ethos of the Prussian officer of duty, honor, and loyalty to the Fatherland and served heroically throughout the war. His writings then provided the intellectual justification for a future generation of even more vicious Nazi front fighters. Sassoon, although an instinctively courageous fighter, as his nickname "Mad Jack" suggested, was far too intelligent, sensitive, and independent an individual to accept the platitudes that politicians and press offered as justifications for war by 1917. Sassoon courageously rejected the entire enterprise. His friend Robert Graves, equally aware of both the dangers and the ambiguities in Sassoon's open stance against the war, tried to protect his friend as he struggled to deal with similar feelings. Jünger suffered innumerable wounds, always to return to the war, and both Graves and Sassoon, though wounded, would return to service. Remarque, author of perhaps the most acclaimed war novel of all time, *All Quiet on the Western Front*, published in 1929, did not soldier long before grievous wounds precluded his further service at the front. *All Quiet*, like other literature, extols the comradeship and alienation that all front-line soldiers experienced, but in the context of a wasteful, senseless slaughter that inexorably consumes all its protagonists and led the Nazis later not only to condemn the book as anti-war, but also to ban the movie and place Remarque on trial. These representations of the war certainly reflect accurately the response of a certain segment of society – the young, middle-class, educated intelligentsia that the war scarred and traumatized. Their attitudes likely did not represent the majority sentiment of war veterans, but their writings created powerful representations and myths of the war experience that continue to evoke feelings decades after the war.

It would be easy to lose the postwar experience of many of the veterans in such myths, but the experience varied with the individual. Beyond the many disabled and ailing pensioners on government rolls, large numbers of former soldiers suffered from post-traumatic stress. Veterans, whose memories kept them awake at night, encountered others in their same predicament as they walked the streets of towns and cities. Some, unable to communicate, withdrew from society; others either could not find work or keep jobs if they secured them. For many, return to the bosom of loving families, an understanding community, and previous work proved sufficient salvation; for others, nothing could save consciences ravaged by the guilt of random survival when they had seen friends mangled or torn to bits, or subconscious minds whose dreams conjured such horrors that they feared sleep. Some, coal-miners, for example, who had led such deprived and dangerous prewar lives that war seemed no riskier, returned to endure more of the same degrading existence. Finally, in numbers that grew with distance from the event, many a veteran would celebrate the war as the high point of his life, the escape from a humdrum daily existence, the confrontation with the ultimate danger – death – which he had survived and surmounted.

Among the artists' representation of war, C.R.W. Nevinson's works *Returning to the Trenches 1914* and *French Troops Resting 1916* portray the war's mechanization and dehumanization of men. The soldiers, their faces angular, their uniformed bodies and packs geometrical, their metal helmets and implements gleaming, their cleanliness and precision striking, have become cogs in the machine of war. William Barnes Wollen's painting *Canadians at Ypres* strikes a heroic image, as the men, handsome, shaven, and clean, rise from their trench to counter-attack an onrushing and undifferentiated mass of Germans. In John Nash's painting *Oppy Wood, 1917*, a stark and barren landscape, punctuated by the splintered stumps of a few destroyed trees, dwarfs two British soldiers, the one standing on the fire step, the other on duckboards at the bottom of a deep, cleanly cut trench that leads to the entrance of a well-fortified bunker. Everything – the soldiers, the trees, even the dirt – is immaculate. John Singer Sargent's painting *Gassed* captures a line of blinded soldiers, their eyes covered, bandages round their heads, each with his hand or hands on the shoulders or back of the man in front, surrounded by blinded troops lying about on the ground. A soccer game proceeds in front of tents in the background. The soldiers, whether standing or prone, in their bandages and uniforms, exude a purity and calm, their fine, handsome, and boyish features at peace.

In these paintings one searches in vain for the pain and agony, the blood and gore, the fear and panic, the lust and savagery of men in war. The mud and slime, debris, decay, and disorder have disappeared. In general men do not become machines, stay clean, or suffer heroically and stoically when wounded. They bleed, vomit, scream, curse, soil themselves. The photography of the war depicts it no more graphically than the art, as the war antedated combat photography. Certainly, graphic pictures of corpses abound, but invariably of dead enemy. Otherwise, men are marching or riding to and from war, firing artillery, or rising and charging into the unknown.

Among the war artists, the German Otto Dix, who served as a machine-gunner on the Eastern and Western Front during the war, almost alone captures the truly gruesome nature of the First World War. Dix viewed the war as apocalypse, which destroyed, deformed, and mutilated the human body. Only after the war did he realize how profound a shock the war imparted, as for years afterward he crawled constantly through the ruins of war in his dreams. Dix's collection *Der Krieg. Radierwerk 1924* and his *Triptychons*, in which wild, unshaven, barely human men reduced to the state of animals, not machines, live among the dead in a gruesome and grotesque wasteland, in which the wounded lie or flee in abject terror, the dying suffer ghastly wounds, exemplifies the ability of an artist to capture the essence of war better than his peers and the photographers of the time. *Der Krieg* ends with a sketch of a German soldier raping a nun, the sort of atrocity that Entente propaganda relished, but here the final atrocity in a collection that demonstrates the atrocious nature of the war.

THE START OF A THIRTY YEARS' WAR?

The obvious links between the First and Second World Wars have given rise in some historical circles, particularly in France, to the concept of a "thirty years' war," with a "twenty years' peace" in between. The connection of the Great War to the rise of fascism and the disarray in the democracies leads ultimately to the question of the relationship of the Great War to its successor, the Second World War. After the First World War, a weakened Britain preoccupied with its empire and an isolationist United States intent on withdrawing all presence except financial from Europe left a gravely wounded France to confront an embittered, unrepentant, and only temporarily impaired Germany. The manner of Germany's resurgence, in particular after the Great Depression with Hitler's rise to power, resulted in another, larger war. This time, to avoid repeating the result of the first war, the Allies fought to unconditional surrender, occupied Germany, and tried German war criminals for their transgressions against humanity.

John Keegan, referring directly to the "legacy of political rancour and racial hatred so intense," to Adolf Hitler, "demobilised front fighter" who on 18 September 1922 vowed "vengeance!" for the two million fallen Germans in the First World War, ultimately judged the Second World War "the direct outcome of the First" and "in large measure its continuation."[99] "Totalitarianism," Keegan considered "the political continuation of war by other means."[100] He concludes: "The First World War inaugurated the manufacture of mass death that the Second brought to a pitiless consummation."[101] Systems of forced labor, censorship, justification by an elaborate ideology, and the perversion of language began with colonialism in Africa, intensified during the war, and became part and parcel of totalitarian systems of Nazi Germany and Soviet Russia. Images of the Great War abounded in the Second World War, in particular that of the hardened front fighter. Sons of soldier fathers retread the same ground as the parent, in some cases where the father had died. In particular, the bloody struggle in the rubble of Stalingrad resurrected German historical recollections of Verdun.

By the mid-1920s many Frenchmen believed that the Germans would come again. The small classes of French conscripts in the late 1930s, the result of the soldiers killed in 1914–18, provided palpable evidence of the Pyrrhic nature of France's victory in 1918. The French collapse in 1940 and the Vichy Regime overshadowed their valiant sacrifice in 1914–18. The only major French figure of 1914–18 still alive, Marshal Philippe Pétain, capitulated to and collaborated with the Germans. The pessimistic old soldier believed that he saved France from further blood-letting at the hands of an even more formidable Germany.

Yet Charles de Gaulle, Pétain's early protégé, refused to accept defeat in 1940 and proclaimed a resistance from Britain. De Gaulle, who attributed the German defeat in 1918 to moral collapse, believed in the concept of a thirty years' war. If the invasion of 1940 continued the Germans' war of 1914–18, de Gaulle's resistance resumed his unfinished war. Captured as an infantry captain at Verdun, he had spent the rest of the war attempting to escape from German captivity. Col. de Gaulle, proponent of a professional, armored, elite force, had a score to settle with the Germans, and continued the struggle from abroad. In all countries the first war generation rose to power to fight the second.

The stability of the Weimar Republic, the various treaties from Locarno in 1925 culminating in the Kellogg–Briand Pact of 1928, and the disarmament movement in the late 1920s and early 1930s offered prospects of a peaceful future. On the other hand, German rearmament proceeded apace. Certainly the year 1929 posed a distinct divide. Foch and Clemenceau died that year. German conservative and former monarchist Gustav Stresemann, whose ministerial policies balancing between Russia and the western powers enabled the peaceful establishment of Weimar Germany's position, also died that fateful year. Poincaré lived until 1934, ending his life in his bed facing east, convinced that the Germans would come again.

The mid-point between Versailles in 1919 and the outbreak of war in Europe in 1939, the year 1929 also marked the onslaught of the Great Depression in the United States. Wall Street exported the disaster to central Europe by calling in American short-term loans initially established in the Dawes Plan of 1924 to stabilize the German mark. Central Europeans had invested them in long-term projects. German and other economies consequently collapsed like a house of cards, the harshness of their depression second only to that in the United States. Within a decade, Germany had experienced hyperinflation and Great Depression, the former growing directly from the war, the latter indirectly from the financial connections established in postwar agreements. Furthermore, the outcome of the war of 1914–18 thrust the United States prematurely into a position of global financial leadership that it lacked the expertise to assume.

Adolf Hitler and the Nazis rose to power as a result of the depression in Germany in 1933. The Weimar Republic had already undertaken rearmament, and the German Army's junior officer corps had become Nazi by 1930. Hitler's unlimited ambitions and rabid anti-Semitism, all discussed openly in *Mein Kampf* in 1925, made another war highly likely. Hitler, no "typical German statesmen" as A.J.P. Taylor once contended, differed from his predecessors Bismarck and Stresemann in the unlimited nature of his aims and his plans to use Germany as the instrument to create his Aryan super-state.

The proponents of a "thirty years' war" focus entirely on European affairs. Attention to East Asia, where the war of 1914–18 diminished the presence of the European imperial powers, leaving the region open to the Japanese, strengthens but nuances the case for a thirty-year conflict. Japan displayed the same unlimited ambitions in Asia as Hitler's Germany did in Europe, but even earlier, in 1931. The Japanese Army's naked aggression in Manchuria and China elicited warnings from the United States that heightened long-term Japanese naval concerns about American power in the Pacific. These concerns culminated ultimately in the Japanese attack on Pearl Harbor on 7 December 1941, after which Hitler declared war on the United States.

Until 1941, two separate wars raged – the Japanese conquest of east Asia, and the Nazi conquest of western Europe. In 1941, with Hitler's invasion of Russia in June and the Japanese attack on Pearl Harbor in December, the two merged into a world war. Although a global perspective thus undermines the notion of a twenty years' peace, it substantiates the idea of a thirty years' war. Since conflict continued in eastern Europe at least until 1921, and certainly began at the latest in Asia by 1931, a global perspective reduces the era of peace within the thirty years' war to ten years.

INTO THE TWENTY-FIRST CENTURY

W.E.B. DuBois, writing in 1903, presciently argued that the problem of the twentieth century would be the "color line." DuBois would later locate the roots of the war in European imperialism in Africa. The color line, etched by the poverty and arrested development engendered by European colonial and imperial domination, demarcates a global divide that will remain the problem of the twenty-first century as well. Two world wars did little to lessen this gap, although they did force the imperial powers to relinquish their empires.

The lingering effect of the First World War proves evident even upon the historians who write about it. Many dedicate their books to the members of their family who fought and died in it. Niall Ferguson observes "The first World War remains the worst thing the people of my country have ever had to endure,"[102] that twice as many Britons were killed in it as in the Second World War. It remains "the forgotten war" to many Americans, who fail to note that the war was "a watershed in American history," a first step on America's road to "globalism" and a war in which the American financial contribution was "immense and arguably decisive."[103]

In diplomacy the notion of a League of Nations based on collective security and international solidarity certainly heralded a new era of international relations, despite the League's failure to prevent war in the 1930s. The League represented a step, however flawed, on the road of international cooperation toward the United Nations.[104] Historian Jon Jacobson suggests that the legacy of Versailles was a "seventy-year crisis" of European civil war, the rise of communism and fascism, inflation and depression, a second world war, and a bipolar system that ended only in 1989.[105] Even then, war in the Balkans in the 1990s awakened the specter of the origins of the Great War.

The First World War, with its ceremonies, monuments, and memorials, has more recently attracted scholars of mourning, who analyze the artifacts and relate them to their cultural, social, and political contexts, at national and even regional levels. This specific focus accords with a more general tendency among historians to dichotomize between the military and political history of the war and the social, economic, and cultural, with the emphasis increasingly on the latter fields. Such a dichotomy impedes fuller comprehension of the war, because all the fields interact.

Even to the less analytical observer, the powerful, barrel-chested eagles that guard the entrance to the American cemetery at Romagne impart a feeling of triumph. In contrast, the often mournful statues of European memorials include dead soldiers in their presentation. These initial impressions correspond to the contrasting experiences of the United States and Europe in the war: the former short and victorious; the latter long and debilitating, whether victor or vanquished.

Triumphs and memorials notwithstanding, the Great War imparts a sense of a tragedy of enormous proportions. Europeans, in their hubristic determination to rule the rest of the world, destroyed their own. The class-bound and imperialist governments of the time willingly consigned the men of their countries and empires to unparalleled slaughter, and expended their wealth and knowledge to improve and increase the implements of destruction. Their arrogance and exhortatory, excessive propaganda drove them to become the agents of their own annihilation. Their approaching exhaustion and collapse finally ended the conflict. The Great War originated in imperialism; the victors gained in empire, while the losers not only lost their empires but also their own imperial states. Disillusion and despair gripped all, because any reason, any aim, any goal, any gain, and any commemoration paled before the havoc they had wrought. No peace in the conditions of 1919 could lay to rest the demonic passions that four years of war had evoked. The war had solved no problems before it and left many more in its wake, which gave rise to its even more destructive spawn.

The First World War remains with us today. At Ypres, in Belgium, under the arch commemorating British Empire war dead, a trumpeter sounds the Last Post, as British schoolchildren in their uniforms place wreathes in the niches of the arch. Near Péronne in the Somme region, travelers on the *autoroute* and the high-speed railroad pass numerous battlefields and cemeteries hidden by the rolling terrain and small groves of trees. The noise and activity of road and rail contrast with the peaceful quiet of the land. Here the dead – French, African, British, Dominion, Indian, and German soldiers – rest in well-kept cemeteries, large and small. Occasionally ordnance long buried in the soil explodes, killing the unfortunates who unearthed it, a reminder that the war still reaps a grim harvest eighty years later. Along the country roads in the Meuse-Argonne region, yellow signs with a red line through the names on them mark the site of towns the war destroyed, never to rise again.

War, though large entities wage it, exacts its price from the individual and family. In summer 2000 I decided to visit the tiny French town where my Great-Uncle Thomas won the Distinguished Service Cross and the *Croix de Guerre* in 1918. He died in his thirties, leaving memories and medals. Cemeteries – African, French, and German – dotted the way. Despite the steady rain, I stopped frequently to walk among the stone and wood markers and to read the entries in the visitors' books kept in small vaults at the cemetery entrance. In one cemetery lies a father killed in 1915 who left five orphans, the youngest 20 months old. His only daughter, then 7 years old, would in turn have a daughter, the note's author, whom the Second World War would orphan – at the age of 7. Some descendants had just located the graves of their loved ones in 1999, while others still searched in vain for the final resting place of their dead. One short note, written firmly and legibly, left me in tears and will remain with me forever, just as the Great War should with us.

17 July 2000.
To you, my father whom I never knew, I have traveled far to see you again for the last time (if you only knew how much I have missed you).
. . . (I'm eighty-six years old!) and I don't think I will be able to travel easily.
Your daughter whom you often wrote.
Émilienne Raspault to her father Émile Raspault (killed in action 1915)

NOTES

1 THE ORIGINS OF WAR, 1871–1914

1 (London, 1995), 84.
2 (New York, 1996), 213.
3 Eric Hobsbawm, *The Age of Empire, 1875–1914* (New York, 1987). Arno J. Mayer, *The Persistence of the Old Regime: Europe to the Great War* (New York, 1981). George Lichtheim, *Europe in the Twentieth Century* (New York, 1972), 31.
4 Crook, *Darwinism*, 1–24.
5 Lindqvist, *Exterminate*, 2–3.
6 Boemeke *et al.*, *Anticipating*, 246.
7 Boemeke *et al.*, *Anticipating*, 392.
8 *Chronicle of Higher Education*, "Leopold's Congo: A Holocaust We Have Yet to Comprehend," May 12, 2000, B4.
9 Crook, *Darwinism*, 25.
10 Friedberg, *Titan*, 220.
11 Hobson, *Imperialism*, 11, 154–7, 174–5, 159, 282, 211, 222, 227, 136–7, 311–12.
12 Boemeke *et al.*, *Anticipating*, 247.
13 Offer, *Agrarian*, 173–5, 188–97, 204–5, 209.
14 Friedberg, *Titan*, 24–6.
15 Friedberg, *Titan*, 137.
16 Friedberg, *Titan*, 248, 259.
17 Friedberg, *Titan*, 278.
18 Keegan, *First World War* (*FWW*), 28.
19 Boemeke *et al.*, *Anticipating*, 348–61, quote 361.
20 Adams, *Adventure*, 59–61.
21 Eckart Kehr, *Battleship Building and Party Politics in Germany* (Chicago, 1975).
22 Holger H. Herwig, *'Luxury' Fleet. The German Imperial Navy 1888–1918* (London, 1980).
23 George Dangerfield, *Strange Death of Liberal England* (London, 1935).
24 Kent, *Gender*, 262.
25 Oron J. Hale, *The Great Illusion, 1900–1914* (New York, 1971). L.L. Farrar, Jr., *The Short War Illusion: German Policy, Strategy and Domestic Affairs, August–December 1914* (ABC-Clio, 1973).
26 Balesi, *Adversaries*, *passim*.
27 Ferguson, *Pity*, 1.
28 Hobson, *Imperialism*, 214.
29 Adams, *Adventure*, xiv.
30 Adams, *Adventure*, 6–8.
31 Kent, *Gender*, 236–7.
32 Adams, *Adventure*, 59–61.
33 Adams, *Adventure*, 72.
34 Schoellgen, *Escape*.
35 Boemeke *et al.*, *Anticipating*, 167–87 *passim*, quote 187.
36 Darrow, *French*, 12.
37 Darrow, *French*, 9–46.
38 Stromberg, *Redemption*. Crook, *Darwinism*.
39 Boemeke *et al.*, *Anticipating*, 363–4.
40 Chickering and Förster, *Great War*, 299–300.
41 Ferguson, *Pity*, 20–30, quote 30.
42 Ferguson, *Pity*, 140, 132, 136–7, 105–25.
43 Morrow, *Great War*.
44 Friedberg, *Titan*, 295, ftn. 8.
45 Kojevnikov, "Great War," 1–2.
46 Halpern, *Naval FWW*, 4.
47 Keegan, *FWW*, 19.
48 See Clarke, *War*, *passim*.

49 Offer, *Agrarian*, 322–30, quote 324.
50 Ferguson, *Pity*, 83–7.
51 Ferguson, *Pity*, 83–7.
52 See Paul Kennedy, *The Rise of the Anglo-German Antagonism 1860–1914* (London, 1980).
53 Offer, *Agrarian*, 232.
54 Ferguson, *Pity*, 83–7.
55 Offer, *Agrarian*, 221–5, 253–7, 294, 265–9.
56 Offer, *Agrarian*, 226–9, 235, 239, 241, 243, 285–310, 4–7.
57 Cited in Friedberg, *Titan*, 293–4.
58 Friedberg, *Titan*, 301–2.
59 Ferguson, *Pity*, 67.
60 Ferguson, *Pity*, 56–67, 103–4.
61 Boemeke *et al.*, *Anticipating*, 393.
62 Joll, *Origins*, 164.
63 Boemeke *et al.*, *Anticipating*, 366.
64 Snyder, *Ideology*, *passim*.

65 Keegan, *FWW*, 27.
66 Gerhard Ritter, *The Schlieffen Plan* (New York, 1959).
67 Echevarria, "Legacy," 1–8; *Clausewitz*.
68 Friedberg, *Titan*, 275.
69 Ferguson, *Pity*, 83–7.
70 Keegan, *FWW*, 23.
71 Offer, *Agrarian*, 322–30.
72 New York, 1967. New York, 1975.
73 Ferguson, *Pity*, 161–4, 168–73.
74 Ferguson, *Pity*, 145–51.
75 Offer, *Agrarian*, 352.
76 Keegan, *FWW*, 46–7.
77 Keegan, *FWW*, 426, 3.
78 A18.
79 Prior and Wilson, *FWW*, 26.
80 Joll, *Origins*, 167.

2 1914. THE "BIG SHOW" OPENS

1 Chickering and Förster, *Great War*, 117.
2 Macdonald, *1914*, 418.
3 See Fritzsche, *Germans*, 20–2. Ziemann, *Front*, 463.
4 Fritzsche, *Germans*, 13–29.
5 Cornwall, *Undermining*,16–22.
6 Macdonald, *1914–1918*, 38.
7 Macdonald, *1914*, 82, 88.
8 Macdonald, *1914–1918*, 17–20.
9 Macdonald, *1914–1918*, 22.
10 Mosier, *Myth*, 111.
11 Chickering and Förster, *Great War*, 301–3, 325.
12 Macdonald, *1914*, 333–8.
13 Hirschfeld, Krumeich, and Renz, *"Keiner,"* 56–9.
14 Chickering and Förster, *Great War*, 117–18.
15 McPhail, *Silence*.
16 Stone, *Eastern*, 94.
17 Sondhaus, *Conrad*, 139–63.
18 For this and following material, see Fromkin, *Peace*, 40–109, and Karsh, *Empires*, 105–40. On war, see Erickson, *Ordered*, 7–22.

19 Halpern, *Naval WWI*, 23.
20 Halpern, *Naval WWI*, 36.
21 Wilson, *Decisions*, 223.
22 Halpern, *Naval WWI*, 93.
23 Halpern, *Naval WWI*, 83.
24 Farwell, *Africa*, 163, 165.
25 Chickering and Förster, *Great War*, 410.
26 Chickering and Förster, *Great War*, 438–41.
27 Moyer, *Victory*, 81–2.
28 Chickering and Förster, *Great War*, 49.
29 Chickering and Förster, *Great War*, 352–3.
30 Chickering and Förster, *Great War*, 248–540.
31 Chickering and Förster, *Great War*, 289.
32 Chickering and Förster, *Great War*, 37–41.
33 Jeffery, *Ireland*, 6–12.
34 Offer, *Agrarian*, 315.
35 Chickering and Förster, *Great War*, 65.
36 Kent, *Making Peace*, 12.
37 Macdonald, *1914–1918*, 53.

38 Kent, *Making Peace*, 29, 14–30 *passim*.
39 Gullace, "Propaganda," 714–40.
40 Gullace, "Propaganda," 715.
41 Gullace, "Propaganda," 729.
42 Chickering and Förster, *Great War*, 80.
43 Lincoln, *Passage*, 43–4.
44 Chickering and Förster, *Great War*, 134–5.
45 Christian S. Davis, "For *Freiheit, Kultur,* and *Humanität.* The Viennese Jewish Outlook on the First World War, 1914–1915," MA thesis, (University of Georgia, 1998), *passim*.

46 Hanna, *Mobilization*, 78–105.
47 Macdonald, *1914*, 381, 421.
48 Macdonald, *1914*, 420.
49 Mosier, *Myth*, 120–1.
50 Macdonald, *1914–1918*, 46–7.
51 Macdonald, *1914–1918*, 52.
52 Macdonald, *1914–1918*, 116–17.
53 Miquel, *Poilus*, 179–84.
54 Hanna, *Mobilization*, 62.
55 Adams, *Adventure*, 100.
56 Hirschfeld *et al.*, "*Keiner*," 59.
57 Macdonald, *1914*, 418.
58 Chickering and Förster, *Great War*, 140.
59 Lincoln, *Passage*, 89–103.

3 1915. AN INSIGNIFICANT YEAR?

1 Omissi, *Indian*, 32.
2 Tuffrau, *1914–1918*, 73.
3 Tuffrau, *1914–1918*, 90.
4 Erickson, *Ordered*, xv.
5 Chickering and Förster, *Great War*, 438–41.
6 Mosier, *Myth*, 175–6.
7 Mosier, *Myth*, 175.
8 Miquel, *Poilus*, 208–9.
9 Macdonald, *1914–1918*, 84.
10 Chickering and Förster, *Great War*, 95–111.
11 Miquel, *Poilus*, 178, 228.
12 Miquel, *Poilus*, 233.
13 Macdonald, *1914–1918*, 104–6.
14 Omissi, *Indian*, 7.
15 Omissi, *Indian*, 27–8.
16 Omissi, *Indian*, 32.
17 Omissi, *Indian*, 45.
18 Omissi, *Indian*, 98.
19 Omissi, *Indian*, 61, 63, 80.
20 Omissi, *Indian*, 110.
21 Omissi, *Indian*, 102.
22 Mills, *Strange War*, 54–5.
23 Balesi, *Adversaries*, 88.
24 Mosier, *Myth*, 162.
25 McPhail, *Silence*, 55.
26 Herwig, *FWW*, 147.
27 On *Ober Ost*, see Liulevicius, *War Land*, 1–125.
28 Herwig, *FWW*, 158.

29 Panayi, *Minorities*, 57–8.
30 Erickson, *Ordered*, 95–104.
31 Melson, *Genocide*, 148.
32 Moorhouse, *Hell's Foundations*, 124–40.
33 Macdonald, *1914–1918*, 73.
34 Macdonald, *1914–1918*, 99–100.
35 Turkish figures from Erickson, *Ordered*, 94.
36 Williams, *Anzacs*, 110.
37 Panayi, *Minorities*, 263–74.
38 Williams, *Anzacs*, 23–5, 82–3.
39 Williams, *Anzacs*, 110.
40 Page, *Chiwaya War*, 16.
41 Şaul and Royer, *African*, 1, 14, 24–5.
42 Şaul and Royer, *African*, 127–8.
43 Şaul and Royer, *African*, 141–58.
44 Şaul and Royer, *African*, 158–72.
45 Farwell, *Africa*, 107.
46 Halpern, *Naval FWW*, 103.
47 Halpern, *Naval FWW*, 48.
48 Hardach, *FWW*, 39–41.
49 Halpern, *Naval FWW*, 191.
50 Halpern, *Naval FWW*, 139.
51 Halpern, *Naval FWW*, 150.
52 Downs, *Gender*, 32–3.
53 Downs, *Gender*, 35.
54 Chickering and Förster, *Great War*, 46.
55 Kent, *Making Peace*, 31–41.

56 Following from Levine, "Battle," 104–30.
57 Levine, "Battle," 110.
58 Omissi, *Indian*, 104.
59 Omissi, *Indian*, 114.
60 Omissi, *Indian*, 119.
61 Omissi, *Indian*, 123.
62 Omissi, *Indian*, 127.
63 Omissi, *Indian*, 42.
64 Vance, *Death*, 198–9.
65 Downs, *Gender*, 26.
66 Downs, *Gender*, 30.
67 Hardach, *FWW*, 88–9.
68 Downs, *Gender*, 40.
69 Lunn, *Memoirs*, 66.
70 Chickering and Förster, *Great War*, 252–3.
71 Procacci, "Protest," 34.
72 Tomassini, "Mobilization," 59–63.
73 Coetzee and Coetzee, *Authority*, 3–12.

74 Tomassini, "Mobilization," 36–7.
75 Chickering and Förster, *Great War*, 50.
76 Daniel, *War*, 24–5, 26–9, 58–60.
77 Davis, *Home Fires*, 48–113 *passim*.
78 Chickering and Förster, *Great War*, 354.
79 Liulevicius, *War Land*, 165–70.
80 Florinsky, *End*, 52.
81 Hardach, *FWW*, 92–4.
82 Kojevnikov, "Great War," *passim*.
83 Wynn, *Progressivism*, 22.
84 Wrigley, *FWW*, 115.
85 Hardach, *FWW*, 62.
86 Downs, Gender, 16,18.
87 Chickering and Förster, *Great War*, 85.
88 Chickering and Förster, *Great War*, 140–1.
89 Chickering and Förster, *Great War*, 120.

4 1916. TOTAL WAR

1 Chickering and Förster, *Great War*, 119.
2 Farwell, *Africa*, 294.
3 Miquel, *Poilus*, 281.
4 Morrow, *Great War*, 134.
5 Herwig, *FWW*, 297–9.
6 Chickering and Förster, *Great War*, 101–2.
7 Chickering and Förster, *Great War*, 113–14.
8 Mosier, *Myth*, 230.
9 Lunn, *Memoirs*, 139.
10 Lunn, *Memoirs*, 137.
11 Macdonald, *1914–1918*, 155, 160–1.
12 Morton and Granatstein, *Marching*, 52.
13 Keegan, *FWW*, 296.
14 Macdonald, *1914–1918*, 169–71.
15 Macdonald, *1914–1918*, 178.
16 Omissi, *Indian*, 228.
17 Omissi, *Indian*, 257–8.
18 Morton and Granatstein, *Marching*, 135.
19 Mosier, *Myth*, 233.
20 Herwig, *FWW*, 209, 213.
21 Rauchensteiner, *Der Tod*, 373.

22 Omissi, *Indian*, 144, 165.
23 Omissi, *Indian*, 232, 159–60, 168, 199.
24 Fromkin, *Peace*, 168–98.
25 Şaul and Royer, *African*, 212.
26 Şaul and Royer, *African*, 230.
27 Şaul and Royer, *African*, 4–5.
28 Farwell, *Africa*, 266.
29 Farwell, *Africa*, 297–8.
30 Halpern, *Naval FWW*, 316.
31 Halpern, *Naval FWW*, 319.
32 Halpern, *Naval FWW*, 328.
33 Halpern, *Naval FWW*, 333.
34 Halpern, *Naval FWW*, 336.
35 Downs, *Gender*, 64–5.
36 Kent, *Making Peace*, 82.
37 Hennessy, *Ireland*, 198. See also Jeffery, *Ireland*, 37–58.
38 Kent, *Making Peace*, 42–5.
39 Gardner, *Line*, 111–12.
40 Gardner, *Line*, 115.
41 Kent, *Making Peace*, 59–60.
42 Kent, *Making Peace*, 60–61.
43 Kent, *Making Peace*, 62, from n.20.
44 Kent, *Making Peace*, 67.
45 Kent, *Making Peace*, 63–73.

46 Wilson, *Myriad*, 392.
47 Wilson, *Myriad*, 406.
48 Wilson, *Myriad*, 418.
49 Downs, *Gender*, 50.
50 Downs, *Gender*, 52.
51 Downs, *Gender*, 60.
52 Lunn, *Memoirs*, 103.
53 Page, *Africa*, 37–8.
54 Lunn, *Memoirs*, 106–86.
55 Godfrey, *Capitalism*, 56.
56 Miquel, *Poilus*, 302.
57 Becker *et al.*, *14–18*, 137–43.
58 Roberts, *Reconstructing*, 19.
59 Roberts, *Reconstructing*, 31.
60 Roberts, *Reconstructing*, 33.
61 Procacci, "Protest," 36.

62 Moyer, *Victory*, 148.
63 Davis, *Home Fires*, 179, previous material 114–69.
64 Rauchensteiner, *Der Tod*, 371.
65 Rauchensteiner, *Der Tod*, 391.
66 Rauchensteiner, *Der Tod*, 397.
67 Rauchensteiner, *Der Tod*, 405.
68 Lincoln, *Passing*, 215.
69 Lincoln, *Passing*, 312, above from pp. 215–37, 261–312.
70 Dickinson, *Ordered*, 119–53.
71 Chickering and Förster, *Great War*, 488–90.
72 Gullace, "Propaganda," 743.
73 Macdonald, *1914–1918*, 181–2.

5 1917. CLIMAX

1 Lincoln, *Passage*, 312.
2 Herwig, *FWW*, 345.
3 Lemarchand, "Lettres," 80.
4 Herwig, *FWW*, 346.
5 McPhail, *Silence*, 75–87, 163–84.
6 Lemarchand, "Lettres," 92.
7 Lemarchand, "Lettres," 53.
8 Lemarchand, "Lettres," 79.
9 Lunn, *Memoirs*, 139.
10 Lunn, *Memoirs*, 139.
11 Lunn, *Memoirs*, 139.
12 Miquel, *Poilus*, 326–7.
13 Keegan, *FWW*, 329.
14 Lemarchand, "Lettres," 94–6.
15 Chickering and Förster, *Great War*, 316.
16 Chickering and Förster, *Great War*, 287–8.
17 Macdonald, *1914–1918*, 210–1.
18 Keegan, *FWW*, 358. Chickering and Förster, *Great War*, 104. Mosier, *Myth*, 282–3.
19 Keegan, *FWW*, 361.
20 Macdonald, *1914–1918*, 243–7.
21 Macdonald, *1914–1918*, 247.
22 Macdonald, *1914–1918*, 248.
23 Keegan, *FWW*, 368.
24 Mosier, *Myth*, 284, 289. Mosier cites 190,015 British deaths on 289.
25 Chickering and Förster, *Great War*, 291–5.

26 Liulevicius, *War Land*, 186–8.
27 Fromkin, *Peace*, 234–5,263–7.
28 Erickson, *Ordered*, 71.
29 Fromkin, *Peace*, 226–8, 309–10.
30 Fromkin, *Peace*, 267–301.
31 Farwell, *Africa*, 319.
32 Herwig, *FWW*, 316.
33 Offer, *Agrarian*, 354–61.
34 Herwig, *FWW*, 317.
35 Chickering and Förster, *Great War*, 189.
36 Lincoln, *Passage*, 316.
37 Keegan, *FWW*, 336.
38 Lincoln, *Passage*, 341.
39 Lincoln, *Passage*, 405–10.
40 Rauchensteiner, *Der Tod*, 413–20.
41 Herwig, *FWW*, 275–83.
42 Rauchensteiner, *Der Tod*, 487, 498.
43 Rauchensteiner, *Der Tod*, 451–69.
44 Herwig, *FWW*, 275–83.
45 Rauchensteiner, *Der Tod*, 498.
46 Davis, *Home Fires*, 193, 196, 199–200.
47 Davis, *Home Fires*, 181.
48 Davis, *Home Fires*, 204.
49 Davis, *Home Fires*, 172.
50 Davis, *Home Fires*, 191.
51 Chickering and Förster, *Great War*, 354–61.
52 Davis, *Home Fires*, 190–1, 214–18.
53 Downs, *Gender*, 147, 166–85.

54 Downs, *Gender*, 119–46.
55 Stovall, "Color Line," 765.
56 Stovall, "Color Line," 746.
57 Stovall, "Color Line," 749.
58 Chickering and Förster, *Great War*, 256–9.
59 Balesi, *Adversaries*, 90.
60 Chickering and Förster, *Great War*, 254–8.
61 Wilson, *Myriad*, 507.
62 Chickering and Förster, *Great War*, 200–1; Wilson, *Myriad*, 537–8.
63 Kent, *Making Peace*, 82.
64 Kent, *Making Peace*, 74–96.
65 Hennessey, *Ireland*, 158–201.
66 Morton and Granatstein, *Marching*, 190, 212.
67 *The Observer*, Sunday, 11 November 2002, on www.observer.co.uk
68 Wilson, *Myriad*, 514.
69 Chickering and Förster, *Great War*, 390–7.
70 Chickering and Förster, *Great War*, 494–9.
71 Chambers, *Army*, 211–13.
72 Chambers, *Army*, 156.
73 Barbeau and Henri, *Unknown*, 42–3.
74 Barbeau and Henri, *Unknown*, 72.
75 Barbeau and Henri, *Unknown*, 86.
76 Erickson, *Ordered*, 157.
77 Erickson, *Ordered*, 155–7.
78 Erickson, *Ordered*, 157–80.
79 Chickering and Förster, *Great War*, 192.
80 Chickering and Förster, *Great War*, 237–9.
81 Chickering and Förster, *Great War*, 211, 214, 218–19, 224.
82 Downs, *Gender*, 78.

6 1918. DENOUEMENT

1 Liulevicius, *War Land*, 205.
2 Mead, *Doughboys*, 247.
3 Barbeau and Henri, *Unknown*, 117.
4 Chickering and Förster, *Great War*, 323.
5 Schreiber, *Shock*, 18–29, quote on 19.
6 Morton and Granatstein, *Marching*, 198.
7 Keegan, *FWW*, 399.
8 Keegan, *FWW*, 400.
9 Keegan, *FWW*, 404.
10 Macdonald, *1914–1918*, 273–4.
11 Mosier, *Myth*, 318.
12 Macdonald, *1914–1918*, 281.
13 Barbeau and Henri, *Unknown*, 111.
14 Barbeau and Henri, *Unknown*, 116.
15 Macdonald, *1914–1918*, 294–5.
16 Doughty, "Numbers," 6, 7.
17 Schreiber, *Shock*, 32, 41, 43, 58, 62.
18 Triplet, *Youth*, 216.
19 Carlo D'Este, *Patton: A Genius for War* (New York, 1995), 259.
20 D'Este, *Patton*, 261.
21 Triplet, *Youth*, 187.
22 Triplet, *Youth*, 188.
23 Triplet, *Youth*, 125–6.
24 Triplet, *Youth*, 230.
25 Triplet, *Youth*, 268–9.
26 Barbeau and Henri, *Unknown*, 121.
27 Barbeau and Henri, *Unknown*, 138.
28 Keegan, *FWW*, 374.
29 Chickering and Förster, *Great War*, 340–2.
30 Chickering and Förster, *Great War*, 325–6.
31 Bessel, *Germany*, 46–7.
32 Mosier, *Myth*, 328.
33 Liulevicius, *War Land*, 205.
34 Liulevicius, *War Land*, 206.
35 Herwig, *FWW*, 384.
36 Chickering, *Imperial*, 171–2.
37 Salzman, *Judson, passim*.
38 Mead, *Doughboys*, 275.
39 Mead, *Doughboys*, 281.
40 Rauchensteiner, *Der Tod*, 568–9.
41 Rauchensteiner, *Der Tod*, 616.
42 Chickering and Förster, *Great War*, 189; Bessel, *Germany*, 39.
43 Davis, *Home Fires*, 224–5.
44 Herwig, *FWW*, 381.
45 Moyer, *Victory*, 232–72.

46 Moyer, *Victory*, 282.
47 Procacci, "Protest," 54.
48 Carls, *Loucheur*, 64–71.
49 Downs, *Gender*, 41, 47.
50 Downs, *Gender*, 143.
51 Carls, *Loucheur*, 89–92.
52 Lunn, *Memoirs*, 139–40.
53 Page, *Africa*, 43.
54 Dallas, *Tiger*, 549.
55 Dallas, *Tiger*, 542, 552.
56 Kent, *Gender*, 284–5.
57 Wilson, *Myriad*, 642.
58 Downs, *Gender*, 41.
59 Kent, *Gender*, 280.
60 Morton and Granatstein, *Marching*, 204.
61 Morton and Granatstein, *Marching*, 206.
62 Panayi, *Minorities*, 275–86.
63 Wynn, *Progressivism*, 79.
64 Schaffer, *America*, 31,58.
65 Keene, *US and FWW*, 3.

66 Keene, *US and FWW*, 40–1, 44.
67 Boemeke *et al.*, *Versailles*, 217.
68 Boemeke *et al.*, *Versailles*, 279–82.
69 Boemeke *et al.*, *Versailles*, 284–5.
70 Boemeke *et al.*, *Versailles*, 72–3.
71 Keegan, *FWW*, 414.
72 Boemeke *et al.*, *Versailles*, 608.
73 Boemeke *et al.*, *Versailles*, 86.
74 Chickering and Förster, *Great War*, 343–4.
75 Macdonald, *1914–1918*, 316.
76 Mead, *Doughboys*, 344–5.
77 Schreiber, *Shock*, 133, 139.
78 Becker *et al.*, *14–18*, 84.
79 Offer, *Agrarian*, 1, 23–4, 2, 38, 53.
80 Chickering and Förster, *Great War*, 80.
81 Herwig, *FWW*, 447.
82 Audoin-Rouzeau and Becker, *Guerre*, 31.
83 Audoin-Rouzeau and Becker, *Guerre*, 32-3.

7 THE POSTWAR WORLD: A "PEACE TO END PEACE"?

1 Fromkin, *Peace*, frontispiece quote.
2 Boemeke, *et al.*, *Versailles*, 143.
3 Boemeke *et al.*, *Versailles*, 205–7, 212.
4 Boemeke *et al.*, *Versailles*, 402.
5 Boemeke *et al.*, *Versailles*, 223–4.
6 Offer, *Agrarian*, 386.
7 Offer, *Agrarian*, 400–1.
8 Boemeke *et al.*, *Versailles*, 479–83.
9 Boemeke *et al.*, *Versailles*, 301.
10 Boemeke *et al.*, *Versailles*, 137.
11 Boemeke *et al.*, *Versailles*, 382, 386–7.
12 Boemeke *et al.*, *Versailles*, Nicolson quote on 136, last quote on 166.
13 Boemeke *et al.*, *Versailles*, 343.
14 Boemeke *et al.*, *Versailles*, 351.
15 Boemeke *et al.*, *Versailles*, 543.
16 Boemeke *et al.*, *Versailles*, 360–1, 587, 590–1.
17 Boemeke *et al.*, *Versailles*, 535–46.
18 Boemeke *et al.*, *Versailles*, 500–1.
19 Boemeke *et al.*, *Versailles*, 337–8.
20 Boemeke *et al.*, *Versailles*, 398, 360–1.

21 Boemeke *et al.*, *Versailles*, 470.
22 Boemeke *et al.*, *Versailles*, 524.
23 Boemeke *et al.*, *Versailles*, 404.
24 Boemeke *et al.*, *Versailles*, 425–6.
25 Boemeke *et al.*, *Versailles*, 436, 439.
26 Boemeke *et al*, *Versailles*, 441–2, 444–5, 447.
27 Boemeke *et al.*, *Versailles*, 486–8, 490.
28 Boemeke *et al.*, *Versailles*, 470, 496–9, 502–5.
29 Boemeke *et al.*, *Versailles*, 182, 243.
30 Boemeke *et al.*, *Versailles*, 536.
31 Boemeke *et al.*, *Versailles*, 233–5.
32 Boemeke *et al.*, *Versailles*, 310.
33 Boemeke *et al.*, *Versailles*, 471.
34 Boemeke *et al.*, *Versailles*, 523–32.
35 Roberts, *Reconstructing*, 216.
36 Kent, *Making Peace*, 3.
37 Downs, *Gender*, 1–14.
38 Downs, *Gender*, 198, 200.
39 Downs, *Gender*, 206.
40 Downs, *Gender*, 214–15, 202–25.
41 Roberts, *Reconstructing*, ix.
42 Roberts, *Reconstructing*, 1–16.

43 Roberts, *Reconstructing*, 105.
44 Roberts, *Reconstructing*, 110.
45 Roberts, *Reconstructing*, 91, 107.
46 Roberts, *Reconstructing*, 84–5, 46–87.
47 Roberts, *Reconstructing*, 153.
48 Roberts, *Reconstructing*, 46, 116, 123, 166–8.
49 Kent, *Making Peace*, 5.
50 Kent, *Making Peace*, 5–6.
51 Kent, *Making Peace*, 97–9.
52 Kent, *Making Peace*, 110, 97–113.
53 Kent, *Making Peace*, 115.
54 Kent, *Making Peace*, 140–3, also in general 121–39.
55 Grayzel, *Identities*, 2–4.
56 Grayzel, *Identities*, 6–10.
57 Frevert, *Women*, 168–204.
58 Parsons, "Right-Wing," 3, n.3; 4, ns 6, 7; 72, n.53.
59 Parsons, "Right-Wing," 15, n.12; 27, n.9; 31, n.18.
60 Parsons, "Right-Wing," 41, n.44; 44, n.53.
61 Parsons, "Right-Wing," 59, n.19; 60, n.24.
62 Parsons, "Right-Wing," 75, n.63; 76, ns 67–8.
63 Parsons, "Right-Wing," 90.
64 Stovall, "Color Line," 737–69, *passim*.
65 Chickering and Förster, *Great War*, 260. Martin, *France*, 48.
66 Barbeau and Henri, *Unknown*, 175.
67 The following footnotes (67–76) are cited in traditional style because graduate student Michael Pack's unpublished seminar paper on American intellectual precursors of Nazism served as my original source for this material.
68 (New York, 1920).
69 *The Revolt against Civilization* (NP, ND, 67–72), quote on 120.
70 Lothrop Stoddard, *The Rising Tide of Color against White World-supremacy* (New York, 1920), 13, 26, 123, 181, 190.
71 Stoddard, *Clashing Tides of Color* (New York, 1935), 125.
72 *Revolt*, 152, 134, 198–9, 208–9, 224, 233, 250, 261, 253.
73 Mike Hawkins, *Social Darwinism in European and American Thought, 1860–1945: Nature as Model and Nature as Threat* (Cambridge, 1997), 246. Stefan Kuhl, *The Nazi Connection: Eugenics, American Racism, and German National Socialism* (Oxford, 1994), 61.
74 Peter Viereck, *Meta-Politics: The Roots of the Nazi Mind* (New York, 1965) 254–5. Joachim Fest, *The Face of the Third Reich: Portraits of the Nazi Leadership*, trans. Michael Bullock (New York, 1970), 99. Hans Günther, *The Racial Elements of European History*, trans. G.C. Wheeler (London, 1927), ftns 172, 235, 245, 248, 249.
75 Hawkins, *Darwinism*, 244, 246. Kuhl, *Nazi*, 60, 85. Grey Brechin, "Conserving the Race: Natural Aristocracies, Eugenics, and the U.S. Conservation Movement," *Antipode*, 28, 3 (1996), 233.
76 Kuhl, *Nazi*, 62.
77 Boemeke *et al.*, *Versailles*, 465–8.
78 Dickinson, *War*, 206–58. Wrigley, *FWW*, 114–16.
79 Popplewell, *Intelligence*, 287–8.
80 Boemeke *et al.*, *Versailles*, 572, 578, 584.
81 Lewis, *DuBois*, 574–8. MacMillan, *Paris 1919*, 104–5.
82 Boemeke *et al.*, *Versailles*, 494–5.
83 Şaul and Royer, *African*, 301–14.
84 Lunn, *Memoirs*, 187–205, 215, 229–35.
85 Page, *Chiwaya*, 135–8, 164–6, 203–6, 226.
86 Mathews, "WWI," 493–502.
87 Crowder, "FWW," 311, 283–311.
88 Elkins, "Caribbean," 99–103.
89 Simon Rogers, *The Guardian*, Wednesday, 6 November 2002, www.guardian.co.uk
90 Prasad, *Muslims*, 86.
91 Popplewell, *Intelligence*, 301, 317; Brown, *India*, 220.
92 Sarkar, *India*, 101–226.
93 Fritzsche, *Germans*, 90.
94 Fritzsche, *Germans*, 189–94.

95 Fritzsche, *Germans*, 208.
96 Fritzsche, *Germans*, 209.
97 Fritzsche, *Germans*, 209.
98 Ziemann, *Front*, 462–72.
99 Keegan, *FWW*, 3, 9.
100 Keegan, *FWW*, 8.

101 Keegan, *FWW*, 4.
102 Ferguson, *Pity*, xxi.
103 Ferguson, *Pity*, xxiii–v.
104 Boemeke *et al.*, *Versailles*, 507–22.
105 Boemeke *et al.*, *Versailles*, 451.

SELECT BIBLIOGRAPHY

Among the many fine works available on the First World War, the literature listed below proved particularly helpful to the author, and bibliographies of these studies can lead the interested reader to further sources. The short bibliographical commentaries concluding many of the sections indicate works that the author found to be of special interest or merit.

GENERAL HISTORIES, ESSAY AND DOCUMENT COLLECTIONS

Audoin-Rouzeau, Stéphane and Annette Becker. *La Grande Guerre 1914–1918*. Paris: Gallimard, 1998.

Becker, Jean-Jacques. *L'Europe dans la Grande Guerre*. Paris: Belin, 1996.

Becker, Jean-Jacques, Gerd Krumeich, Jay Winter, Annette Becker, and Stéphane Audoin-Rouzeau (eds). *1914–1918. La très Grande Guerre* Paris: Le Monde Editions, 1994.

Beckett, Ian F.W. *The Great War 1914–1918*. London: Longman, 2001.

Cecil, Hugh and Peter H. Liddle (eds). *At the Eleventh Hour. Reflections, Hopes and Anxieties at the Closing of the Great War, 1918*. London: Leo Cooper, 1998.

—— *Facing Armageddon. The First World War Experienced*. London: Leo Cooper, 1996.

Chickering, Roger and Stig Förster. *Great War, Total War. Combat and Mobilization on the Western Front, 1914–1918*. Cambridge: Cambridge University Press, 2000.

Coetzee, Franz and Marilyn Shevin-Coetzee (eds). *Authority, Identity, and the Social History of the Great War*. Providence: Berghahn, 1995.

Ellis, John. *Eye-Deep in Hell. Trench Warfare in World War I*. New York: Pantheon, 1976.

Ferguson, Niall. *The Pity of War*. New York: Basic Books, 1999 [1998].

Hardach, Gerd. *The First World War 1914–1918*. Berkeley: University of California Press, 1977.

Haythornthwaite, Philip A. *The World War I Source Book*. London: Arms and Armour, 1996 [1992].

Higonnet, Margaret R., Jane Jenson, Sonya Michel and Margaret C. Weitz. *Behind the Lines. Gender and the Two World Wars*. New Haven, CT: Yale University Press, 1987.

Horne, John (ed.). *State, Society and Mobilization in Europe during the First World War*. Cambridge: Cambridge University Press, 1997.

Howard, Michael. *The First World War*. Oxford: Oxford University Press, 2002.

Isnenghi, Mario. *La Premiere Guerre Mondiale*. Florence: Casterman, 1993.

Keegan, John. *The First World War*. New York: A.A. Knopf, 1999.

Kruse, Wolfgang (ed.). *Eine Welt von Feinden. Der Grosse Krieg 1914–1918*. Frankfurt: Fischer, 1997.

Lyons, Michael J. *World War I. A Short History* (2nd edn). Upper Saddle River, NJ: Prentice Hall, 2000.

Macdonald, Lynn. *1914–1918. Voices and Images of the Great War*. London: Penguin, 1988.

Michalka, Wolfgang (ed.). *Der erste Weltkrieg. Wirkung, Wahrnehmung, Analyse*. Munich: Piper, 1994.

Morrow, John H. Jr. *The Great War in the Air. Military Aviation from 1909 to 1921*. Washington, DC: Smithsonian, 1993.

Mosier, John. *The Myth of the Great War. A New Military History of World War I*. New York: HarperCollins, 2001.

Offer, Avner. *The First World War: An Agrarian Interpretation*. Oxford: Clarendon Press, 1989.

Palmer, Alan. *Victory 1918*. New York: Grove Press, 1998.

Panayi, Panikos (ed.). *Minorities in Wartime. National and Racial Groupings in Europe, North America, and Australia during the Two World Wars*. Oxford: Berg, 1993.

Prior, Robin and Trevor Wilson. *The First World War*. London: Cassell, 1999.

Robbins, Keith. *The First World War*. Oxford: Oxford University Press, 1985.

Rousseau, Frédéric. *La Guerre Censurée. Une histoire des combattants européens de 14–18*. Paris: Seuil, 1999.

Stevenson, David. *The First World War and International Politics*. Oxford: Oxford University Press, 1988.

Stokesbury, James. *A Short History of World War I*. New York: William Morrow, 1981.

Stone, Norman. *The Eastern Front, 1914–1917*. New York: Scribners, 1975.

Strachan, Hew. *The First World War. Vol. I: To Arms*. Oxford: Oxford University Press, 2001.

—— (ed.). *The Oxford Illustrated History of the First World War*. Oxford: Oxford University Press, 1998.

Toland, John. *No Man's Land. 1918 – The Last Year of the Great War*. New York: Smithmark, 1980.

Tucker, Spencer C. *The Great War, 1914–1918*. Bloomington: Indiana University Press, 1998.

Wall, Richard and Jay Winter (eds). *The Upheaval of War. Family, Work, and Welfare in Europe, 1914–1918*. Cambridge: Cambridge University Press, 1988.

Winter, Jay, Geoffrey Parker, and Mary R. Habeck, (eds). *The Great War and the Twentieth Century*. New Haven, CT: Yale University Press, 2000.

Wrigley, Chris (ed.). *The First World War and the International Economy*. Cheltenham: Edward Elgar, 2000.

Of the above works, the studies by Audoin-Rouzeau and J-J. Becker provide excellent information on the European scene from the perspective of important French historians. Chickering and Förster's masterful collection of essays proves indispensable to study of the war on the Western Front, while Kruse's volume offers fascinating essays from a German perspective. Keegan's work provides a first-rate military history of the land war, while Macdonald's oral history, although primarily British in focus, offers insightful recollections from Dominion and German soldiers. Mosier's work revises notions of which side won the military conflict in favor of Germany, Ferguson's iconoclastic study poses and attempts to answer fundamental and fascinating questions about the war, while Offer proposes a unique perspective on the significance of agrarian and naval issues for the origins and outcome of the war. Finally, Strachan's edited volume on the war provides a fine collection of essays, while his three-volume study in progress promises to be the magisterial work on the Great War.

PREWAR AND ORIGINS

Adams, Michael C.C. *The Great Adventure. Male Desire and the Coming of World War I*. Bloomington: Indiana University Press, 1990.

Berghahn, V.R. *Germany and the Approach of War in 1914*. New York: St. Martin's Press, 1993 [1973].

Boemeke, Manfred, Roger Chickering, and Stig Förster (eds). *Anticipating Total War. The German and American Experiences, 1871–1914*. Washington, DC: The German Historical Institute; London: Cambridge University Press, 1999.

Buchholz, Arden. *Moltke, Schlieffen, and Prussian War Planning*. Oxford: Berg, 1991.

Clarke, I.F. (ed.). *The Great War with Germany, 1890–1914*. Liverpool: Liverpool University Press, 1997.

Crook, D.P. *Darwinism, War and History: The Debate over the Biology of War from the "Origin of Species" to the First World War*. Cambridge: Cambridge University Press, 1994.

Echevarria, Antulio J. II. "An Infamous Legacy: Schlieffen's Military Theories Revisited," *Army History*, No. 53 (summer–fall 2001), 1–8.

—— *After Clausewitz: German Military Thinkers before the Great War*. Lawrence: University Press of Kansas, 2000.

Friedberg, Aaron L. *The Weary Titan. Britain and the Experience of Relative Decline, 1895–1905*. Princeton, NJ: Princeton University Press, 1986.

Geiss, Immanuel. *July 1914. The Outbreak of the First World War: Selected Documents*. New York: Norton, 1967.

Hermann, David G. *The Arming of Europe and the Making of the First World War*. Princeton, NJ: Princeton University Press, 1996.

Hobson, J.A. *Imperialism*. Ann Arbor: University of Michigan Press, 1965 [1938].

Hochschild, Adam. *King Leopold's Ghost. A Story of Greed, Terror, and Heroism in Colonial Africa*. Boston, MA: Houghton Mifflin, 1999.

Joll, James. *The Origins of the First World War*. London: Longman, 1984.

Keiger, John F.V. *France and the Origins of the First World War*. New York: St. Martin's Press, 1983.

Kennedy, Paul M. (ed.). *The War Plans of the Great Powers, 1880–1914*. Boston, MA: Allen & Unwin, 1985 [1979].

Lewis, David Levering. *The Race to Fashoda: European Colonialism and African Resistance in the Scramble for Africa*. New York: Weidenfeld & Nicolson, 1987.

Lieven, D.C.B. *Russia and the Origins of the First World War*. New York: St. Martin's Press, 1983.

Lindqvist, Sven. *'Exterminate All the Brutes.' One Man's Odyssey into the Heart of Darkness and the Origins of European Genocide*. New York: New Press, 1996.

McCullough, Edward E. *How the First World War Began. The Triple Entente and the Coming of the Great War of 1914–1918*. New York: Black Rose, 1999.

Miller, Steven E., Sean M. Lynn-Jones and Stephen Van Evera (eds). *Military Strategy and the Origins of the First World War*. Princeton, NJ: Princeton University Press, 1991.

Pick, Daniel. *War Machine. The Rationalisation of Slaughter in the Modern Age*. New Haven, CT: Yale University Press, 1993.

Schoellgen, Gregor (ed.). *Escape into War? The Foreign Policy of Imperial Germany*. Oxford: Berg, 1990.

Snyder, Jack. *The Ideology of the Offensive. Military Decision Making and the Disasters of 1914*. Ithaca, NY: Cambridge University Press, 1984.

Steiner, Zara S. *Britain and the Origins of the First World War*. New York: St. Martin's Press, 1977.

Stevenson, David. *Armaments and the Coming of War. Europe 1904–1914*. Oxford: Clarendon Press, 1996.

Stromberg, Roland N. *Redemption by War. The Intellectuals and 1914*. Lawrence: Regents Press of Kansas, 1982.

Turner, L.C.F. *Origins of the First World War*. New York: Norton, 1970.

Williamson, Samuel R. Jr. *Austria-Hungary and the Origins of the First World War*. London: Macmillan, 1991.

Wilson, Keith (ed.). *Decisions for War, 1914*. New York: St. Martin's Press, 1995.

Beyond the standard studies of military and diplomatic history cited above, certain works proved stimulating. Boemeke, Chickering, and Förster offer an outstanding collection of essays on Germany and the United States, while McCullough's revisionist interpretation of the origins of the war lays the blame squarely on the Entente Powers. Adams perceptively studies the culture that prepared British and American youth for war, while Stromberg elucidates with clarity the intellectuals' exaltation of war as a solution to contemporary problems in 1914. Friedberg provides great insight into the strains of imperial overstretch in England at the turn of the century, while Crook presents a nuanced study of the influence of Darwinism on ideas of war. Hobson remains one of the most indispensable studies of imperialism. Finally, Hochschild's marvelous study of Belgian imperial depredations in the Congo and Lindqvist's probing historical meditation on the connection between imperialism and genocide should be required reading on imperialism.

CULTURE

Becker, Jean-Jacques, Gerd Krumeich, Jay Winter, Annette Becker, and Stéphane Audoin-Rouzeau *1914–1918. La très Grande Guerre*. Paris: Le Monde Editions, 1994.

Dagen, Philippe. *Le Silence des peintres. Les artistes face à la Grande Guerre*. Paris: Fayard, 1996.

Eksteins, Modris. *Rites of Spring: The Great War and the Modern Age*. New York: Doubleday, 1990.

Mosse, George L. *Fallen Soldiers. Reshaping the Memory of the World Wars*. Oxford: Oxford University Press, 1990.

Paris, Michael (ed.). *The First World War and Popular Cinema, 1914 to the Present*. New Brunswick: Rutgers University Press, 2000.

Roshwald, Aviel and Richard Stites (eds). *European Culture in the Great War. The Arts, Entertainment, and Propaganda, 1914–1918*. Cambridge: Cambridge University Press, 1999.

Tate, Trudi. *Modernism, History and the First World War*. Manchester: Manchester University Press, 1998.

Winter, Jay. *Sites of Memory, Sites of Mourning. The Great War in European Cultural History*. Cambridge: Cambridge University Press, 1995.

Wohl, Robert. *The Generation of 1914*. Cambridge, MA: Harvard University Press, 1979.

In a selection of excellent studies, Ecksteins, Mosse, Winter, and Wohl provide particularly stimulating works on European culture and the Great War.

NAVAL WARFARE

Campbell, John. *Jutland. An Analysis of the Fighting*. New York: The Lyons Press, 2000.

Gordon, Andrew. *The Rules of the Game. Jutland and British Naval Command*. Annapolis, MD: Naval Institute Press, 1996.

Gray, Edwyn. *The Killing Time: The U-Boat War, 1914–1918*. New York: Scribner's, 1972.

Halpern, Paul G. *A Naval History of World War I*. Annapolis, MD: Naval Institute Press, 1994.

—— *The Naval War in the Mediterranean, 1914–1918*. London: Allen & Unwin, 1987.

Hough, Richard. *The Great War at Sea, 1914–1918*. London: Oxford University Press, 1983.

Padfield, Peter. *The Great Naval Race: The Anglo–German Naval Rivalry, 1900–1914*. New York: David Mckay, 1974.

Tarrant, V.E. *The U-Boat Offensive, 1914–1945*. Annapolis, MD: Naval Institute Press, 1989.

Terraine, John. *Business in Great Waters: The U-Boat Wars, 1916–1945*. London: Leo Cooper, 1989.

Yates, Keith. *Flawed Victory. Jutland, 1916*. Annapolis, MD: Naval Institute Press, 2000.

Of the works on naval history, Paul Halpern's volumes are absolutely outstanding and essential, while one notes the interest in the battle of Jutland during recent years.

CONTINENTS AND COUNTRIES

Africa (and the West Indies)

Balesi, Charles J. *From Adversaries to Comrades-in-Arms: West Africans and the French Military, 1885–1918*. Waltham, 1979.

Crowder, M. "The First World War and its Consequences," in A. Adu Boahen (ed.) *General History of Africa. VII Africa under Colonial Domination*. Heinemann, California: UNESCO, 1985 (pp. 283–311).

Elkins, W.F. "A Source of Black Nationalism in the Caribbean: The Revolt of the British West Indies Regiment at Taranto, Italy," *Science and Society*, 34 (1970), 99–103.

Farwell, Byron. *The Great War in Africa, 1914–1918*. New York: W.W. Norton, 1986.

Gifford, Prosser and Wm. Roger Louis (eds). *Britain and Germany in Africa. Imperial Rivalry and Colonial Rule*. New Haven, CT: Yale University Press, 1967.

—— *France and Britain in Africa. Imperial Rivalry and Colonial Rule*. New Haven, CT: Yale University Press, 1971.

Lunn, Joe. *Memoirs of the Maelstrom. A Senegalese Oral History of the First World War*. Portsmouth, NH: Heinemann, 1999.

Mathews, James J. "WWI and the Rise of African Nationalism: Nigerian Veterans as Catalysts of Political Change," *Journal of Modern African Studies*, 20, 3 (1982), 493–502.

Michel, Marc. *L'Appel à l'Afrique. Contributions et reactions à l'effort de guerre en A.O.F. (1914–1919)*. Paris: Sorbonne, 1982.

Miller, Charles. *Battle for the Bundu. The First World War in East Africa*. New York: Macmillan, 1974.

Page, Melvin E. (ed.). *Africa and the First World War*. New York: St. Martin's Press, 1987.

—— *The Chiwaya War. Malawians and the First World War*. Boulder, CO: Westview Press, 2000.

Şaul, Mahir and Patrick Royer. *West African Challenge to Empire. Culture and History in the Volta–Bani Anticolonial War*. Athens: Ohio University Press, 2001.

Page's collection of essays and study of the Chiwaya War prove very useful, while Farwell offers a highly readable account of the war in East Africa. Lunn's work on Senegalese memoirs and Şaul and Royer's recent study of the Volta–Bani War offer illuminating insights on Africans and the war, and the latter work contains exciting revelations about wartime imperialism from a historical and anthropological perspective.

Australia and New Zealand

Williams, John F. *Anzacs, the Media, and the Great War*. Sydney: University of New South Wales Press, 1999.

Austria-Hungary

Cornwall, Mark. *The Undermining of Austria-Hungary. The Battle for Hearts and Minds*. London: Macmillan, 2000.

Kann, Robert A., Bela K. Kiraly, and Paula S. Fichtner (eds). *The Habsburg Empire in World War I*. New York: Columbia University Press, 1977.

Rauchensteiner, Manfried. *Der Tod des Doppeladlers. Oesterreich-Ungarn und der Erste Weltkrieg*. Graz: Verlag Styria, 1993.

Rozenblit, Marsha L. *Reconstructing National Identity. The Jews of Habsburg Austria during World War I*. Oxford: Oxford University Press, 2001.

Sondhaus, Lawrence. *Franz Conrad von Hoetzendorf: Architect of the Apocalypse*. Boston, MA: Humanities Ltd, 2000.

Rauchensteiner's magisterial work proves indispensable on the Dual Monarchy. Cornwall's work on propaganda presents valuable information on its subject and on the empire, while Sondhaus's biography of Conrad presents a fascinating portrait of the key military personage in Austria-Hungary.

Canada

Morton, Desmond and J.L. Granatstein. *Marching to Armageddon. Canadians and the Great War 1914–1919*. Toronto: Lester and Orpen Dennys, 1989.

Schreiber, Shane B. *Shock Army of the British Empire. The Canadian Corps in the Last 100 Days of the Great War*. Westport: Praeger, 1997.

Vance, Jonathan F. *Death So Noble: Memory, Meaning, and the First World War*. Vancouver: University of British Columbia Press, 1997.

Morton and Granatstein's study provides a well-written and illustrated overview of Canada and the war, while Schreiber's work shows the role and value of the Canadian Corps in the BEF during the victorious advances in the final months of the war.

France

Becker, Jean-Jacques. *La France en guerre 1914–1918. La Grande Mutation*. Paris: Editions Complexe, 1988.

Bernard, Philippe and Henri Dubief. *The Decline of the Third Republic, 1914–1938*. Cambridge: Cambridge University Press, 1988.

Carls, Stephen D. *Louis Loucheur and the Shaping of Modern France, 1916–1931*. Baton Rouge: Louisiana State University Press, 1993.

Comte, Arthur. *Joffre*. Paris: Perrin, 1991.

Dallas, Gregor. *At the Heart of a Tiger. Clemenceau and his World 1841–1929*. London: Macmillan, 1993.

Darrow, Margaret H. *French Women and the First World War. War Stories of the Home Front*. Oxford: Berg, 2000.

Douglas, Allen. *War, Memory, and the Politics of Humor. The Canard Enchaîné and World War I*. Berkeley: University of California Press, 2002.

Downs, Laura Lee. *Manufacturing Inequality. Gender Division in the French and British Metalworking Industries, 1914–1939*. Ithaca, NY: Cornell University Press, 1995.

Duroselle, Jean-Baptiste. *Clemenceau*. Paris: Fayard, 1988.

—— *La Grande Guerre des Français. 1914–1918*. Paris: Perrin, 1994.

Godfrey, John F. *Capitalism at War. Industrial Policy and Bureaucracy in France, 1914–1918*. Leamington Spa: Berg, 1987.

Goldberg, Nancy Sloan. *"Woman, Your Hour is Sounding." Continuity and Change in French Women's Great War Fiction, 1914–1919*. New York: St. Martin's Press, 1999.

Hanna, Martha. *The Mobilization of Intellect. French Scholars and Writers during the Great War*. Cambridge, MA: Harvard University Press, 1996.

Horne, John. *Labor at War. France and Britain 1914–1918*. Oxford: Clarendon Press, 1991.

Lemarchand, Lionel J-M. "Lettres militaires censurées de 1917. Une place dans la littérature et l'histoire." Diss., University of Georgia, 1987.

McPhail, Helen. *The Long Silence. Civilian Life under the German Occupation of Northern France, 1914–1918*. London: I.B. Tauris, 2001 [1999].

Martin, Benjamin F. *France and the Après Guerre, 1918–1924. Illusions and Disillusionment*. Baton Rouge: LSU Press, 1999.

Miquel, Pierre. *La Grande Guerre*. Paris: Fayard, 1983.

—— *Les Poilus. La France sacrifiée*. Paris: Plon, 2000.

Pedroncini, Guy. *Pétain. Le soldat et la gloire 1856–1918*. Paris: Perrin, 1989.

Roberts, Mary Louise. *Civilization Without Sexes. Reconstructing Gender in Postwar France, 1917–1927*. Chicago, IL: University of Chicago Press, 1994.

Schnor, Ralph. *La France dans la première guerre mondiale*. Paris: Nathan, 1997.

Smith, Leonard V. *Between Mutiny and Obedience. The Case of the French Fifth Infantry Division during World War I*. Princeton, NJ: Princeton University Press, 1994.

Stovall, Tyler. "The Color Line behind the Lines: Racial Violence in France during the Great War," *American Historial Review*, 103, 3 (1998), 737–69.

Tuffrau, Paul. *1914–1918. Quatre Années sur le Front. Carnets d'un combattant*. Paris: Imago, 1998.

Three of the deans of French historical studies, Becker, Duroselle, and Miquel, have written substantial histories of France in the Great War, and Duroselle and Dallas have penned detailed biographies of the indomitable Clemenceau. Pedroncini, another leading historian of the war, has authored the standard biography of Pétain, and Comte, that of Joffre. Miquel's work on Les Poilus *shows clearly the sacrifice expected of, and given, by French soldiers, while Lemarchand's dissertation poignantly shows their sentiments during* 1917, *and Tuffrau's memoir exemplifies a number of excellent published recollections of French soldiers. Downs, Grayzel (see section on Great Britain), and Roberts offer essential works on gender, while Stovall's* AHR *article presents path-*

breaking material on race in wartime France. Finally, McPhail's study of northern France under German occupation fills an essential gap in historical awareness of occupied France.

Germany

Bessel, Richard. *Germany after the First World War*. Oxford: Clarendon Press, 1993.

Chickering, Roger. *Imperial Germany and the Great War, 1914–1918*. Cambridge: Cambridge University Press, 1998.

Daniel, Ute. *The War from Within. German Working-Class Women in the First World War*. Trans. Margaret Reis. Oxford: Berg, 1997.

Davis, Belinda J. *Home Fires Burning. Food, Politics, and Everyday Life in World War I Berlin*. Chapel Hill: University of North Carolina Press, 2000.

Feldman, Gerald D. *Army, Industry, and Labor in Germany 1914–1918*. Princeton, NJ: Princeton University Press, 1966.

—— *The Great Disorder. Politics, Economics, and Society in the German Inflation, 1914–1924*. Oxford: Oxford University Press, 1993.

Frevert, Ute. *Women in German History from Bourgeois Emancipation to Sexual Liberation*. Oxford: Berg, 1990.

Fritzsche, Peter. *Germans into Nazis*. Cambridge, MA: Harvard University Press, 1998.

Herwig, Holger H. *The First World War. Germany and Austria-Hungary, 1914–1918*. London: Arnold, 1997.

Hirschfeld, G., G. Krumeich, and I. Renz. *"Keiner fühlt sich hier als Mensch . . .". Erlebnis und Wirkung des Erstern Weltkrieges*. Frankfurt: Fischer, 1996.

Horne, John and Alan Kramer. *German Atrocities, 1914. A History of Denial*. New Haven, CT: Yale University Press, 2001.

Kihntopf, Michael P. *Victory in the East. The Rise and Fall of the Imperial German Army*. Shippensburg: White Mane, 2000.

Liulevicius, Vejas Gabriel. *War Land on the Eastern Front. Culture, National Identity and German Occupation in World War I*. Cambridge: Cambridge University Press, 2000.

Mommsen, Wolfgang J. *Imperial Germany, 1867–1918. Politics, Culture, and Society in an Authoritarian State*. London: Arnold, 1995.

Moyer, Laurence V. *Victory Must Be Ours. Germany in the Great War*. London: Leo Cooper, 1995.

Nevin, Thomas. *Ernst Jünger and Germany. Into the Abyss, 1914–1945*. Durham, NC: Durham University Press, 1996.

Nipperdey, Thomas. *Deutsche Geschichte 1866–1918* (2 vols). Munich: Beck, 1993.

Paschall, Rod. *The Defeat of Imperial Germany, 1917–1918*. New York: Da Capo, 1994.

Stürmer, Michael. *Das Ruhelose Reich. Deutschland 1866–1918*. Berlin: Siedler, 1983.

Verhey, Jeffrey. *The Spirit of 1914. Militarism, Myth and Mobilization in Germany*. Cambridge: Cambridge University Press, 2002.

Welch, David. *Germany, Propaganda and Total War, 1914–1918. The Sins of Omission*. New Brunswick: Rutgers University Press, 2000.

Ziemann, Benjamin. *Front und Heimat. Ländliche Kriegserfahrungen im südlichen Bayern 1914–1923*. Essen: Klartext, 1997.

Chickering and Herwig offer essential reading on wartime Germany; Bessel, on postwar Germany; while Hirschfeld, Krumeich, and Renz present an outstanding collection of essays most of which concern wartime Germany. Feldman has written indispensable studies of the military and the economy, while Davis's fine work on Berlin shows the effects of war on the German capital. Fritzsche and Verhey explain the power of the myth of 1914 in Germany, the former all the way to the Nazi era, while Ziemann penetrates behind myth in his study of Bavarian peasant soldiers. Finally, Horne and Kramer's long-awaited study of German atrocities in Belgium probes the facts underpinning the propaganda, while Liulevicius's excellent monograph on the German occupation on the Eastern Front makes clear the extent of Hindenburg and Ludendorff's plans for the east.

Great Britain

Bourke, Joanna. *Dismembering the Male. Men's Bodies, Britain, and the Great War*. Chicago, IL: University of Chicago Press, 1996.

Constantine, Stephen, Maurice W. Kirby and Mary B. Rose. *The First World War and British History*. London: Edward Arnold, 1995.

Culleton, Claire A. *Working Class Culture, Women, and Britain, 1914–1921*. New York: St. Martin's Press, 1999.

Gardner, Brian (ed.). *Up the Line to Death. The War Poets 1914–1918*. London: Methuen, 1986 [1964].

Grayzel, Susan R. *Women's Identities at War. Gender, Motherhood, and Politics in Britain and France during the First World War*. Chapel Hill: University of North Carolina Press, 1999.

Griffith, Paddy. *Battle Tactics of the Western Front. The British Army's Art of Attack, 1916–1918*. New Haven, CT: Yale University Press, 1994.

Gullace, Nicoletta F. "Sexual Violence and Family Honor: British Propaganda and International Law during the First World War," *American Historical Review*, 102, 3 (1997), 714–47.

Hynes, Samuel. *A War Imagined. The First World War and English Culture*. New York: Atheneum, 1991.

Kent, Susan Kingsley. *Gender and Power in Britain, 1640–1990*. London: Routledge, 1999.

—— *Making Peace. The Reconstruction of Gender in Interwar Britain*. Princeton, NJ: Princeton University Press, 1993.

Levine, Philippa. "Battle Colors: Race, Sex, and Colonial Soldiery in World War I," *Journal of Women's History*, 9, 4 (1998), 104–30.

Macdonald, Lynn. *1914. The First Months of Fighting*. New York: Atheneum, 1988.

—— *1915. The Death of Innocence*. London: Headline, 1993.

—— *Somme*. London: Michael Joseph, 1983.

—— *They Called It Passchendaele*. London: Macmillan, 1983.

—— *To the Last Man. Spring 1918*. New York: Carroll and Graf, 1999.

Mills, C.P. *A Strange War*. Gloucester: Alan Sutton, 1988.

Moorhouse, Geoffrey. *Hell's Foundations. A Town, Its Myths, and Gallipoli*. London: Hodder & Stoughton, 1992.

Ouditt, Sharon. *Fighting Forces, Writing Women. Identity and Ideology in the First World War*. London: Routledge, 1994.

Parsons, Gregory S. "Right-Wing Ideology and the Language of Anti-Bolshevism in Great Britain, 1918–1924." MA thesis, University of Georgia, 1994.

Sheffield, Gary. *Forgotten Victory. The First World War: Myths and Realities*. London: Review, 2002.

Thom, Deborah. *Nice Girls and Rude Girls. Women Workers in World War I*. London: I.B. Tauris, 2000.

Travers, Tim. *How the War Was Won. Command and Technology in the British Army on the Western Front, 1917–1918*. London: Routledge, 1992.

—— *The Killing Ground. The British Army, the Western Front and the Emergence of Modern Warfare, 1900–1918*. London: Allen & Uniwn, 1987.

Wilson, Trevor. *The Myriad Faces of War. Britain and the Great War, 1914–1918*. Cambridge: Polity Press, 1986.

Wilson's detailed macro-history paints a marvelous portrait of Britain at war, while Moorhouse's micro-history shows the effect of Gallipoli on the town whose regiment won "Six VCs before breakfast." Kent, Culleton, Grayzel, Thom, and Bourne provide excellent and well-written studies of gender, while Gullace's AHR article imaginatively approaches the ingredients in British propaganda. Travers, Griffith, and Sheffield revise notions of an incompetent British Army to show how the BEF improved to its victorious status in 1918, while Macdonald's oral histories make for marvelous reading and insights into the lives and thoughts of British soldiers.

India

Brown, Judith M. *Modern India. The Origins of an Asian Democracy*. Oxford: Oxford University Press, 1994 [1985].

Omissi, David (ed.). *Indian Voices of the Great War. Soldiers' Letters, 1914–18*. London: Macmillan, 1999.

Popplewell, Richard J. *Intelligence and Imperial Defense: British Intelligence and the Defense of the Indian Empire, 1904–1924*. London: Frank Cass, 1995.

Prasad, Yuvaraj Deva. *The Indian Muslims and World War I*. New Delhi: Janaki Prakashan, 1985.

Sarkar, Sumit. *Modern India 1885–1947*. Delhi: Macmillan India, 1983.

Omissi's outstanding collection of Indian soldiers' letters is both informative and moving, while Popplewell offers an informative study of British intelligence operations in and about India.

Ireland

Caulfield, Max. *The Easter Rebellion. Dublin 1916*. Boulder, CO: Roberts Rinehart, 1995 [1963].

Fitzpatrick, David (ed.). *Ireland and the First World War*. Gigginstown, Ireland: Lilliput, 1988.
Hennessey, Thomas. *Dividing Ireland. World War I and Partition*. London: Routledge, 1998.
Jeffery, Keith. *Ireland and the Great War*. Cambridge: Cambridge University Press, 2000.

Italy

Procacci, Giovanna. "Popular Protest and Labour Conflict in Italy, 1915–18," *Social History*, 14, 1 (1989), 31–58.
Tomassini, Luigi. "Industrial Mobilization and the Labour Market in Italy during the First World War," *Social History*, 16, 1 (1991), 59–87.

Japan

Dickinson, Frederick R. *War and National Reinvention. Japan in the Great War, 1914–1919*. Cambridge, MA: Harvard University Press, 1999.
Nish, Ian H. *Alliance in Decline. A Study in Anglo–Japanese Relations 1908–23*. London: The Athlone Press, 1972.

The Ottoman Empire and the Middle East

Erickson, Edward J. *Ordered to Die. A History of the Ottoman Army in the First World War*. Westport, CT: Greenwood Press, 2001.
Fromkin, David. *A Peace to End All Peace. The Fall of the Ottoman Empire and the Creation of the Modern Middle East*. New York: Henry Holt, 1989.
Karsh, Efraim and Inari Karsh. *Empires of the Sand. The Struggle for Mastery in the Middle East, 1789–1923*. Cambridge, MA: Harvard University Press, 1999.
Kayali, Hasan. *Arabs and Young Turks. Ottomanism, Arabism, and Islamism in the Ottoman Empire, 1908–1918*. Berkeley: University of California Press, 1997.
Kent, Marian (ed.). *The Great Powers and the End of the Ottoman Empire*. London: Frank Cass, 1996 [1984].
McCarthy, Justin. *The Ottoman Peoples and the End of Empire*. London: Arnold, 2001.
Melson, Robert. *Revolution and Genocide. On the Origins of the Armenian Genocide and the Holocaust*. Chicago, IL: University of Chicago Press, 1992.

Erickson provides a much needed history of the Ottoman Army's war, while Fromkin's detailed and well-written history clearly shows the relationship between the war and the formation of the modern Middle East.

Russia

Fitzpatrick, Sheila. *The Russian Revolution*. Oxford: Oxford University Press, 1994 [1982].

Florinsky, Michael T. *The End of the Russian Empire*. New York: Collier, 1961 [1931].

Keep, John L.H. *The Russian Revolution. A Study in Mass Mobilization*. New York: Norton, 1976.

Kenez, Peter. *Civil War in South Russia, 1918*. Berkeley: University of California Press, 1973.

—— *Civil War in South Russia, 1919–1920. The Defeat of the Whites*. Berkeley: University of California Press, 1977.

Kojevnikov, Alexei. "The Great War, the Russian Civil War, and the Invention of Big Science," ms., 1–49.

Lincoln, W. Bruce. *Passage through Armageddon. The Russians in War and Revolution 1914–1918*. New York: Simon & Schuster, 1986.

—— *Red Victory. A History of the Russian Civil War*. New York: Simon & Schuster, 1989.

Pipes, Richard. *A Concise History of the Russian Revolution*. New York: Knopf, 1995.

Rabinowitch, Alexander. *The Bolsheviks Come to Power. The Revolution of 1917 in Petrograd*. New York: Norton, 1978.

Rutherford, Ward. *The Russian Army in World War I*. London: Gordon Cremonesi, 1975.

Salzman, Neil V. (ed.). *Russia in War and Revolution. General William V. Judson's Accounts from Petrograd, 1917–1918*. Kent: Kansas State University Press, 1998.

Wildman, Allan K. *The End of the Russian Imperial Army. The Old Army and the Soldiers' Revolt (March–April 1917)*. Princeton, NJ: Princeton University Press, 1980.

—— *The End of the Russian Imperial Army. The Road to Soviet Power and Peace*. Vol. II. Princeton, NJ: Princeton University Press, 1987.

Florinsky's history remains valuable after nearly three-quarters of a century, while Lincoln's marvelous works present detailed and readable accounts of Russian events.

United States

Barbeau, Arthur E. and Florette Henri. *The Unknown Soldiers. African-American Troops in World War I*. New York: Da Capo Press, 1996 [1974].

Braim, Paul F. *The Test of Battle. The American Expeditionary Force in the Meuse–Argonne Campaign*. Newark: University of Delaware Press, 1987.

Bristow, Nancy K. *Making Men Moral. Social Engineering during the Great War*. New York: New York University Press, 1996.

Cashman, Sean Dennis. *America in the Age of Titans. The Progressive Era and World War I*. New York: New York University Press, 1988.

Chambers, John Whiteclay II. *To Raise an Army. The Draft Comes to Modern America*. New York: Free Press, 1987.

Coffman, Edward M. *The War to End All Wars. The American Military Experience in World War I*. Madison: University of Wisconsin Press, 1986.

Doughty, Robert A. "More than Numbers. Americans and the Revival of French Morale in the Great War," *Army History*, 52 (spring 2001), 1–11.

Early, Frances H. *A World Without War. How U.S. Feminists and Pacifists Resisted World War I*. Syracuse, NY: Syracuse University Press, 1997.

Eisenhower, John S.D. *Yanks. The Epic Story of the American Army in World War I*. New York: Free Press, 2001.

Ellis, Edward Robb. *Echoes of Distant Thunder. Life in the United States, 1914–1918*. New York: Kodansha International, 1996.

Farwell, Byron. *Over There. The United States in the Great War, 1917–1918*. New York: W.W. Norton, 1999.

Foglesong, David S. *America's Secret War against Bolshevism. U.S. Intervention in the Russian Civil War, 1917–1920*. Chapel Hill: University of North Carolina Press, 1995.

Greenwald, Maurine Weiner. *Women, War, and Work. The Impact of World War I on Women Workers in the United States*. Ithaca, NY: Cambridge University Press, 1980.

Herries, Meirion and Susie. *The Last Days of Innocence. America at War, 1917–1918*. New York: Random House, 1997.

Hawley, Ellis W. *The Great War and the Search for a Modern Order. A History of the American People and their Institutions, 1917–1933*. New York: St. Martin's Press, 1992.

Keene, Jennifer D. *Doughboys, The Great War, and the Remaking of America*. Baltimore: Johns Hopkins University Press, 2001.

—— *The United States and the First World War*. London: Longman, 2000.

Kennedy, David M. *Over Here. The First World War and American Society*. New York: Oxford University Press, 1980.

Kennedy, Kathleen. *Disloyal Mothers and Scurrilous Citizens. Women and Subversion during World War I*. Bloomington: Indiana University Press, 1999.

Knock, Thomas J. *To End All Wars. Woodrow Wilson and the Quest for a New World Order*. Princeton, NJ: Princeton University Press, 1992.

Koistinen, Paul A.C. *Mobilizing for Modern War. The Political Economy of American Warfare, 1865–1919*. Lawrence: University Press of Kansas, 1997.

Lewis, David Levering. *W.E.B. DuBois. Biography of a Race. 1868–1919*. New York: Henry Holt, 1993.

McCartin, Joseph A. *Labor's Great War. The Struggle for Industrial Democracy and the Origins of Modern American Labor Relations, 1912–1921*. Chapel Hill: University of North Carolina Press, 1997.

Mead, Gary. *The Doughboys. America and the First World War*. Woodstock: Overlook Press, 2000.

Meigs, Mark. *Optimism at Armageddon. Voices of American Participants in the First World War*. New York: New York University Press, 1997.

Schaffer, Ronald. *America in the Great War. The Rise of the War Welfare State*. Oxford: Oxford University Press, 1991.

Schneider, Dorothy and Carl J. *Into the Breach. American Women Overseas in World War I*. New York: Viking Press, 1991.

Trask, David F. *The AEF and Coalition Warmaking, 1817–1918*. Lawrence: University Press of Kansas, 1993.

Triplet, William S. In Robert H. Ferrell (ed.) *A Youth in the Meuse-Argonne. A Memoir, 1917–1918*. Columbia: University of Missouri Press, 2000.

Wynn, Neil A. *From Progressivism to Prosperity. World War I and American Society*. New York: Holmes & Meier, 1986.

Zeiger, Susan. *In Uncle Sam's Service. Women Workers with the American Expeditionary Force, 1917–1919*. Ithaca, NY: Cambridge University Press, 1999.

Zieger, Robert H. *America's Great War. World War I and the American Experience*. New York: Rowman and Littlefield, 2000.

Schaffer, Wynn, Zieger, and Keene, among others, provide excellent accounts of America at war, while Coffmann, Braim, Eisenhower, Mead, and Trask present the history of the American military effort, the AEF, and finally the AEF's role in the allied coalition. Finally, Triplet's recently published memoir presents an unvarnished account of a young soldier's experience in the AEF.

Versailles

Boemeke, Manfred, Gerald D. Feldman, and Elisabeth Glaser (eds). *The Treaty of Versailles. A Reassessment after 75 Years*. Cambridge: Cambridge University Press, 1998.

Henig, Ruth. *Versailles and After. 1919–1933*. London: Routledge, 1995 [1984].

Mee, Charles L. *The End of Order. Versailles, 1919*. New York: Dutton, 1980.

MacMillan, Margaret. *Paris 1919. Six Months that Changed the World*. New York: Random House, 2001.

Boemeke, Feldman, and Glaser present an outstanding collection of essays in a retrospective on Versailles, while MacMillan offers a detailed history of the conference and its important personages.

INDEX